D1233803

The Tragedy of Afghanistan

The Tragedy of Afghanistan

The Tragedy of Afghanistan

A First-hand Account

RAJA ANWAR

Translated from the Urdu by
Khalid Hasan

VERSO

London · New York

*Dedicated to the memory of Zulfikar Ali Bhutto
and to all those who have fallen in
the struggle against military dictatorships
in Pakistan*

This edition published by Verso 1988
© 1988 Verso
All rights reserved

Verso
UK: 6 Meard Street, London W1V 3HR
USA: 29 West 35th Street, New York NY 10001-2291

Verso is the imprint of New Left Books

British Library Cataloguing in Publication Data
Anwar, Raja, *1948-*
    The Tragedy of Afghanistan : a first-hand account.
    1. Afghanistan
    I. Title
    958′.1044

ISBN 0-86091-208-6

US Library of Congress Cataloging in Publication Data
Anwar, Raja, 1948-
    The tragedy of Afghanistan

    1. Afghanistan–History–Soviet occupation, 1979-
I. Title.
DS371.2.A59   1988   958′.1044   88-6074
ISBN 0-86091-208-6

Typeset by Leaper & Gard Ltd, Bristol, England
Printed in Great Britain by Bookcraft (Bath) Ltd, Midsomer Norton, Avon

Contents

Translator's Note

Raja Anwar and I have at least one thing in common: we were both associated with Zulfikar Ali Bhutto, Pakistan's only genuinely elected Prime Minister, who was overthrown by the army on 5 July 1977 and executed on 4 April 1979 after a trial which was a travesty of justice. We have both lived in exile, though fate has been kinder to me than to Raja Anwar. But had Anwar not undergone imprisonment in Kabul, he might never have produced this unique document, which is likely to become the basic work of reference on that unhappy country. Its greatest merit lies in its honesty. I have no hesitation in claiming that this is the only truthful book written on Afghanistan: as such, it will undoubtedly please no one: neither the two factions of the People's Democratic Party of Afghanistan, nor the so-called 'Mujahideen' leadership, the Soviet Union, the United States and certainly not the regime now in control of the country to which both author and translator belong – Pakistan.

It was towards the end of 1986 that I learned Raja Anwar was in Frankfurt writing a book on Afghanistan. Muzaffar Sheikh, a mutual friend also living in Frankfurt, put us in touch and after congratulating Anwar on being 'alive' (thanks to the *Sunday Times*, I had for a number of years believed he had been killed by the Soviets in Afghanistan), I asked him about the book. He told me he had done nothing except work on it since leaving Afghanistan early in 1984. He said he would like me to translate the book into English, and agreed to send a few chapters for me to look at. On receiving ninety-three pages written in beautiful Urdu script on lined A4 sheets, my first reaction was: no, I can't do it. The task was intimidating. If the act of writing is painful, the ordeal of translation is doubly so. However, I finally decided to go ahead because I was just as keen as the author to see the book in English. I also felt it deserved to reach an international audience.

I began my translation in February 1987, and it has taken exactly five months for the work to be accomplished. Since during this period I was also working full time for a news agency in Vienna, the labour of translation has filled every moment of my spare time. Proper names have presented something of a problem. There are no agreed or uniform English spellings for Afghan (nor for that matter most Muslim) names, and I have therefore devised my own – the only virtue of this being consistency. In Urdu and Persian, this problem does not arise because there is only one way in which words (including proper names) can be spelled.

I must most sincerely thank Audrey Haylins and Khalid Shaikh who typed most of the manuscript more than once. Without them this book would have been inordinately delayed. I also acknowledge with gratitude the extreme patience and understanding shown by my wife Juanita and our children Jeffrey and Jahan who for several months heard only my typewriter and saw nothing of me. But the hard work has been worth it, because I believe Raja Anwar has produced something approaching a masterpiece of contemporary history.

Khalid Hasan, Vienna, July 1987

Author's Foreword

I lived in Afghanistan from June 1979 to January 1984, and spent the period between October 1980 and March 1983 in jail. These were the most painful, the most trying years in Afghan history. I am glad to have been there to observe events at close quarters before, during, and after my imprisonment. In jail I came to know many rebels, as well as members of Hafizullah Amin's family and his former Ministers. During the nine months I spent in Kabul after my release, I heard many inside stories and met a large number of important figures. I have tried to transfer this knowledge and experience to the pages that follow with detachment and honesty. It is, of course, for the reader to judge the degree of my success.

I have no desire to speak about my imprisonment and the personal suffering resulting from it. Such were Afghanistan's conditions during those years that anything could have happened to anybody. As my account reveals, both factions of the People's Democratic Party of Afghanistan used their time in power to offer the 'hospitality' of prison to their rivals. That such 'hospitality' was also extended to foreigners like myself and others is therefore understandable. However, I must acknowledge with gratitude the role played in my release by certain western socialist figures, in particular the Labour MP Ron Brown, who used his good offices with the Afghan government. It was efforts such as these, together with certain internal circumstances, which eventually persuaded my hosts to release me from their great 'lost luggage' facility, otherwise known as Kabul's Pulcharkhi Prison.

Pulcharkhi is in itself a vast and fascinating subject. This is not the place to recount in detail my experiences in that extraordinary jail – which included countless hunger strikes so that I could be allowed to walk along its high and impregnable walls, sit in the sun, talk to other prisoners, or be given paper and pens to write 'poetry'. After a couple of months in Pulcharkhi, I was perhaps the 'freest' of its inmates, which was why I was able to get to know people of every school of thought and political inclination.

During my stay in Afghanistan, I had the opportunity to meet, and often to deal with, major and minor leaders of both factions of the PDPA. I also enjoyed great kindness and consideration at the hands of smaller functionaries of the Party (in stark comparison with senior figures), both inside and outside the prison: this despite my openly critical attitude towards both Brezhnev and Karmal.

After Karmal's arrival on the scene, minor Party workers started asking themselves if the Soviet Union had any ideological, moral or natural right to use brutal physical force to play politics in Afghanistan. After 1981, the junior Party functionaries, who were the greatest victims of the war, had begun to criticize the Kremlin – though under their breath. After watching the Red Army and Soviet advisers at close quarters, their idealism had been shattered. After all, these workers had been taught that the Soviet Union was peopled not by mortals but by angels: which is as absurd as telling the people of Europe that the Soviet Union consists entirely of cannibals. With the possible exception of Karmal and his Ministers and advisers, by 1984 almost all members of the Party had lost hope in the future of the Revolution.

Failure can often be turned to success by accidents of history. Were such a miracle to take place in Afghanistan at some time in the future, it is certain that no PDPA government could ever hope to gain mass popular backing. Socialism has been one of the main casualties of Soviet intervention. There is talk that a 'national' government might be set up under the former King Zahir Shah: this is perhaps the only way for the Afghan rebels and the Kremlin to end the war. But what an irony of history: the Afghan 'revolution' which overthrows a republic ends with the restoration of the monarchy! The truth, however, is that neither the Kremlin nor the rebels can any longer afford the luxury of time-consuming solutions. Prolongation of war will produce no results, only more bloodshed and destruction on both sides.

I want to thank all those Afghan friends in whose company I have been privileged to spend long nights in prison and many pleasant days of freedom. I can hope to forget the bitterness of the past and the personal suffering I went through in jail while I see before me the smiling faces of my Afghan friends and relive the affection I received from them.

I also want to recall the days spent in Kabul with my many Pakistani friends who were constrained to seek refuge and who are now scattered here and there: Mir Murtaza Bhutto (in exile), the late Shahnawaz

Bhutto, Shaukat Ali (in exile), Sohail Sethi (in exile), Qayoom Butt (in exile in Britain), Rashid Nagi (in exile in Canada), Safdar Hamdani (in exile in Canada), Sheikh Gul Mohammed (in prison in Pakistan), Zubair Shad (in prison in Pakistan), Arshad Awan (in exile in Holland), Tajbar Khan (in prison in Pakistan), Kausar Ali Shah (in exile), the late Pervez Shinwari and the late Baba Mohsin.

My translator Khalid Hasan I cannot thank enough for the hard work he has put into the book. In fact he has been the 'midwife' to this work. Had it not been for his efforts and constant encouragement, I would never have been able to complete it.

Raja Anwar, Offenbach, July 1987

Introduction

Afghanistan has posed one of the major world crises of the 1980s: since the advent to power in April 1978 of the People's Democratic Party of Afghanistan (PDPA), that country has been marked by intense internal conflicts, and by a growing involvement of external powers. Most of the western coverage of the war has presented it in straightforward terms as a conflict between one nation, the Afghan people, and a foreign invader, the USSR, and has attributed the crisis to the conflict between these two. The solution to the problem would therefore appear to lie in the withdrawal by the USSR of its forces from Afghanistan, to be followed by democratic determination by the Afghan people of the kind of government and international alignment they would prefer.

This analysis, appealing as it is, is fundamentally flawed, for at least three reasons. It is the great merit of Raja Anwar's book that he enables us to see how much more internationally complex and internally determined the Afghan crisis really is. In the first place, the war in Afghanistan began not as a war between one nation and an external invader, but as a conflict between Afghans, a rivalry between an incipiently interventionist state in Kabul and other groups in society, a conflict that grew during the early 1970s, persisted through the coups of 1973 and 1978, and finally exploded into civil war in 1979. Many of those involved in the guerrilla opposition to the Soviet forces after the intervention of December 1979 had been active against the central government both before and after April 1978: this was particularly true of Gulbudin Hikmatyar and his *Hizbe Islami*. The PDPA came to power in an attempt to accelerate the transformation and modernisation of Afghan society, with an impatience and a lack of experience born both of the frustrated reforms of Daud, who had preceded them, and of the long stasis of the Zahir Shah period. It was this paralysis, of which the intelligentsia and the upper echelons of the state apparatus were especially conscious, that led to the civil war into which, at a later stage, the USSR was drawn.

It is here that the second corrective emphasis of Anwar's book lies. His portrait of life within the PDPA, never before provided, offers powerful insights into the mentality and strategy of the Afghan revolutionary movement. On the basis of his first-hand knowledge of political processes in Kabul in the late 1970s, Anwar paints a unique and detailed picture of the background to the intra-PDPA crisis of 1978–1979 and the Soviet intervention of December 1979: never before has the argument so clearly been put that it was the adventurism and mismanagement of PDPA leaders Taraki and Amin, not some Soviet strategic plan, that drew the Soviet forces into Kabul. Faced with the prospect of seeing the PDPA swept away by the guerrillas, the Brezhnev leadership believed it could save the reforming state by simultaneously introducing Soviet forces and moving the PDPA away from its more provocative social reforms. It was the contradiction within that decision – which, far from stabilising the PDPA, provoked great internal and external opposition – which in the longer run was to confound Soviet expectations.

The third important shift of perspective proposed by Anwar relates to the question of Afghan nationalism itself. The phenomenon of nationalism in Afghanistan can be looked at in at least three ways. It can be seen first of all in terms of the widespread resistance to the Soviet forces after December 1979 on the part of different sectors of Afghan society on what is said to be a 'national' basis. As Afghans, they wanted foreign forces to leave their country. It is doubtful, however, how far such a pan-Afghan sentiment pre-existed the war and indeed how far it developed during the war: as much as identifying with one Afghan nation with common culture and interests, the guerrilla groups fought on the basis of particularist nationalisms: they identified with specific sub-groups, ethnic and tribal, within Afghan society. Thus they fought the Soviet forces as Tajiks and Hazaras, Uzbek and Pushtuns, as much as Afghans, with the added factor that if not now then in the future they would as likely be fighting each other on these particularistic 'national' bases. The very term 'Afghan' was normally used to refer to only one of these groups, the Pushtuns.

However, there exists in Afghanistan a third variety of nationalism, namely that of the republican modernisers who from 1973 onwards sought to overcome the backwardness of their country and introduce many of the changes they saw as overdue. This kind of nationalism is apparent in other semi-colonial countries in which modernising elites challenging traditional monarchies and oligarchies have sought to accelerate the kinds of changes that had been initiated in part elsewhere during periods of direct colonial rule: in North Yemen after 1962, in Ethiopia after 1974, and, earlier, in Thailand after 1932. Here national- ism consists not so much in struggle against an external power as in a reforming and democratic attempt to bring the nation into contact with international trends and processes of development. Such impatient revolutions from above can lead to arbitrary and precipitate reforms, provoking significant sections of the population into opposition to modernisation and change: this is exactly what happened in Afghanis- tan, as in the earlier instances. Part of the determination exhibited by the PDPA in transforming Afghanistan after April 1978 was therefore a product of this reforming nationalism. The reaction to it, under the banner of 'Islam', expressed social opposition to reform of Afghan society, not religious belief.

Anwar's book takes us inside the leadership of the Afghan revolu- tion in a way that no previous account has done: he provides precisely the kind of insight that someone close to, but not directly involved in, the leadership of that period can evoke. Sympathetic as he is towards the overall goals of the April 1978 revolution, he nonetheless draws a critical portrait of the crimes and follies, personal and strategic, of the initial PDPA leadership and of the reckless manner in which they squandered the opportunities of the immediate post-April period and then plunged the PDPA into a murderous factional spiral. The lessons that he draws about the dangers of such factionalism are as relevant to other cases of self-inflicted crisis, such as Grenada and South Yemen, as they are to the grotesque aberrations of the PDPA.

The special strength of Anwar's study lies in its account of the period preceding and immediately following the Soviet intervention. His later narrative is of necessity based on secondary material and adds less to what is already known. His central argument on the post–1979 period, that the PDPA regime was doomed by the very fact of the Soviet inter- vention to assist it, must remain controversial, given the multiple factors that subsequently came into play. Evidence from Afghanistan suggests that between 1983 and 1986 the PDPA regime had begun to gain some ground, politically and militarily, and that for reasons of political align- ment and convenience, larger numbers of Afghans had begun to collaborate with the organs of party and state. Whether this could have led to a longer term consolidation – permitting a withdrawal of Soviet forces – is open to question, but it seems that in 1986 the trend turned significantly against the Kabul regime and its Soviet allies, in at least three respects. First, the military balance swung in favour of the guer- rillas, as a consequence of the deployment of ground-to-air missiles provided by the USA (Stinger) and the UK (Blowpipe, Javelin). This robbed Soviet and Afghan government forces of their air superiority. Secondly, the move by the USSR to encourage 'national reconciliation' between the PDPA and the opposition set off a new round of factionalism within the ruling party itself: as with the replacement of Amin by Babrak Karmal in late 1979, so the replacement of Babrak by Najibullah in May 1986 opened uncertainties within the Party that weakened the appeal of new policies and undermined the credibility of the regime. Thirdly, there was a clear shift within the USSR itself away from the unmovable commitment of the Brezhnev years and towards an admission of Soviet limits and an urgent desire to withdraw – both because of the war's unpopularity within the USSR and also because of the effects of the Soviet role on US-Soviet relations. The combination of these three factors – military, political, and strategic – led the USSR in 1986 to proclaim its willingness to withdraw, and in 1987 to detach this commitment from any guaranteed survival of the PDPA regime itself.

Whatever the course and consequences of a Soviet withdrawal from Afghanistan, the commitment of the Red Army in that country must appear as one chapter in a longer history of conflict within the country itself, a history in which external forces and influences have played an exacerbating role, but in which the determining factors have been intrinsic to the society. Moreover while Soviet influence may be reduced, it is unlikely to disappear entirely, and other regional forces with long-established interests in the country have shown little sign of abandoning their interest: Pakistan, heir to the interventionist propensities of the British raj, has long sustained the conservative opposition in Afghanistan; and Iran, combining Islamic internationalism with hegemonic aspirations harking back to Iranian conquests of the eighteenth century, sees in Afghanistan a new arena for the export of Khomeini's revolutionary message. The USA and China can also retain their accesses. As long as the issue of political power within Afghanistan is unsettled, these external forces will search for openings to pursue their own policies.

Raja Anwar draws his own lessons from the tragedy of contemporary Afghanistan, two of which are of special relevance in the wider context of the late 1980s. One is the disastrous consequences that follow from precipitate attempts to impose reforms from above, and the risk that, aside from the loss of human life involved, such attempts will mobilise the population behind regressive leaderships. The other lesson has to do with the reality of internationalised counter-revolutionary intervention in the contemporary world, evident in Afghanistan, as in Cambodia, Angola and Nicaragua. Indigenous in its origins, the Afghan civil war acquired an international character from the late 1970s onwards and mobilised the USA and its allies, in this case including China, in support of the counter-revolution. The consequences of that mobilisation in Afghanistan and internationally have still to be seen: they may constitute yet another ominous chapter in the history of the Afghan conflict.

Fred Halliday, London, February 1988

1

Early History

The region known in early history as Khorasan, came to form the geographical basis of modern Afghanistan in the mid-eighteenth century. Literally, Afghanistan means the land of the Afghans. However, it should be made clear that the term Afghanistan has generally been employed to connote the Pushtun nation. It was, in fact, the people of Iran who originally coined the term Afghan to refer to Pushtuns. In ancient Iranian, the word Afghan was used to describe a tribal chief, warrior or hero. In Persian, it has meant unruliness and upheaval. Some medieval historians also employed the term Afghan satirically to suggest that the Pushtuns were an unruly lot. As for the Iranians, whether they used the term Afghan by way of an admission of Pushtun gallantry, or as an expression of lighthearted contempt, the term gradually lost its original meaning and came to be accepted as a description of the Pushtuns.

The Pushtuns are called Afghans in Afghanistan and their language Afghani, rather than Pushtu. In Afghanistan today, there live about seven million ethnic and sub-cultural groups which are non-Pushtun, and though they claim Afghan citizenship, they do not describe themselves as Afghans, but as Tajiks, Hazaras, Uzbeks, Turkomans, Hiratis, Aimaqs or Nooristanis.

The emergence of a change in productive economic relations, and the evolution of a socio-historical consciousness among Pushtun tribes, led them to the concept of a single nation. It was also at this point that the tribal system of joint land ownership gave way to the institution of feudalism and individual ownership. However, neither this important social development nor its aftermath is so straightforward as to allow us simply to declare Afghanistan a feudal society in the classical sense – an error which most western intellectuals and the Marxist leaders of the present ruling order have made with such tragic consequences. The intricate political and social currents which have formed the Afghan national entity will be analyzed in greater detail later in this book.

There are conflicting theories about the racial, historical and geographical origins of the Afghan tribes. In 1839, B. Dorn expressed the view that the Paktyes mentioned by Herodotus in his *Istoria* were the real ancestors of modern-day Afghans (Pushtuns).[1] A later theory claimed that the Afghans were the descendants of the 'Pakhta' tribes to whom the Vedic scriptures also make reference. According to the Vedas, these tribes inhabited the northwestern parts of India, which would roughly place them in modern Afghanistan. If this theory is accepted, then the Afghans should trace their origins to the Indo-Aryan tribes.[2]

The Soviet historian Gankovsky has a different explanation which is not only less myth-ridden but far more plausible:

> The formation of the union of largely East-Iranian tribes which became the initial stratum of the Pushtun ethnic group dates from the first millennium A.D. and is connected with the Ephtalite Confederacy. In the areas north of the Hindu Kush, some of the tribes of this Confederacy participated in the formation of the nationalities who inhabit Middle Asia today.[3]

If Gankovsky's theory is accepted then this historical riddle is easy to solve. The existence of Ephtalite or Abdali tribes among the Pushtuns, no less than among the Uzbeks, Turkomans and Lokaiis, points to historical proximity and racial intermix. Jarring is also agreed that the presence of the Ephtalite tribes among the Uzbeks, Turkomans, Lokaiis and Pushtuns is sufficient to establish the important role played by the East Iranian tribes of the Ephtalite Tribal Confederacy in the racial formation of the present-day Pushtuns.[4]

After the fall of the Ephtalite Tribal Confederacy, some of its splinter sections moved to the Koh-i-Suleman area and settled there. They can truly be described as the ancestors of the Pushtun people.

Known to their neighbours as Pushtuns, meaning the inhabitants of Pusht, these tribes gradually began to identify themselves by this name when any of their members moved into other areas, either as military conquerors or immigrants. Koh-i-Suleman was not a particularly hospitable region, but since it was home to the Pushtun tribes, they never forgot it, even when they had trekked away from it. About the Koh-i-Suleman range Babur writes: 'These hills are extremely ugly, misshapen, diminutive and forgettable. Perhaps no uglier mountain range exists elsewhere in the world.'[5]

During the thirteenth and fourteenth centuries, the Pushtuns spread to

Ghazni, the plains of Peshawar and the suburbs of Kabul. By the fourteenth and fifteenth centuries, they were to be found in Kandhar, in Zhobe, Loralai and Shal (today's Quetta in Pakistan), and a hundred years later in Swat, Kurram and Panjkora.

A number of factors came together to confer national identity on the Pushtun tribes in the ensuing period and, by the eighteenth century, external conditions had become ripe for an independent Pushtun or Afghan state. By this time, their once-formidable neighbours, the Iranian monarchy and the Mughal dynasty at Delhi, were at the end of their tether. The Turkoman and Tajik emirates were also tottering. The establishment of a Pushtun nation state had become an historical necessity. Internally, moreover, because of their protracted struggle against foreign rulers, the Pushtuns were now fully conscious of their political and national identity.

The traditional Pushtun tribal system had turned into a feudal order over the years. In the eighteenth century, every Pushtun tribe had its own territory, grazing grounds, water source and fort. The fort was always built at the site of the water source because, for economic survival, it was essential to protect it from rival tribes. Initially, the forts were considered the joint property of the tribe, but as time passed they came to be treated as the personal estate of the head of the tribe. In a Pushtun tribe, there is no head or leader as such, but each branch or *khel* of the tribe has its own elder or Malik. If a tribe has ten *khels*, it will have an equal number of heads or Maliks. They meet in council, called a *jirga*, where important matters, internal and external, are deliberated upon and decided, such as making war on a rival tribe or suing for peace. The high moral and social position enjoyed by the head of a tribal *khel* had with time been transformed into economic overlordship, thanks to the annexation of rival territory through battle. By the middle of the eighteenth century, a feudal system had come firmly into existence, consolidated with the help of cheap or unpaid labour performed by the remaining inhabitants of the conquered territories, Pushtun farmers and, sometimes, slaves.[6] The stage for a Pushtun state had been set. What was needed was a man of destiny, a hero, to accomplish the task.

History sometimes throws up the right person at the right moment. So it was in Afghanistan. The man who laid the foundation of the first Afghan state was born at Multan (now in Pakistan) in the second decade of the eighteenth century. His name was Ahmed Shah Saddozai. He is still remembered by the Afghans as Baba or father. It was he who founded the Abdali kingdom. At a very young age, he commanded 5,000 troops in Nadir Shah's army and at the age of only twenty-five, he laid the foundations of modern Afghanistan.

Ahmed Shah was born into the Saddozai branch of the Barakzai tribe which in turn was a branch of the Popalzai Pushtun tribe. He was a descendent of Asadullah Khan Barakzai whom the Saffayid kings of Iran had appointed head of the Abdali tribes. The Saddozai tribe takes its name from Asadullah. This remarkable ancestor of Ahmed Shah was much in favour at the Iranian court and this connection and its attendant benefits were responsible for the later importance and powerful position of the Saddozai branch. Among the Pushtuns, blood must be avenged with blood and yet no Abdali will ever shed the blood of a Saddozai, no matter how grave the score to be settled. This is because the Saddozais were made Abdali chiefs on the basis of a royal Iranian decree.[7]

After the death of Nadir Shah, the Iranian court fell into disarray. In 1747, a historic *jirga* of Pushtun tribes, held at Kandhar, laid the foundations of the first national Afghan/Pushtun State. This assembly of elders lasted for nine days, according to contemporary accounts. However, it was unable to decide who the first head of the new state should be. There were two candidates, namely, Ahmed Shah Saddozai and Haji Jamal Khan Barakzai. The latter was not only older, but commanded a larger following, in terms both of numbers and armed men, than his rival. According to tribal tradition, seniority in age and greater armed strength are to be treated as deciding factors in such situations. Ahmed Shah was not only young but his tribe numbered no more than 5,000. When the *jirga* found itself in a deadlock, it broke normal tradition and decided to leave the decision to a holy man who was the keeper of the shrine where this assembly was being held. This old man, who was a Punjabi by birth and thus a non-Pushtun, entered the assembly hall, it is said, with an ear of young wheat in his hand. This he placed on Ahmed Shah's head. The assembled tribal leaders, including Haji Jamal Khan, taking the gesture as the final choice, declared their allegiance to Ahmed Shah, the first head of the first Afghan State. It was the same holy man who conferred the title Durrani on Ahmed Shah, who made it part of his name. All his life, he never wore a crown, but an ear of young wheat in his turban. He never declared himself king, though he not only conquered many kingdoms but was responsible for restoring many defeated kings to their thrones.

One mistake needs to be rectified here, because it has been repeated in most western scholarly writings on Afghanistan. It has been asserted that the rule of the Durrani tribe came to an end in 1978. It must be made clear that there are no such tribes as Durrani among the Pushtuns. This was merely an honorific title conferred on Ahmed Shah, who, in turn, conferred it on many Pushtun and non-Pushtun tribes. Among them were Yusufzais, Mehmands, Khattaks and some others whom he grouped together under the name Bar Durrani or Highland Durrani. In 1753 or 1754, he conferred the title Durrani Bamzai on the non-Pushtun Kurdish tribe Kubushan. Until 1978, power in Afghanistan lay with the Barakzai, Saddozai and Ahmedzai branches of the Popalzai tribe. The Popalzai were themselves an offshoot of the Abdali tribe.

Ahmed Shah was a wise, prudent and simple ruler. During his reign, the boundaries of the Afghan state stretched beyond Afghanistan across what is now Pakistan to the River Beas. In the Third War of Panipat, Ahmed Shah defeated an army three times the size of his own. However, after having crushed the Marathas, he restored the Delhi throne to the decadent and powerless Mughals. This act of royal munificence is difficult to comprehend because the eastern Pushtuns had fought the Mughals for as long as two hundred years. However, this kiss of life turned out to be futile as the Mughal dynasty was never again able to find its feet.

Ahmed Shah returned to Kandhar. At the time of his departure from Delhi, he is said to have recited a verse

The Delhi throne indeed is beautiful
But does it compare with the Kandhar mountains!

The Third Panipat War changed the balance of power in India. By destroying the burgeoning might of the Maratha empire, Ahmed Shah also demolished the last bulwark against the rising tide of British influence from the East. The Marathas never recovered from this defeat and the Mughals could no longer muster the power to defend their throne or the future of India. It was only a matter of time before the British would capture Delhi while the tottering pretenders to the Mughal throne made futile calls to Ahmed Shah's warring successors to save them from the onslaught. Many historians think that if Ahmed Shah had decided to fill the existing power vacuum by assuming power at Delhi, India might have been spared enslavement to the British. However, Ahmed Shah was only mortal, and after his death, his battling successors might not have been able to hold on to power. After all, not only did they savage each other following Ahmed Shah's death, but one of them actually allowed himself to be placed on the throne at Kabul with the help of the British. Perhaps the greatest favour Ahmed Shah could have done to India's future would have been not to fight and win the Third War of Panipat.

At this point, one must mention a Pushtun controversy which later became the cause of bitter hatred and strife between Afghanistan's two major tribes, the Ghilzai and Popalzai.

According to one Pushtun tradition, all Pushtuns are the direct offspring of Qais Abdul Rashid, who is said to have been converted to Islam at the hands of the Holy Prophet Mohammed (570-632) himself.[8] According to this legend, Shah Hussain, the son of the ruler of Ghaur, had an illicit affair with Bibi Mato, the grand-daughter of Qais Abdul Rashid. Their offspring came to be known as Ghilzai Pushtuns (in Pushtu, *ghilzai* literally means the offspring of sin). If this legend is to be trusted, the Ghilzais are Pushtun only from the maternal side, since Shah Hussain was not a Pushtun. The Ghaur connection also implies that the ancestral territory of the Ghilzais was Khalaj. There is other historical evidence to suggest that the Ghilzais were of Turkish origin and came under the influence of the Pushtuns because of common blood bonds among the women of the two groups.[9]

In any case, this legendary belief in the original illegitimacy of the Ghilzais became the cause of bitter social and political friction between this tribe and the Popalzais. Two hundred years of Afghan history are characterized by fratricidal, internecine warfare between the Ghilzais and the ruling Popalzai tribe. Throughout this period, the Ghilzais were denied all higher state appointments. In fact, the very word Ghilzai came to mean rebel and enemy, although Ahmed Shah publicly declared that the Ghilzais and Abdalis were deserving of equal respect: 'All are as one man, the Abdalis and the Ghilzais'.[10] Despite Ahmed Shah's almost poetical tribute to the Ghilzais, they did not receive fair and equal treatment during his reign. He himself ordered that all Ghilzai tribes should be led by Abdali chiefs. This 'administrative change' was designed to keep the 'unreliable' Ghilzais under direct Abdali control. However, the Ghilzais never accepted Abdali overlordship and continued to fight bravely against the ruling order. During the feudalistic tribal rule of the Abdalis, the majority of Ghilzais remained, as before, nomadic cattlemen or farm labourers.

With the birth of independent India and Pakistan in 1947, the Ghilzai nomads were instrumental in the formation of a new economic sector. Because of their constant movement across the borders, they became the natural carriers of smuggled goods between Afghanistan and Pakistan. After 1978, the majority came down to settle in Pakistan. Today, most smuggled goods markets (popularly called Baras) in that country are run by Ghilzais. Their women hawk smuggled cloth and other items from house to house. The Ghilzais of Katwaz have been moneylenders for several hundred years and can be seen (and done business with) in any major Pakistani or Indian city.

I have summarized the legend regarding the origins of the Ghilzai, and told something of their history, because Afghanistan's first revolutionary party was born under the roof of a Ghilzai Pushtun. The party was the People's Democratic Party of Afghanistan (PDPA) and its founding General Secretary, who became the first head of the Afghan April Revolution, was Noor Mohammed Ghilzai, born in the Taraki branch of the Ghilzai tribe. Taraki's disciple, assassin, and successor Hafizullah Amin was also a Ghilzai from the Kharoti branch of the clan. If one looks back at the previous 225 years of Afghan history, one cannot but be struck by the fact that the Ghilzais ruled the country for only one year and nine months. It is understandable that Taraki and Amin, who carried generations-old memories of exploitation and discrimination, should have become impatient revolutionaries. The radical and ill-considered land reforms initiated by them are also to be linked to their Ghilzai background. It was their rebellious disposition which prompted them to declare immediate war on the feudal order dating back to the Abdali years of power, and though this may not be the only factor which can explain their conduct in office, it is too important to be ignored.

The traditional hatred between the Abdalis and the Ghilzais took new forms after the 1978 revolution. Unable to accept a Ghilzai as their ruler, it was only natural that the Abdalis should rebel against the revolutionary government. On the other hand, since the Ghilzais made up 50 per cent of the Pushtun population, attempts to press them into the service of the Revolution do not have to be viewed as a plunge into tribalism. It was perhaps the logical and objective approach which Taraki and Amin failed to adopt.

There have been three rulers in Afghan history who lost their thrones because they tried to move away from established tradition. The first was Ahmed Shah's grandson and Taimur Shah's son, Shah Zaman, who was deposed by his step-brother Shah Mahmood and blinded because he openly attempted to lessen the influence of feudal tribal chieftains at his court. The second was Amir Amanullah Khan, who had to abdicate because he tried to introduce modern ideas to Afghanistan. The third victim was Sardar Daud Khan, who fell to his assassins because he tried to find a compromise between tradition and modernity.

In 1747, Ahmed Shah was elected to rule Afghanistan by a council, or *jirga*, of tribal elders, all of them holders of great feudal wealth and power. He took good care of the tribal *sardars*, or chiefs, by keeping them in important and influential positions. However, he was always wary of the Barakzai chiefs who, he felt, might prove a danger in the future. In order to reduce the influence of the head of the tribe, Haji Jamal Khan, he brought about the administrative separation of the

Achakzai branch from its Barakzai clan. After Ahmed Shah's death his son Taimur Shah ruled for twenty-five years and, following his father's example, kept the tribal sardars happy by offering them important positions at his court. However, no sooner had his son Shah Zaman come to power than he declared war on his step-brothers since, being older, they were all contenders for the throne. The head of the powerful Barakzai tribe, Sardar Painda Khan (son of Haji Jamal Khan), was active in his support of Shah Mahmood, Shah Zaman's step-brother. To teach him a lesson, Shah Zaman had Painda Khan's eyes taken out. There was a revolt, spearheaded by the blinded Sardar's sons, which only ended when Shah Mahmood avenged his mentor's pain and humiliation by blinding Shah Zaman after overthrowing him.

The Barakzai tribes were led by Painda Khan's eldest son Fateh Khan. There was bitter conflict between Ahmed Shah's grandsons for power and during this time of fratricidal tribal war, Fateh Khan emerged as the king-maker. He helped Shah Mahmood ascend the throne. One of his early moves was to shift the capital from Kandhar to Kabul. Shah Shuja, Shah Zaman's real brother, took this opportunity to occupy Kandhar and declare himself king, but was beaten in battle and fled to Punjab. Shah Mahmood was once again in control of the kingdom, thanks mainly to the help of Fateh Khan. However, he repaid his benefactor by having his eyes gouged out. Following this cruel act, the leadership so far exercised by Fateh Kahn fell into the hands of his younger brother, Sardar Dost Mohammed Khan. The conflicts which followed turned Afghanistan into a bloody bullring until the crown finally fell like scattered fruit at the feet of Painda Khan's numerous sons.

2

The British and Afghanistan

Till the time of Shah Zaman, Ranjeet Singh of Punjab used to pay tribute to the Kandhar court, but as soon as inter-tribal conflict broke out in Afghanistan, he declared himself Maharaja or king. The ousted Shah Shuja, Ahmed Shah's grandson, sought refuge at Ranjeet Singh's court at Lahore. At first, the Sikh ruler showed him great hospitality but before long divested him of all the treasures he had brought with him, including the incomparable diamond, *Koh-i-Noor*, or 'mountain of light'.

Shah Shuja settled down in Ludhiana, a town now in the Indian Punjab. In 1838, the first official delegation from the Czarist court arrived in Kabul and sought an audience with Amir Dost Mohammed Khan. After getting rid of Ahmed Shah's sons and grandson, Painda Khan's twelve sons had carved up Afghanistan into their own separate fiefdoms, none of them willing to choose or accept one ruler for the entire country. The British had come to the conclusion that given Afghanistan's anarchic conditions, any growth in Russian influence would go against their interest. Although at this point in history Ranjeet Singh's empire stretched from the Beas river in Punjab to Peshawar in the northwest, the British could already foresee these areas becoming part of their growing Indian empire. British overtures to Shah Shuja began almost immediately after the arrival of the Russian mission to Kabul.

In 1838, a 'treaty of friendship' was signed between Shah Shuja, Ranjeet Singh and the British, under which Shah Shuja offered formal allegiance to the British. The treaty also promised some parts of Afghanistan to Ranjeet Singh. It was also agreed that Shah Shuja would be helped to the Kabul throne jointly by Ranjeet Singh and the British. The British Governor General, Lord Auckland, declared at Simla that

'His Majesty Shah Shuja-ul-Mulk would enter Afghanistan in the company of his troops and the army of the British Empire would protect him from foreign interference and a rebel opposition.'[1] Lord Auckland also expressed the hope that Shah Shuja's 'loyal subjects' would help him in his bid. A mercenary army, consisting of four rifle and two cavalry battalions, was raised for Shah Shuja by the British to be paraded as the mock conquerers of Afghanistan. Finally, a *lashkar* of about 90,000 to 100,000 men, 'led' by Shah Shuja and commanded by British officers (accompanied by their entourage of Indian servants), entered Afghanistan through Baluchistan, having earlier marched through Sind on horseback, camels, elephants and mules. The illiterate but very wily Ranjeet Singh did not, however, allow this army to use his territories.

On 25 April 1839, the British army captured Kandhar and Amir Dost Mohammed Khan's brother, Konhdel Khan, fled the city. Shah Shuja was now the 'real' king of Afghanistan. The famous Soviet historian Nafatula Khalfin describes the coronation of Shah Shuja thus:

> On his left were British officers in red and gold full dress coats and on his right, barely half a dozen bedraggled, partly-clothed Afghan followers. Not more than a hundred Afghans had arrived to see Shah Shuja's entry into the city ... even among these one could hear grumbling against the infidel invaders. After his coronation ... the puppet signed an agreement ... on the permanent presence of British troops in Afghanistan and the establishment of British control over its foreign relations.[2]

Ironically, this account would need only a change of names and dates to apply almost to the letter to Babrak Karmal's arrival on the scene in our times.

In August 1839, Shah Shuja entered Kabul with his 'friendly army'.[3] Amir Dost Mohammed Khan had 12,000 cavalry, 2,500 infantrymen and 45 artillery guns. He fled Kabul to start a guerilla war against the British. However, he found the going hard and surrendered, agreeing (in vain) to accept the legitimacy of Shah Shuja's accession to the throne. He was put under arrest and exiled to British India. However, an armed insurrection was started against the British by the Ghilzais in Kalat Ghazni, causing much damage to the occupying army. In the suburbs of Kabul, Amir Dost Mohammed Khan's sons, Wazir Akbar Khan, Amin Logari and Mir Masjidi, became the leaders of the Afghan national struggle. There was a spate of surprise attacks on the British troops, though Lord Auckland kept assuring his government that the new occupant of the throne in Kabul would soon be recognized by the neighbouring states of Bokhara and Kunduz as an 'independent' ruler.[4]

When the British first began their military moves against Afghanistan, the British Resident in Baluchistan said to the Khan of Kalat, in an effort to elicit a reaction, 'The British army has entered Kabul without firing a bullet.' The worldly-wise Mir Mehrab Khan, instead of answering, began to stare at the sky. The Resident made another attempt 'You make no answer. You seem lost in thought.' The old Khan replied, 'Yes, I am thinking. You people have entered this country, but how will you get out?'[5]

The old man was perhaps not too far off the mark. Two years later, an Englishman writing home bewails the lot of the British army in Afghanistan. His letter makes prophetic reading:

> The plan was for Shah Shuja to ascend to this ancestral throne and the (British) army to return to India. The job was done two years ago, but we are still here. The government cannot bear the tremendous cost of holding Afghanistan. Unrest is growing all over the country ... Our posts are being attacked. Our soldiers are being killed. Can we leave Afghanistan in such a state, and on the other hand, will it change and will the country calm down? Never. At least we won't live to see it. I cannot tell you how the people hate us, anyone who kills a European is considered as a saint ... We must go back with a loss of honour.[6]

Afghanistan had turned into a virtual hell for the British in less than three years. The powerful British administrator MacNaughton was shot dead by Wazir Akbar Khan and Shah Shuja was overthrown by the rebellious Afghan people.[7] The British, not about to give up, signed another 'treaty of friendship' with the detained Dost Mohammed Khan and agreed to return him to Afghanistan. Wazir Akbar Khan took a large number of British women and children hostages, and in the ensuing struggle, the British lost 20,000 men and about £16 million. The most grievous damage was inflicted on them by the Ghilzai tribes. Writing of the humiliation of the British army in Afghanistan, Karl Marx noted:

> January 13, 1842. On the walls of Jalalabad ... the sentries espied a man in a tattered English uniform on a miserable pony horse, and the man was desperately wounded; it was Dr Brydon, the sole survivor of the 15,000 [British troops] who had left Kabul three weeks before. He was dying of starvation.[8]

In 1843, Amir Dost Mohammed Khan arrived in Kabul and was installed on the throne. One of his first moves was a military campaign against the Ghilzais who were staging attacks in the Swat area (now in Pakistan) in an attempt to dislodge the British. Maharaja Ranjeet Singh was dead and the former Afghan territories were now under British control. Dost Mohammed Khan, instead of trying to wrest control of occupied Afghan territories from the British, was reminding the British of their obligations to him under the 'friendship treaty'. He had even put Amin Logari and Mir Masjidi Khan in prison. His son, the nationalist crown prince Wazir Akbar Khan, was also poisoned. Although the British were against the heir to the throne, some historians hold the father responsible for the murder. (According to Khalfin, the hatred of the people for the foreign British army and the 'stooge' government was evidence enough that Afghanistan was not free:

> Afghan historian Ahmed Ali Kohzad was fully justified in claiming that the reign of Shah Shuja should in reality be called the British Occupation of the country. The country was being held by foreign troops and the people were eager to give expression to their disgust both morally and materially.[9]

The Soviet historian's account is significant because its publication came two years after Babrak Karmal was brought into power by Soviet troops, and the anti-soviet camp was using the same line of argument to 'prove' that Afghanistan no longer existed as a sovereign state.)

In 1848, the British occupied Punjab and thereby gained control of the Afghan areas annexed by the Sikhs. The British now physically stood at the borders of Amir Dost Mohammed Khan's territories. In 1855 and 1857, he signed 'friendship renewal' treaties with the British, in effect formalizing their occupation of Afghan areas. This was the beginning of what later came to be called the Pushtunistan problem. Until 1900, these annexed Pushtun areas were a part of Punjab. In 1901, Lord Curzon grouped them together to form the administrative unit he called the North West Frontier Province (NWFP).[10]

The year 1857 was a golden opportunity for Amir Dost Mohammed Khan to regain control of his annexed territories. India was in a state of turmoil and an armed uprising was in the offing. The decadent kings, Maharajas and local chieftains, could not change India's destiny, but the popular rebellion, when it came, hit the British like a shock-wave. In that year of the 'Mutiny', the Pushtun areas were cleared of armed British presence. The British hero, Colonel Nicholson, who defeated the mutineers of Delhi, had arrived in the Mughal capital from a cantonment in the Pushtun areas. If Dost Mohammed Khan had attacked the British from the northwest, it would have been difficult for the besieged British garrisons to survive the onslaught from two sides. However, Dost Mohammed Khan was occupied with less onerous matters. By protecting the undefended British rear, he played his role of 'trusted ally and friend'.

While Dost Mohammed Khan kept his part of the bargain, his British 'allies' had other ideas, eventually issuing an ultimatum to his son and successor, Amir Sher Ali Khan, to accept the presence of a permanent British Mission in Kabul. This was part of the new 'forward policy' aimed at making the northwest of India an integral part of the Empire. Amir Sher Ali Khan was in a tight spot. His brothers, Afzal Khan and Azam Khan, and his nephew Abdul Rahman Khan, in keeping with the family tradition, were engaged in armed uprisings against his rule. Even his eldest son, Yaqub Khan, rose against him but was captured and put in prison. His nominated successor, an infant, was poisoned in 1878. Amir Sher Ali, now certain that the moves against him were largely British-backed, decided to make overtures to Czarist Russia, and a Russian mission came to Kabul to open talks.

This was the main cause of the British ultimatum of 1878, demanding a permanent diplomatic and military presence at Kabul. Two weeks before the expiry of the British ultimatum on 9 November 1878, the British Prime Minister told a meeting at Guildhall, London: 'The British Northwest Frontier is a haphazard affair ... Britain desires a change in this state of affairs.'[11]

In December 1878, a British army numbering 35,000 invaded Afghanistan through Khyber, Kurram and Bolan. Amir Sher Ali Khan released his rebel son Yaqub Ali Khan from jail and, putting him in charge of the state, left for Petersburg fully determined to organize an international conference with the help of the Russians to invite world attention to the British invasion. Unfortunately, he did not make it. He fell ill on the way and died at Mazar Sharif in February 1879.

In May 1879, under the Gandmak, a treaty signed between Amir Yaqub Ali Khan, his heir, and the British, the bordering Afghan areas of Pashin, Sibi, Khyber, Kurram and Michni were annexed. (These frontier areas now lie under the administrative jurisdiction of the Pakistan government and are still called Agencies as in British times. Internally, they continue to be autonomous and the Pakistani laws do not apply here.) Amir Yaqub also agreed to accept British control over Afghanistan's external relations and to step up mutual trade and commerce. Under the treaty, the author of the scheme, one Cavagnari, was not only appointed ambassador to Kabul, but like his predecessor MacNaughton, he virtually exercised the powers of the king. On 2 September 1879, Cavagnari was assassinated in his embassy by Afghan soldiers and an angry mob. The British retaliated by re-occupying Kandhar. Clashes between British troops and Afghans became commonplace around Kabul's outlying areas. At Maiwand, Sardar Ayub Khan inflicted a crushing defeat on the British. One of the great romantic figures of this battle was a Pushtun girl named Malali who had fearlessly advanced towards the enemy waving a flag fashioned out of her headscarf, and been killed. Many Pushtun girls to this day are named after her and a school or institution in practically every Afghan city bears witness to her memory.

The British, worried about the rising power of Sardar Ayub and tired of the ineffectual Amir Yaqub Khan, were on the lookout for another Pushtun leader to get them 'honourably' out of the Afghan imbroglio. Before long, they had found one — Amir Yaqub's first cousin, Sardar Abdul Rahman, who in 1880 entered Afghanistan from the north. Sardar Abdul Rahman knew the area well and, using past contacts, he assembled a large army but, instead of attacking Kabul, confined himself to skirmishes with British troops away from the capital. He was a cunning and patient man. In the meanwhile, the British defeated his arch rival Sardar Ayub Khan at Kandhar, thus making way for the old campaigner.[12] In 1880, they formally recognized him as the new Afghan ruler. Yaqub Ali Khan was exiled to India.[13] In 1893, the Durand treaty was signed between Amir Abdul Rahman and the British.

The Durand Line continues to be the international boundary between Afghanistan and Pakistan. This division has been the subject of many controversies and interpretations in the last hundred years. To the Afghans, it is a symbol of imperial *diktat* but Pakistan, following the British view, maintains that it is an international frontier. Whatever the interpretation, it is difficult to deny that the Durand Line is an unnatural and culturally divisive demarcation of the frontier which has shattered the Pushtun cultural and political entity. The Pushtuns, regardless of which side of the Line they were on, never accepted it and were constantly in revolt against the British. In a hundred years, the British fought nearly a hundred campaigns against the Pushtuns. The Khyber Afridis alone fought eight battles against the British between 1850 and 1908.[14]

Having already surrendered large Pushtun areas to the British, Amir Abdul Rahman spent the next many years embroiled in minor but bloody military actions against smaller tribes and nationalities. His first victims, not unexpectedly, were the Ghilzai Pushtuns who had always fought the British because of their free and rebellious nature. He next directed his attention to the Hazara tribes which claimed descent from the Mughals. His soldiers seized their lands and houses and killed the men without remorse. Those who were able to sought shelter in Iran and Quetta (now Pakistan).

To ensure that they should know no peace, Amir Abdul Rahman forced the Ghilzais to settle in areas peopled by the Hazaras. Noor Mohammed Taraki was born of one of the forcibly-settled Ghilzai tribes in this area only seventeen years after Abdul Rahman's death.

Amir Abdul Rahman Khan not only shed much Muslim blood, but fulfilled his religious 'obligations' even more thoroughly by attacking the Kafirs, an ancient nature-worshipping ethnic sub-nationality which spoke the Pashai language, and converting them to Islam at the point of the sword. Although the history of Afghanistan is not short on bloody rulers, Amir Abdul Rahman must rank as the bloodiest of them all. He was one of history's worst sadists. He was particularly fond of blowing up his victims by having them tied to the front end of a cannon or crucifying them in the town centre. Often, he would throw them in iron cages placed in public squares so that people could watch them die slowly of heat and starvation. Another favourite device was to throw the victim into a waterless well, so small that he could hardly stand in it.[15] It is said that many of the intended victims used to prefer suicide to capture.[16] The stories of his reign of terror are still told in Kabul. When he died in 1901, his son set free 10,000 prisoners. It should be pointed out that the population of Kabul at the time was between 100,000 and 125,000.

The story of Amir Abdul Rahman Khan has been told in some detail because since 1980 there has been much distortion of history. The sudden rise of 'Afghan friendship' in the United States has led to some amazing tinkering with established facts. Amir Abdul Rahman has been canonized as an Afghan national hero. He has been credited with a 'last will and testament' which says: 'My last word to you, my son and successor, never trust the Russians'.[17] The 'last will and testament', there is compelling evidence, was penned not in 1901 but in 1980. It is difficult to believe that a man who owed his accession to power to having sold national honour to the British should depart the world on this patriotic note. Chances are that his actual 'will and testament' enjoined upon his son to remain loyal to the British crown.

Amir Habibullah Khan, the new ruler of Afghanistan, was denied his monthly stipend by Lord Curzon, the Indian Viceroy, on the ground that his father Amir Abdul Rahman's stipend had been given to him in his 'personal' capacity. It was made clear that the practice could only be revived if he came to India and offered to sign and maintain a pledge of friendship. Amir Habibullah Khan at first considered it undignified to travel to India for the grant of his stipend, but in 1904 he sent his son, Sardar Enyatullah Khan, to Delhi to plead on his behalf. In 1905, an Afghan-British treaty was signed, incorporating and renewing all the old treaties. Amir Habibullah Khan's stipend was restored and a sum of £40,000 paid to him by way of arrears.

The British were perhaps history's wiliest and most cynical rulers. They knew how to deal with princes. From 1842 until 1919, every

Afghan Amir was dependent on British grants, stipends and privy purses. While the purchase of the Afghan rulers was never a problem, the hardy Pushtun people, nurtured on ancient and individualistic tribal traditions, were outside both their circle of influence and their comprehension. It took the British a long time and much sacrifice and suffering to understand the fundamental difference between the Afghan rulers and the Afghan people. Within their tribes and in their ancestral areas, the people of Afghanistan were completely free. The rulers of Kabul and Kandhar were not competent by tradition to interfere in the free and autonomous existence of the Afghan tribes. Whenever a foreign power entered Afghan territory, the Afghan tribesmen rallied round their leaders and headmen to resist the invaders. The tribes were constituted – and continue to be constituted – as military units. Ultimately, the British learnt from experience and granted internal independence to the annexed tribal areas so as to rule them with relative ease.

3

Into Modern Times

In many ways, Amir Habibullah Khan was different from his father. It was during this time that Afghanistan's first school, Habibia (named after him), was set up at Kabul. So was the first power station and the first pumping station for irrigation. The country's first printing press and first newspaper also date back to this time – not to mention clandestine political organizations founded by the supporters of 'constitutional monarchy'. In a tribal society like that of Afghanistan, there could be no more than a handful of proponents of 'constitutional monarchy'. Notwithstanding the fact that this harmless group posed no threat to Amir Habibullah, he hanged its leaders Mohammed Sarwar Khan, Syed Johar Khan, and Lal Mohammed Khan and jailed several hundred of their sympathizers.

The outbreak of the war in 1914 created many complications for Amir Habibullah Khan. A Jang Party was formed by his heir apparent Amanullah Khan and his brother Sardar Nasrullah Khan, both of whom were convinced that since the British were occupied in war, it was a God-sent opportunity to win back captured Afghan areas.[1] However, Amir Habibullah Khan did not favour this course of action. On 2 October 1915, a German and Turkish delegation arrived in Afghanistan via Iran. The delegation which included two Indian nationalists, Kanwar Mohinder Partab and Barkatullah, handed Amir Habibullah Khan a letter from the German Kaiser which promised him all military assistance if he made war on the British, and expressed the hope that he would make a determined effort to regain his lost Afghan territories. To please his son and brother, Amir Habibullah Khan signed an agreement of sorts with the delegation, but he was still not prepared to attack the embattled British. On the contrary, in reply to a letter from King George V, he wrote on January 6, 1916: 'I can assure you that we will remain neutral and keep our pledge to the last.'[2]

On 29 January 1916, he declared at a *jirga* that he would not make war on the British, causing great disappointment to his son, his brother and the people at large. He said war was a bloodthirsty monster which he would not allow to enter Afghanistan. Amir Habibullah Khan was probably the first Afghan ruler who forswore war on humanitarian grounds. However, the plea for peace went contrary to the temperament of the Afghan people, apart from the fact that his refusal to lead hostilities proved of more benefit to the British than to peace. In order to avoid going to war, he came out with a number of impossible preconditions. He told the German-Turkish delegation that he would declare war on the British only if a large contingent of German and Turkish troops was sent to Afghanistan, armed with long-range artillery. Another precondition was the pre-existence of a popular and widespread revolt against the British in India.

In 1919, when encamped on a hunting trip at Qila Gosh in Laghaman, Amir Habibullah was pounced upon and killed. In the power struggle which followed on his murder, Amir Amanullah Khan emerged triumphant, and established himself as Afghan history's only reformist, liberal, progressive and nationalist king. On 13 April 1919, he summoned all ambassadors resident in Kabul and declared the 'complete independence and autonomy' of Afghanistan.

The British did not take this development seriously at first. Not being unmindful of the new ruler's Barakzai lineage and traditions, they were convinced that this was a ruse to ask for an increase in his stipend. In a letter to him, the Viceroy of India, instead of offering any comment on his declaration of independence, went into a long paean of praise for his ancestors, finally expressing the hope that the good relations established by his ancestors with the British would continue during his reign as well. He also offered to open talks on trade and other matters. (Ironic as it may now seem, the first country to recognize the new Afghanistan on 27 April 1919 was the Soviet Union[3] whose delegation to the Paris Peace Conference in March 1919, proposed, on the explicit instructions of Lenin, that international guarantees should be given that the Afghan government would not be overthrown by any external power through the use of force).[4]

Amir Amanullah Khan's declaration of independence and autonomy had come at a bad time for the British, who were soon forced to take it seriously. On 13 April 1919, hundreds of peaceful political dissenters had been massacred at Jallianwala Bagh, Amritsar, India. The protests which had followed had swept across India's major cities of Bombay, Delhi and Lahore. An Afghan declaration of independence at this point could only be viewed by the Indians as an example to be followed. To put pressure on the new Afghan ruler, the British ordered the deployment of 750,000 troops all along the Durand Line, in an operation involving some 400,000 transport animals.

In military terms, the third British-Afghan war, which began on 6 May 1919, was one of the most uneven contests ever fought. The British force was fifteen times the size of the Afghan army. It was armed with mortars, tanks and aircraft. In addition, it had behind it the experience of four years of the First World War. The Afghan army had nothing more lethal than nineteenth-century guns. The British bombed Kabul. It was the first time the poor, backward Afghans had seen an aircraft. They had nothing to defend themselves against this 'engine of the devil' and used ordinary guns and artillery in vain attempts to bring these strange, lethal death machines down.

The fighting began on three major fronts. At Khyber the tribal militia raised by the British rebelled and occupied the area. However, the British counter-attacked and not only regained control, but pushed back the Afghans nearly twenty kilometres into their own territory. At Kandhar also, the British attack was successful. There was heavy fighting around the Afghan post of Spin Boldak, which the British eventually captured.

At Khost, the Afghan army fought valiantly and advanced as far as the cantonment town of Tal. In this engagement, the military governor of Paktia, General Nadir Khan, emerged as a hero. This was more due to his tribal contacts than to his abilities as a commander. He had excellent relations with the tribal chiefs of Paktia province. As hostilities began, he pressed the local tribes into service. Thirty thousand armed Waziri tribesmen, who were settled in British-occupied territories, marched to his aid;[5] and they were joined by other tribesmen. According to Erland Jaenson,

> Large sections of the tribes were carried away by a mixture of enthusiasm for the Afghan cause and the hope of loot. Militia forces in the tribal territory mutinied, a large part of Waziristan had to be given to the Afghans and the Khyber Pass was closed by tribal *lashkars*.[6]

Emboldened by these successes, tribal parties began to carry out daring raids into British territories. In 1919, according to one estimate, a total of 611 raids took place, resulting in 298 killed, 392 wounded, and 463 abductions. Property worth 300,000 rupees was damaged and of the invading tribal fighters 119 were killed, 80 injured, and 40 taken prisoner.[7] Most of these raids were carried out behind British lines and the main targets were British and Indian officers.

Afghan communications were so bad that it took at least three days for a signal or an order to reach from Kabul to the front. As a result, the Afghan commander at Khyber was only ordered to open hostilities three days after the war had actually begun.[8] At that time, there was not even a single metalled road in the entire country. There were no telephone or wireless links either. The Saddozai and Barakzai rulers had kept their people free of these 'instruments of the devil' and 'works of the infidel'.

The golden opportunity lost in 1914 was not so easy to regain in 1919. The British were no longer involved in a world war. They were not only free of any military worries elsewhere in the world, but were the victors of the Great War. The German Kaiser and the Turkish Sultan, who only a few years ago had offered full military support to the Afghans, had been divested of their crowns. The Afghans stood alone. The war which the father had lost without a fight, his son could not have won merely by initiating it. However, despite these tremendous disadvantages and their meagre numbers, the Afghans were able to keep the British running in circles in guerilla warfare. But this was to remain the extent of the Afghan 'victory'. The British were not keen for a prolonged war; therefore, on 3 June 1919, both sides agreed to a 'ceasefire'. After three years of negotiations, the two sides signed the Treaty of Rawalpindi in 1923. Amir Amanullah Khan recognized the Durand Line, while the British recognized Afghanistan as an independent and sovereign state. In order to show their goodwill, the British presented him with a squadron of ten aircraft. This was the founding of the Afghan Air Force.[9]

Amir Amanullah Khan was the antithesis of his Barakzai forefathers. He was an intellectual, an admirer of modernism, a nationalist, and a reformer. He was the first Afghan ruler to don western clothes, as did his queen, Surraiya. The queen had grown up in Turkey during her father's exile. Her father, Mahmood Beg Tarzi, had only been allowed to return to his homeland during the reign of Amir Habibullah Khan. He was the first man in Afghanistan to bring out a newspaper. He was a popular figure at the court, which was how his intimacy with Amanullah Khan had begun.[10] It was during Amir Habibullah Khan's life that both his sons had married the two Tarzi girls. The marriage had brought Amir Amanullah Khan even closer to Tarzi. When he came to the throne, he appointed him his Foreign Minister. Unlike his ancestors, Amir Amanullah Khan contented himself with one marriage. He also put an end to the disgraceful practice which required the Hazara tribes to present their most beautiful young maidens to the Afghan royal family as a mark of loyalty. He went on a tour of Turkey, England, Germany and the Soviet Union. Intellectually, he was in sympathy with the religious and social reforms brought about in Turkey by Ataturk

Mustafa Kamal. Against 'friendly advice' given him at a banquet in Buckingham Palace not to visit Moscow, he went direct from London to the Soviet capital, thus becoming the first foreign ruler to visit 'red Moscow'. Kalinin gave him the red carpet treatment. In Amir Amanullah's view, the Soviet Union and Turkey were to be considered reliable friends. He appointed General Ghulam Nabi Charkhi ambassador at Moscow and the General's brother his envoy to Ankara. In 1921, he signed a Treaty of Friendship with the Soviet Union, following it up a year later with a Treaty of Non-Interference and Non-Aggression.

After his return from a foreign tour in 1928, Amir Amanullah Khan decided to announce a set of liberal reforms to eradicate outdated tribal and semi-tribal customs. In Kabul, where until 1980 half the women still went around in *purdah*, Amir Amanullah tried in 1928 to declare the custom illegal. He ordered that any woman found wearing a veil on the street should be immediately divested of it. What the reformist king failed to understand was that he could not change the visible aspects of social and religious traditions without first changing the infrastructure of his society. Social change is a slow and intricate process. It takes generations to bring about the complete eradication of old ideas, customs and traditions, even if a change in productive forces and economic relations has already taken place. Afghan tribal society was not yet ready to don the mantle of western liberalism. This was in contrast to Turkey, where Mustafa Kamal's social and religious reforms had taken root because the country had moved away from the tribal state centuries earlier. By the end of the nineteenth century, Turkey was a decadent feudal power ripe for liberal change.

The British, who had not forgiven Amanullah Khan his friendship with the Soviet Union, were looking for an opportunity to discredit him. This soon presented itself in the form of a wave of religious revolts, first inspired by the reactionary fanatic, Hazrat Shor Bazar, against his 'godless' ways.

The man who was to play the decisive role in the fall of Amanullah Khan now appears on the scene. He was a Tajik from Kalakan by the name of Bacha Saqao.[11] He was an illiterate and uncouth petty thief who had found his way to Para Chanar (now in Pakistan) in search of a livelihood, where, according to Afghan accounts, he had been in jail on a theft charge. He arrived in Kalakan when the unrest began. He soon organized a rag-tag band of followers, all out-of-work men, and began to raid government treasuries across the region. His power and local influence grew rapidly. Amanullah Khan's government was already semi-paralyzed by the growing movement against its reforms. The power and nuisance value of Saqao could no longer be ignored. All police cases pending against him were, therefore, dropped by the government and he was appointed administrator of the Kalakan area. Taking full advantage of his new position, Bacha Saqao raised a well-armed force of supporters, all paid out of the government treasury. As the agitation against Amir Amanullah Khan grew in intensity, Bacha Saqao moved with his soldiers to Kabul and captured it without much trouble. At that time, Amanullah Khan was busy quelling revolts in the outlying Ghazni and Kandhar provinces. Bacha Saqao ordered the Afghan Air Force to bomb Amanullah Khan's army but the pilots, instead of obeying their orders, dipped their wings in salute to Afghanistan's first and last nationalist and reformist king.[12]

It is a strange coincidence that Bacha Saqao's real name was also Amanullah. When he entered Kabul, he was ceremonially turbaned as a mark of religious honour by the Pir of Tagao, how also conferred on him the title of 'Ghazi Amanullah, Khadim-i-Deen', or 'the holy warrior Amanullah, servant of the faith'. However, his influence did not extend beyond Kabul. Had Amanullah Khan not decided to leave the country in disillusionment with his people, it would not have been impossible for him to recapture Kabul.

One of the first acts of Bacha Saqao was the closure of all educational institutions and schools. The salaries formerly paid to the teachers began to be paid to religious 'scholars' or *ulema*. However, Bacha Saqao failed to understand the basic Afghan psyche. The Pushtun majority could never accept him as their ruler because he was a Tajik by origin, not a Pushtun. Even if he had started to go round the streets of Kabul with a Quran over his head for protection, the Pushtuns would have surely killed him.

To aid Amir Amanullah, the Charkhi brothers, accompanied by Afghan students who were studying abroad, entered Afghanistan through north Iran, but as soon as they learned that the king had gone into exile, they pulled back into the Soviet areas. At that time it was futile to expect any assistance from Stalin, who was busy liquidating his predecessor's Central Committee. If General Charkhi had decided to advance towards Kabul instead of returning to the Soviet territories, he would have been able to occupy Kabul before General Nadir Khan, though it is not clear if he had any personal ambition to rule Afghanistan. It is also possible that he returned to seek Soviet help as he was a Logri Pushtun, but in the northern part of the country the population consisted mainly of non-Pushtun tribes who would not have supported him. Whatever the reason, his retreat brought him to his death and General Nadir Khan to the throne at Kabul.

General Nadir Khan, who was ambassador in Paris, rushed back to British India and declared at the famous Mahabat Mosque in Peshawar the launch of a *jihad*, or holy war, against Bacha Saqao. He also promised that if he succeeded, he would bring back Amir Amanullah Khan, the hero of the Pushtuns in the British-occupied areas, to the throne. Taking advantage of this popular feeling, Nadir Khan recruited his army from amongst the Afridi, Waziri and other tribes.[13] Thus it was that the British came to allow a man who had fought against them only ten years earlier, to assemble an attacking force from the sensitive tribal territories for the express purpose of restoring the Afghan crown to their old enemy Amanullah Khan.

As expected, General Nadir Khan's first camp was based at Paktia where the Gilani family, a relatively new arrival in the area, was the 'spiritual' leader of the reactionary movement against Amir Amanullah Khan. The Gilanis had settled at Paktia during British times and, therefore, it cannot be ruled out that their arrival had British blessings. Such 'spiritual' leaders and families had earlier been employed by the British in India to further the ends of British rule.

With the help of the Gilanis, Nadir Khan assembled a large tribal *lashkar* at Paktia. He also used the anti-Tajik feelings of the tribesmen to consolidate popular support. Since areas outside the capital were now under the jurisdiction of local administration or tribal chiefs, Nadir Khan was able to reach Kabul easily.[14] Bacha Saqao, after making Nadir Khan sign a pledge of safe passage and life on a copy of the Quran, stepped down. However, in the new ruler's books there was no pardon for enemies. He inaugurated his reign with the murder of Bacha Saqao and, instead of declaring the formerly-proclaimd 'defender of the faith' a martyr, Hazrat Shor Bazar welcomed Nadir Khan with open arms. In recognition of the 'great religious services' of Hazrat Shor Bazar, Nadir Khan appointed his younger brother (father of an exiled Afghan leader in Pakistan, Sibghatullah Mujadaddi) his Minister of Justice.[15] Next on his list was General Ghulam Nabi Charkhi who was openly critical of Nadir Khan since he had gone back on his promise of restoring the Afghan throne to Amir Amanullah Khan. Nadir Shah invited him to his palace and, according to popular accounts, there was an altercation between the two. General Charkhi was not prepared to accept him as king. He called him a cheat and a man without honour. Nadir Khan, in reply, pulled out his gun and shot him dead. In keeping with time-honoured Pushtun tradition, even an enemy, if invited to your house or found there, is not to be killed. However, Amir Habibullah Khan's former security commander was now His Majesty Nadir Shah and, being a king, was free to do as he wished. He now ordered the Paktia *lashkar* to move into the Tajik area of Kalakan where hundreds of Tajiks were massacred and their women and possessions taken away.[16] To reward the people of Paktia province,

Nadir Shah made them exempt from compulsory military service, the only Afghan province to have that privilege.[17] He also made a law under which his own military officers were to be directly recruited from this province. Furthermore, he exempted the feudal landlords of Paktia from land revenue levies.

History has its own ironies and lessons. On 27 April 1978, at exactly midday, the last ruler of the Nadir Khan dynasty, and the founder's nephew, Sardar Daud Khan, had his palace attacked. The tank commander, one Major Aslam Watanjar, who fired the first shell, was a Paktia Pushtun who had been declared the 'loyalest of the loyal' by Nadir Shah. Since the officer corps in the Afghan army mostly consisted of Paktia Pushtuns, they became the first to join the PDPA when it began its political work among the defence forces. After Noor Mohammed Taraki and Hafizullah Amin, the leadership of the Khalq group was assumed by a man by the name of Syed Gulabzoi who also belonged to Paktia (he was a junior commissioned officer in the Afghan Air Force). The current Secretary General of the PDPA, Dr Najibullah Khan, is also from Paktia, as is Haji Chamkany, who became the President of Afghanistan in November 1986.

After Nadir Khan's assumption of power, the British government gave him £170,000 to enable him to deal with the country's grave economic crisis. Not only did Nadir Shah invite religious reactionaries to become part of the ruling order, but he put mosque *imams* on the government pay-roll. Under the Ministry of Justice, he constituted a special board made up of *ulema*, assigning to them the responsibility of adapting the syllabi to 'Islamic values': the real task of this board was to denounce all modern and progressive ideas as 'un-Islamic'. However, his own son (Zahir Khan), brother (Shah Mahmood), and nephews (Sardar Abdul Wali, Sardar Taimur Shah, Sardar Naeem Khan and Sardar Daud Khan) were sent for education to the 'un-Islamic' educational institutions of France. Nadir Khan alone is not to be blamed for this duplicity. His successors followed faithfully in his footsteps.

Every progressive policy of the past and everything associated with Amir Amanullah Khan was systematically dismantled. The Amania School at Kabul was renamed Najat or 'salvation' School. However, Nadir Shah could not entirely obliterate the former ruler's progressive legacy. The Najat School itself became a breeding ground for Afghan nationalists.[18] The founders of the Afghan Zalme movement were all former students of this school. This secret organization was committed to the return of Afghan areas annexed by the British across the Durand Line. According to the followers of this movement, Nadir Khan was no more than a tool of the British who had been brought to power to undo

Amir Amanullah Khan's nationalistic and progressive reforms.

Although the progressive group born during the rule of Amanullah Khan was limited in numbers and consisted only of educated Afghan youth, it never accepted Nadir Khan's accession to the throne. The walls of Kabul were lined with graffiti against Nadir Khan.[19] One of Amir Amanullah Khan's most committed supporters, the father of the well-known PDPA woman leader Dr Anahita Ratebzad, was caught distributing a pamphlet entitled 'The British Jackal'.[20]

It was one of the former students of the Najat School who, in 1933, murdered Nadir Khan's brother, Sardar Mohammed Aziz Khan, in Germany. The murdered man, Afghanistan's ambassador, was Sardar Daud Khan's father.[21] The same year, the British ambassador in Kabul was attacked and the credit claimed by the Afghan Zalme. In November of that year, it was Nadir Khan's turn at last. He was peppered with bullets by a young cadet (also a former student of the Najat School) while he was inspecting a parade at the Military Academy. This young cadet was the adopted son of General Ghulam Nabi Charkhi, who had no natural children of his own. The young man, in keeping with Pushtun tradition, had avenged the death of his 'father'. Nadir Khan's Prime Minister was his own brother Hashim Khan who killed his brother's young assassin after torturing him in jail for a long time. Those who know say that Nadir Khan's brother and nephews visited the assassin in prison and asked him which finger he had used to pull the trigger. When he stuck out his index finger, it was chopped off. Then he was asked with which eye he had taken aim and the culprit eye was gouged out. They say that he was killed slowly with different parts of his body being hacked away during interrogation and questioning.[22] Nadir Khan's brothers then put his fifteen-year-old son Zahir Khan on the throne. He was given the title 'Al-Mutwakkal Billah', which meant 'the one who places his trust in God'. It may be mentioned that the author of this title was none other than Hazrat Shor Bazar, who had conferred the titles of 'defender of the faith' and 'warrior of Islam' on Bacha Saqao.[23]

After Nadir Khan's murder, real power came into the hands of his brothers. The boy king was no more than a convenience. While mercilessly suppressing his enemies at home, Sardar Hashim Khan maintained what at first sight appeared to be a non-partisan foreign policy. There were simultaneous understandings with both the British and the Soviet Union. The rise of National Socialism in Germany in 1933, while coinciding with the undoing of the post-war arrangements and laying the foundations of a greater conflict, also saw the beginning of German involvement in Afghanistan. It is obvious that the anti-British past of the Afghans interested the Nazis as well as, perhaps,

Afghanistan's 'Aryan' beginnings. The word Aryan is still current in the country as a reminder of claimed Afghan racial origins.

In 1936, the German government extended a loan of DM27 million to Afghanistan in return for the purchase of German arms by the latter. A year later, a joint Afghan-German company was set up to prospect for minerals in the country and the German airline Lufthansa opened an office at Kabul. The armaments factory in Baghlan and the Afghan National Bank had German advisers for the first time.[24] However, if the Germans thought that the Afghan ruling dynasty would make war on the British for the return of their territories, they were mistaken: in keeping with their Barakzai tradition and history, they opted for defending the 'naked back' of the British.[25] This was perhaps the third opportunity after 1857 and 1914 that the Afghans lost to reclaim what belonged to them.[26]

In 1946, Sardar Hashim was replaced by Sardar Shah Mahmood. He was the last on the long list of Nadir Khan's brothers. Zahir Shah's older uncle had now been replaced by his younger uncle. Power still lay in the iron claws of the family. While the nephew was king, the uncle was Prime Minister and the cousin (Sardar Daud Khan) Defence Minister. The other cousins were all generals of the army.

However, Shah Mahmood, compared to his less educated brothers Nadir Khan, Hashim Khan, and Shah Wali Khan, was more sophisticated (he had studied in France) and more liberal in his views. One of his first acts as Prime Minister was the release of political prisoners. He also held elections to the seventh parliament in a relatively free manner. In 1950, he ordered press and censorship laws to be considerably eased. It was the first time since Amir Amanullah Khan's days that the small and suppressed group of Afghan intellectuals and political thinkers had felt their identity publicly recognized. This limited group of Afghan intellectuals was neither young in years, nor too influential. It was in 1920-21 that the first Afghan students had been sent abroad for education. The University of Kabul was established in 1932. There was a shortage of trained teachers in the country and quite a few German and French teachers had been imported.[27] While imparting instruction, they had managed to spread western ideas among their pupils. The cumulative result of these changes was the establishment during Shah Mahmood's liberal rule (1946-52) of the Tehrik-i-Naujawanan-Baidar (TNB), or the Movement of the Enlightened Youth. Its founders were middle class in origin and most of them had received a more or less liberal education and been exposed to western ideas. It was a loose kind of political movement. Its manifesto was published in 1947 by Abdul Rauf Benawa. Its declared aims included the removal of outdated customs, superstition and ideas, grant of legal rights to women, construction of a society free of external pressures, restoration to the people of the right to decide their future, eradication of bribery and corruption, an end to injustice, development of national industry, and diversion of national revenues to public welfare projects. It was the TNB which used the term 'Free Pushtunistan' with reference to the Pushtuns living on the other side of the Durand Line in British India (now Pakistan).

The TNB manifesto was actually the flowering of the tender plant whose seeds Amir Amanullah Khan had sown against such odds twenty years earlier. In 1950, the first student union in the history of Afghanistan was set up. A number of symbolic plays satirizing the misdeeds of the royal family and the misuse of Islam for the perpetuation of unjust government were staged by the students, leading the government to impose a ban on the union in November 1950. The French-educated Shah Mahmood and Zahir Shah (the latter had constructed a palace in Italy at the cost of millions of dollars and he has been residing there since 1973) obviously considered the students' right to criticize their society 'un-Islamic'. Another former student of the Najat School, who appeared on the scene during these years, was Babrak Karmal, later to become the leader of the Parcham faction of the PDPA and the third President of Afghanistan after the revolution. Another product of these years was a student named Hafizullah Amin.

In 1951, after press restrictions were somewhat eased, a number of journals were brought out, all favouring the TNB. Among these were: *Angar, Nadai Khalq, Owlas, Watan,* and *Payam-i-Afghanistan.* These publications did not come out regularly. In fact, until 1968 there was no regular daily newspaper in Afghanistan. Papers like the *Kabul Times, Hewad, Anis,* and *Haqiqat-i-Inqilab-i-Saur* were most irregular in their publication. Nearly thirty years after the establishment of the TNB and five years after the Afghan revolution, there were only eleven newspapers and journals being published in Kabul and no more than eighteen newspapers and forty-two journals coming out of other towns and cities, figures which demonstrate the limited influence of Afghan middle-class intellectuals on the general population even today.[28] In 1951, it was negligible. However, even the very moderate criticism offered by these limited circulation publications was too much for the government to take. Shah Mahmood, divesting himself of his French liberal robes, ordered a ban on the publication of all these papers. The editors were put in prison or exiled.[29]

It is a tragedy of Asian rulers – 'revolutionaries', 'populists', kings or generals, educated at home or abroad – that as long as they are in power all they wish to hear or read is sycophantic praise from their subjects. The moment they are removed from power, they begin to make eloquent speeches about 'freedom of expression'. Although this game has been played endlessly in Africa and Latin America as well, Afghanistan's rulers occupy a place which is all their own. Yesterday, Taraki, Karmal and Amin wanted 'freedom of expression'. Today it is the Zahir Shahs, the Mujadaddis and the Gilanis who seek that same 'freedom'.

The TNB was crushed by the government. In 1953, there was a palace revolution in Kabul. The new generation of the Nadiri dynasty had decided to get rid of its elders. Zahir Shah and Sardar Daud Khan conspired together to remove their uncle Shah Mahmood. Consequently, Sardar Daud became Prime Minister. He was not only Zahir Shah's first cousin, but also the husband of his sister. Daud Khan threw into prison what supporters of the TNB still existed. Had this movement not been so summarily suppressed, at best it would have assumed the harmless form of, say, the Progressive Writers Movement in India in 1935. However, in its suppression lay the seeds of its future assumption of political power. It not only became the cause of the 1978 revolution but also led it. The most vociferous supporter of Free Pushtunistan was the publisher of the journal *Angar*, Faiz Mohammed Faiz, a Pushtun from Kandhar, who was good friends with a quiet, good humoured, unassuming writer, working as an assistant director at the Bakhtar News Agency. This was Noor Mohammed Taraki, destined to become the founder of the People's Democratic Party of Afghanistan (PDPA) in 1965 and the head of government from 1978 to 1979. After the failure of the TNB, he was banished to the United States on a diplomatic assignment. However, soon after his arrival he held a news conference at which he denounced the ruling Afghan government and resigned his post.

Another TNB activist, Babrak Karmal, a student leader at the Kabul University, spent three years in jail from 1953 to 1956. When he entered the jail he was not more than an emotional young man but in jail he took the name Karmal, which, in Pushtu, means 'comrade of the workers'. In 1965 Karmal became the first Deputy Secretary General of the PDPA and a member of Parliament from 1965 to 1973. He was Afghanistan's most controversial head of government during his six years of power (1980-86).

In the 1950s, a young army cadet who was a Marxist by conviction was also put in jail. His name was Ustad Amir Akbar Khyber Khan and he has been credited with converting Karmal to Marxism. Ustad Khyber later became the editor of the newspaper *Parcham* and was generally known as the ideological 'pundit' of the Parcham faction. It was his murder which became the immediate cause of the Afghan revolution in 1978. Others who turned to revolution under the influence of the TNB were Ghulam Dastgir Panjsheri, Tahir Badakhshi and Shuruhullah Shahpur.

The editor of *Watan*, Mir Ghulam Mohammed Ghubar, was also jailed for his TNB sympathies. Ghubar had been an advocate of progressive ideas since Amir Amanullah Khan's times. In jail, he wrote a massive book on the history of Afghanistan which remains the only history of the country written from a progressive point of view by an Afghan.[30] It has been described as the bible of Afghan history. Two of Ghubar's assistants on the *Watan* newspaper – Abdul Hai Aziz and Mir Sadiq Farhang – were to become members of Parliament from 1965 to 1973 and held ministerial portfolios at the Ministry of Planning.[31]

The editor of *Nadai Khalq*, Dr Abdul Rahman Mahmoodi, was also a member of Parliament and a staunch supporter of the TNB. His political affiliations kept him in jail through the entire duration of Sardar Daud's premiership (1953-63), and he died only three months after his release of a kidney ailment. His brother Dr Abdul Rahim Mahmoodi and his nephew Dr Abdul Hai Mahmoodi founded the first pro-Peking communist party of Afghanistan in 1964, three months after his death.[32] Dr Abdul Rahman Mahmoodi is the only communist leader who is still considered a hero and martyr by both pro-Soviet and pro-China Afghan communists. After the April Revolution, he was paid warm public tribute.[33]

The Soviet historian R.T. Akhramovich, analyzing the TNB, writes:

> Not possessing a distinct organizational structure and noted for its mixed membership, the movement at first was more like a trend made up of diverse social views and sentiments; and often the only thing which was common to all of them was the desire to find a way to get rid of the confusion obtaining in the country. This movement became a centre of social ideas, around which began the consolidation or polarization of forces on a class basis.[34]

Despite this reference to the 'mixed membership' of the organization, there is no historical record or indication or document listing its membership. It is not surprising that Akhramovich sees it as having been made up of 'diverse' elements and views: Soviet historians, tied as they are to the apron-strings of the official truth, see every progressive movement in the world as 'diverse' and full of 'confusion', unless the name of the current head of the Kremlin is part of its manifesto! Given Afghanistan's internal conditions at the time, the TNB was undeniably a manifestation of progressive and revolutionary thinking.

4

Genesis of the Pushtun Problem

The return of annexed Pushtun areas across the Durand Line was always an Afghan demand. However, the first time the term 'Independent Pushtunistan' became a part of the current political vocabulary was in 1947, the year of British withdrawal from India. Some American writers, such as Anthony Arnold, have mistakenly held the TNB responsible for the concept of Independent Pushtunistan, but history offers no evidence in support of this view.[1] The concept of Independent Pushtunistan was borrowed by the TNB from the Khudai Khidmatgars (God's Servants) of the North West Frontier Province (in Pakistan). On 21 June 1947, a resolution was passed at a meeting of Khudai Khidmatgars at Bannu (NWFP) calling for the establishment of an Independent Pushtunistan. This meeting was also attended by members of the NWFP Assembly and leaders of the Pushtun Zalme, the youth wing of the Khudai Khidmatgars.[2] The very concept of Pushtunistan when a state of Afghanistan (which also means land of the Pushtuns) was already in existence was a tragic admission of the fact that 125 years of foreign occupation and the unjust Durand Line had divided the Pushtun people into two units, despite their cultural, historical, linguistic and geographical oneness.

The Pushtun leaders of NWFP were in a unique and painful dilemma during the fateful years of 1946-47. It was not possible for them to return to their past – which was Afghanistan – with their eyes closed, because 125 years of Sikh and British slavery had created deep, if not unbridgeable, chasms between them and their blood brothers to the east. Nor was it easy for them to accept the future, which meant union with the Punjab in the new state of Pakistan, when all they had in common with it was a shared history of colonial slavery. Enslavement involves no choice, but freedom does. This was the dilemma of the

30

Pushtun leaders in 1946 and 1947. They ended up accepting the Durand Line as the geographical boundary of the Pushtun nation while weaving the dream of a separate state called Pushtunistan.

In 1947, the government of Afghanistan made a last ditch effort to negotiate with the British for the return of Pushtun areas which were now to constitute part of Pakistan.[3] However, the Afghan cause had been lost long before 1947. The British were not prepared to entertain the claim, nor did a 'return to the homeland' movement of any note exist in the Pushtun area to the east of the Durand Line. While the NWFP Pushtuns were joined to the west by history and culture, by 1947 their material links with India were well-established. In strictly practical terms, an NWFP Pushtun felt closer to the subcontinent than to Afghanistan. Consequently, the Afghan government was obliged to support an Independent Pushtunistan. Erland Jaenson writes:

> It must be stressed here that the Afghan position did not coincide with that of Abdul Ghaffar Khan, since the latter demanded independence of the NWFP, but did not advocate accession to Afghanistan. However, the Afghans subsequently also supported the demand for Pushtunistan.[4]

In their search for a new national identity, the authors of the Pushtunistan concept seemed to view themselves in the mirror of Afghanistan's past. They were prepared to accept Afghan support for their idea rather than Afghanistan itself. According to Qazi Ataullah, a former NWFP Minister of Finance, 'Afghanistan was a Muslim state and the Pushtuns had more in common with that country than with Punjab. Therefore, there was nothing wrong in the Afghan support for the Pushtunistan Movement'.[5] Jaenson's book on Afghanistan quotes Amir Nawaz Jalia as saying that in 1942, Khan Abdul Ghaffar Khan was dead set against any scheme which would mean accession of the Pushtun areas to Afghanistan. According to Jalia, Ghaffar Khan said, 'We do not want to be one with those naked people' (namely Afghans)[6] – which confirms that a Pushtunistan on the non-Afghan side of the Durand Line was the new nationalist ideal of the Pushtun people. Historically, of course, those 'naked people' were not only the focal point of Pushtun nationalism but also the creators of the first Pushtun state in the world. Moreover, the family in power in Afghanistan in 1947 was related to Khan Abdul Ghaffar Khan's Mohammedzai tribe. The dream of an Independent Pushtunistan was the natural reaction of the NWFP Pushtuns to the Barakzai rulers of Afghanistan who, in order to save their throne, had bartered away half their people to the British.

To sum up, the idea of Pushtunistan was neither a creation of the

Afghan government nor the brain child of the TNB. In fact, the support lent to the idea by the Afghan government and the TNB was in complete contradiction to their past standpoints. The Afghan view of the geographical boundaries, shape and future of Pushtunistan was unclear and vague. The Afghans saw Pushtunistan as the first sign of the undoing of the Durand Line. During my five-year stay in Afghanistan, I came to feel that to most Afghans, Pushtunistan meant only the disappearance of the Durand Line, although the true begetters of the idea had taken the existence of the Durand Line as the basis of their new national identity. The tragedy of the leaders of independent Pushtunistan lay in the fact that the support it received from the Afghan people was not reflected in equal measure in the NWFP. One important reason for this contradiction was that the authors of the idea became the victims of political and psychological confusion at a most delicate point in history. These Pushtun leaders, instead of devoting themselves without reservations to the establishment of an independent Pushtun state, could only see a future for themselves in an undivided India. They raised the Pushtunistan slogan at a time when India was on the verge of being divided into two independent countries. That is why they were unable to win popular support for the boycott of the referendum held in NWFP on the eve of partition. And although, as a result of the referendum, NWFP became a part of Pakistan, the Punjabi-Mohajir (refugees from India) policy, born out of partition, refused to accord the Pushtuns an identity of their own within the new state. Perhaps this was the new rulers' way of 'serving' Islam and Pakistan. Three of the four units constituting the present Pakistan (Punjab, Sind and Baluchistan) are known by their racial, linguistic and cultural origins, but even today the province of the Pushtuns has no name. It was the British who christened it the North West Frontier Province – an administrative description – a name which has remained unchanged forty years after independence.

In 1951, the first serious crisis occurred in Pakistan-Afghanistan relations. At this time of great tension between the Muslim League government in the NWFP and Ghaffar Khan's Khudai Khidmatgars, Sardar Daud Khan, the Afghan Defence Minister, infiltrated Afghan troops dressed as ordinary tribals into Pakistan's tribal areas. His being chosen as Prime Minister in 1953 was an indication that he would play the Pushtunistan card to exploit the sentiments of the Afghan masses, and as expected he made Pushtunistan the cornerstone of his new foreign policy. An analysis of the situation in this region after the end of World War II will be instructive here.

The year 1947 marked the end of British rule in India and the emergence of the independent states of India and Pakistan. To the south of Afghanistan, Iran was beginning a new chapter in its history as a major oil-exporting country. To its northeast, China was about to be rid of both its Japanese occupiers and Chiang Kai-Shek under the leadership of Mao Tse-Tung. Its northern neighbour, the Soviet Union, which had survived the holocaust of the War, was now a major power. It was, therefore, no longer possible for Afghanistan to live in isolation from the fateful developments taking place all around its borders. Like Amir Amanullah Khan before him, Sardar Daud decided to break out of the confining circle of the past. Afghanistan needed outside help in every sector of national life. It is true that its three neighbours, China, Pakistan, and India, were still busy licking their colonial wounds, but the time had also perhaps come for Afghanistan to pay the price of the freedom for whose protection it had denied itself all modern knowledge and development.

Afghan–US relations began after World War II.[7] In 1946, the two countries signed their first agreement for the construction of a dam on the river Hilmand. Between 1951 and 1953, many advances occurred in their bilateral relations. Two long-term technical assistance treaties were signed. However, the nature of Pakistan-US relations impeded closer ties between the two countries. In 1947, Afghanistan had opposed Pakistan's membership of the United Nations on the plea that the new state was in occupation of Afghan areas. On this basis, Sardar Daud successfully built his relations with India, Pakistan's rival. The existence of the Kashmir dispute between the two countries of the subcontinent was used by Daud to bring himself even closer to India. Because of the Kashmir problem, Pandit Nehru tended to view the Pushtunistan question from a sympathetic point of view. As a *quid pro quo*, Daud lent open support to India in its dispute with Pakistan over Kashmir. The Afghan Prime Minister was also keen to obtain arms and made approaches to the United States. However, the Eisenhower administration not only gave a disappointing answer to him, but advised him to solve the Pushtunistan problem with Pakistan. A copy of the US President's letter was sent to Pakistan to please the new ally.[8] The US did, however, propose to Afghanistan that if it wished to obtain American arms, it should join the Baghdad Pact. Daud could not do so because of Pakistan's presence in the Pact. Many years later *Le Monde*, commenting on the attitude of the United States towards Afghanistan during those years, wrote:

> At the beginning of his premiership, he (Daud) asked the US to mobilize and equip the military forces of Afghanistan. The US made it subject to Afghanistan joining CENTO (Baghdad Pact). Daud, despite the fact that he was an anti-communist, did not accept the proposal forwarded to him and instead asked for military assistance from the USSR.[9]

Some American authors have insisted since 1980 that if the United States had agreed to help Afghanistan at the time, the country might have been saved from the revolution and the events of 1980. However, this wisdom after the event does not take into account the situation as it then existed. Also, US aid is no guarantee against revolutions. Iraq itself, where the Baghdad Pact was born, underwent an anti-American revolution led by Abdul Karim Kassem not long after the Pact was signed. The name of the Pact was changed to CENTO, the Central Treaty Organization. Another pillar of this military treaty, Iran, became the most implacable enemy of the United States in 1979. Even if Daud had been given US military aid, there is no guarantee that an anti-US revolution would not have taken place in Afghanistan.

After World War II, the United States laid the foundations of its role as a world power on the crumbled edifice of European colonialism. It had little understanding of the contradictions and dissensions in the newly-decolonized countries, nor did it have any colonial experience as such. Not only were these countries the victims of industrial, educational and economic backwardness, but European colonialism had left behind a legacy of border disputes and unsolved territorial questions. The national boundaries of these countries had been drawn up by the colonial powers to suit their own needs. Consequently, many nations and countries now stood divided, and the newly-independent countries were born with either inherited or artificially-created problems. The Durand Line and Kashmir were just two of these. The United States, the neo-colonialist power, seemed to be more interested in geography than history. Its aid to the new states was not intended for the establishment of democratic institutions or the solution of regional problems, but to create a military line-up against the Soviet Union through 'defence' treaties. Pakistan was an early recruit to this crusade against communism.

While the United States, under the distorted logic of McCarthyism, considered it nothing short of heresy even to shake hands with a communist country, the Soviet Union had opted for an open-door policy. Daud was rebuffed by the United States for his 'neutralism', but the Soviet Union received his request for assistance with both enthusiasm and generosity. Transcending ideological considerations, the Soviet Union, unlike the United States, also managed to establish close relations with India. The Soviet philosophy seemed to boil down to this: extend economic assistance now and allow time for the generation of political support. (It helped Pakistan, Turkey and Iran with the establishment of heavy industries like steel at a time when these countries were active members of US-sponsored anti-Soviet pacts. The first Soviet-aided steel mill was set up in Pakistan when mutual relations were at an all-time low because of Pakistan's support for the Afghan rebels.)

In January 1954, the first Afghan-Soviet agreement involving long-term credit was signed. In 1981, Afghanistan owed its ally more than 1.49 billion dollars.[10] In 1984, the Karmal government, in a review of bilateral relations, stated:

> The period after 1954 was the period of fundamental expansion in Soviet-Afghan relations. It was during this period that relations with the Soviet Union found new grounds.[11]

It was after 1953 that the direction in which Afghanistan would go in the future was set. With Soviet assistance came Soviet advisers and Soviet ideas. The educated Afghan class – teachers, journalists, writers, engineers and army officers – began to be influenced by this close encounter and it was this class which took over power in 1978 through a military revolution.

Soviet aid was not without its concomitants, of course. As early as 1954, the number of articles critical of the United States that the Afghan press published far outnumbered those which questioned Soviet policy or actions.[12] In 1955, the Non-Aggression and Cooperation Treaty between the two states was extended. (It had first been signed in 1921, as mentioned elsewhere.) In the same year, the border confrontation between Afghanistan and Pakistan assumed grave proportions. Sardar Daud's recalcitrant attitude on Pushtunistan led Pakistan to close the Karachi port to landlocked Afghanistan, forcing Daud to sign a trade agreement with the Soviet Union. Contacts grew rapidly after that. Air links were established in March 1956, a border security treaty signed in 1958, followed by agreements on telecommunications (February 1959), road building (May 1959), bridge construction (July 1959), power generation (August 1959), cultural exchanges (March 1960), construction of river ports (May 1960), and a press service (December 1960). In April 1962, another agreement was signed for the construction of modern housing in Kabul.[13]

However, the treaty which in retrospect perhaps made the 1978 Revolution possible was signed in 1956.[14] This related to the modernization and rearmament of the Afghan army, including training of the Afghan officers in the Soviet Union. This far-reaching treaty too was a direct result of the 1955 confrontation between Afghanistan and Pakistan. It is ironic that Pakistan's pro-western feudal rulers should have signed defence pacts which did not serve the country's national interest. On the one hand, these pacts with the United States forced Daud to go into the Soviet orbit and, on the other hand, they led India to go back on its earlier commitment to hold a referendum in the disputed Kashmir state to decide its future alignment. Pakistan's border disputes lay with Afghanistan and India and yet it had signed US-sponsored treaties which were directed against the Soviet Union and China.

Under the Afghan-Soviet pact of 1956, between 1956 and 1977 the Soviet Union supplied weapons to Afghanistan worth 600 million dollars, and about 3,700 Afghan officers, or one-third of the entire officer corps, received training in the Soviet Union. Many of these officers were deeply influenced by the Soviet way of life and ideas and it was they who became the motivating force behind the 1978 revolution.[15]

It was with Soviet help that Afghanistan launched its first five-year development plan in 1956. There was absolutely no industry in the country before that, which is why it was included among the world's thirty-five least developed states. Before 1950, there was no facility to generate electric power, nor an irrigation scheme, much less a machine-tool factory.[16] The 1956 development plan was followed by three more five-year plans and what industry now exists in the country results from these. Some ideas of the Soviet contribution to Afghanistan's economic progress can be had from the fact that nearly 70 per cent of the funding of the four development plans came from Soviet sources.[17] The importance accorded to relations with Afghanistan was reflected in the 1955-56 visit to Kabul of Soviet leaders Khrushchev and Podgorny. The Daud years (1953-63) were the beginning of Afghanistan's economic and industrial development as well as of long-term Soviet influence. There was to be no turning back from the course which Daud had set. Between 1975 and 1978, however, he was to make an effort to arrest Afghanistan's slide into the Soviet orbit, but paid for it with his life when he was killed by those very army officers whom he had sent to the Soviet Union for training.

In 1961-62, tension gripped the region following the Sino-Indian border dispute and its eruption into hostilities and the breakdown of diplomatic relations between Afghanistan and Pakistan. Ambassadors were recalled and, once again, Pakistan closed its sea ports to Kabul. The cause, as before, was Pushtunistan and the Durand Line dispute, but perhaps the contribution of the Sino-Indian conflict has not been given the importance it deserves in the creation of this situation. It can be argued that the Durand Line controversy was reactivated in order to pressure Pakistan's President, Field Marshal Mohammad Ayub Khan, not to try to take advantage of India's difficulties. Ayub's pro-Chinese Natural Resources Minister, Zulfikar Ali Bhutto, rushed to Swat, where the President was holidaying, and tried to persuade him to take action to settle the old Kashmir dispute with India by taking advantage of its vulnerability. However, Ayub rejected the suggestion.[18]

If it was the Soviet Union which had signalled Daud to reactivate the Pushtunistan issue to exert pressure on Ayub, then it had failed to read Ayub's character. Nothing could have induced this loyal American ally to take advantage of India at a time when it was engaged in hostilities with a communist state. Ayub's response finally came in an offer to India of 'joint defence' against the communist menace, which Nehru rebuffed. Instead of attacking Kashmir in 1961-62, when success was almost assured, Ayub did so in 1965 and not only lost Kashmir, but US patronage as well.

The first twenty years of King Zahir Shah's rule had been spent trying to deal with his hierarchy of uncles. Though he managed to get rid of them in 1953 with the help of his cousin and brother-in-law Daud, personally he did not benefit much from it. Daud Khan was not one of those who believed in sharing power. Consequently Zahir Shah's next ten years were also spent, like the previous twenty, diverting himself with women and good living.

Daud Khan brought the country perilously close to war with Pakistan on two occasions, and it is reasonable to assume that Zahir Shah decided at some point to get rid of the 'family connection' in the running of the kingdom. For the first time in his reign, he began to tour the country in 1962. The purpose of this departure from earlier practice was to establish direct and personal relations with influential tribal leaders. In March 1963, he demanded Daud's resignation and, quite unexpectedly, Daud offered it to him quietly. Zahir Shah had already taken the precaution of appointing his son-in-law Marshal Abdul Wali as the commander-in-chief and unofficial head of the Ministry of Defence, just in case Daud created difficulties before or after his resignation.

Zahir Shah then set up a commission to give Afghanistan a new constitution and after the acceptance of its recommendations (made with surprising speed), he announced a new constitution in October 1964. Under this dispensation, although Parliament was declared the fountainhead of all power, no clear division was made between the powers of the King and those of Parliament. This lack of clarity was to prove fatal. It neither helped Parliament to become truly powerful, nor did it make the King a constitutional ruler. Political parties were allowed to be formed under the new law, but Zahir Shah never signed the parliamentary bill which would have formalized the arrangement. However, he did implement Article 24 of the constitution which forbade any member of the royal family to take part in politics, join a political party, become a member of Parliament, a minister of the cabinet or a supreme court judge. This article was a result of Zahir Shah's bitter experience stretching over thirty years with his intrusive family.

That Zahir Shah's 'democratic' experiment ultimately failed was due not only to his lack of ability to clarify his own constitution's fundamental clauses, but also to the material conditions of Afghan society. Afghanistan was pitifully short of both education and industry. There was only one university in the entire country and it was not authorized to award degrees even in the two national languages, Pushtu and Persian. (Even in 1978, it could only offer degrees in a few limited subjects.)[19] The industrial backwardness of the country was pathetic. Until 1962, the number of industrial workers did not exceed 20,000.[20] The Afghans, subjected to the crushing burden of feudalism and tribal custom for centuries, did not possess the qualities which are basic to the establishment of representative government. The Parliament, predictably, became the domain of the same feudalistic and illiterate reactionary tribal leaders who were responsible for the plight of the Afghan people. In the 1969 elections, one-third of the members returned were illiterate. Some were so ignorant that, even today, stories of their foibles are common in Kabul. One tribal leader elected from Wardak made the following speech:

> Since no Minister has been elected from my area Wardak, it is my humble request to the King that in keeping with his promise, he should choose the next Secretary General of the United Nations from this area. Our biggest problem is the narrow road which runs through our settlements. So far, three of my trucks have met accidents on this road . . ..

The story was that at the time of the election of the leader of the house, some tribal sardars had made all kinds of promises, one being that the member from Wardak would be 'appointed' UN Secretary General by the King.

5

The Birth of Afghan Communism

The 1964 constitutional reforms gave Afghan middle-class intellectuals a unique opportunity to express themselves. If the 1946-53 reforms had brought them to birth, this second set of reforms set them on their feet. Despite the political repression of the Daud years, this minuscule class was able to carve out an identity for itself. In terms of the country's population the number of intellectually conscious Afghans was small, but as nearly 90 per cent of the educated minority was settled in Kabul, its influence was significant.[1] However, it must not be forgotten that the influence of these men did not extend beyond the capital.

PDPA sources have confirmed that as early as 1956, some leading progressive and left-wing figures has set up secret 'study circles'. These 'circles' did not have a given course of study or membership, nor did they extend beyond personal acquaintances and friends of the organizers.[2] Although Daud Khan had established close relations with the Soviet Union, it did not follow that he was willing to allow communist ideas to be preached openly. His sole objective was to get as much assistance from the USSR as possible. So eminent a communist as Dr Abdul Rahman Mahmoodi spent the entire period of Daud's rule in prison, as mentioned earlier. Babrak Karmal and Ustad Amir Khyber Khan, it is true, were released in 1956 but they were not identified as Marxists at the time. The 'study circles' were the only avenue open to frightened left-wing intellectuals and political workers to meet and exchange ideas.

By 1963, these left-wing intellectuals had become bolder and were beginning to meet in more public places. In 1963-64, there were four or five active study circles. One was run by Dr Abdul Rahim Mahmoodi and Dr. Abdul Hadi Mahmoodi, brother and nephew respectively of Dr Abdul Rahman Mahmoodi, who in 1946 had founded the first pro-

Peking communist party known as Sazeman-e Azadi Bakhsh-e Mardom-e Afghanistan (SAMA).[3] Another familiar face was the former TNB activist, diplomat and progressive writer, Noor Mohammed Taraki, who had returned to the country in 1953 after resigning his diplomatic post in the United States and had since been active in spreading his Marxist ideas. In 1963-64, those who could be said to be under his influence included Dr Shah Wali, Dr Saleh Mohammed Zeary, Karim Misaq, Abdul Mohammed, Ismail Danish, Abdul Rashid Arayan and Dr Mohammed Zahir.[4]

According to Parcham group sources, the Karmal-Khyber study circle was set up in 1960. Karmal got out of jail in 1956 and spent the obligatory two years (1957-59) in the army before entering Kabul University at the age of thirty-one to complete his degree.[5] His appeal to the young was obvious. Not only was he the oldest among them, but he had spent many years in jail. He was by now a mature and committed Marxist and it was during his years at Kabul University that he began to recruit the future leaders of the Parcham faction. In 1960, Sultan Ali Kishtmand was also at the Kabul University and was drawn to Karmal's circle. He and Karmal later worked together at the Ministry of Planning. Noor Ahmed Noor, son of a prosperous land-owning family from Panjwai (Kandhar), also met Karmal at the University.[6]

Another prominent member of the Karmal group was Anahita Ratebzad, a medical student at the University in 1957-63, and daughter of Ahmed Ratebzad, one of Amir Amanullah Khan's diehard supporters. Her closeness to Karmal was to lead to her divorce from her husband.[7] Parcham party sources indicate that Mir Ghulam Mohammed Ghubar was another of Karmal's companions, and that Tahir Badakhshi also began his socialist journey in one of Karmal's study circles: Before 1963, Ghulam Dastgir Panjsheri and Shuruhullah Shahpur were running a further study circle, as was Tahir Badakhshi (comprising mostly students from Badakhshan province). Another small study circle was run by Mohammed Zahir Ofaq.

In 1963-64, barring the Mahmoodi brothers, all the other activists of these study circles felt that the time had come to make a common platform, although the atmosphere was far from auspicious for such a risky initiative. When the formation of political parties was made legal under the 1964 constitution, they thought the last hurdle had been removed. Five weeks after the announcement, the group had not only prepared the basic documents of the new progressive party, but also worked out its administrative structure.[8]

On a cold winter morning in early 1965, thirty of these men met at Noor Mohammed Taraki's house to form the Hizbe Democratic Khalq Afghanistan, or the People's Democratic Party of Afghanistan (PDPA)[9] (the Soviet writer Arunova mistakenly says the number was twenty-seven)[10]. On the face of it, this was a small group, but in only thirteen years it was to father the Afghan revolution. While they sat in Taraki's house on that historic day, it could not have occurred to any of them that in the not-too-distant future some of them would become mortal enemies. Perhaps they were not even aware of the tremendous role history was to choose for them to play.

Although administrative details had been worked out earlier, there was some tension between Taraki and Karmal. The founders of the new party chose Taraki as the first General Secretary and Karmal as the First Secretary, a fair and balanced decision which nonetheless left Karmal dissatisfied. He felt that he had been overlooked for the top post because of his youth and that Taraki had been chosen because of his 'white hair'.

While this gathering agreed to grant full legal and political rights to women, there was no woman member. Begum Taraki was there, but she was merely serving tea to her husband's comrades.[11] While one can attribute the lack of a woman founder of the new Party to the highly segregated nature of Afghan society, how does one explain that there was not a single representative of the 'working class' at the meeting that day? In 1978, thirteen years and four months after the formation of the Party, not even a single member of the thirty-strong Central Committee was a representative of either workers or farmers. In July 1986, of the eight members of the Politburo, not one could be said to represent the working classes. After 1980, a number of nominations were made to the Central Committee (ironically from the ranks of the middle class) which were supposed to represent labour (Sattar Purdilli for one), but the fact is that twenty-two years after the foundation of the Party, no member of its provincial or central committees or of the Politburo belongs to the 'salt of the earth'.

The founding fathers of the Party, as stated earlier, were all members of different 'study circles', and when the Party was actually formed, they became its office-bearers and leaders. In fact, Article 3 of the Party constitution confirms that the original committee was chosen so as to give representation to every study circle. It reads:

> Acceptance of membership can only take place on an individual basis through the constituency (i.e. cell). However, the Central Committee in exceptional cases can accept the group membership of candidates.

At the time of the PDPA's formation, no known left-wing group was unrepresented on it. The Mahmoodi brothers had already formed the pro-China communist party, this being the high point of Sino-Soviet

Table 1

Former Study Circle	Name of Central Committee Member	Nationality
Taraki	1. Noor Mohammed Taraki	Pushtun
	2. Saleh Mohammed Zeary	Pushtun
Karmal-Khyber	1. Babrak Karmal	Tajik[12]
	2. Sultan Ali Kishtmand	Hazara
Panjsheri	1. Ghulam Dastgir Panjsheri	Tajik
	2. Shuruhullah Shahpur	Uzbek
Karmal-Badakhshi	1. Dr Tahir Badakhshi	Tajik

Party Secretariat

General Secretary: Noor Mohammed Taraki

First Secretary: Babrak Karmal

tension. The provision for 'group membership' included by the PDPA seems not to have been made in case, at a later date, the Mahmoodi brothers were to wish to join the Party. However, the Central Committee members chosen from various 'circles' were endowed with extraordinary powers through this clause to merge their respective circles into the PDPA. In later years, the PDPA made full use of this provision. Many groups left and came back to the Party under this *carte blanche.*

The Party's founding congress elected a seven-member Central Committee (see Table 1). In addition, four 'member candidates' of the Central Committee were also chosen. While Zamir Safi was connected with the Karmal group, Dr Mohammed Zahir, Dr Akbar Shah Wali and Karim Misaq were aligned with Taraki. Four important persons were not present at the congress. Hafizullah Amin was studying in the United States, Ustad Amir Akbar Khyber Khan had been appointed an instructor at the Police Academy, Kabul, Anahita Ratebzad was preoccupied with the dissolution of her marriage and Ismail Danish was out of Kabul because of his job.[13]

The foundation documents of the Party were published in the Party organ *Khalq.*[14] The founding congress had decided to bring out this magazine with Taraki as senior editor and Baraq Shafi as editor. Reviewing the past political struggle in Afghanistan, a *Khalq* article said:

The exploited sections of our people, our national leaders, those who advocated constitutional monarchy and the followers of liberal ideals have fought gallantly for an end to feudalism, the eradication of colonialism and neo-colonialism, internal reaction and injustice. However, unhelpful international and domestic conditions forced them to suffer temporary defeats ... History has now chosen progressive and nationalist forces to accomplish the mission of resolving these fundamental contradictions.[15]

The basic mission of the party was described as the resolution of Afghan society's 'fundamental contradictions'. It is interesting to note that while the founders of the Party were all diehard communists, they refrained from mentioning Marxism or Leninism, and mentioned socialism only once in passing ('We will never relinquish our aim of realizing a complete society which can only be accomplished through socialism.'[16])

For the industrial development of the country, the Party had chosen state capitalism which it believed would turn Afghanistan, within the span of a lifetime, into an industrial society. The Party had also promised to set up a 'national government' on the principle of a united national front to fulfil its programme:

The political pillars of the national government of Afghanistan would consist of a united national front representing all the progressive, democratic and nationalistic forces, that is workers, farmers, enlightened and progressive intellectuals, craftsmen, the petit bourgeoisie and national capitalists.[17]

According to the official Soviet line, it is not possible for underdeveloped Third World countries to bring about a socialist revolution because they lack an industrial labour class. Such states are, therefore, advised to work towards a socialist revolution through the formation of a 'nationalist government', organized by a 'united nationalist front' which can lead them through the 'national democratic phase'. The national democratic phase means the eradication of feudal landholdings, nationalization of import and export corporations, nationalization of major industries held in private hands and the promotion of state-held industries. Without undertaking any deep or serious analysis of the class structure or basic contradictions of the Afghan society, the PDPA Marxist intellectuals were content to make the 'national democratic phase' integral to the Party's general programme as enunciated in its foundation documents.

The PDPA, then, was a platform of Afghan Marxist intellectuals, but it wore the figleaf of national democratic objectives. In terms of its manifesto, it was no different from the liberal-leftist National Awami Party in Pakistan. However, unlike that party, its leadership was not in the hands of nationalists. After the Revolution, Taraki told a press conference that 'in a technical sense' there was no communist party in Afghanistan. In a 'technical' sense he was right.[18] In terms of its name and programme, the PDPA was a national democratic party. However, unlike 'popular and democratic' parties, it was not willing to throw its membership open. The Marxist founder of the Party set up an ideological seminary through which the prospective member had to pass before being accepted. Article 3 of the PDPA constitution said:

> The candidate will spend a probationary period of furthering his party education, raising the level of political and ideological consciousness and broadening his outlook of the party objectives. The candidate, depending on his own class background, will spend between four months and a year on probation ... if a probationer ... does not show up his worth to be a full member, the relevant official or the party organization may reject his application or extend his period of probation.[19]

Moreover, an application for Party membership could only be considered if it was supported in writing by two Party members.

On the question of foreign relations, support for the Soviet Union and maintenance of Afghanistan's neutrality were made part of Party policy. (The limited knowledge of the founders about the outside world can be judged from the fact that in the foundation documents, Burma had been described as a socialist country.[20]) A Khalq party pamphlet issued in 1975-76 said:

> Since the very beginning, the PDPA has had a Leninist attitude towards Parliament and parliamentary campaigns. While it rejects bourgeois parliamentarianism, it supports the revolutionary use of the parliamentary platform.[21]

Elections to Parliament were to be held in 1965. In order to use the opportunity and the atmosphere generated by it, the PDPA needed funds. However, with the Party leadership in the hands of the jobless Taraki, the homeless Karmal and other equally poor comrades whose ability to run their households was nothing short of a miracle, this appeared almost impossible. The elections were being held only nine months after the Party's formation. But there was one way out. Taraki and Karmal visited Moscow soon after it became clear that elections would take place.[22] It was also during this visit that it was arranged that a collection of Taraki's short stories *Zindigi-i-Nau* (New Life) would be published in Moscow and smuggled to Afghanistan.[23] It must have been as a result of help obtained from the Soviets that the PDPA fielded eight candidates in the September 1965 elections.

Elections to the lower house of Parliament were held in 1965 and since political parties still had no legal cover, the PDPA fielded its candidates on an individual basis. Tribal chiefs, Khans and feudal landlords, sceptical about the promised 'autonomy' of Zahir Shah's Parliament, took little interest in the proceedings, which is the main reason the election results were such an unexpected triumph for the Party. Three PDPA candidates (Babrak Karmal, Noor Ahmed Noor and Faizan) won their seats. Anahita Ratebzad was also returned from one of the four seats reserved for women. (The Khalq group was later to claim that Ratebzad was not a Party member. Whether in a technical sense she was or she wasn't, she was very much a part of the PDPA.)

Four PDPA candidates, namely Noor Mohammed Taraki, Sultan Ali Kishtmand, Abdul Hakim Jozjani and Hafizullah Amin, failed to get elected. Amin had joined the Party after his return from the United States. Since 1950, he had been a teacher at different Kabul institutions and at the teacher training school. He had, therefore, a large number of former students to draw support from. Even after having been absent from the scene for so many years, he only lost by fifty votes. It is interesting to note that winning PDPA members later joined up to form the Parcham group and those who lost established the Khalq faction. The only exception was Kishtmand who remained loyal to Karmal, though he was among the losers. Faizan, who had won, later left politics altogether.

In October 1965, the lower house began its first session. Zahir Shah invited Dr Mohammed Yusuf who had earlier headed the cabinet of Ministers to form a government. However, there was bitter criticism in the house of his past 'misdeeds and corruption'. It became increasingly clear that he would find it hard to obtain a vote of confidence from the house. On 24 October 1965, at the PDPA's instigation, particularly that of Karmal, a group of students burst into Parliament, shouting angry slogans against Dr Yusuf. They occupied the members' seats and there was total pandemonium. Karmal rose dramatically, his sleeves rolled up, and began to address the intruders. Karmal was not only a member from Kabul city, but also considered himself the spokesman of the younger generation and the first rebel student leader in Afghan history (which he was).[24] Soldiers were called in and the house was cleared.[25]

The next day, the students marched in protest against the heavy-handed manner in which the soldiers had dealt with them. Troops were called in and, to disperse the students, they opened fire, killing three people, one of them a passer-by. The students made flags of the blood-spattered shirts of their slain companions and marches began to set forth from Kabul's educational institutions every day. These agitations made the Yusuf government totally ineffective, forcing Zahir Shah to appoint Hashim Maiwandwal Prime Minister.[26] Maiwandwal, a western-style social democrat, went immediately after his appointment to Kabul University and addressed the students, assuring them of his support for their demands and welfare.

Dr Yusuf's fall was the first political victory scored by the Afghan students. The event symbolized the birth of mass petty-bourgeois radicalism. The Marxist intellectuals of the PDPA took it as the beginning of a socialist revolution.

One student of the Habibia School who was one of the leading figures during the *Soyem Aqrab* (the name given to the October 1965 protests)[27] was a close friend of Karmal's brother, Mahmood Baryali. This Pushtun youth from Paktia prided himself on being Karmal's most eminent disciple. Following the Revolution, he was appointed Ambassador to Iran. After 1980, he rose from being a mere member of the Central Committee to join the Politburo. By profession he was a doctor, but he was made head of intelligence. This devoted and admiring Karmal follower was no other than Dr Najibullah Khan who, at the young age of thirty-seven, successfully eliminated his former mentor. This mentor-disciple relationship has played an important role in the history of the PDPA: both Taraki and Karmal were ousted by their disciples.

The political career of Dr Najibullah, the fourth Secretary General of the PDPA, can be said to have begun with the *Soyem Aqrab* movement. Among his companions of those days was a young student named Khalil Zimer who became a member of the Parcham group Central Committee in 1972. When in 1976 the two factions agreed to an alliance, he left the Party and joined Sardar Daud Khan's National Party because he was against the alliance. One of the charges against Zimer is that it was he who informed Daud of the alliance between the two factions.[28] Soon after the April 1978 Revolution, he was arrested. Both groups of the Party were unwilling to forgive him his 'treachery'. He stayed in the Pulcharki prison through Taraki's, Amin's and Karmal's years in power. By December 1982, he had once again become a Marxist-Leninist. During the author's many conversations with him in jail, he kept insisting that the conferral of the highest national honours on Brezhnev by the leaders of Afghanistan and Eastern European communist countries on what proved to be his last birthday was a recognition of his 'services to Marxism' instead of a graceless political joke and an untimely effort at a revival of the cult of personality.[29] Since Zimer had grown to political maturity under Karmal, for him the head of the Kremlin could do no wrong. He had spent nearly ten years in the Parcham group and was extremely well informed about its inner and outer workings. In 1981, Dr Najibullah sent for him and assured him that 'respected comrade Karmal' was studying his case. Then he was sent back to Pulcharkhi. When the writer left Afghanistan in January 1984, he was still there, suffering from acute syphilis and stomach disorders.

In accordance with the decision of the PDPA founding congress, the Party brought out its official organ called *Khalq*. With a blazing red masthead, it appeared in April 1966, but after only six issues its licence to publish was revoked on 22 May 1966. It had neither advocated violence nor printed any criticism of Zahir Shah which could be taken exception to, but it had printed the PDPA manifesto, the foundation documents and an account of policy objectives. It also published articles by Karmal, Kishtmand, Taraki, Baraq Shafi and Suleman Laiq. After the paper was banned, a meeting was called at Taraki's house to consider the situation. Karmal is said to have described *Khalq*'s masthead as leftist adventurism and observed that 'instead of flying the red banner, we should have tried to reassure Zahir Shah that we were not communists. Not only would it have been wise but it would have saved the paper from closure.'[30]

Taraki was the chief editor of *Khalq*, so it was he whom Karmal was accusing of 'leftist adventurism'. Karmal's criticism, which was not endorsed by the majority of the Central Committee membership, indicated the basic differences in approach and tactics between Taraki and him. Karmal maintained that in view of the prevailing circumstances, which were most unfavourable, the Party should move carefully under the umbrella of its national democratic programme. It should not allow itself to fall a victim to official action before it had consolidated its strength and unity. Karmal seems to have assumed that Zahir Shah's government was so naive that it did not know what the real programme of the PDPA was. The fact is that the government did know, and did not wish to permit the Party to propagate its communist views under liberal pretexts. When Taraki later made an application for a fresh licence, this was refused by the Minister of Information and Culture,[6] because your new paper will have the same purpose and objectives as *Khalq*. You cannot be allowed to print the *Khalq* under another name.'[31]

6

The Karmal-Taraki Break

The closure of *Khalq* was the beginning of the Karmal-Taraki break. There were no ideological or qualitative differences between these two men as regards the nature of the Afghan social and political struggle. Their basic policy prescriptions were almost identical. Both considered the Soviet Union their ideological leader and they were equally committed to the PDPA's national democratic programme. It was only a difference of tactics that divided the two Marxists. Karmal did not wish to scare the ruling elite. He wanted to take advantage of their internal contradictions and move cautiously towards the Party goal without attracting too much attention. Taraki did not believe, either, that the Party should storm ahead with its guns blazing. Like Karmal, he wanted to spread PDPA ideas through press and Parliament. However, in his speeches and writings, he tended to be bolder, taking a more open line.

To understand the two men and their eventual break, we must analyze their social origins and those of their followers. While both of them hailed from the salaried middle class, there were basic differences in their social background. Karmal's father, General Mohammed Hasan, had retired as the Military Governor of Paktia province in 1965. His close friend Noor Ahmed Noor was born in a well-to-do land-owning family of Kandhar. Another close companion, Suleman Laiq, had been born in the famous Mujadaddi family. Sibghatullah Mujadaddi's sister, the niece of Hazrat Shor Bazar, was his wife.[1] Anahita Ratebzad's husband, Dr Qamaruddin Kakar, was King Zahir Shah's personal physician. Amir Akbar Khyber, after his release from jail in 1956, was employed as an instructor at the Kabul Police Academy. Jilani Bakhtiari, Karmal's brother-in-law, was a high government official whose house the group had used since June 1966 for cell meetings (nominally devoted to the promotion and study of the Pushtu language).[2] To sum up, almost all members of the Karmal group belonged to the city-bred, high-ranking upper-middle class. Najibullah, who later joined the Parcham faction and succeeded Karmal in 1986, was born to a high-ranking embassy official.

Another crucial element in Karmal's development which must not be overlooked is that although he and many of his older friends had been forced into exile from their families because of their political views, they had never entirely liberated themselves from their middle-class upbringing, nor moved away from its social circle. Members of the Taraki group, by contrast, mostly belonged to the lower-middle, salary-earning class. They also tended to have rural rather than urban backgrounds. Despite the influence of educated Pushtuns in the Taraki group, the presence of men like Ghulam Dastgir Panjsheri (Tajik), Jozjani (Uzbek), the Alamyar brothers (Farsiban), Mansur Hashmi (Arab), and Ismail Danish (Arab) can only be explained by the rural background and lower-middle class origins which they shared with Taraki.[3] Taraki's influence was particularly strong in institutions where the majority of the students came from rural areas, while Karmal's group was stronger in Habibia, Najat and various departments of the Kabul University where the students hailed from the well-off, city-bred middle class.

The Karmal and Taraki groups were differentiated, then, by background (urban and rural) and by class origins (upper-middle and lower-middle) and consequently held dissimilar and opposing attitudes. Even on a cultural level, these distinctions were evident after the revolution. In the one and a half years when the Khalq group was in power (April 1978 to December 1979), radio and television programmes were dominated by artists from a rural background – Pushtu folk singers, or such artists as Tawwakli (Hazara folk music) and Gulbaz Badakhshi (Badakhshani folk singer). Kabul-born performers hardly found any work on the state-owned radio and TV. During the Karmal era, the pendulum swung the other way. The weekly Pushtu movie on television was discontinued and folk singers were not given more than half an hour a week.

In 1966, 'in order to put an end to Karmal's unprincipled and factional intrigues, Taraki finally decided to increase the membership of the Central Committee.'[4] After much bitter debate, the following additions were made: Noor Ahmed Noor, Suleman Laiq, Baraq Shafi, Abdul Hakim Jozjani, Ismail Danish, Mohammed Zahir Ufaq, Abdul Mohammed and Hafizullah Amin. Not unexpectedly, these new members did not hail from the working class or the peasantry. They were poets, writers, journalists, teachers or engineers. The Marxist founders of the Party, instead of broadening the class base of the organization, appeared quite unable to break out of their middle-class circle, and rather than expand the Party, they chose to expand the Central Committee in order to bring one another down.

However, the expansion in the size of the Committee did not resolve the Karmal-Taraki differences. In order to consolidate his position, Karmal began to campaign for the inclusion in the Committee of Anahita Ratebzad and Ustad Amir Khyber Khan, both of whom had good independent grounds for being enlisted. However, Taraki saw this proposal as a Karmal ruse to increase his voting strength in the Committee and opposed it.

On 7 August 1966, while this bitter in-fighting was still in progress, Karmal made a speech in Parliament describing Zahir Shah as 'Asia's great progressive king':

> It is the duty of each and every Afghan subject to pay his heartfelt respects to such a King who, I dare say, is considered the most progressive of all the kings in the monarchist countries of Asia. This is the right which we sincerely believe in and revere, and no-one can deprive us of this right to respect such a progressive King ... It should be well to entrust the honourable Assembly, in contact with the Ministry of Finance, to render new Terms of the Royal Court, so that the authority and prestige of our King will be established and preserved.[5]

It seemed that Karmal had launched this new line without taking the Party into his confidence. The purpose was to convince Zahir Shah that he, Karmal, was not a communist. What effect the speech had on the King, it is difficult to say. In any case, the entire house was engaged in a sort of sycophantic competition to please the King. However, in the already divided party, Karmal's speech became the subject of a bitter controversy. To portray Karmal as a 'royalist', Taraki had the speech printed and distributed as a Khalq pamphlet. Commenting on the incident in 1976, the Khalq group claimed that 'Karmal's pro-monarchist speech was shocking even to the most reactionary deputies because, fearing public opinion, they could not have expressed their pro-monarchist sentiments so explicitly.'[6]

Karmal's speech may perhaps have surprised the reactionaries, but it should not have caused such a 'shock' to the Khalq faction. One of its leading lights, Hafizullah Amin, was to use more or less the same words for Zahir Shah later.[7] In any case, students of communist parties would know that such somersaults are not unusual at all. If the communist Tudeh party of Iran, despite being on the Shah's hit list, could describe his 'White Revolution' as a 'progressive step' (simply because he had just signed a steel mill and gas sale deal with the Soviet Union), surely Karmal and Amin could also praise their king, the last years of whose rule had not been at all bad, compared to the reign of the Shah.

In August 1966, Karmal sent a written note to the Party announcing his resignation both from the Central Committee and as First Secretary of the PDPA. As reasons, he cited the non-inclusion of Anahita Ratebzad and Ustad Amir Khyber in the Committee and the *Khalq* masthead (Taraki's 'adventurist' tactics).[8] This was a calculated move. He controlled four votes in the Committee, while Taraki could rely on only two. Ghulam Dastgir Panjsheri, the seventh member, was likely to side with Karmal. Karmal was sure that the Committee would not accept his resignation, which would lead not only to Taraki's humiliation, but to his possible elimination.

Karmal deputed Sultan Ali Kishtmand to hand over his resignation to the Committee.[9] On 24 September 1966, a session was called to consider it. It did not take Taraki long to divine Karmal's game.[10] After all, he was an old hand at this kind of infighting and was not about to be upstaged by the younger man. Both Panjsheri and Tahir Badakhshi were Tajiks, though they came from different areas. Because both claimed against the other to represent the Tajiks on the Committee, it was clear to Taraki that they would never vote on the same side. Therefore, the moment Kishtmand, Shahpur and Badakhshi began to argue against accepting Karmal's resignation, Panjsheri, as expected, moved over to Taraki's side. The Committee was now evenly divided, with Taraki, Saleh Mohammed Zeary, and Panjsheri favouring the acceptance of the resignation. A casting vote was needed which was Karmal's own.

Through a brilliant move, Taraki turned Karmal's own vote against him. According to Khalq leaders who spoke to the author in the Pulcharki prison in Kabul (most of them were pro-Amin men), Taraki argued that communist party posts were always accepted on a voluntary basis and since Karmal had resigned voluntarily, he had already cast his vote in favour of the acceptance of his resignation. The legality of Taraki's interpretation apart, he won the first round that day on the basis of this technical point. Although Karmal and his friends never accepted this decision, Taraki was certainly the victor in the first open conflict between the two.

Karmal's resignation was not backed by any political sincerity; nor had it been tendered in the interests of the Party, but only to steal a march over his arch rival Taraki. The 24 September meeting did not resolve anything really. In name, the Party was still one, but the lines were now clearly drawn. This, one might add, was in keeping with the standard traditions of all middle-class-oriented ideological parties.

After the acceptance of the resignation,, to his rivals Karmal was no more than an ordinary member of the Party. For the next eleven years, Taraki took care to keep the dangerous number two position unfilled.[11] However, if Taraki was now confident that he would be able to tie up Karmal to the first tree in the Party backyard, he was quite wrong. Taraki was no Mao, nor Karmal a Deng Xiao Ping who could quietly bide his time as an ordinary member of the Party after being removed from the Central Committee. To regain his lost position, Karmal once again used the bourgeois platform of the Parliament. On 30 November 1966, he made a deliberately provocative speech in the house which led to scuffles among the deputies. Both Karmal and Anahita Ratebzad were slightly injured and taken to the Ibne Sina Hospital in the city. As arranged by Karmal, his followers, the students Mahmood Baryali (Karmal's brother), Najibullah, Abdul Wakil and Khalil Zimer, went round the Kabul schools and colleges distributing pre-printed pamphlets.[12] Besides being a member of Parliament, Anahita Ratebzad was also the director of the Malali Girls' School. As reports reached the school of her 'serious injuries', an angry procession of girl students was hurriedly organized and began to make its way towards the hospital.[13] Elsewhere in the city further student processions had been formed, all marching towards the Ibne Sina Hospital.

Here was the opportunity Karmal had been waiting for. He appeared to his young supporters, duly bandaged, and addressed them, making full use of his oratorical gifts. Khalil Zimer told the author that even Taraki came to the hospital to enquire after Karmal. This could have been a good moment to forge party unity, but instead the students' processions became the cause of a new dispute. It turned out that the pamphlets handed out that morning had urged the formation of processions in the name of the Central Committee. According to Zimer, the moment Taraki came to know of the 'appeal', he sent his men round with instructions to clarify that no such appeal had gone out from the Central Committee.[14] However, despite Taraki's efforts, it was quite clear that Karmal commanded an important student following. Even if no appeal had been made in the name of the PDPA Central Committee, it is likely that the students would still have come out to see the injured 'hero'.

It is possible that Karmal staged the demonstrations in order to rehabilitate his image after his pro-Zahir speech to Parliament, as well as to regain his position in the Party.[15] While Taraki saw Karmal's actions as only directed at ousting him from his top Party position, it is also possible that Karmal was at the same time trying to carve out for himself a larger popular constituency than the narrow-based PDPA provided. In both his parliamentary speeches, it was Zahir Shah's ineffective Prime Ministers that Karmal had singled out for attack. He had carefully refrained from saying anything against the King – whom, indeed, he had gone out of his way to praise. His two performances were example and evidence of his middle-class opportunism.

Almost all the Central Committee members went to the hospital to enquire after the 'injured' Karmal. Some of them, such as Panjsheri and Mohammed Zaher Ofaq, took this opportunity to discuss Party unity with Karmal. These members belonged to smaller tribes and nationalities, and to them the Taraki-Karmal dispute was not, therefore, of fundamental significance. However, it was a nuisance because they were being forced to take sides. They felt that the best way of avoiding a choice was to bring back Party unity. The student agitations had proved helpful to Karmal. Some of the Party's Marxist intellectuals were once again prepared to grant the certificate of a 'revolutionary' to him since agitational politics was considered the practical implementation of Marxist philosophy.

Karmal now felt that the time had come to make a frontal attack on Taraki. He argued that since Taraki had tried to stop the student processions, he had acted not as a Party member, but as a friend of the regime. He added that the situation could only be resolved by a vote of confidence in him (Karmal) by the Central Committee.[16] This was a clever tactical move. He was not asking the Party for the revival of his former posts, but for a formal expression of confidence. Normally, the Party should have had no difficulty in granting him that.[17] Some Parcham sources claim that at this point Karmal was sincere in seeking to end the schism in the Party. Had Taraki been more far-sighted, perhaps the Party would have been spared the infighting and break-up which followed. However, Taraki was not prepared to accept Karmal. Being a Ghilzai, he simply could not bring himself to forgive Karmal's public praise for the King;[18] nor could he view Karmal's return to his former position in the Party as anything but his own undoing.

He therefore decided to take on Karmal. This time, however, it was not to be so easy. The next few weeks were spent by both adversaries in attempts to win the support of the less partisan members of the Committee such as Panjsheri, Badakhshi, Shahpur, Jozjani and Ofaq. The three first named held the key votes. In the Karmal resignation affair, Panjsheri had sided with Taraki and Badakhshi with Karmal. However, in the 'vote of confidence' imbroglio, Panjsheri and Jozjani began to negotiate with Karmal, with Panjsheri assuring him of his 'permanent' support. Since Panjsheri had moved to the Karmal camp, it was only natural that Badakhshi should go over into Taraki's arms.

The impasse continued. While Panjsheri, Shahpur and Kishtmand stayed with Karmal, Zeary and Badakhshi sided with Taraki. No decision was possible. As for the prospective Central Committee candidates, the position of the two claimants was evenly balanced. In the end, the Karmal vote of confidence was not put to discussion before a full plenary session of the Committee. According to both Khalq and Parcham sources, the line-up was: for Taraki: Shah Wali, Karim Misaq, Hafizullah Amin, Ismail Danish, Abdul Mohammed, and Dr Mohammed Zahir; for Karmal: Noor Ahmed Noor, Baraq Shafi, Suleman Laiq, Zamir Safi, and Abdul Hakim Jozjani. The writer has been unable to establish if Mohammed Zahir Ofaq was neutral or with Karmal. He did not, however join the Karmal group then or later.

Political parties, like individuals, can often wonder after the event what all the heat and dust was about. When I discussed the 'confidence/no confidence' rigmarole of those days with Khalq leaders in Kabul's Pulcharki jail years later, some of them could only smile sheepishly in answer.

The break finally came in May 1967, when two parties, both calling themselves the People's Democratic Party of Afghanistan (PDPA), were set up, though their manifestos, constitutions and objectives were identical. Karmal formed a separate Central Committee with himself as head and Taraki followed suit. Both groups, their briefcases chock-full of complaints against each other, went for arbitration to their mentors. Both were keen to establish that the other was 'anti-Soviet'. Soviet embassy officials in Kabul advised them to resolve their differences.[19] This was good and timely advice, but it was not properly taken. A meeting of the representatives of the two groups was arranged. Karmal appointed Panjsheri and Jozjani as his spokesmen and Taraki nominated Misaq and Shah Wali. The four peacemakers met at Taraki's house to consider a 'package deal' proposed by Karmal demanding the restoration of his two Party posts and the inclusion of Anahita Ratebzad and Ustad Amir Akbar Khyber Khan in the Central Committee.

Instead of rejecting Karmal's proposal out of hand, Taraki came out with a 'third alternative'. He suggested that, first of all, the two groups should formulate a joint programme against the Zahir Shah regime. He argued that only unity in practice could lead to Party unity. What Taraki was trying to prove was that the real cause of the dispute did not lie in personal differences, but in the 'strategy and thinking' of the two factions. As a matter of fact, not only were their basic politics identical, but their strategies were not much different either. As mentioned earlier, no peasant or worker was represented on either group, nor was there any divergence of views on the role of the working class in the emancipation of Afghanistan and the correct interpretation of the socio-economic background of the country. Their disagreement merely boiled down to what colour the masthead of the Party paper should be and whether Zahir Shah should be denounced or praised in public.

After discussions lasting over many days, the four representatives signed the formula proposed by Taraki. According to a Khalq pamphlet, 'At the end of the discussions, an agreement was reached. Unity of action is to be achieved as a first step to pave the way for full unity. Babrak vetoed the agreement.'[20]

Karmal had appointed Panjsheri and Jozjani as his spokesmen – instead of Kishtmand and Noor – so that in the event of the decision going against him, he should have the freedom of veto. His two nominees did not really belong to his group: they had in fact all along tried to persuade Karmal to reach a settlement with Taraki. Karmal had also been fairly certain that the negotiations would fail, which in his book meant fail to meet his demands. He could not have expected Taraki, who only a few months earlier had refused to grant him a vote of confidence, to agree to the package deal proposed by him. He also hoped that after the failure of the negotiations, the two emissaries Panjsheri and Jozjani would join his group. What happened was completely contrary to his expectations, as the old lion Taraki caught him by the tail.

Despite the ardent desire of the Soviet embassy for a settlement, an accord had once again eluded the two sides. It was not only the beginning of long and painful Party strife, but an indication of the lack of influence of the Soviet embassy on internal Party conflicts. It is possible that responsible Soviet officials were unable to see the grave consequences of the Taraki/Karmal rivalry at the time. However, their reaction to the impasse was 'pragmatic'. They decided to continue their financial support to both Taraki and Karmal. If the Soviet analysis was that at some future point the two groups would come together, then it can only be said that they were ignorant of the nature of tribal influences on the psychological make-up of Marxist intellectuals.

Not only did the Party break into the two Khalq and Parcham factions in the middle of 1967, but a number of splinter groups comprising smaller nationalities also emerged. As for the negotiators, Jozjani returned to Taraki and stayed with him. However, Panjsheri and Shahpur had other ideas. The former, saying goodbye to both factions, set up his own shop. It was called Groh-i-Karagar, or the workers' group. He even managed to gain a toehold in the industrial areas of Mazar Sharif and Pul Khumri. His solo flight, however, was short-lived and in 1968, he rejoined Taraki's Khalq group. It was not actually a rejoining but an 'alliance' or a 'joint front'. It was secretly agreed that Panjsheri would remain a member of the PDPA Central Committee, as well as the leader of his group, until 'complete unity' was achieved through 'joint action'. The two had also agreed that while the workers' group would be treated as an 'internal affair', it would carry out its work in the name of the PDPA. Some members of the group were also given PDPA posts at local levels.

Both Taraki and Panjsheri had their own distinct following now. They were also cool men by temperament. Their personal relationship remained steadfast until the end. According to my information, the Panjsheri workers' group was in existence even during the Karmal years.[21] In September 1982, the Provincial General Secretary of the Mazar-e-Sharif PDPA was sentenced to death at Pulcharkhi. (This was the only instance during Karmal's days of a Parcham worker being sentenced to death.) The man had been charged with the murder of two members of the workers' group. Panjsheri put so much pressure on Karmal to take action that he finally had to agree to hang one of his own followers.[22] Since Panjsheri was always considered more or less neutral in the Khalq-Parcham dispute, it was he who, in May 1986, was requested by the PDPA's fourth General Secretary, Dr Najibullah, to write the joint history of the Party.[23]

After the Taraki-Karmal break, Mohammed Zahir Ofaq also left the Party and set up a group called Jamiat-e-Inqlabyun (the Revolutionary Party). After the revolution, Ofaq continued the work of his group or party secretly and in the last days of Karmal – around 1984 – attempts were being made to bring him back to the PDPA. In the 19th plenary session of the Central Committee in July 1986, it was announced that he had been made a permanent member of the Committee. At the same meeting, his group formally allowed itself to be absorbed by the PDPA.[24]

Panjsheri's entry into the Khalq group in 1968 led to the logical exit of Badakhshi who accused Khalq of Pushtunism and formed his own party which he named Sitm-e-Milli. He began to organize youth in his native Badakhshan province against the Pushtun 'domination of Afghan politics'. The Tajiks of the area found Badakhshi's anti-Pushtunism attractive. Between 1973 and 1978, while Daud was in power, Badakhshi launched an armed struggle for the 'rights of national minorities'. During those years, a number of Sitm-e-Milli youths came to Pakistan and were given financial and military help.[25] Although Badakhshi himself, after leaving the PDPA, became a committed Tajik nationalist, the Badakhshani youths who came to Pakistan seemed inclined towards the Chinese line. (After the April Revolution, there is some evidence of a Badakhshi-Karmal political understanding against the Taraki government. Badakhshi was arrested in September 1978 and murdered at Pulcharkhi in February 1979. The Badakhshan Tajiks were enraged and tried to capture the city of Faizabad. The Afghan Air Force bombed the city and its vicinity for many days. The former Governor of the province, Mansur Hashmi, spoke to the writer in the Pulcharkhi jail about those 'terrible' days.) In 1980 Badakhshi's wife (Kishtmand's sister) was put in charge of all Afghanistan handicraft factories in Kabul. The main handicrafts factory, located near the Shehr-i-Nau general post office in Kabul, became the meeting place of Sitm-e-Milli workers during the Karmal years. In November 1983, one faction of the Sitm-e-Milli activists rejoined the PDPA.

In November 1983, Karmal, commenting on the PDPA breakup, said: 'Why the two of us with the same constitution, the same manifesto, the same desire for international cooperation, and the same enemies broke apart can only be attributed to an imperialist conspiracy.'[26] If Karmal was making an indirect reference to Hafizullah Amin, then he should have remembered that until 1967, Amin was only a junior contender for the PDPA Central Committee. He was not in a position to vote for or against Karmal's 'package deal', nor was he included in the negotiating team formed by Taraki. The fact is that if Taraki was responsible for the break-up of the Party to the extent of say 30 per cent, the rest of the 'credit' belongs to Karmal himself, while Amin was the child of this break-up.

The Soviet writer Arunova, discussing the infighting in the PDPA, writes:

> Difficult conditions of semi-legal activity, attacks by reactionary circles and ultra-left groups, repression on the part of the authorities, the small number and weak organization of the working class, the low level of class and political consciousness of workers, the incomplete process of class formation – all these complicated the institution and formation of the PDPA – and for that reason it did not escape its growing pains.[27]

This analysis begs the question. After all, in the Third World, with the exception of India, Sri Lanka and Japan, progressive movements have always been 'semi-legal'. There is no developing country where the communist party has been allowed to carry out its work free of interference. But in Afghanistan, except for the forcible eviction of Karmal and Ratebzad from Parliament, the PDPA leaders, cadres and workers were not attacked. The Soviet analyst is wrong, then, in attributing the Party's 'growing pains' to 'repression on the part of the authorities'. From 1 January 1965 to April 1978, only three party members were jailed, namely, Saleh Mohammed Zeary, Ghulam Dastgir Panjsheri and Karim Misaq – and this was between 1969 and 1973. The Khalq group did not blame the government alone for these prison sentences, but hinted at a conspiracy between Karmal and the government. Zahir Shah released Misaq after two years because of a nervous disorder: Misaq's second jail term came when Karmal was in power and the Red Army was in Afghanistan to protect that power. Ironically, the decadent institution of kingship proved more humane than the 'revolutionary' regime which showed no mercy to a former comrade suffering from a nervous breakdown. Taraki and Amin committed their excesses against their Parchamite opponents before the arrival of the Soviet Army: Karmal did not spare the Khalqites during his rule. Moreover, while only three PDPA leaders were in jail for varying terms during Zahir Shah's rule, in Daud's second term Taraki and Karmal were in jail for only two days and Amin for one. If the situation in Afghanistan is compared to what happened in Chile or Indonesia, the PDPA struggle appears to have been relatively painless.

Arunova is right when he speaks about the weakly-organized working class. However, the PDPA made no effort to bring this class into the Party. Its claim after the April Revolution that the working class had grown to political maturity under its wings was no more than a boast. Arunova has also made the mistake (perhaps deliberate) of crediting the Party with various workers' strikes which took place during the liberal reform period (1963-73).[28] Most of these strikes took place in 1968. Louis Dupree has counted nineteen workers' strikes between May and June 1968.[29] Pro-Peking communists claim that it was they who organized 80 per cent of the strikes in the Kabul factories. This is borne out by the fact that Dr Rahim Mahmoodi and Dr Hadi Mahmoodi were arrested in 1969 for their role in a strike which hit the largest state factory in Janglak.[30] The majority of workers in Kabul belonged to the Hazara tribe. Religiously, they were Shi'as. The Mahmoodi brothers tried to organize them on a tribal and religious basis instead of raising their class consciousness. The Hazaras are still considered the main recruiting ground by pro-Peking communists who, after 1980, launched an armed struggle against Karmal in the Hazarajat region. Consequently, there is much weight in the claim that it was the pro-Peking communists who were responsible for most of the industrial strikes in Kabul back in the late 1960s and early 1970s.

The one well-founded point made by Arunova relates to the 'low level of class and political consciousness' of the Afghan working classes, mainly due to the incomplete process of class formation in the Afghan society. However, from the basic documents of the PDPA to the political record of its two groups there is not a single mention anywhere of the existence of this difficulty. Nowhere is it identified as a problem in the struggle which the Party was supposedly trying to lead.

As in other parts of the world, Afghanistan in the years 1965-70 was swept by student protests. According to the rulers of the times, these protests were a kind of influenza which had spread from one country to the next. Afghanistan, the land of kings, had always been free of such foreign epidemics. Therefore, the student protests, when they came, caused both surprise and anxiety to the rulers. On 21 May 1968, a joint procession of students of the Kabul University, the School of Nursing, the School of Technology and the Teachers' Training School was fired upon by the police and one student was killed. The students made his blood-drenched shirt into a flag and processions became the order of the day.[31]

More serious student unrest began in May 1969, quickly spreading from Kabul to the smaller towns. These demonstrations completely disrupted normal life in the country. Since the government had announced elections for September/October, it thought the safest course was the closure of all schools, colleges and other institutions. All educational establishments remained closed from May until November 1969. This did not solve the problem, because when the students returned to their home towns and cities, they continued to organize processions.[32] Some of the popular student demands were quite non-political. They included postponement of examinations, simpler examination papers, concessional marking, issue of degrees without examinations, etc., etc. However, student leaders of those days say that these demands were made only to attract the common students.[33]

Between 1965 and 1973, the focus of both pro-China and pro-Soviet communists remained educational institutions. Because of these heady and defiant demonstrations against established authority, the left wing was in a state of euphoria at the time, confident that it was only a matter of time before students would move out of their schools and colleges, waving red banners. Revolution, they said excitedly, was round the corner. In 1968-69 the Karmal organ *Parcham* and the Mahmoodi brothers' *Shola-e-Javed* (the official paper of the pro-Chinese communist party, SAMA, which was set up in 1964) were locked in a contest for the students' undivided attention. The Taraki Khalq group could not join the fray because it did not have a paper of its own. In any case, the Khalq group was in the grip of a mental inertia during those days. However, the Khalq and the Shola-e-Javed groups were one in their lack of admiration for the Parchamites. Some western writers have seen this as the formation of a regular political alliance, which is a mistake. This was one of the rumours spread by the Parcham group at the time to win Soviet support.

According to the leaders of the two factions, whom time and circumstance brought together in 1980 in the same cell of the Pulcharkhi jail, the Khalq-Javed unity slogan was raised by a student who was a member of neither. This seems to be true because the division between the two at the time was bitter. How could a simple student, carried away by all those red banners, have known anything about the ideological niceties of the Soviet-Chinese dialectical debate?

In Daud's second term, Shola-e-Javed supporters were singled out for punishment. He hanged Dr Rahim Mahmoodi and a number of his pro-Peking followers. A pro-China communist Majid Kalkani (who came from the same area as Bacha Saqao) initiated an armed struggle against the Daud regime, which continued during the years in power of Taraki, Amin and Karmal. In 1980, he was arrested and executed by firing squad along with some pro-Amin Khalqis, the men whom he fought for nearly two years. Both the Tajik Maoist and pro-Moscow communists, it is said, shouted 'Long live Marxism-Leninism' before being put against the wall and shot.

After 1968, the pro-China group began to fragment. Among the many splinter groups formed as a result were SAMA, Paykar, Angar, Rahi, Jahanmordan and Khorasan.[34]

The Marxist intellectuals of the PDPA, like those of the pro-China SAMA, believe that the 'international situation' is more important than the situation at home. Instead of trying to analyze and solve the problems of their own people, they prefer to parrot official lines issued from Moscow and Peking and to claim that they alone are the true inheritors of that divine foreign wisdom. In the eyes of pro-China communists, Soviet 'social imperialism' is humanity's greatest enemy, while whatever comes out of Peking is the last and immutable word of revelation.[35] According to the PDPA doctrine, 'the sole criterion of being a progressive, a lover of peace and a revolutionary lies in friendship with Lenin's great country, the Soviet Union.'[36] If that is so then both the late Mrs Indira Gandhi and the present Prime Minister of India, Rajiv Gandhi, should be included among the world's great revolutionaries! The Afghan communists, one found, tended to be more Chinese than the Chinese and more Russian than the Russians.

The pro-Peking group believes that the first enemy of the people is Soviet 'social imperialism' and 'imperialism' itself. Next on the list is the struggle between the dominant and exploiting Pushtuns and the suppressed sub-nationalities (like the Tajiks): Class struggle takes third place on the list of priorities.[37] It is interesting to note that with the exception of SAMA, Afghanistan is not part of the name of any pro-China Afghan faction. This is because if the word Afghanistan is used, it is an indirect admission that Afghanistan is the home of Afghans or Pushtuns. The pro-China communists are not prepared to concede that.[38] In fact, one pro-China group employed the ancient name of the area (Khorasan) to identify itself. This was a direct negation of the concept of a modern Afghan state.[39]

The key to these divisions lies in the foreign policies of China and of the USSR. On a state level, relations have always existed between Afghanistan and the Soviet Union, whether in the time of Amir Amanullah, Nadir Khan, Zahir Shah or Karmal. It has, therefore, been incumbent on the Soviet Union to support only those movements and groups which believe in a strong centre. The Soviet Union has been unwilling to recognize the bitter struggle between the different nationalities which make up Afghan society. Not only would a change in this policy have meant bad relations with the ruling circles in Kabul; it might have led to the destabilization of Afghanistan, so sensitively close to the Soviet Union.

The Chinese, however, with whom Afghanistan's relations are relatively recent, have made the nationalities question the cornerstone of their Afghan policy in the hope that it would earn them broad-based Afghan support.

Across the Durand Line in Pakistan, it has been another story. After the 1962 war with India, regardless of the regime in power, Pakistan-China relations have remained close. Consequently, in Pakistan the Chinese policy has been exactly contrary to the one followed in Afghanistan. It has been the Soviet Union which has been responsible for raising the nationalities question in Pakistan. The Bangladesh movement of 1970-71 was described by the Soviet Union as a movement of 'national liberation', whereas to China it was a blatant example of Indian 'expansionism'. At the time of the Indo-China war in 1962, India and the Soviet Union came even closer, which is why the Soviet Union has refused to acknowledge the nationalities question in India, while China has found no difficulty in discovering Naga and Mizo 'national liberation movements' in the northeast of India. Beyond India, in Burma, the Soviet-Chinese contradictions have once again been highlighted.

These are only three examples, but they can be multiplied. They demonstrate that both the Soviet Union and China consult their state foreign policy interests of the moment to determine the character of revolutionary movements elsewhere in the world. If the state is friendly, the nationalities question is made subservient to federal unity. If it is unfriendly, the nationalities question is pushed to the forefront. International communist movements have kept dancing blindly to these dissonant and confusing Soviet-Chinese ideological tunes through the last two decades. The PDPA and SAMA in Afghanistan have been no exception in this respect. The leadership of the 'class war' was, as expected, in the hands of the dominant Pushtun nationality, while the proponents of the nationalities question were the smaller nationalities which were ill-served by the federalist principle. The great upholder of the rights of nationalities was SAMA which was led by non-Pushtuns.

Between May 1967 and July 1977, the Karmal and Taraki groups had evolved into separate political parties – the Parcham and the Khalq. This divide was to prove auspicious for Karmal. He was given permission in 1968 to publish his party organ, also called *Parcham*. It began to come out under the editorship of Ustad Amir Khyber Khan and Suleman Laiq with Karmal, Ratebzad and Kishtmand as regular contributors. This period was the party's youthful phase. Khalq workers now admit that after 1967, the Karmal group was bigger than theirs and more effective.[40] After his separation from Taraki, Karmal conducted himself with his usual care. The policy of his paper *Parcham* was also to play safe. Louis Dupree, writing about that period, said:

> Babrak and Parcham appear to be agreed that a milder revolutionary approach to socialism is to be preferred to violent overthrow. Parcham believes that all sectors of the Afghan population can contribute to the defeat of 'feudalism and imperialism' and promotes the creation of a 'united democratic front' to work for change within the framework of the constitutional system.[41]

To Karmal, the dream of putting an end to feudalism and imperialism, while staying within the ambit of constitutional kingship, and setting up alliances with all political and social groups of Afghan society, was not unrealistic. Being a product of the middle-class, high-ranking bureaucracy, he was well aware of the crisis gripping the ruling class. He hoped to find a niche for his 'united front', taking advantage of the contradictions of the ruling class and the vacuum created by them in the body politic. However, he must have known that the royal house of Afghanistan was not about to abdicate. And while it was true that the King had earned the enmity of his entire family by stripping its members of state offices, he had failed to fulfil his promise of sharing power with Parliament. This had created a situation of great uncertainty in the country. Karmal hoped to take advantage of this political vacuum and the alienation of members of the ruling family from power politics. He was also hoping that some disgruntled elements of the royal house would join him. His calculations were not so far off the mark: it was Sardar Daud who made a 'united front' with him a few years later.

It was of course paradoxical that according to the Party manifesto, it was the exploited classes of Afghan society with whom a 'united front' was to be established, whereas Karmal was eager to set up this front with members of the ruling classes! According to his Parchamite followers, this was a matter of 'tactics' only, and Karmal undoubtedly did use his intimate understanding of the inner contradictions of the ruling classes to his own political advantage. His rivals were more naive and more doctrinaire.

Expounding his position in *Parcham*, Karmal writes:

[The party] views the national democratic phase of the social revolution not as a period of consecutive reforms but as the legitimate material and political preparation for the socialist revolution.[42]

By 'preparation', Karmal meant not the preparation of the masses for the looming battle, but the search for a back entrance to the citadel of power. Later the revolutionaries of the Khalq and Javed factions were to follow in Karmal's footsteps. However, at the time, both of them denounced Karmal for his time-serving politics. He was described as a 'court sycophant' and his party was called the 'royal communist party'. To project himself as a progressive-liberal leader instead of a diehard communist was one of Karmal's characteristics and an integral part of his political persona. Even after 1980, he kept trying to present himself as an open-minded reformer. During the liberal reform period of Zahir Shah, he did manage quite successfully to be popularly viewed as a liberal and progressive parliamentarian. The American 'Afghanologist' Louis Dupree (who was expelled from the country after the revolution after being charged as a 'CIA agent') wrote of Karmal in 1971 that 'those who know him believe that if he is not really a leftist, he is independent'.[43]

In 1971, the famous Indian socialist leader, the late Jai Prakash Narayan, invited Karmal to visit India. The invitation could only have been extended due to Karmal's image as a non-communist and a social democrat. After parting company with Taraki, Karmal's flirtation with liberalism had intensified. After the 1969 student agitations, Karmal decided to modify his image further. But although his organ *Parcham* was without a red masthead and tended to follow a fairly safe policy, it was closed down. His so-called milder strategy could save neither the paper nor his credentials as a 'revolutionary'. He was, however, fortunate that there was no new Karmal under his wing at the time, as he would have done to him what he did to Taraki when *Khalq* was banned. The man who was to topple Karmal eighteen years later was still a student at the Habibia School.

The 1969 elections proved fatal for the Karmal group in terms of its parliamentary presence. Ratebzad had not run for office because she was quite sure she would not be returned. Noor, Laiq and Kishtmand were soundly beaten. However, Karmal kept his seat. It has been said that one reason the Karmal group fared so badly was the enthusiastic participation in the elections by tribal chiefs and big landlords. This is not a very convincing argument, because in the same elections, Hafizullah Amin inflicted a crushing defeat on a feudal Mullah in Paghman. Panjsheri, Misaq and Zeary of the Khalq group were unable to take part because they were in jail.[44] Taraki and Jozjani ran but, as in the past, lost. The reason for the defeat of the Khalq and Parcham stalwarts was that the constituencies they chose to run for they had not lived in for years, settled as they were in the distant Kabul. In Afghan society, what mattered were not election programmes, but personal relations on the basis of tribe, nationality and domicile. Karmal's constituency was Kabul. Not only were most of his supporters resident there, but Kabul was comparatively free of the social and tribal pressures so strong in outlying areas. Thus Karmal won easily. Amin ran from a suburban Kabul constituency where his entire family was settled. He was not in 'exile' from his native area but very much a part of the community where he chose to contest.[45]

Let us now turn to the situation in the Khalq group following the dissensions which became so pronounced after May 1967. After Karmal's exit, the group had fallen into anonymity. Until 1969, it had neither a paper nor a parliamentary existence. It did have two clandestine publications (*Junbish* and *Rahnuma*), according to its leaders.[46] However, their circulation must have been quite limited, compared with *Parcham* and *Shola-e-Javed*.

During those days of political eclipse. Taraki's greatest find was Amin. It can be safely said that if the group had not had the patient Taraki and the hard-working Amin, it would not have lasted six months. Karmal's departure opened the doors of the Central Committee to Amin. In 1968, the membership of the Committee was: Taraki (General Secretary), Panjsheri, Zeary, Shah Wali, Misaq, Jozjani and Amin.[47] The alternate candidates were: Mansoor Hashmi, Abdul Ahad Wolse, M.K. Soma, Abdul Rashid Aryan, Hasam Paiman, Dr Abdul Karim Zarghun and Ismail Danish.[48] Amin was the most junior member of the Committee. However, five of the alternate members were proposed by him.[49] Aryan was from Kandhar and under the influence of Zeary, while Dr Zarghun was a Taraki nominee. Zarghun and Amin could not get along because they were both hot-tempered Pushtuns and possessed equally intense and domineering personalities.[50] Zarghun was thrown out of the Party after he published a pamphlet critical of Amin.

Following the April Revolution, Zarghun tried to make a number of suggestions to the Party through Ismail Danish. According to Danish, these related to a new strategy which the Party was recommended to follow.[51] Both Danish and other Khalq group leaders have said that Zarghun was arrested in late 1978 because of his backing of anti-government terrorist groups. Amin was successful in turning every major Khalq leader, including Taraki, against Zarghun. After the revolution, the intelligence department came under Amin's charge and the head of the service, Sarwari, was said to be in his pocket. The intelligence report which apparently became the basis of Zarghun's arrest could well have been authored at Amin's insistence. Most personal and political opponents picked up during those days were shot or hanged without the formality of a trial. Amin had a more terrible fate awaiting Zarghun. He was locked in a refrigeration chamber where he froze to death.[52]

Amin had his unforgiving, barbaric side, but he was also a man of great personal magnetism and tremendous organizational ability. Without those qualities, he could never have become Taraki's number two after Karmal's exit, considering that he was the most junior member of the Central Committee. The political loyalties of the members of that Committee can be judged from the fact that, with the exception of Panjsheri, Zeary, Danish and Aryan, all the rest were put in the Pulcharkhi prison in 1980 following Amin's murder, under the charge of being 'Aminists'.

Before joining the party, Amin had served as head of the Teachers' Training School at Kabul. This institution played an important role in the life of the Khalq party. Not only were many of its teachers his close personal friends, but hundreds of his former students were spread throughout the country as teachers. It was because of Amin's close links with this 'teachers' factory' that Taraki once described Khalq as a 'teachers' party'. Amin's association with educational institutions and the Ministry of Education continued even after he had joined the Party. There is no doubt that it was Amin who first challenged Karmal's influence in his stronghold – the schools and colleges of Kabul. Not only that, but during this dark period in Khalq's life, Amin toured the country, renewing old friendships with former colleagues and students. He, more than anyone, was responsible for spreading the influence of the Khalq group in Afghanistan. In 1969, Amin was returned to Parliament, where he came face to face with Karmal. The Karmal-Amin rivalry can be traced back to this point in time. Karmal could see the makings of a dangerous claimant to power in Amin.

Karmal's tour of India in 1971 at the invitation of Jai Prakash Narayan caused another Party dispute. Not unexpectedly, the Khalq group sent a telegram to Narayan saying that Karmal had nothing to do with the PDPA.[53] The same year, the Khalq group presented a two-point 'peace formula' to Karmal and the other pro-Soviet factions. It said:

> 1.   All those individuals and groups which believe in the aims and the organizational and ideological principles of the PDPA, as set forth by the First Congress, are invited to join the party ranks ...
>
> 2.   All those parties and forces which are combating feudalism and imperialism, but do not agree with the ideological and organizational principles of the PDPA, while preserving their own ideological and organizational principles, may form a 'United National Democratic Front' with the PDPA.[54]

PDPA here meant the Khalq group. (As stated earlier, both groups described themselves as the real PDPA.) Although this open invitation was sent to both Badakhshi's Sitm-e-Milli and Ofaq's Jamiat-e-Inqlabyun, it was really directed at the Parcham group.[55] At this time, neither the Khalq nor the Parcham had a paper of their own, so the 'invitation' had to be published in the journal *Razakar*, whose columns were subsequently used by the two rivals to conduct a debate.[56]

This public controversy created more bitterness than unity. While talking to Khalq leaders in the Pulcharkhi prison, the writer came to the conclusion that what Taraki wanted to achieve through this 'unity call' was the isolation of Karmal. Had Karmal accepted his offer, it would have meant that he had admitted his deviation. If he refused to cooperate, it was argued, he would damage his political reputation and name. It seemed to me while talking to these men that even after so many years, this Khalq-Parcham debate still appeared to them to have been the greatest issue facing the Afghan people at the time. It is doubtful if this controversy held any interest for the common citizen. It was no more than a typical inter-Marxist verbal and tactical fight. Karmal withdrew from the debate first. It had not damaged him, and it had brought no benefit to Taraki.

Another purpose of Taraki's move appears to have been to demonstrate to Karmal that, despite the intrigues, Khalq was alive and doing well. If it did not have a larger following than Karmal's, it no longer had the low profile it had after the 1967 break. Taraki was sufficiently confident at this stage to believe that even if Karmal decided to accept his invitation and return to the fold, his own authority in the Party would remain unchallenged. Karmal did not fall into the trap.

Had Karmal been able to look beyond the immediate controversies surrounding the two groups in 1971 and done a deal with Taraki, perhaps the Party could have buried the hatchet once and for all. It is ironic that in November 1983, Karmal tried to put out with his bare hands the fires which he himself had ignited. To quote him:

> What is it that is being said about the Party? Who are the Khalqis and Parchamis? Let me make it clear to you that those who call themselves Khalqis and those other Parchami comrades who have failed to correct their ways have made equally serious mistakes. In our book, no-one has a right to claim superiority over others. Well, how then should the Party leadership have dealt with the situation? It needed time to fight free of the crushing burden of errors made in the past, personal vendettas and misleading actions. However, some people [meaning the Khalqis] interpreted the conciliatory attitude of the leadership as weakness. Some of them thought that the Party leadership lacked the authority to take action. Not only did they spread these false ideas among their friends, but they also tried to influence public opinion. These people under the garb of Party unity, in fact, tried to sabotage the Party, the revolution, the government of the workers of Afghanistan and our international obligations [meaning relations with the Soviet Union].[57]

Karmal made this speech four years after overthrowing the Khalq government with the assistance of the Red Army. He was also telling the Soviet Union that by criticizing him for his lack of strength, the Khalq faction was trying to imply to the people that the real power in Afghanistan lay in the hands of the Soviet army. Behind the 1979 Soviet operation there might have lurked the desire to pressure the two factions into unity. Karmal's message to the Kremlin was that the Khalqis were not only trying to despoil the Party and weaken the government, but sabotaging the Party's 'international obligations' to the Soviet Union. He wanted Soviet blessing to crush the Khalqis.

While in 1971 he had rejected the two-point Khalq formula, in November 1983 he was calling himself the 'first Khalqi'. Addressing a Party meeting, he said:

> Of all the people assembled here, Comrade Baraq [Shafi] would remember that when he was editor of the journal *Khalq*, it was I who had used the word 'Khalqi' – and that was the first time it had been used – in an article entitled 'Ways and Means'. [Baraq Shafi, who was present, said: 'Yes, that is true. You wrote it.'] So, comrades, tell me: if I was the first man in the Party to use the word, then am I not the first Khalqi? I am not saying this in a light vein … the real problem is not what word was used when but what the word meant.[58]

Karmal was right in saying that what mattered was not the word but what it stood for. However, as always, he found factionalism only in the word Khalq and those who followed Taraki. After 1980, Karmal and the Parcham group claimed the sole ownership of the PDPA with

Karmal as the 'honoured revolutionary'. The Parchamis used to boast that Karmal was the only 'great revolutionary' outside the eastern bloc for whose assistance the Red Army had taken the trouble to march in.

In 1971, however, these fateful developments were some years away. Karmal was not interested in an alliance with Taraki. He was in search of an ally whose shoulder he could use to fire the gun which would inaugurate the 'national democratic phase' of the revolution. He was to find that man in Sardar Daud Khan.

7

The End of Kingship

Zahir Shah's 'democratic experiment' in a tribal society resulted in economic catastrophe for the country. The establishment of the first Assembly immediately led to a steep fall in foreign credits. Between 1967 and 1971, externally-raised loans shrank from 62.2 million dollars to 27.5 million.[1] This amounted to the sudden withdrawal of the life-support systems which had kept the economy breathing. The shrinkage in external assistance caused a concomitant loss in employment opportunities. Things soon reached a point where there were simply no jobs for graduates. The economic situation worsened further with the drought which hit the country in 1971-72, leaving in its wake the most terrible famine in Afghan history. According to one estimate, it left nearly 500,000 dead, or one out of every twenty Afghan citizens. The United States sent a shipment of 200,000 tons of wheat, but as so often happens, it arrived after the catastrophe had claimed most of its victims. The December 1971 India-Pakistan war led to delays since the port of Karachi was closed. The Afghan bureaucracy also contributed its bit. As for the donor, instead of consigning its food surplus to the sea, it placed it in ships bound in the general direction of Aghanistan while making no serious effort to ensure that the food reached the starving Afghans in time. If Karachi was closed, Iran's Bandar Abbas port could easily have been used for docking.

In Afghanistan, this unprecedented economic disaster was bound to lead to changes in the citadel of power. Four groups were now busy in palace intrigues. The first contender for power was Sardar Daud Khan, former Prime Minister and the country's most diehard Pushtun nationalist and reform-minded politician. Zahir Shah's cousin, commander-in-chief and son-in-law, Abdul Shah Wali, was also lurking in the wings. There were rumours too about the ambitions of another former Prime Minister, Dr Mohammed Yusuf, whose politics were based on religious fundamentalism. Yet another former Prime Minister, Hashim Maiwandwal, leader of the social democratic Masawaat Party, was mindful of the opportunity which had arisen. Zahir Shah must have decided that the clock had come full circle, because in July 1973 he left on a European tour and took up residence at his Italian palace. On the night of 17 July, a detachment of army officers loyal to Daud, and led by Major Faiz Mohammed Faiz of the Afghan commandos, occupied the royal palace without encountering much resistance. Abdul Shah Wali, who was at a cocktail party arranged by the Iraqi embassy that evening, was taken into custody by two officers, Engineer Abdul Aziz Mohtat and Engineer Pacha Gul Wafadar.[2] The Daud takeover was a sort of domestic arrangement and no more than seven soldiers were killed during the coup.[3]

Daud's first and last great historical achievement was his announcement that kingship in Afghanistan had ended. Addressing a press conference on 24 July 1973, he declared the country a 'Republic', promising to bring in a new constitution and hold fresh elections. He also outlined his foreign policy. Although by 1973 Brezhnev's Asian Security Plan enunciated in 1960 had become one of diplomacy's more forgettable stories, Daud went out of his way to emphasize its need and importance, thus betraying his tilt towards Moscow. It should, of course, be borne in mind that during the 1960s, China considered the Plan a device to encircle it. However, by 1973, China's external situation had changed. It was not only a member of the United Nations, but the fifth occupant of the Security Council which it had once described as a 'luxury coach'. China's anti-Soviet policy had at last borne fruit and in 1971, nine years after the Sino-Soviet rift, the United States had opened its arms to the former enemy by flying Henry Kissinger to Peking. This development had made the Asian Security Plan an irrelevance. By reserving his comments on the Treaty of Hilmand, which involved the construction of a dam on the Hilmand river to benefit both Afghanistan and Iran, Daud was indicating that his Iranian options were open. Daud also made it clear at his press conference that Pakistan was the only country with which Afghanistan had a dispute over the Pushtunistan question. It was evident that, as in 1951, 1955 and 1962, Afghanistan under Daud would be willing to go to any length to pursue the Pushtunistan question.

Daud declared himself Afghanistan's President and Prime Minister while emphasizing that the true bastion of power was a fifty-member Central Committee which he had nominated. At its first session, the Committee, under Daud's chairmanship, chose the country's first 'republican' cabinet 'unanimously'. One need not add that 'unanimous' decisions are the norm with such Central Committees and 'Revolutionary Councils'. The Central Committee, whose membership, unlike its decisions, had not been made public, also put the portfolios of foreign affairs and defence in Daud's hands.

It is noteworthy that for the first time in Afghan history, a separate portfolio was created by Daud for Border Areas. This might have been a direct response to the establishment in neighbouring Pakistan of a Ministry of Frontier Regions and Tribal Affairs, headed by Major General (retired) Jamal Dar Khan. For all practical purposes, both these ministries were active in the semi-autonomous tribal agency areas of the Durand Line. After independence in 1947, Pakistan had declared these regions a part of its geographical territory. By setting up the new Ministry, Daud had thrown a challenge to Pakistan. It is of note that India gave Daud Rs. 40 million (about $4 million) to help him set up the new Ministry.[4]

A few weeks after the Daud revolution, King Zahir Shah wrote him a letter. It was addressed to 'His Excellency Sardar Daud Khan, President of the Republic of Afghanistan' and not only did it contain a formal abdication announcement, it also stated the former King's acceptance of the 'new Republic' in his capacity as a common Afghan citizen. This letter was made full use of in the Afghan media.[5] However, Zahir Shah was to make another bid for power after the April 1978 Revolution, when in 1980 he expressed his support for reactionary figures like Sibghatullah Mujadaddi, Mohammed Ahmed Gilani and Maulvi Mohammed Nabi.

Parcham leaders claim that it was they who in 1971-72 persuaded Daud to come out of retirement and stage a revolution. In fact, many Parcham Party workers believe to this day that Daud was really one of them, but changed his colours after getting into power. Karmal himself once went as far as almost to describe Daud as a member of his party. The forging of the Daud connection was part of Karmal's political strategy, apart from being a political necessity. However, nothing could be further from Daud's thoughts than membership of Karmal's party. It is true though that during the crisis of 1971-72, Afghan army officers trained in the Soviet Union had begun to congregate around Daud. Many of them considered him not only the mentor of the Afghan armed forces, but a man capable of transforming Afghanistan into an ideal progressive society. Karmal's relations with Daud date back to those years. To Karmal, Daud must have appeared as the saviour he had waited for so long to protect him as he embarked on his revolutionary journey through the hostile valley of Afghan feudo-tribalism. In 1953-63, Daud had also been responsible for giving a new and fateful turn to Soviet-Afghan relations. Karmal was justified in believing that Daud would continue to maintain the policy he had himself authored, especially when Parcham was also included in his entourage with the same ideological orientation.

Daud also commanded a certain political credibility in the country because of his Pushtunistan policy. He was one of its heroes. Not only did royal blood flow in his veins, but his administrative experience stretched over several decades. Daud, unlike other members of his family, was not given to carnal pleasure nor did he hanker after wealth and material possessions. As an administrator he was dictatorial, but in a class sense he was liberated. Politically he was a progressive. After Amir Amanullah Khan, he was the second Afghan leader to have brought his wife out of *purdah*. According to Parcham sources, he was an advocate of agricultural reform. (After getting into power, he began the process by distributing his ancestral lands in Paghman. Perhaps he naively believed that other feudal landlords would follow suit and distribute their holdings among their tenants. However he was unable to persuade them to do so either through personal example or through official pressure.)

In Karmal's eyes, Daud not only embodied the end of kingship, he was the simplest and most effective vehicle for Parcham's itinerary through the 'national democratic revolutionary' phase. Karmal must also have been mindful of Daud's advancing years and the fact that he was a loner who had no party or movement to back him. If Karmal played his cards right, Daud would come to depend on his Party during his rule — and after his departure from the scene, the Party would be seen as the rightful heir and would be in a position to complete the next phase of the revolution.

Parcham leaders still maintain that if Daud Khan had not modified his basic policy (that of remaining in the Soviet orbit), there would have been no need to bring about a revolution against him. They believe that the 1978 Revolution was not only a continuation of the 1973 revolution, but an effort to correct its course. The April Revolution, to use one of Karmal's favourite phrases, was the 'new phase' of the Daud revolution. Since Khalq had no role to play in the Daud takeover, it considered it neither 'revolutionary' nor 'democratic', but a palace coup or an internal arrangement. There is not a single Parcham Party leader or worker the author has met who did not regret Daud's killing during the 1978 Revolution. On the other hand, one cannot recall a Khalq sympathizer who was not thrilled at Daud's violent end and who did not consider it both expected and deserved. Since many military officers who played a leading role in the Daud takeover were later to be found in Parcham ranks, some western writers have assumed that they were always Parchamites. Closer study, however, suggests that the Karmal group's first contact with these officers took place during private meetings at Daud's house.[6] Some who were present state that during these informal get-togethers, the grave crisis facing the country used to be the main topic of conversation. These meetings were to culminate in the 1973 revolution. Daud Khan must have viewed this disparate group of malcontents as his constituency. These young military hotheads had no political organization of their own. The only organization proper which was part of the Daud 'cell' was the Parcham group. Its distinct political line must have held much appeal for these young Soviet-trained officers aching to do something to rescue their crisis-stricken country. Gradually, but inexorably, they seem to have outgrown their fascination with Daud and become part of the Parcham group and its political aspirations. Daud, after all, was a product of the ruling feudalistic order where personal loyalty took precedence over ideological ties. It is unlikely that it ever occurred to him that his young Turks were no longer under his spell, or that their allegiance to him had waned. Their outward deference for him might have misled him.

After the 1973 revolution, the Parcham group set up an office in the Hotel Spinzar at Kabul. This was the only instance of a political group operating openly after the 1973 change. Even the staff of this government-owned hotel was recruited from amongst Parcham sympathizers, and the number of Parchamites employed at ministries headed by army officers was sizeable.[7] However, after Daud's arrival, life became hard for pro-China and radical left-wing elements. Tahir Badakhshi's Sitm-e-milli Party was on Daud's hit list. Consequently, a large number of supporters of Sitm-e-Milli, Shola-e-Javed, Hizab-Islami (led by Gulbudin Hikmatyar), Jamat-e-Islami (led by Burhanuddin Rabbani) and Harkat-e-Islami (led by Maulvi Mohammed Nabi) began to move across to Pakistan. Daud also arrested, not unexpectedly, his old opponents Abdyul Shah Wali, Dr Mohammed Yusuf, Musa Shafiq and Hashim Maiwandwal.

In October 1973, the government released a report entitled 'Maiwandwal's confession and suicide'. According to its contents — which were widely publicized by the official media — Maiwandwal had conspired to overthrow the government and, after being caught and following a full confession, had committed suicide in jail in mysterious circumstances.[8] The Khalq group maintains that Maiwandwal had returned to the country from abroad to seek an alliance with Daud. Karmal being Daud's 'political conductor' at the time, he arranged to have Maiwandwal involved in the conspiracy case and arrested on the basis of a report prepared by the Ministry of the Interior. Khalq workers strongly believe that a Daud-Maiwandwal truce would have eliminated Karmal from the scene. It should be mentioned that the

Interior Ministry was headed by the pro-Karmal Faiz Mohammed Faiz and quite a large number of Parchamites had been inducted into its investigation and intelligence wings. Parchamites, however, deny these allegations but in private conversations they call Maiwandwal an 'imperialist agent' who wanted to 'betray and mislead the people in the name of social democracy'. In Europe, one hundred years of reform have blurred the dividing line between conservatives and social democrats. However, in Afghanistan, social democracy did not stand for the same things it does in Europe. It is difficult to understand why the Parcham was so distrustful of Maiwandwal when it was falling over backwards to strike an alliance with Daud. Maiwandwal was a much better man than Parcham's new ally.

Although it is not easy to say with certainty how Maiwandwal died, a careful study of Afghan publications of the time can perhaps throw some light on this incident. *The Republic of Afghanistan Annual 1973-74* carries a report on the Maiwandal affair under the caption 'The Continuing Revolution'. It is obvious that the nameless author is a Parchamite, so pronounced is the political slant of his argument. The article also gives the reader an insight into the real reasons behind Maiwandal's arrest.

> Such documents cannot always be obtained. Such plots cannot always be discovered unless noble human beings remain revolutionaries until they die. The friends of revolution [undoubtedly the term refers to Parchamites who were the only friends Daud's revolution could claim] in Afghanistan serve as [a] paramount and eternal example for preserving and protecting the revolution. The traitor's clique [meaning Maiwandwal] wanting to topple the revolution and liquidate the patriots thinks of ways to disrupt and undermine the confidence and unity of the revolutionaries. They [that is Maiwandwal and his friends] make promises and indulge in conspiracies – oblivious of the fact that the distance between the revolutionary and a betrayer of the country cannot be eliminated by money and position. The revolutionaries collaborate with them [Maiwandwal's men], they learn all there is to know, and light is shed on all angles, with no speck of dust remaining. They [meaning the Parchamites] say: surrender you base men, traitors and merciless murderers. The revolution governs you and it is the revolution that will remain eternal. They all confess because their voices are recorded and their documents captured ... After his confession Maiwandwal commits suicide in his cell.[9]

It appears that the report was originally written in Persian, because in that language past perfect is often rendered as pesent indefinite, a practice the English translator has unconsciously followed. It is quite obvious that Maiwandwal was charged with trying to wreck the Daud-Parcham alliance. If this official account is to be believed, some

Parcham people made contact with Maiwandwal and, after prising out information from him, had him arrested. Once again, in the first six months of the Daud revolution, terms such as 'friends of the revolution', 'defenders of the revolution' and 'revolutionary' were exclusively reserved for the Karmal group. Daud did not have a party of his own and the only political group attached to him was Karmal's Parcham which missed no opportunity to shower itself with these revolutionary epithets. The two men denounced in the official media as collaborators of Maiwandwal – namely Abdul Razzaq and Khan Mohammed – were totally unknown, connected neither with the army nor with politics. There can be little doubt that the 'credit' for Maiwandwal's arrest belongs to the Karmal group. However, a final judgement as to whether he killed himself or was killed is not so easy to make.

After Daud took power, Karmal, Anahita Ratebzad and Noor Ahmed Noor became members of his inner circle. The Parchamites assert that Karmal was Daud's unofficial adviser of foreign affairs. The three were also members of the fifty-strong Central Committee set up by Daud.[10] However, it is interesting that no better-known Parchamite, including Karmal, accepted any government position under Daud. On the other hand, a large number of Parcham supporters and fellow travellers were found jobs in the central ministries and the lower rungs of the bureaucracy. There appears to be truth in the Parcham claim that what Daud wanted was for Karmal to agree to become his Deputy Prime Minister, but Karmal declined the overtures most tactfully. He did not wish to come to power through Daud but to use Daud to advance the cause of his revolution. At the time Khalq had charged that after 'obtaining profitable positions in the Daud regime, Parcham has begun to spread word that there is no need for the Party to exist, as the Republican government itself is engaged in fulfilling the goals set by the Party. Under the circumstances, any continuation of Party activity amounts to treachery against the new Afghan Republic.'[11]

Karmal's objective appears to have been two-fold. By spreading these rumours (no formal press statement was ever issued), he wanted to assure Daud that to the Parcham its own existence was far less important than Daud's republican revolution. (Karmal, more than anyone, was fully conversant with the feudalistic mentality of the ruling Afghan classes and he knew that Daud could never accept or tolerate the presence of an heir apparent in the wings). Secondly, he wanted to force the Khalq group out of the political arena while simultaneously strengthening his own Parcham group. About this time, he appointed Noor Ahmed Noor the head of the Party's military wing.[12] The Khalq group alleges that in order to eliminate it, Karmal had prepared a detailed plan in league with one of his followers, Major Zia Ahmed Zia, Daud's guard commander. The possibility cannot be ruled out: had Karmal been able to do a Maiwandwal on Khalq by using Daud, he would not have given the matter a second thought.

After the April Revolution, the Khalq group, falsifying much past evidence, insisted that it had never supported Daud. This crown of thorns was squarely placed on Karmal's head. The Khalq claim, though not surprising, was a crude effort to rewrite the past in the light of the present. Khalq's own literature of the Daud years contradicts its later professions of innocence.

> The PDPA [this means Khalq, since both factions laid claim to the title PDPA] published a communique on the very first day of the announcement of the new regime and alerted its own members to defend the Republic against the intrigues of imperialism and the reactionary forces ... In the opinion of the PDPA, this programme [a reference to Daud's first address] could be achieved by a government composed of a 'United Front' including the PDPA. However, up to now no steps have been taken in this direction.[13]

Parcham sources confirm that soon after differences developed between Daud and Karmal, Khalq addressed a letter to Daud containing a unilateral offer of its services. As far as Daud was concerned, however, Khalq did not have much of a political identity, nor was he overly keen to offer the hand of friendship to a group subservient to the Kremlin. It was only natural that he rejected or failed to take notice of the 'generous' Khalq offer of cooperation.

While the Khalq leadership dreamt in vain of closer ties with Daud, even Karmal, the wiliest of Afghan politicians, was unable to prolong his Daud honeymoon beyond six months. In 1974, Mohtat and Wafader were eased out of their cabinet posts, while Karmal, Anahita Ratebzad and Noor were gently removed from Daud's 'inner circle'. In 1975, Daud divested Jilani Bakhtiari, Sharq and Faiz of their ministerial portfolios. The same year, he removed nearly forty Soviet-trained officers from the army.[14] (One of those dismissed was Asadullah Sarwari.) The Vice Commander of the Afghan Air Force, Lt. Col. Abdul Qadir, was sent to manage a government-owned butchery. In other words, by 1975, Daud had liquidated every known Parchamite from the government. He had also got rid of all those officers who had helped him to seize power in 1973. However, he was not able to eliminate the hundred or so Parcham sympathizers and party cadres who occupied minor, and sometimes sensitive, posts in various departments and ministries.

When Daud visited Pakistan in 1976, one of his security staff was an officer named Yaqubi, who became an adviser to Dr Najibullah (1980-

85) and has been in charge of the ministry responsible for intelligence since 1986.[15] He is also a member of the Politburo. He told the author in 1983 that he began to work for Daud under instructions from the Parcham party.[16] Similarly, the commander of the Presidential Guard, Major Zia Ahmed Zia, was also a Parchamite who occupied his sensitive post until the 1978 revolution. There is no doubt that Karmal was well and regularly briefed by his men in the government on Daud's thinking, strategy and secrets.

Afghanistan's neighbouring countries had undergone many changes between 1953 and 1973. Twenty years before, the Shah of Iran had been installed on his throne through the good offices of the CIA, but in 1973, like the mythological bull, he could be said to be carrying the entire burden of the region on his horns. Iran's next door neighbour Pakistan had been torn asunder two years earlier and what was once its western wing was now the entire state. To Afghanistan's north and northwest, its two giant neighbours, China and the Soviet Union, were engaged in a fearful war of nerves, daring each other to strike first. While at his first press conference Daud had implied his friendship for the Soviet Union, this did not mean that he had closed the door on other options. By making no comment on the Treaty of Hilmand, he had left the window open for Iran to make an overture.

The Shah of Iran began to drop hints in 1973 of massive offers of aid to Daud, who, after some initial hesitation, signed a billion dollar loan agreement with Tehran a year later. This money was to be spent on laying a railway line from Kabul to the Iranian port of Bandar Abbas. Daud must have found great satisfaction in the fact that this single Iranian loan (which, it was promised, would be doubled) was more than the total external aid given to Afghanistan since the end of the Second World War. However, in practical terms, no more than $10 million was handed over as part of the Treaty of Hilmand. This new turn in Kabul–Tehran relations led to a break in Daud's association with Parcham. Karmal was wise enough to know that the Iranian credit would be accompanied by 'advisers' and that there would be a political give and take.

One major reason for Daud's disenchantment with the Soviet Union (which western commentators do not seem to have taken into account) was the Pushtunistan problem. Pushtunistan had always been the focal point of Daud's politics. In 1973, he felt that an ideal situation existed on his eastern borders as far as the Pushtunistan question was concerned. In December 1971, 54 per cent of the people of Pakistan had separated to form their own independent state, Bangladesh.

It was only natural that the constituent provinces of the new Pakistan should wonder why they, being distinct cultural, linguistic and historical entities, should not follow the Bangladeshi example. Pakistani Pushtun and Baluch leaders, long suffering under the hegemonistic centrist rule of Punjabi vested interests, felt that perhaps the time had come to fulfil their old dream of a separate national identity.

After the breakup, the federal government in Pakistan was inherited by the Pakistan People's Party (PPP). In the NWFP and Baluchistan provinces, the emerging leadership was in the hands of Pushtun and Baluch nationalists. While the PPP foreign policy was oriented towards Peking, the Pushtun and Baluch leaders believed in forging closer ties with the Soviet Union, Afghanistan and India. In domestic terms, too, while the PPP was federalist, the National Awami Party (NAP) of the Pushtuns and Baluchis stood for the vindication of the rights of smaller nationalities. In 1973, the federal government of the PPP suspended the NAP ministry in Baluchistan, which led to the NAP government in the NWFP resigning in protest. These three events – the breakup of Pakistan, the ousting of the NAP government in Baluchistan and the NWFP, and Daud's assumption of power – became the basis of renewed Pakistan–Afghanistan conflict. After the dismissal of the NAP government in Baluchistan, the Baluch sardars and the Baluch people took up arms against the central authority. Conditions in the NWFP were also tense. This new situation was more than Daud had ever hoped for. He ordered the establishment of a training camp at Kandhar for Baluch liberation fighters. Between 10,000 and 15,000 Baluch youths were trained and armed there.[17] In October 1973, Daud renamed one of Kabul's central squares 'Chowk Pushtunistan'. A Pushtunistan national flag was duly unfurled at the ceremony. The sudden arrival in Kabul for political asylum of the NAP General Secretary and famous Pushtu poet, Ajmal Khattak, was a godsend for Daud.[18]

The Marri and Mengal tribes in Baluchistan were well armed and well positioned and they inflicted considerable damage on the Pakistan army. In the NWFP, the movement did not reach the stage where army troops would have been needed. The opposition in the province involved terrorist bombs. The PPP leader Hayat Mohammed Sherpao was killed by a time-device at a student meeting at Peshawar University.[19] Since the spreading revolt in Baluchistan could well get out of hand, the Pakistani generals presented an Afghan invasion plan to Zulfikar Ali Bhutto, the Pakistan Prime Minister, involving a quick occupation of certain Afghan areas, including Jalalabad.[20] The idea was that with the success of the action, Daud would be forced to accept the Durand Line and withdraw his support from Baluch and Pushtun nationalists. The 'conquered territories', it was argued would not only prove a good bargaining chip, but reinstate the image of the Pakistan army which had suffered a humiliating defeat in Bengal at the hands of India. While the

Pakistani generals, with their limited knowledge of history, were incapable of foreseeing the consequences of their adventurism, the astute Bhutto, a perceptive student of history, had no difficulty in doing so. He took little time in chucking this naive plan in the waste-paper basket and decided to tackle Daud politically.

Bhutto also wanted to take advantage of the tribal contradictions of Baluch society. His first move was the appointment of Nawab Mohammed Akbar Bugti as Governer of Baluchistan. Bugti had been a life-long and passionate advocate of independent Baluchistan (and perhaps still is), but as soon as he became Governor, he turned into an equally determined enemy of Baluch freedom fighters. After Bugti, the Governorship of the province was given to the Khan of Kalat, whose brother, Prince Karimuddin, was living in Kabul and was a committed supporter of the Baluchistan fighters. There were also age-old differences between the Baluch and the Pushtun residents of the province. Abdul Samad Achhakzai's Pushtun Khwa National Awami Party was a child of this chasm between the two tribal entities. Although some passionate Pushtun youths, such as Bismillah Khan Kakar, were fighting shoulder to shoulder with the Baluchis, Achhakzai's party did not support the Baluch insurrection. It is ironic that all his life, Achhakzai was considered one of the leading exponents of the rights of Baluchistan, but when the lines were drawn, instead of fighting in defence of his earlier beliefs, he chose to go to Islamabad to 'confer' with Bhutto. The Pushtun Khwa NAP did not alter its stance at least until the murder of Achhakzai.

Bhutto, when appointing Jam Sahib of Lasbela Chief Minister of the province, had not overlooked the fact that the ousted NAP chief Minister, Ataullah Mengal, now one of the leaders of the insurrection, was a close relation of Lasbela. No other Pakistani politician in history had a better understanding of tribal psychology than Bhutto. He knew that a tribal sardar was only considered a leader as long as he did not accept the hegemony of another sardar. His recruitment of the Khan of Kalat was aimed at eliminating any chances of Baluch tribal chiefs coming under one banner held by such a central and respected Baluch figure as the Khan. This appointment also ensured that inter-tribal enmities would continue. Bhutto reduced the Baluch liberation movement into a 'tribal revolt' by the Marris and Mengals and the Pushtunistan issue to a few bomb blasts. It is also true that while on the one hand he was subjected to criticism in the context of Pushtun and Baluch rights, he received strong support from the 'federalists'. However, a critical examination of this brilliant politician's actions would need a separate study.

To counter Daud's bomb blasts in the NWFP, Bhutto set about

establishing contacts with both extreme left- and right-wing elements in Afghanistan.[21] It was Pakistan's financial assistance which enabled Gulbudin Hikmatyar, Maulvi Ghulam Nabi and Sitm-e-Milli activists to start minor insurrections in Wardak, the Panjsher Valley and Badakhshan respectively. Bhutto had placed Pakistan in a position to stage its own bomb blasts in Jalalabad and Kabul. However, the essential differences between the situations of 1973 and 1978 should be clarified at this point. It was not Bhutto's intention to help overthrow the Daud regime. However, after 1978 it was the prime objective of Pakistan's military government to dismantle the April Revolution. Bhutto attempted to make Daud desist from his adventurism in Baluchistan and NWFP by using his opponents against him on a limited scale. He did not advise them to seek US or Chinese patronage. That is why very few people know that the present Afghan Mujahideen leadership was resident in Pakistan during Bhutto's time. The only objective Bhutto was following was to force Daud to come to the negotiating table, whereas after 1978 the only objective of the Pakistani military leaders was to avoid negotiations and sabotage the regime in Kabul.

Bhutto's tour of the Soviet Union led to Daud's eventual disenchantment with Moscow. Bhutto held detailed discussions on the Afghan situation with Soviet leaders. Bhutto took the following line of argument: 'For the first time in history, there are five governments from Afghanistan to Burma which, without being communist, are anti-imperialist with the word "socialism" a part of their manifestos. Unfortunately, all five of these nationalist and progressive governments have also inherited a number of disputes dating back to colonial times. It is incumbent on the Soviet Union, on the basis of progressive principles, as well as for the sake of its international obligations, to use its influence to help settle these disputes on the negotiating table. For the first time in Pakistan's history, there is an anti-imperialist and progressive government in power. The existence of this government is not in conflict with Soviet interests. This government has signed the Simla agreement with India on the basis of equality. Similarly, it is keen to open a dialogue with Daud. The people of Pakistan, therefore, hope that the Soviet Union will not disappoint them and will in fact use its moral pressure on Afghanistan not to employ Soviet arms against Pakistan.'

During his Soviet visit, Bhutto further told Brezhnev that Daud perhaps did not understand that the four nationalities – Pushtuns, Punjabis, Baluchis and Sindhis – inhabiting Pakistan were also a part of the population of three other neighbouring countries. If Pakistan broke up, it could lead to an unprecedented crisis in the entire region.[22]

Bhutto was extremely happy with his Moscow visit. 'I have cut the string which flew the [Afghan] kite,' he said on his return.[23]

It was Daud's bad luck that neither the Baluch nor the Pushtun leaders were able to mobilize the kind of mass support which Sheikh Mujibur Rahman had generated in East Pakistan, nor was the occupant of power in Islamabad a brainless general of the Yahya Khan variety. Nor did Daud have the power or the ability to play the sort of midwife role India played in East Pakistan in 1971. A prisoner of the old Soviet-Afghan equation, he believed that the Soviet Union would always continue to support his country on the Pushtunistan issue. Therefore, when he was told by Moscow to negotiate with Pakistan, his irate reply was: 'We understand our own problem best.'[24]

Pakistan's pro-American governments had managed to bring into being a hostile triangle composed of Delhi, Kabul and Moscow, which, it was maintained, was the unchangeable political reality of the region. If Bhutto did not entirely succeed in demolishing this triangle, he certainly modified its dangerous angles. India did not offer to help Daud either, at the time of the Baluchistan insurrection. Had it merely moved its troops to its frontiers with Pakistan, it would have been impossible for Bhutto to continue army operations in Baluchistan. Not only was it difficult for India to do so because of the 1972 Simla Accord, but its own internal situation did not permit of such adventures. The Soviet Union did not help Daud. The only 'evidence' of Soviet interference in Baluchistan was a diary written in Russian, which one of the army detachments captured from a 'conquered' rebel area. When it was translated, it turned out to be the personal notes of a Baluch student who had studied in the Soviet Union. Had the Soviets really wished to intervene, it would not have taken them more than a few weeks to send the Pakistani army packing to Islamabad. Without Soviet help, Daud was in no position either to arm the Baluchis or to liberate Pushtunistan. Bhutto also used the Shah of Iran's influence to persuade Daud to negotiate with him. The Baluch movement was, of course, no cause for joy in Tehran because a 'Greater Baluchistan' also meant the liberation of Iranian areas inhabited by the Baluchis. There was no Pushtunistan-style dispute between Pakistan and Afghanistan on their common boundary in Baluchistan. In any case, for Daud a free Baluchistan was no substitute for a free Pushtunistan. He was also frustrated at the reaction of the Pakistani Pushtuns of the NWFP. They seemed to have once again rejected the idea of Pushtunistan, although what was now left of Pakistan was in dire economic and political straits. Daud, as well as the leadership of the National Awami Party, failed to understand that unlike the Baluchis, the Pushtuns were no longer a subjugated national minority, but very much a part of Pakistani society in terms of their economic interests. The Pushtun component of the Pakistan army was nearly 20 per cent. More than one million Pushtuns lived and worked in Sind and Karachi. Pushtun trade interests were well integrated in Karachi and Punjab. How could they abandon all that and start marching behind Daud?

In June 1976, Daud stood at Kabul airport waiting for Bhutto's arrival.[25] He had been in power exactly two years and eleven months and was tired. The iciness which had characterized relations between the two countries had melted. Daud was now willing to make peace. Frustrated by the Soviet attitude over Pushtunistan, he had not only agreed to negotiate with Pakistan, but had established close links with the Shah of Iran. However, close relations with Tehran were not without their *quid pro quo.* They meant becoming part of the American police post manned by the Shah in the region. Kissinger arrived in Kabul in August that year. A joint communique issued at the end of the visit said: 'The US expresses its understanding of Afghanistan's position. The two sides noted the similarity of the views and aims of the Afghan and American leaders.'[26]

Obviously, the United States had taken note of the change in Daud's policy. Coincidentally, it was at about the same time that Anwar Sadat had begun his political journey towards Washington. Daud's Camp David was to consign the Pushtunistan issue to oblivion. On 17 August 1976, a smiling Daud landed at Islamabad airport and said:

> Pakistani brothers, I can assure you that we came to your country with the utmost goodwill and sincerity ... We will be able to solve our political problems and one day we will live together as very close and intimate brothers.[27]

The blueprint of the Daud–Bhutto parleys was disappointing from an Afghan point of view. Bhutto, instead of conquering Jalalabad and making it the basis of a political settlement with Afghanistan, had offered Daud the release of the detained NAP leadership as his part of the bargain. Daud had abandoned his advocacy of an independent Pushtunistan and Baluchistan and was now content with the release of Pushtun and Baluch leaders in return for his acceptance of the Durand Line as the international boundary between the two neighbours. (However, Bhutto and Daud were removed from power one after the other in 1977 and 1978 and the understanding they had reached remained unimplemented.) Daud's disavowal of Pushtunistan was the greatest retreat of his political career. It was because of the Pushtunistan issue that he had found his way to the Soviet camp and it was the same issue which made him get out of it. Both Parcham and

Khalq sources confirm that Daud had decided to ask India and Egypt to train Afghan military officers, instead of their having to be sent to the Soviet Union. Both countries also possessed Soviet weapons, but were free of Soviet 'ideological contamination'.

Under Article 123 of his constitution, Daud formed a new cabinet in 1977. It included such anti-communists as Ghulam Haider Rasuli, who was made Minister of Defence, and Abdul Qadir Nooristani, who was given the Interior portfolio. Daud had spent most of his time in office chasing the Pushtunistan mirage and had failed to bring about any noteworthy material or industrial progress to his country. The standard of living of the average citizen had not improved and Daud had failed to keep the army happy due to his internal and external policies. Daud had started out with a vow to end nepotism and yet it was his brother Sardar Naeem Khan whom he had made his unofficial Minister of Foreign Affairs. Nor had he been able to end the hold of the Mohammedzai family over the army. Promotion in service was not based on seniority or ability, but on family connections. One reason army officers had welcomed Daud was the hope that he would put an end to such ills. They had all turned against him by the end of his rule. Daud, sick in body and mentally tired, had not perhaps realized that though it was easy to get into power with the help of the army, it was very difficult to keep an army which had once tasted power away from the presidential palace.

8

The Takeover Plan

Daud's five and a half years in power were spent waiting for that cheque for one billion dollars the Shah of Iran had waved at him. The economic plight of Afghanistan was to become the major reason for Daud's failure and the April Revolution.

According to a 1977 survey, for a population of 15 million there were 3,728 schools, 237 of them exclusively for girls. Not more than three or four per cent of girls from the rural areas ever attended a primary school; 76 per cent of Afghan children never had the opportunity to receive an education. Only 2 per cent of the Afghan GNP was spent on education. In terms of literacy, Afghanistan occupied the 127th place in the world.[1] As for public health facilities, it was 119th; 50 per cent of the children died before their fifth birthday. For every 16,000 Afghans, there was only one doctor; 80 per cent of the country's doctors were concentrated in the capital Kabul. Health facilities in the provinces were pathetic. In Ghazni province, there was one doctor for every 49,333 people. The ratio in Gaur province was one to 59,333. In Parwan province there was one hospital bed for every 30,100 people, while the ratio in Arzqan province was one to 48,000. Only 0.65 per cent of the national income was earmarked for health.[2] In 1978, per capita income was 157 dollars, probably the lowest in the world.[3]

Total electricity generation in the country was only 776 KWH, 55 per cent of which was consumed in Kabul. Almost the entire rural population of Afghanistan was without electrical power. In terms of electricity consumption, Afghanistan was the world's most backward country.[4] The total number of vehicles in 1975-78 was 60,517. There were only 20,851 telephones, 12,582 of them in Kabul.[5]

The agricultural sector was a disaster. Out of the country's population of 15 million, 13 million were landless. Of the 28,000 villages, 20,000 were owned by feudal families. In the words of Karmal's brother, Mahmood Baryali:

> In the year 1978, with the low level of social welfare, Afghanistan had the lowest economic index in the world with a per capita income of 157 dollars, a per capita GDP of 241 dollars, a gross agricultural product of 127 dollars per head, a gross industrial product per capita of 48 dollars, per capita export of 27.7 dollars, a per capita energy consumption of 47 KWH.[6]

Under these economic conditions, had the PDPA made any effort to absorb the exploited Afghan masses in its ranks, the April Revolution could have generated widespread and spontaneous popular support. However, the Party had remained content with its disenchanted middle-class recruits, while offering only lip service to the 'toiling masses'.

In 1974-75, Daud's 180 degree foreign policy turn was a bitter disappointment for Karmal. The Parchamites, who not long ago had conferred the title of 'great revolutionary leader' on Daud, could not get over their sense of disbelief. However, they were not alone. The 'new Daud' was of equal concern to the Soviet Union which in 1975 finally succeeded in encouraging the two rival PDPA factions to open negotiations.[7] It was not an easy task to bring these two ideological groups under a single administrative umbrella. Both sides had agreed that no announcement would be made to their workers until the conclusion of the talks. While on the one hand this was intended to save their skins from Daud's secret services, it was also meant to spare themselves possible pressures from their cadres. After all, for ten long years, both leaderships had carried out poisonous propaganda against the other and encouraged their workers to follow suit. Both Karmal and Taraki were afraid that their workers might receive the news of the parleys negatively. One point made by Khalq as discussions opened was that Parcham should relinquish what official posts its workers or sympathizers still held. According to Khalq sources, it was the view of the Party that Parcham could only be re-admitted after it had severed all ties with the ruling order.[8] While these discussions were in progress, Parcham issued a statement in the name of the Central Committee. Denouncing this as a violation of agreed conditions, Khalq terminated the negotiations, stating that 'the talks regarding reunification proved useless as a result of the sabotage and the unprincipled position of the Parcham group'.[9]

However, Daud's changed foreign policy and Soviet pressure for PDPA unity were factors neither group could ignore. According to the writer's information, the role of conciliator was played by Iranian Tudeh Party leader Ehsan Tabari. This second attempt at Khalq-Parcham unity proved successful: on 3 July 1977, the two sides agreed to form a single administrative organization. Central Committees were merged. Taraki was made General Secretary, as in the past, and Karmal was given the post of First Secretary. According to the writer's information, there were 30 members of the new joint Central Committee (see Table 2).[10] Taraki's official biography describes this grand reconciliation as follows:

> The unity consisted of two parts. First, unity in connection with civilians, secondly, unity among the armed forces. In the case of the former, unity was achieved in all organizations belonging to Khalqis and Parchamis with equal rights for each group.[11]

If the 1977 agreement is studied closely, it will be apparent that it carried the seeds of future discord. Although under pressure the two groups had agreed to set up a unified administrative structure, what they had really done was to divide the new offices in equal measure. Khalq had finally agreed to accept Anahita Ratebzad and Ustad Amir Akbar Khyber Khan as members of the Central Committee and Karmal had acknowledged Taraki as General Secretary. In practical terms, it was not a reunification but an alliance. The reconciliation was confined to civilian posts in the government; the armed forces had been carefully kept out of its ambit. Khalq maintained that Parcham had no following

Table 2

Khalq Group	Parcham Group
1. Noor Mohammed Taraki, General Secretary	1. Babrak Karmal, First Secretary
2. Saleh Mohammed Zeary	2. Ustad Amir Akbar Khyber Khan
3. Ghulam Dastgir Panjsheri	3. Sultan Ali Kishtmand
4. Dr Akbar Shah Wali	4. Anahita Ratebzad
5. Hafizullah Amin	5. Noor Ahmed Noor
6. Ismail Danish	6. Suleman Laiq
7. Abdul Hakim Jozjani	7. Baraq Shafi
8. Abdul Karim Misaq	8. Majid Sarbuland
9. Hassan Paiman	9. Abdul Wakil
10. M.K. Soma	10. Sarwar Yorish
11. Mansur Hashmi	11. Fida Mohammed Dehnashin
12. Abdul Rashid Aryan	12. Abdul Quddus Ghaurbandi
13. Yasin Bunyadi	13. Nizamuddin Tehzib
14. Abdul Ahad Wolesi	14. Mahmood Baryali
15. Abdul Mohammed	15. Najibullah

in the armed forces to speak of and hence the 50 per cent principle of parity was not applicable there. Parcham was indeed weakly represented in the armed forces, but it was still insistent that the parity principle should apply to the army as well.

It was also demanding that Hafizullah Amin should be removed from his party post, which put him in charge of the armed forces.[12] During Karmal's 10-year absence from the Party, Amin had carved out an important place for himself. In Amin, Karmal had already seen a rival who could challenge him one day. He was also resentful of his influence in the Khalq group, not to mention his army contacts. However, to push Amin down the pecking order was no easy task, either for Karmal or Taraki. The writer learnt in 1980 from pro-Taraki leaders of the Khalq faction (and this was also confirmed by senior Parcham figures) that in July 1977, Taraki was all but ready to sacrifice Amin at the altar of Party unity. They claimed that Taraki had asked for a year to remove Amin from his armed forces Party assignment. He wanted to use the time to take over Amin's contacts, lists and documents. Taraki supporters may have come to believe this following Taraki's murder at the hands of Amin. It is difficult to see what possible compulsion Taraki could have had in 1977 to get rid of Amin. As for Karmal's pressure, Taraki might well have told him that he would get rid of Amin to keep Karmal happy. There is an indication of Karmal's pressure regarding Amin in Taraki's biography.

> [Taraki] defended him [Amin] against all sorts of intrigues and propaganda. He always shielded comrade Amin against the treacherous or erroneous blows ... by some elements who meanwhile took pride in belonging to the Party.[13]

As is evident, this account was published when relations between Taraki and Amin were close. There may be an element of political exaggeration in the depiction of Taraki's attitude towards Amin. However, in 1977, even if the relationship between the two men was not as fraternal as the official account would have us believe, it was by no means bad, as later alleged. It must be borne in mind that in the great Khalq-Parcham controversy, facts and personalities are so intertwined that it is not always easy to disentangle them.

After 1980, Parcham sources claimed that as early as 1977, they had tried to warn Taraki that Amin was not only a CIA agent, but had close links with Daud's intelligence apparatus. It was said that he had had Daud assassinated hurriedly during the revolution because he was afraid that if Daud lived, he would expose his (Amin's) past.[14] While it is true that Amin was a highly ambitious and extremely callous man who never forgave enemies, if he really was part of Daud's intelligence network, then neither a living nor a dead Daud could have saved him from exposure. If there is any truth in this charge, there is little doubt that the Parcham faction would have had solid evidence of it in hand after the revolution, because both the Defence and the Interior Ministries were given to its members.

It seems that the Parcham 'misunderstanding' flowed from rumours of Amin's close ties with Colonel Pacha Gul Sarbaz of the Afghan military intelligence. Sarbaz was in charge of reporting the activities of both Parcham and Khalq. What the Parchamites did not know was that the Soviet-trained colonel was an active PDPA member.[15] He was to play an important role in helping the Party at some of the most decisive moments of the April 1978 Revolution. Amin was extremely careful when operating in the army as part of his Party duties. His line in the army was that if right-wing elements tried to overthrow Daud, the Party would fight on his (Daud's) side. Since there were enough Parchamites in the army they might have taken this to mean that Amin was working for Daud. However, this was a carefully worked out Khalq strategy which was intended to keep Daud's agents off its back. Khalq's objective all along was not to save Daud but to stage a revolution against him. The following excerpt from Taraki's biography is significant:

> Comrade Taraki had appraised Afghan society on a scientific basis and had intimated to the Party since the 1973 coup that it was possible ... to wrest power through a short cut, as the classical way in which the productive forces undergo different stages to build a society based on 'socialism' would take a long time. This short cut would be utilized by working exclusively within the armed forces. Previously, the army was considered as the tool of the dictatorship of the despotic ruling class and it was not imaginable to use it before toppling its employer. However, Comrade Taraki suggested to use it [the army] to topple the ruling class.[16]

There is no evidence that Taraki was the first man to 'intimate' after Daud's 1973 takeover that the ruling class's armed forces should be employed to overthrow the ruling class itself. The lesson of military revolution was learnt by Karmal in Daud's school and after 1973, the Khalq group followed it to the letter. If revolution through military means is the true interpretation of Marxist ideology, then the credit should go to the Daud-Karmal alliance. Since the Taraki biography was published during his days of power, Amin (the man behind the production of such literature) seems to have gone out of his way to credit his 'great teacher' with every glorious achievement.[17]

Taraki's biography once again proves that the Party, instead of mobilizing Afghanistan's peasants, workers and nomads, was essentially looking for 'short cuts' to revolution. If before 1973 it was wooing the intellectuals to bring about a revolution, after 1973 it was looking for comrades in military cantonments. (The same Party, afraid of even the shadow of the masses, placed the responsibility of protecting both its government and the April Revolution after 1980 with the Kremlin.) While it is true that class formation had yet to come to full realization in Afghanistan, Afghan society was not unmarked by the age-old struggle between the rulers and the ruled. It is another matter that this struggle did not correspond to text book socialism. And while Karmal tried to move towards revolution with the help of Daud in 1973, Taraki used the army for the same purpose in 1978. The PDPA believed that after taking over the state, it would place the resources of the state at the people's disposal and thus win their allegiance. It wanted, in other words, to give birth to the child of revolution first and bring into being the mother of that child, the people, afterwards. And that is exactly what it did.

After 1973, Khalq began active political work in the army. No-one could have been better qualified for this delicate task than Amin. With amazing speed, Amin began to recruit army officers into the Party. The material conditions in the army also suited Khalq. Before the revolution, nearly one-third of the officer cadre was Soviet-trained.[18] Most of these men were not only familiar with revolution, but desirous of bringing it to their country. When Daud threw out every senior and junior army officer who had played any part in bringing him to power, it caused a major setback to the Parcham group because the vast majority of these men had become sympathetic to it. However, the Khalq group now made use of the disaffection Daud's action had caused in the army. Unlike Karmal's Parcham, Khalq was not a part of the government. And Amin was a far more intelligent and well-connected man than his Parcham counterpart Noor Ahmed Noor. He also differed from Noor in being a brilliant organizer. According to Taraki's biography, by 1976 Amin had brought the military wing of the Party to a point where it could easily, with a certain number of casualties, take over the government.

So, in 1976 Comrade Amin presented to the great leader his written views to the effect that the PDPA could with a certain number of casualties on the part of the armed forces topple the Daud government and wrest political power. However, Comrade Taraki with his profound farsightedness asked Comrade Amin to wait till the objective and subjective conditions in the country were ripe and the Party had grown still stronger.[19]

It is strange to hear a party talk about subjective and objective conditions becoming ripe when it had no appreciation or understanding of either. Perhaps to Taraki the mere recruitment of army officers disenchanted with Daud amounted to the ripening of subjective and objective conditions. However, if strength were be based on the number of adherents from the army, then, certainly, the Taraki group was much stronger than Karmal's in 1977-78.

Taraki, Karmal and Amin are all agreed that the revolution had been planned for July-August 1978 (the fifth Afghan month).[20] Parchamites later claimed that Amin had created such conditions that the timetable for the revolution had to be advanced to April. They maintained that Amin had changed the time-frame because he was afraid of losing his position and influence in the army following the Khalq-Parcham accord. As stated earlier, both Taraki and Amin were reluctant to extend the accord to include the army. On 27 April 1978, the accord was already nine months old. The planned revolutionary coup was still three months away. However, no joint Khalq-Parcham effort was visible as far as the army was concerned. There is no evidence that this would have come about even if the Revolution had taken place at the agreed time in July-August.

Before examining the April Revolution, we must consider the extent of Soviet influence on the literate sections of Afghan society which provided the bulk of pro-Soviet cadres belonging to the educated middle class to the PDPA. A fair portion of the Afghan officer corps and the majority of professionals in the civil services had been educated in the Soviet Union. Between 1965 and 1978 no less than 750 engineers went to Russia and returned with higher degrees. The Soviet Union laid the foundation of professional studies in Afghanistan. There were Soviet instructors at every professional institute in the country. The Kabul Polytechnic was set up in 1967 as a symbol of Afghan-Soviet friendship. There were at least 50 Soviet instructors at this institute. By 1978, its graduates numbered 871. In 1971 and 1974 respectively, two Soviet-funded institutions – the Gas Technicum Mazar Sharif and the Auto Technicum Kabul – were established. The number of Soviet instructors at these two establishments was 55. Before the April Revolution, 1,096 Afghans had completed training at these two facilities.[21] As for other sectors, the following excerpt is instructive:

> With the assistance of the USSR (before April 1978) construction work started on 174 major projects in productive areas ... For instance, 60 per cent of the public sector production and 60 per cent of power generation was produced through Soviet-made plants. Similarly, 60 per cent of the major roads were constructed and asphalted with the help of the Soviet Union and 65,000 persons were trained in skilled and unskilled jobs ... In the course of

the development plans the government spent 70 billion Afghanis, half of which (or more than 2.25 billion dollars) came from the Soviet Union.[22]

It is clear that Soviet influence was widespread in Afghanistan among educated and professional people on the eve of the April Revolution.

9

The April Revolution

The armed forces' leading cadres were trained under Comrade Amin in making preparations for the Revolution in such a manner that they themselves did not feel that the time for action was approaching fast.
('Our Saur Revolution', *Kabul Times*, 24 May 1978)

It was only through Party unity that for the first time in Afghan history, we established a new society by changing the old. This was not a simple task. However, the Saur Revolution only succeeded after the Party had unified itself by ending factional differences.
(Babrak Karmal's address to Party and government officials, November 1983, *Da Watan Paigham*, Organ of the Democratic Youth Organization, Kabul 1984, p. 13)

On the night of 17-18 April 1978, two unknown men on motorcycles knocked at the front door of Ustad Amir Akbar Khyber Khan's house. As he opened it, they pointed their revolvers at him and led him to the road. Then they shot him dead. This was a political murder: Ustad's life was free of personal enmities. From his early youth until his death, he had remained a committed advocate of socialist views. The Daud government laid the responsibility for the murder on the Hizbe Islami. The PDPA organized a funeral procession in which about 15,000 mourners took part. Winding through the streets of Kabul, it ended in a rally at Zar Nigar Park in Shehr-i-Nau. It was addressed by both Taraki and Karmal, who held imperialism responsible for Khyber's murder. They also vowed that every drop of his blood would be avenged.[1]

However, in 1980, Karmal declared that Amin had been responsible for Khyber's murder. According to this new Parchamite disclosure, two brothers, Siddiq and Arif Alamyar, had killed Khyber at Amin's instance. It was further alleged that the murder had been committed because Amin wanted to force through the revolution before the agreed date. The Karmal government later arrested the Alamyar brothers, charging them with Khyber's murder, and hanged them in June 1980. Two younger Alamyar brothers also spent time in the Pulcharkhi prison. Captain Shafiq Alamyar shared a cell with the author in 1980-81. He always kept a newspaper picture of his executed brother Arif Alamyar in his wallet. He told the writer that his brothers were innocent. Other inmates of the jail also confirmed this. The two accused never confessed to the murder and the prosecution was unable to produce any hard evidence. Although it is difficult to say with certainty who did murder Khyber, had the normally vengeful Amin decided to plan a murder, he would rather have got rid of Karmal than the harmless Khyber. Not only would Karmal's removal have changed the timetable of the revolution, it would have removed the author of the timetable himself from the scene.

Immediately after the April events, both Khalq and Parcham believed – at least this was their public position – that Daud's Interior Minister Nooristani, under the influence of his West German advisers, had Khyber murdered so that the government could judge the extent of unity between the two PDPA factions and the popular support they enjoyed. It was further said that the Daud government wanted to incite the Party to come out in the open so that it could round up its leadership more easily. The theory is not so far-fetched: when the Daud government did arrest the PDPA leadership, the impression given was that the Party had walked into the trap laid for it. As for the Karmal regime, after executing the Alamyar brothers the Amin story was forgotten and the official media began openly to accuse the Daud government of Khyber's murder. Reference to certain German police officers and advisers was also made in this context:

> In early April 1978, one of Afghanistan's popular leaders, Mir Akbar Khaiber, was assassinated by the Daud regime. A few days later Daud had virtually all leftist leaders arrested. At that time Afghan police had West German police officers as advisers.[2]

Nothing happened for one week after Khyber's funeral procession. The interval was used by Daud to plan the crackdown. He wanted to watch the situation carefully and to identify the quarters where PDPA support lay so that it could all be dealt with comprehensively. Army cantonments were most carefully watched. Daud, a cool man, instead of launching a blitzkrieg against the Party, decided to pick up its leaders. Amin, the most dangerous figure in the PDPA, was the last to be arrested – a fateful decision by the Daud regime.

After Khyber's funeral, it had been agreed between Taraki and Amin that Taraki's arrest should be treated as a signal for the revolution's launch.[3] On the night of 25-26 April, Taraki, Karmal, Panjsheri, Jozjani and Dr Zamir Safi were picked up. When the police knocked on Amin's door, he hurriedly handed over the detailed plan prepared by him for the takeover to his wife, instructing her to hide it under the mattress in the children's bedroom. The police searched the house quite thoroughly, but did not find any incriminating documents. Amin was not taken that night. However, he was put under house arrest. As soon as the police left, Amin asked his eldest son Abdul Rahman to go to Karta Chahar (where Taraki lived) and find out what was happening. The boy reported on his return that Taraki had been picked up earlier that evening.[4]

This was the signal for the revolution, but because of the police watch on his house, Amin could not pass the word to PDPA collaborators in the armed forces. His family says he did not sleep a wink that night. In the morning, he gave the plan to his son to take to Faqir Mohammed Faqir.[5] But while the boy was preparing to leave, Faqir himself came to visit Amin. Since he bore a close physical resemblance to Abdullah Amin, Amin's elder brother, the soldiers, mistaking him for Abdullah, let him in. Handing over the plan to Faqir, Amin directed him to get it as quickly as possible to Syed Ghulabzoi, an officer in the Afghan Air Force.

Faqir was the author's neighbour both at Pulcharkhi and Sadarat detention centre. He, Iqbal Waziri and M.A. Soma were in the same interrogation cell, while Abdul Hakim Jozjani, Mansoor Hashmi, Col. Ahmed Jan and Capt. Shaista Khan were kept separately. Other Khalq leaders were not allowed to talk to them. With the exception of Waziri, the rest were men of great personal courage. Faqir, who was once a teacher and had also served as a cabinet minister, was a man of great rectitude. A simple Pushtun, he always seemed to be putting antimony in his eyes and used snuff instead of smoking cigarettes.

Faqir handed over the plan to Ghulabzoi, as instructed by Amin, and Ghulabzoi passed it on to Khalq officers in the Air Force and the 4th Armoured Corps. In Faqir, Amin had chosen a good man for this crucial assignment. He did not have much of a position in the Party and was not on the surveillance list of the police. Similarly, Ghulabzoi was the lowest-ranking uniformed officer in the Party, being a junior commissioned officer. The security services could not even have imagined that an anonymous junior officer of the Air Force would play such a crucial role in the Revolution which would rock Kabul a day later.

According to the plan the Revolution was to begin on 27 April at 0900 hours. As a matter of routine, Afghan officers were picked up by bus every morning to report for duty. Khalq officers used this opportunity to pass on the word to those who did not know. After the crackdown of 25-26 April, the government felt so confident that Defence Minister Rasuli had ordered that the arrest of the communists should be celebrated by officers and men by holding parties and entertainments in the cantonments. However, they were to remain in a state of battle readiness. While these orders must have led Daud to believe that the army was fully behind him, the PDPA used them to its own advantage.

> The Defence Minister had ordered that all armed forces detachments be on [a] war footing and celebrate the occasion the next morning with folk dancing and meetings. This treacherous order proved very useful to the forces of the revolution, as the Khalqi elements participated in these meetings where they contacted their unit commanders for instructions without raising suspicion.[6]

On the evening of 26 April, Amin was moved from his residence to a detention centre. Before he was taken away, Engineer Zarif came to see him, but the police being on the alert refused to let him in. Then he saw one of Amin's little children playing outside the house and asked him to tell his father: 'I will be waiting for a message from you in the cafe across the street.' A while later, Amin's older son Abdul Rahman walked into the cafe and told Zarif: 'My father asks you to inform Khayal Mohammed Katwazi and Saleh Mohammed Zeary that as soon as the Revolution gets underway, they should try to reach the radio station.' (Babrak, the little boy who had taken Zarif's message, used to come to the author in jail for English lessons.)

The morning of 27 April dawned on Kabul with the sky a clean, washed blue and the sunlight dancing in the streets. Unaware of the fateful historic change which was to overtake them in a few hours, the people of Kabul were drinking their morning tea and whiling away the time in conversation in the city's lively cafes. The cabinet had begun a meeting at 9 o'clock under Daud's chairmanship to consider the situation arising out of the arrest of the communist leaders. The majority – including Daud – was in favour of passing the death sentence on the arrested men. A heated discussion was in progress about the pros and cons of the proposed course of action.[7] Radio Kabul had already announced that the PDPA leadership had been arrested on charges of treason and conspiracy to overthrow the government. The arrested leaders could have been in no doubt as to the fate which awaited them (with the possible exception of Amin who was expecting a revolution). In Afghanistan's history, the minimum punishment for 'treason' has always been death. Daud and his Defence Minister were confident that by moving decisively, they had rid the country of the communist menace.

The dark, crumbling jail, situated no more than 300 metres from Arg, as the presidential palace was called, was once again playing host to a group of men who had dared question established authority. It is difficult to guess what their thoughts were. Was it going to be the gallows, or had the Revolution of which they had dreamed for many years finally arrived?

The Soviet ambassador had been waiting at the Foreign Ministry since nine o'clock. He was a worried man. In his pocket he carried a strong protest note from his government about the arrest of the PDPA leaders. This was going to be his last effort to save these men from the horrible punishment which he feared awaited them. However, the Foreign Minister, Waheed Abdullah, was in the cabinet meeting at the presidential palace.[8] The ambassador had no option but to wait. Later, Taraki said: 'The news of our Revolution took both superpowers by complete surprise. The Soviet Union was ecstatic and the United States went into shock.' Khalq sources claim that the next day when the ambassador called on Taraki, he handed him the protest note he had been unable to deliver to Abdullah and they both burst out laughing.[9]

At nine o'clock the same morning, Major Mohammed Aslam Watanjar, a short, quiet, well-disciplined officer, stepped into the office of his corps commander, clicked his heels, stood stiffly to attention and saluted him smartly. Then he spoke, 'General, you more than any of us are aware of the delicate situation in the country. Since the army has been put in a state of combat readiness to enable it to deal with any possible reaction to the arrest of the communist leaders, I seek permission to equip my twelve tanks with ammunition so that I can move with my column to defend the Arg (presidential palace) when ordered.'[10]

Watanjar was carrying a loaded gun which he had come prepared to use in case his commander hesitated or refused to issue him the ammunition. However, the commander readily agreed to let Watanjar draw six shells for each of his twelve tanks. The young officer again came to attention, saluted his commander for the last time and left the room. The commander could not have known that he had just passed an order to overthrow the government. By adding a zero to the ammunition release order, Watanjar was able to draw sixty instead of six shells –

sufficient to put 250 tanks at the ready.

According to the plan, at exactly 12 o'clock a squadron of the Afghan Air Force was to buzz the cantonment areas and fly low sorties over the city, including the presidential palace. This was to be the first signal to the armour to storm the palace. Lt. Abdul Qadir of the Air Force, after putting the command of the Bagram air base into the hands of a fellow officer named Hashim, was supposed to jump into a helicopter and land at Kabul airport from where he was to take command of the entire Air Force operation. However, the Air Force was unable to take part in the coup in accordance with the plan, so the official history of the Saur Revolution does not even mention the fact that it was the Air Force which was to give the final assault signal to the army.[11] Asadullah Sarwari, a former Air Force officer, who was the principal Khalq Party recruiter for the Air Force, was present at the Kabul airport all morning, along with Ghulabzoi.[12] According to him,

We had a clear majority following in the Air Force. However, Qadir, instead of handing over the command to Hashim, as arranged, locked himself in his office.[13] It was only when we got into contact with the Bagram base that we realized what the situation was. At about 12.30, two tanks from the 4th Armoured Corps arrived at Kabul Airport to see how we were doing. Watanjar was worried: why had the Air Force failed to move into action as agreed? However, with the help of the two tanks and our other friends, we took control of Kabul airport. We also established contact with Watanjar and a number of tanks were rushed to the Bagram air base. It was only after this detachment arrived at Bagram that we were able to take over the entire Air Force. Qadir, by that time, had also agreed to come out of his office. Although we now controlled the Air Force, we were unable to establish contact with our friends at the anti-aircraft missile base. We could not order our aircraft to fly over the city without the control of this crucial base in our hands. After we took over Bagram, we were able to link up with our friends at the missile base and when they gave us an 'all clear', the first Khalq pilot took off to bomb the presidential palace.[14]

When Sarwari told this to the author in July 1979, Lt. Col. Qadir was in a Khalq prison, so his account may be prejudiced. However, it is a fact that a simultaneous uprising in all cantonments was not achieved because the Air Force failed to take to the skies to signal that the final assault had begun. In the confusion, the 7th and 8th Divisions offered considerable resistance to the rebels. The official history of the Saur Revolution fails to mention these events.

The first column of the 4th Armoured Division, under the command of Maj. Umar, arrived in front of the main entrance to the presidential palace exactly 15 minutes before midday. The cabinet meeting was still going on. Daud was immediately informed of the presence of tanks outside the palace. Getting suspicious, he ordered his Defence Minister Rasuli and the head of the presidential guard, Maj. Zia (who was a secret Parchamite), to investigate what was going on. Maj. Zia went outside and asked Maj. Umar why he was there. He was told that the tanks had come to protect the presidential palace. However, this was not the sort of explanation which could have convinced Rasuli, himself a general of the army. Umar was ordered to return to base. What Umar did was move away from the main gate into a side street. However, in the next few minutes, a large number of tanks from the 4th Corps arrived on the scene and ringed the palace completely. Capt. Watanjar, Maj. Tarun, Maj. Nazar Mohammed, Maj. Mazdoor Yar and Capt. Ahmed Jan were impatiently looking at their watches and scanning the skies for a sign of the missing Air Force.

The people of Kabul called the midday hour 'the hour of the cannon', since traditionally the hour of twelve was sounded by firing a cannon. At exactly twelve o'clock, Watanjar ordered the first shell to be fired at the palace.[15] This was the signal for the entire Corps to start the shelling from all directions. Daud brought the meeting to an end and told his Ministers: 'Whoever wants to escape from the palace to save his life is free to do so.'[16] Daud's palace (which was the former residence of King Zahir Shah) was equipped with the latest anti-tank weapons and guarded by about 2,000 troops. It also had twenty-four T-54 tanks and vast quantities of ammunition. In addition to this, the palace was designed like a fort and it was not easy for an invading force to break through its defences. Two of Daud's colleagues, Defence Minister Rasuli and Interior Minister Nooristani, escaped through the rear gate of the palace and succeeded in reaching their offices to try to organize counter-action. The rest of the ministers sought refuge in the Shahi Mosque in the palace grounds. It is only in times of adversity that the powerful think of God.

The first loyalists to reach the scene were Nooristani's policemen. However, these police were only trained to beat up and kill unarmed people. They had never faced the brute might of the army before. The first four police trucks to reach the Pushtunistan Square were blown up by shells fired from the tanks. The rest sped away helter-skelter.

The news of the assault on the palace soon reached other cantonments in the vicinity of Kabul. Khalq supporters everywhere immediately took over the armouries and command centres. Where their numbers were larger, they rushed some of the troops to the presidential palace to aid the 4th Corps. However, where Khalq support was thin, they merely tried to disarm the others. There was no time for argument, those who resisted were summarily shot and those who offered no resistance were put under arrest. It may be mentioned here that there were only two lieutenant colonels among the rebellious officers (Rafi and Qadir) and they were both members of the Parcham Group. According to Khalq leaders, Rafi and Qadir played no role in the takeover. The majority of Khalq officers consisted of majors or officers even more junior.

Daud's Defence Minister decided that it was not safe to try to organize counter-action from the Defence Ministry. He went round the main cantonments, but found that they were already under the effective control of the revolutionaries. However, he did have some luck with elements of the 7th and 8th Divisions and the 88th Artillery Battery, which agreed to fight the rebels. Rasuli also tried to reach Air Headquarters at Kabul airport but it had been taken over by Khalq officers soon after midday. The Bagram air base was not yet under their control, but the disappointed Rasuli tried to seek help from the Shindan air force base, situated at the southern end of the country.

At about 4.30 p.m. a squadron of twelve aircraft from Shindan arrived in the vicinity of Kabul. According to Sarwari, by this time both Bagram and the missile base had been captured. When the Shindan squadron established contact with Air Headquarters, it was ordered to return to base immediately. (Some western writers have claimed, perhaps rightly, that the squadron did not get into action because there wasn't enough fuel to move in and then return to the safety of the base.[17]) It is not clear why Rasuli did not try to seek help from the Jalalabad base which was much closer than Shindan. Khalq elements have claimed that by that time they had already taken over Jalalabad.

At about 4.45p.m. Rasuli arrived at Dar-ul-Aman at the head of the 8th Division where he encountered tanks from the 4th Army Corps which were advancing towards the Reshkor cantonment. One of the first shells fired by the 4th Corps hit Rasuli's jeep and that was the end of his brief loyalist intervention. Thereupon, one section of the Division joined the rebels, while others continued to fight. Even if Rasuli had managed to reach the presidential palace, it is doubtful if he could have dislodged the rebels. By five o'clock, commando units had also joined the 4th Corps. The Daud forces were routed because their central command was in a state of paralysis. Time was the crucial factor and it was against Daud. Never truer than on that historic morning was Lenin's maxim: 'Victory over time is victory over all.'

A frantic search for the arrested PDPA leaders had meanwhile begun. Officers were not aware that the politicians had all been lodged in Wallaite-Kabul, a municipal detention house no more than 300 yards from the presidential palace. At about 5.30 p.m. Maj. Tarun finally found them. It only needed a few shells to demolish the outer mud walls of the detention centre. The PDPA leaders were brought out and put on tanks. Karmal, unaware of the plan and the extent of Khalq's hold over the army, asked 'Where to?' Amin laughed. 'If you do not wish to come, you are most welcome to stay.'[18]

The radio station was captured between 5.00 and 5.30 p.m. Normal programmes were suspended and a Ravi Shankar sitar recital of the Indian *raga* Malhar, which if sung with devotion, it is said, will bring down rain, put on. Interestingly, this *raga* has sounded the fall of many regimes in Afghanistan. When Daud took over, it was Malhar which was played on Kabul radio. The author himself heard the radio play the *raga* when Taraki and Amin were toppled.

The PDPA leaders were taken to the Kabul radio station. By this time, Qadir and Watanjar had also moved there from Kabul airport. Resistance was dying out, but Karmal was still not sure that the Revolution had really succeeded. Daud was alive and the Kargha and Reshkhor Divisions were continuing to offer spirited resistance. In fact, one detachment from the 8th Division had succeeded in reaching the radio station under the command of Maj. Shamsuddin, but infantry was no match for armour. The major was an apolitical officer and he thought it wise not to fight the rebels when the balance was so heavily in their favour. He not only ordered his soldiers to return to barracks, but went home himself.[19] (Maj. Shamsuddin, ironically, was the guard commander at Pulcharkhi prison during Karmal's time and a number of Khalq leaders who had brought about the Revolution were in his watchful custody, including Jozjani, Faqir, Capt. Ahmed Jan and Lt. Shaista Khan.)

Karmal was of the opinion that until there was complete certainty that the putsch had succeeded, it was inadvisable to stay at the radio station which was a 'sitting duck'. He suggested that they should move to the airport which was more secure. Amin opposed Karmal's proposal vehemently, saying that they should stay close to the scene of action and take direct command of the fighting. He said that at such a crucial juncture, it was necessary for the party leaders to stay close to the officers. Amin's proposal may have been a bit emotional, but it was understandable because it was he who had organized the coup and the Revolution was taking place in accordance with the plan drawn up by him. Karmal, always a careful man, was not prepared to take any chances. Taraki, who was also a cautious man, agreed with Karmal. While Taraki, Karmal and others went to the airport, Amin stayed back, taking control of the makeshift operations room. He established contact with Khalq officers in the cantonments, encouraging them to intensify the pressure.[20] This was to pay him dividends in the future because the army did not forget his personal involvement in the

Revolution. Amin was also to use this incident to denounce Taraki and Karmal, later spreading the story in the army and among Party ranks that Taraki and Karmal had run away to the airport to be able to fly out of the country in case the Revolution failed, while he was willing to die fighting.[21]

Amin and Karmal had another altercation while the fighting was in progress. After spending about an hour and a half at the airport, Taraki and Karmal returned to the radio station. An announcement was now being prepared about the success of the Revolution. Amin was insisting that Taraki should make the announcement because, once the Khalq officers heard his voice, they would take over the rest of the loyalist units. Karmal, on the other hand, was of the view that the announcement should be read by Qadir who had the reputation of a diehard nationalist in the army. He argued that Taraki's direct involvement at this point would be a signal for all reactionary forces to band together and resist the Revolution. He also warned of the presence of right-wing officers in the army. Taraki agreed to Karmal's suggestion, but to keep Amin happy, he proposed that the announcement in Persian should be read by Qadir, while Watanjar should make it in Pushtu. At 7 p.m. the two announcements were broadcast by Radio Kabul. In accordance with Karmal's suggestion, the announcements began with *Bismillah Al-Rahman Al-Rahim* (I begin in the name of God who is most compassionate and merciful). They were so worded as to carry general popular and nationalist appeal. The word Khalq (meaning people) was used only once. If Karmal wanted to keep the reactionary elements guessing as to the exact character of the Revolution, he was successful. On 29 April, a member of the Mujadaddi family (which had sought refuge in Pakistan during Daud's time) issued a press statement, published in the Lahore Urdu daily *Mashriq*, which asserted that the Revolution had been brought about by 'Islam-loving' elements. Over several days, the right-wing sections remained confused and divided over the nature of the change.

When the announcement was being broadcast, planes of the Afghan Air Force finally appeared over Kabul and began to hit the presidential palace with air-to-ground missiles. It was Karmal's proposal that Daud should be captured alive and Taraki and Amin were not opposed to this. However, Daud had refused to surrender and his beleagured loyalist soldiers were fighting a doomed and last-ditch action.

Daud, his relatives and servants were putting up a dogged resistance. Murmurs were heard inside the palace that Daud should not be killed. He should rather be caught alive. However, when the commandos entered Daud's Arg (presidential palace), under the command of 'Khalqi' officers and Daud was told by Comrade Imamudin that the (*sic*) political power was (*sic*) wrested by the PDPA and he ought to surrender, Daud through sheer insanity wounded him with [a] pistol. Upon this incident, the 'Khalqi' soldiers accompanying Comrade Imamudin opened fire on Daud and his associates as a result of which they fell down and the Arg was captured.[22]

Informed Khalq sources gave a different account, saying that when the commandos entered Daud's chambers and asked him to surrender his weapons, he asked: 'Who has brought about the coup?' Lt. Imamudin of the commandos replied, 'The PDPA lays claim to the Revolution.' Daud began to shout abuse and, pulling out his revolver, fired at Imamudin. The commandos then opened fire and killed Daud and his entire family.[23]

The role of the Parchamite officers in the Revolution should also be examined at this point. On 27 April, the presidential guard under the command of Maj. Zia, fought to the last man and the last round. It inflicted heavy damage on the 4th Armoured Corps with its anti-tank missiles. One dedicated Khalq officer, Maj. Umar, lost his life in this engagement. (After the Revolution one of the Kabul colleges was named after him.) Since Maj. Zia, the head of the presidential guard, was a well known Parchamite, after the Revolution Khalq accused Parcham of having defended Daud to the bitter end. Other Parchamite officers from the Kargha and Reshkhor Divisions also fought the revolutionary forces. Parchamites are justified in saying that these officers were never informed that the Revolution had begun. They were under the impression that they were fighting a right-wing uprising. In a similar situation, Khalq loyalists would have done the same, argue the Parchamites.

Moreover, while preparing his takeover 'plan', Amin had consciously kept known Parchamite officers out of it. For instance, Noor Ahmed Noor, the Parcham organizer for the armed forces, was not informed of the 'plan' at all by Amin.[24] Perhaps he was afraid that by taking the Parchamites into his confidence, he might compromise security. Most Khalqites believed that the Parchamite officers were careerists more than they were revolutionaries.[25] The question arises why Qadir was taken into confidence. There are three likely reasons. Firstly, he was not a diehard Parchamite and did not have to await Noor's instructions before joining the revolutionaries. Secondly, he had been humiliated for two years by Daud, who had put him in charge of the central Kabul butchery run for the army. Although he had been reinstated in his former post, he had not forgotten. Thirdly, because of the Afghan Air Force's importance, it was necessary to take him into confidence. However, it appears that Qadir was not aware of Khalq's widespread following in the armed forces, and had not taken the Revolution plan quite seriously, otherwise the Air Force would have come into action at noon instead of several hours later. Officers like Rafi and Shahpur sided with Khalq once the chips were down. As for Maj. Zia, it should not be forgotten that like Daud he was also a Mohammedzai and in the end family ties may have proved stronger. It is not really fair to hold the Parcham group responsible for Zia's refusal to join the coup.[26]

Objectively speaking, the 27 April Revolution was a gamble by Khalq to save its leadership. The bid could have failed. All that the revolutionaries really had going for them was the 4th Armoured Corps. It was the 4th Corps which started the Revolution and it was the 4th Corps which led it to victory. The 7th and 8th Divisions and the Artillery regiments were not with the revolutionaries. The Air Force was the last to join. The evidence is that the Soviet advisers present at the Bagram air base kept themselves strictly uninvolved. Had they encouraged the revolutionaries, the role of the Air Force would have been much more decisive than that of the 4th Corps. However, all accounts written in the west after 1980 see the Soviets as 'active' in the Revolution. Anthony Arnold, flying in the face of facts, writes of 'reports of Soviet pilots' participation in key attacks at the presidential palace ... [as] the planes' unusually accurate rocket fire was beyond the capabilities of Afghan pilots.'[27] Racial prejudice is here coupled with pure fantasy. It is a pity that most American and European writers on Afghanistan have been unable to narrate the facts correctly because of their anti-communist prejudices. They are unwilling to accept that an Afghan pilot could possibly have the skill to fire a missile accurately enough to hit the presidential palace. However, when Afghans join the fight against communists, they are credited with the miraculous ability to bring down Soviet jets with ordinary rifles. And the 'Soviet pilots' who were supposedly firing their missiles at Daud's palace with such deadly accuracy suddenly lose all their skills and are unable to hit the gallant anti-communist Afghan Mujahideen, disgorging all their bombs over barren hills!

The great tragedy of this century's revolutions is their 'official' history. The revolution takes place just once, but its history is rewritten several times. The group in power tries to belittle the contribution of the group which is not in power. One history of the Great October Revolution of 1917 is written by Trotsky who is gallant enough to carry its entire weight on his weak shoulders. Stalin has the history rewritten with no mention of Trotsky's role at all. The group in power in communist states has discovered that the safest targets of criticism are either the living who are out of power or the dead who cannot defend themselves.

Table 3

Name	Position in the Party and Role in the Revolution	Post-Revolutionary Fate
1. Noor Mohammed Taraki	Party's founder General Secretary whose arrest triggered off the April Revolution	Assassinated 8 October 1979
2. Hafizullah Amin	Party Organizer in the armed forces who planned the Revolution and set it in motion	Assassinated 27 December 1979
3. Abdul Rahman Amin	Carried Amin's Revolution 'plan' to Engineer Zarif. Also confirmed Taraki's arrest to Amin	Assassinated 27 December 1979
4. Babrak Amin (age nine in 1978)	Carried Engineer Zarif's message to Amin on 26 April 1978	In jail since 28 December 1979
5. Engineer Zarif	Carried Amin's message to Saleh Mohammed Zeary and Khyal Mohammed Katwazi on 26 April 1978	Hanged in June 1980
6. Faqir Mohammed Faqir	Carried the Revolution's operational 'plan' to Syed Ghulabzoi	In Pulcharkhi prison since 28 December 1979
7. Maj. Daud Tarun	Took part in the Revolution and freed Party leaders from detention on the day	Assassinated in September 1979
8. Babrak Karmal	Party's founder First Secretary. Arrested on 16 April 1978 by Daud	In exile July 1978 to December 1979. Under house arrest from December 1986 to May 1987. Now in Soviet exile
9. Abdul Hakim Sharai Jozjani	Arrested on 26 April 1978 by Daud	In Pulcharkhi prison since 28 December 1979
10. Lt. Col. Ghulam Qadir	One of the commanders of the April Revolution. Announced success of Revolution on radio. Later became Minister	In death cell from August 1978 to December 1979

No.	Name	Role	Fate
11.	Lt. Col. Mohammad Rafi	Fought in the 4th Armoured Corps on 27 April 1978. Later became Minister	In Pulcharkhi prison from August 1978 to December 1979
12.	Maj. Aslam Watanjar	Commanded one of the 4th Armoured Corps columns during the Revolution. Fired the first shell on Daud's palace. Announced the Revolution on radio. Later became Minister	In exile from 14 September to 27 December 1979
13.	Maj. Sher Jan Mazdooryar	One of the 4th Armoured Corps commanders on 27 April 1978. Made Commander of the Corps. Later made Minister	Put under house arrest from 14 September to 27 December 1979
14.	Maj. Mohammed Yaqub	Amin's brother-in-law. Took active part in the 27 April Revolution. Later made Chief of Army Staff	Assassinated on 27 December 1979
15.	Maj. Mohammed Iqbal	Took part in the Revolution. Later made commandant of Amin's Presidential Guard	Assassinated on 27 December 1979
16.	Shahpur Ahmedzai	Took part in the Revolution. Later promoted Lieutenant General	Assassinated after August 1979
17.	Syed Ghulabzoi	Distributed the Revolution 'plan' among army officers. Later made Minister	Forced to go into hiding from September to December 1979
18.	Asadullah Sarwari	Present at Air Headquarters on 27 April 1978. Later made Chief of Intelligence	Forced to go into hiding from September to December 1979
19.	Lt. Iqbal Waziri	Took part in the Revolution. Later made the army's Political Commissar	In jail since 28 December 1979
20.	Capt. Ahmed Jan	Fought in the 4th Armoured Corps during the Revolution	In jail since 28 December 1979
21.	Lt. Shaista Khan	Fought in the 4th Armoured Corps during the revolution	In jail since January 1980

Table 4

Name	Government and/or Party Position	Post-Revolutionary Fate
1. Akbar Shah Wali	Minister, Member Central Committee	In jail since 28 December 1979
2. M.K. Soma	Minister, Member Central Committee	In jail since 28 December 1979
3. Karim Misaq	Minister, Member Central Committee	In jail since 28 December 1979
4. Mansur Hashimi	Governor Badakhshan Province, Member Central Committee	In jail since 28 December 1979
5. Yasin Bunyadi	Member Central Committee	In jail since 28 December 1979
6. Abdul Mohammed	Member Central Committee	In jail since 28 December 1979
7. Hassan Paiman	Member Central Committee	In jail since 28 December 1979
8. Khyal Mohammed Katwazi	Minister, Member Central Committee during Amin's rule	In jail since 28 December 1979
9. Sultan Ali Kishtmand	Minister, Member Central Committee	Sentenced to death and jailed from August 1978 to December 1979
10. Noor Ahmed Noor	Minister, Member Central Committee	In exile from July 1978 to December 1979
11. Anahita Ratebzad	Minister, Member Central Committee	In exile from July 1978 to December 1979. In semi-detention since December 1986
12. Suleman Laiq	Director of Radio and Television, Member Central Committee	In jail from March 1979 to December 1979
13. Nizamuddin Tehzib	Minister, Member Central Committee	In jail from March 1979 to December 1979
14. Majid Sarbuland	Member Central Committee	In jail from March 1979 to December 1979
15. Fida Mohammed Dehnashin	Member Central Committee	In jail from March 1979 to December 1979
16. Sarwar Yurish	Member Central Committee	In jail from March 1979 to December 1979

17.	Abdul Quddus Ghaurbandi	Minister, Member Central Committee	In jail since 27 December 1979
18.	Mahmood Baryali	Member Central Committee	In exile from June 1978 to December 1979. In semi-detention since December 1986
19.	Abdul Wakil	Member Central Committee	In jail from July 1978 to December 1979
20.	Dr. Najibullah	Member Central Committee	In exile from July 1978 to December 1979
21.	Arif Alamyar	Minister, Member Central Committee during Amin's rule	Hanged in June 1980
22.	Sahib Jan Sehrai	Minister, Member Central Committee during Amin's rule	Hanged in June 1980
23.	Abdullah Amin	Governor Northern Zone	Hanged in June 1980
24.	Asadullah Amin	Director of Intelligence, Member Central Committee during Amin's rule	Hanged in June 1980
25.	Maj. Syed Abdullah	Commandant Pulcharkhi Prison	Hanged in June 1980
26.	Sarwar Mangal	Member Central Committee during Karmal's rule	In jail from August 1978 to December 1979
27.	Najmuddin Kehani	Member Central Committee during Karmal's rule	In jail from August 1978 to December 1979
28.	Mohammed Farooq	Member Central Committee during Karmal's rule	In jail from August 1978 to December 1979
29.	Babrak Shinwari	Head of Party Youth Wing and Deputy Minister during Amin's rule	In jail since December 1979

Further, only those who occupy positions of power deserve to be praised.[28]

The PDPA has followed this 'glorious tradition' to the letter. In May 1978, it published a history of the Saur Revolution which revealed that Taraki was its main inspiration and architect and it was his student Amin who had put his 'great teacher's' revolutionary ideas into practice. This brief account, published in booklet form, failed to make any mention of Karmal or his friends, the only exception being Qadir whom the Khalq group considered a casual sort of Parchamite anyway. While it is true that the April Revolution was predominantly the making of Taraki's Khalq, the official history was really no more than a crude attempt to lionize Taraki and Amin.

The second history of the Revolution was written in Amin's time and made no mention of Taraki, Karmal, Watanjar, Qadir, Rafi and Ghulabzoi, none of whom was, of course, in power. Amin also commissioned a nine-hour film on the Revolution in which the central role was played by him. He not only wanted but needed to highlight his contribution to Afghanistan's revolutionary history. In order to ridicule Amin, the Karmal regime later showed certain excerpts from this film on television. In one scene, the police were shown entering Amin's house on the night of 26 April. In accordance with Afghan custom, Amin was filmed sleeping on the floor with his wife and children. Before the arrival of the police, he was shown handing over the 'plan' for the Revolution to his wife for safe custody, while he swallowed a tiny piece of paper himself. The police tried to drag him away, but it did not look quite right and the shot had to go through several retakes. Since Amin was the President of Aghanistan at the time, it was only natural that the actor assigned to play the policeman should have found it rather embarrassing to drag him away like a common criminal. All the retakes of this rather ludicrous re-enactment of history were screened on television at Karmal's orders. In another shot, Amin was shown leaving the prison on a tank. He was not accompanied by either Taraki or Karmal. The entire film revolved around Amin.[29]

Although Karmal did not produce a third history of the Revolution, the official media were directed to establish that while Taraki was a totally forgettable figure, Amin was an 'enemy of the Revolution'. On the occasion of *Soyem Aqrab* in 1981, a semi-documentary was screened on television which, with the generous and frequent use of stills of Karmal, tried to establish that he alone was to be credited with the authorship of the Revolution.[30] The 'authorized version' of the Revolution is currently being written by Panjsheri on a personal commission from Dr. Najibullah. What he writes remains to be seen. Whether he will be able to write at all also remains an open question.

It has been said by Voltaire that every revolution eats up its children, but the April Revolution ate not just its children, but its parents too. Within two years it was unique in the sense that all its major and minor figures had either been murdered, jailed or exiled. Table 3 demonstrates in graphic terms the sad end which awaited the PDPA and the Revolution it had sired on 27 April 1978.

The joint Central Committee set up by the Khalq and Parcham factions in 1977 did not fare any better, as Table 4 shows. Apart from this, many Provincial Governors and army officers, hundreds of party workers and scores of minor officials were either murdered or jailed. Not one of them was killed, jailed or exiled by counter-revolutionary forces. The PDPA alone takes the credit for these bloody events.

In the first nine years of revolutionary rule, only three known Party leaders – Faiz Mohammed Faiz, a Minister (September 1980), Adil Zarmati, an ex-Governor (April 1980), and Abdul Ahad, a member of the Central Committee (January 1987) – could be said to have been possibly assassinated by counter-revolutionary elements. The Party leaders who were neither jailed nor exiled during these nine years number no more than five (Zeary, Panjsheri, Bariq Shafi, Danish and Aryan). Of these Baraq Shafi and Ismail Danish were sent abroad on diplomatic assignments in late 1985.

10

Taraki's Tryst with Destiny and the First Conspiracy

The Afghan peasantry, devoid of all political consciousness and disorganized in class terms, greeted the April Revolution with indifference, which was only natural because it had never occurred to the Party to set up even one peasants' organization across the length and breadth of Afghanistan. Its entire effort in this direction was confined to a few cliché-ridden short stories written by Taraki on peasant-feudal relations. However, there was no opposition to the takeover in the countryside. In the cities, there was widespread public support for the change. In Kabul especially, the people felt that a new order had come into being and their lives would now change for the better. Five years after the Revolution, Karmal tried nostalgically to remind his 'comrades' of those heady days:

> Let us recall how during the first few days of the Revolution, Kabul and all of the country were imbued with the enthusiasm and fervour of the people! Recall how an unforgettable atmosphere full of joy and expectation reigned in the streets, roads, squares and in the common man's household.[1]

What he forgot to add was that during those very days of 'joy and expectation', the Khalq-Parcham rivalry and the bitter Karmal-Amin struggle were at their height. The two old rivals could not even wait for the dust to settle on the Revolution before resuming their suicidal political vendettas. As stated earlier, on 27 April itself there was unpleasantness between Amin and Karmal. However, that day was historic in the sense that Taraki accepted two of Karmal's suggestions which Amin had opposed. Perhaps Karmal felt for the first time that the man he had fought for ten long years was not so bad after all. Amin must have seen it as a clear indication that Karmal's presence in the

Party would be a challenge to him and an impediment to his political ambitions. He could not allow Karmal to gain a hold over Taraki and continue influencing his decisions.

On 1 May 1978 the Revolutionary Council met to choose a cabinet.[2] Taraki was elected Chairman and Prime Minister. The first revolutionary cabinet was:

Chairman of the Revolutionary Council and Prime Minister: Noor Mohammed Taraki
Vice Chairman of the Revolutionary Council and Deputy Prime Minister: Babrak Karmal
Deputy Prime Minister and Foreign Minister: Hafizullah Amin
Deputy Prime Minister and Minister of Communications: Mohammed Aslam Watanjar

The ministerial portfolios were:

Parcham Group

Noor Ahmed Noor (Interior)
Sultan Ali Kishtmand (Planning)
Baraq Shafi (Information and Culture)
Suleman Laiq (Radio and Television)
Anahita Ratebzad (Social Affairs)
Nizamuddin Tehzib (Tribal Affairs)
Abdul Quddus Ghaurbandi (Commerce)

Khalq Group

Akbar Shah Wali (Public Health)
Saleh Mohammed Zeary (Agriculture)
Ghulam Dastgir Panjsheri (Education)
Karim Misaq (Finance)
Abdul Hakim Sharai Jozjani (Justice)
Mohammed Ismail Danish (Mineral Resources and Industry)
M.K. Soma (Higher Education)
Mansur Hashmi (Water and Power)

Two more Parcham sympathizers included in the cabinet were:

Abdul Qadir (Defence)
Mohammed Rafi (Public Works)

Both groups were evenly represented in the first cabinet. On the face of it, the distribution looked fair, though it was not obvious why a backward and underdeveloped country like Afghanistan needed three

Deputy Prime Ministers. The powers of the three deputies had not been outlined either. What the Party had done was to set up not one but three governments within the government in an effort to maintain what it thought was a political balance. Taraki was a sort of federal head of three governments. For the Khalq Ministers, Amin was the Deputy Prime Minister, while the Parchamite members of the cabinet were answerable to Karmal only. Watanjar controlled his army colleagues Qadir and Rafi. No Deputy Prime Minister was supposed to interfere in the working of the Ministries which were not under his direct control. In other words, these three mini-cabinets were really three distinct and conflicting groups.[3] They even used to hold separate sessions. Karmal had succeeded in wresting the army from Amin's direct control, whose portfolio was really a device to distance him from his former constituency, namely the armed forces. This third factor – the armed forces – instead of bringing the Khalq and Parcham factions together contributed to the vivisection of the Khalq group itself.

According to the first announcement made by Taraki, the Revolutionary Council was the true and only repository of political power in the country. While its membership was never publicly announced, it comprised five army men and thirty civilians.[4] The civilians were all members of the joint PDPA Central Committee.[5] The question arises as to why it was felt that the Central Committee should exist under the cover of the Revolutionary Council. After the Revolution, it was the Revolutionary Council which was publicly credited with all decision-making and political power. Since Daud had set up a fifty-member Central Committee in 1973 to run the country, the thinking of the PDPA was that if the term Central Committee was employed, it might give the simple Afghans the impression that the new government was a continuation of the Daud regime.

The second reason why the name of the Central Committee was not used was that the army officers who had brought about the Revolution had joined the government as a third force and none of them was a member of the Central Committee. That is why Taraki stated at his first press conference that the five officers in the Revolutionary Council (Qadir, Watanjar, Ghulabzoi, Rafi and Sarwari)[6] were members of the Party, but did not say what their position in the Party was.[7] Had the Party made the Central Committee the sole and publicly-declared source of political power, these five officers would have been seen as not integral to the power structure. After thirteen years of struggle, the PDPA had only succeeded in inheriting this handful of men in uniform. They were its 'proletariat' and its 'peasantry'. Had the Party tried to make them subservient to the Central Committee, it could not have run the government, or so it believed. However, after some time, these officers were taken on to the Central Committee and the Revolutionary Council gradually disappeared from view. A Party 'Politburo' came into being simultaneously in order to run and control policy when the Central Committee was not in session.

If Karmal had tried to break Amin's power by inducting the army as the third force, Amin was not sitting idle either. He began to develop close personal relations with senior army officers.[8] It was Amin who raised the question of their membership of the Central Committee. He now claimed that the Khalqite officers before the reunification of the party in 1977 had actually been made members of the Central Committee formed by Khalq. Since the 1977 unity meeting had failed to come to an agreement on how the Party should handle and unite its ranks in the army, Karmal was not in a position to counter Amin's argument. As for Taraki, he did not have the courage to contradict Amin, because he was afraid that if he did, he would lose the support of the army. Amin told his soldier friends that although an attempt had been made to 'exile' him by giving him Foreign Affairs, he was still fighting their battles and defending their rights.

Thanks to Amin, this was the main item on the agenda of the 24 May Politburo meeting.[9] Since Amin was not a member of the Politburo, two days before the meeting, he produced an 'official' pamphlet on the April Revolution through the political department of the army.[10] This 'political' department was controlled by his men, as stated elsewhere, and the blow-by-blow account of the Revolution was written at Amin's behest.[11] This account, while highlighting the role of Amin and the Khalq group (which was to some extent correct), contained critical and dismissive remarks about Parcham and its lack of involvement in the Revolution. The pamphlet described the presidential guard as 'Daud's servants', which, considering Maj. Zia's known Parchamite leanings, was an attack on Karmal. Without naming Parcham, the pamphlet accused it of 'political opportunism'. It also made frequent mention of 'Khalq officers' and 'Khalq soldiers' which was an affront to the Parcham group and was received as such. Amin was keen to establish that the Revolution had been brought about by Khalq and its friends in the army. The inference was obvious. While Parcham had played no role in the success of the Revolution, and in fact, had acted 'negatively', it now occupied 50 per cent of the cabinet posts. What was more, membership of the Politburo had been denied to Amin himself and that of the Central Committee to the officers who had toppled the Daud regime. History may not repeat itself, but the PDPA was about to repeat the same old story.

The Politburo meeting of 24 May was characterized by a bitter debate on two issues: the inclusion of revolutionary officers in the

Central Committee and the Amin-inspired pamphlet produced by the Political Department of the army. Parchamites claim that Karmal had warned the Politburo about including the army officers in the higher ranks of the Party. He is said to have told Taraki and the Khalq group that by elevating young and immature officers to the highest positions in the Party, the Revolution and its command would ultimately fall into their hands. (Parchamites happily stressed after 1980 that it was this group of army officers which caused the Taraki-Amin dispute of 1979, leading to the eventual destruction of both). After heated argument, the Politburo agreed to nominate four army officers to the Central Committee.[12] The first mistake had been to accept them as the 'third force' and the second was their inclusion in the Central Committee. However, these two fatal mistakes were natural because neither of the two groups was playing fair or could be said to be motivated by higher principles.

The 'official' account of the Revolution issued at the behest of Amin led, as expected, to bitterness between Taraki and Karmal.[13] By making free use of expressions like 'Khalq officers' and the 'Khalq Revolution' Amin was said to have spread inter-factional bitterness. Karmal proposed that the pamphlet be confiscated and a new pamphlet issued under the supervision of the Politburo. Taraki countered Karmal's objection by asserting that the term 'Khalq' was a true reflection of the Party's oneness, while Parcham was a symbol of factionalism. Taraki, after all, was the founder of the Khalq group. It was also asking too much of him to confiscate the Amin pamphlet, since the term 'great leader' had been used to describe him in that publication for the first time. To flatter Taraki, Amin had also used the epithet 'the great teacher'. Amin's devilish intellect had correctly surmised that as soon as Karmal objected to the pamphlet, it would become evident to Taraki and the Khalq group that he was not willing to accept Taraki as the 'great leader' and members of the Party as 'Khalqis'.

In the beginning, Taraki had tried to remain detached from the growing Karmal-Amin struggle. However, the calculating Amin used flattery to win over Taraki, referring to him in Party and cabinet meetings by such sycophantic titles as 'the star of the east', 'the great thinker', 'the great leader' etc. etc. Lower-ranking members of the Party, taking it as 'official policy', began to use these titles when referring to Taraki. Instead of reprimanding Amin for such blatant flattery, Taraki began to savour the sycophancy. Karmal was no match for Amin in this field. It had taken him ten years to accept Taraki as his senior and he probably needed ten centuries to accept him as the 'great leader'. Like all rulers, it was Taraki's strategy to maintain his power by using the personal enmity which so obviously existed between his two deputies. In fact, he persuaded Karmal not to get worked up over Amin. On Taraki's suggestion, Karmal went to the airport on 8 June 1978 to receive Amin who had gone on his first foreign tour. The arrival story was carried prominently by the press on Taraki's instructions. Parcham workers are mostly unaware of the fact that the proposal to include Amin in the Politburo came from Karmal.[14] This must have been at Taraki's suggestion who perhaps now wanted the cold war between the two to come to an end. Taraki personally exercised no direct political control over the Party, since Khalq was effectively in the hands of Amin and Parcham's undisputed leader was Karmal. All Taraki really had was a fistful of mock-heroic titles conferred on him by Amin.

A meeting of the Revolutionary Council, or the extended Central Committee, on 12 June was the scene of an open clash between the two groups. The first point of dispute was what colour the national flag should be. Khalq had already perfected a red standard, which Karmal had described as another instance of left adventurism. This was a continuation or repeat of the 1966 dispute as to what colour the masthead of the Party paper *Khalq* should be – red or green. The other dispute related to the citizenship of twenty-three members of the former royal family. Karmal was of the view that instead of being stripped of their Afghan citizenship, they should be released and sent into exile in return for a guarantee that they would not take part in politics. To Taraki and Amin, both Ghilzais, such consideration for the tyrannical Barakzai rulers was unthinkable. The Khalq group took the position that in order to keep up the pressure on King Zahir Shah and Daud's son (who had survived because he was studying in France), the royals now in jail should be divested of their citizenship and kept incarcerated. This, it was further argued, would discourage the King and Daud's heir from planning any conspiracy against the Revolution. The Khalq viewpoint eventually prevailed. Party workers and people at large were merely informed of the 'unanimous' decision taken by the Party. Of course, no public acknowledgement of the difference dogging the 'unanimous' decision was made since any such admission could have been construed as 'reactionary'. Moreover, the very decisions supposedly taken according to the communist norms of 'inner party democracy' were later made the basis of bloodshed. Only a few months after these 'unanimous' decisions, Taraki and Amin were accusing Karmal of being 'loyal' to the royal family. Among the first Party decisions reversed by Karmal after coming to power in 1980, were the two relating to the flag and the royal family. In February 1980, the national flag became a tricolour, and this was followed by the release of the twenty-three detained members of the royal family, who were allowed to leave the country.

One of those set free was Zahir Shah's first cousin Taimur Shah. The residence provided by the government to Bhutto's eldest son Mir Murtaza Bhutto was actually the annexe of Taimur Shah's spacious palace. In 1980 this palace (locally known as palace number two) was the residence of the General Officer Commanding of the Soviet Red Army. The writer was present at the annexe in March 1980 when household servants came to inform us that Taimur Shah had arrived to take a last look at his home. After some time he came in, accompanied by the servants. He looked somewhat frightened and did not go to the main palace, appearing to be merely content to take a look at it from the annexe. He went to Italy the next day, but the writer was quite unable to imagine at the time that one day Afghanistan Marxist rulers would reach a point as a result of their short-sighted policies where they would actually ask Zahir Shah and his family to return to the country to 'play their role'.

The 12 June meeting of the Revolutionary Council proved to be the last straw as far as the 'unity' of the Khalq and Parcham groups was concerned. In less than ninety days of the Revolution, both groups had come to the conclusion that it was not possible for them to sleep in the same bed. This situation was known to Party workers as *Do-Rangi* or 'dualism'. Leaders of both groups admit that Taraki requested Brezhnev to use his good offices to bring the two factions together. The Soviet leader was the spiritual head of the two PDPA 'churches', and during the last ten years the Soviet embassy in Kabul had tried hard to give the impression that it was neutral between Khalq and Parcham. Brezhnev, however, instead of agreeing to act as the peacemaker, suggested that the differences between the two should be solved in the Central Committee. There are two versions of this story.

According to the first, in order to settle the *Do-Rangi* dispute, it was decided to call a meeting of the thirty-member joint Central Committee on 17 June. Its number had since been reduced to twenty-nine because of Ustad Amir Akbar Khyber Khan's assassination.[15] It was therefore agreed that Taraki would not take part in the vote, but if there was a tie, he would have the casting vote. The meeting took place and a vote was taken which Karmal lost by two, thanks to Abdul Quddus Ghaurbandi whom Amin had persuaded the night before to side with Khalq. (Karmal's first act after assuming power in 1980 was the jailing of Ghaurbandi for his floor crossing.)

The second story claims that at a Politburo meeting on 24 June, it was decided to send the Parcham leadership out of the country. According to the writer's information, it was Suleman Laiq and Baraq Shafi who were in favour of sending Karmal into exile.[16] (It is significant that on coming to power in 1980, Karmal removed Laiq and

Shafi from the regular membership of the Central Committee, reducing them to 'alternate candidates'. It was probably in 1981 that they were readmitted to the Committee. Laiq, however, edged his way upwards and in May 1986, when Najibullah took over, he became a member of the Politburo.[17] Shafi was stripped of his once-powerful position in the Party and in 1986 was a mere counsellor at the Afghan embassy in Moscow).

If the two versions are married, the facts become clearer. At the 17 June meeting of the Central Committee, it was resolved that state policy would be laid down by Khalq. It was on the basis of this decision that the 24 June meeting recommended the exile of Karmal and other Parcham leaders. However, once again, the Party failed to announce this important decision, which explains why confusion still prevails among Party workers as to what really did transpire at these two meetings.

Karmal's step-brother Mahmood Baryali was the first Parchamite to be sent out. On 27 June 1978 he was appointed ambassador to Pakistan. The people must have seen this as another instance of rewarding friends and family: in Kabul Baryali was known only as Karmal's brother and his membership of the Central Committee was not public knowledge. In July the principal Parcham leaders were all sent out to graze, having been made ambassadors.[18] Soon after, Engineer Nazar Mohammed, Abdul Aziz Mohtat, Pacha Gul Wafadar and Abdul Wakil were also posted as ambassadors. It does not say much for Khalq's wisdom that it had decided to send its worst enemies as ambassadors to some of the world's most sensitive countries as far as Afghanistan was concerned. Noor Ahmed Noor was in the United States, Raz Mohammed Paktain in the Soviet Union, Najibullah in Iran and Baryali in Pakistan. The subsequent role played by the United States, Iran and Pakistan in Afghan affairs owes something to these ill-considered appointments.[19] The choice for Moscow was equally unfortunate from a Khalq point of view. The Soviet Union was not only the Party's political, economic, military and ideological patron, but it was directly involved in all internal disputes. While following the disclosure of what was called the 'Eid Conspiracy Plan', the three Parcham ambassadors in the United States, Iran and Pakistan were relieved of their duties, Paktain remained in his post until 1980 when Karmal took him into his cabinet, paying public tribute to his 'services'.

The ambitious Amin, taking full advantage of inter-group rivalries, had won the first round by having Karmal exiled from the country. Within Khalq he had three possible rivals: Panjsheri, Zeary and Shah Wali. The first was more interested in his workers' organization – Garoh-i-Kargar – than Party in-fighting, while the other two, senior though they were in the Party hierarchy to Amin, were no match for his cunning. In his race for power, he had long ago left them behind.

On 8 July 1978, two days before Karmal was to leave the country, the Politburo met and assigned Amin and Shah Wali the responsibility of reorganizing the Party.[20] Amin was also made First Secretary in place of Karmal. Although Amin had been taken on the Politburo a month earlier, he had deliberately kept the story out of the press because he wanted its release to coincide with Karmal's exit. The newspapers of 9 July carried the announcement of Amin's appointment to the Politburo and his assumption of the office of First Secretary. On 10 July Karmal left Kabul for Prague.[21]

The 8 July meeting of the Politburo also announced the new Party strategy, laid down by Khalq. Karmal's 'united national front' was abandoned in favour of organizing peasants, women and youth directly under the Party on a single platform. The women's wing was put under the charge of a woman named Dil Ara and the responsibility of organizing the People's Youth Organization was given to one of Amin's hand-picked students, Babrak Shinwari. He also appointed his son, Abdul Rahman Amin, a member of the Central Committee of the Youth Organization. His hold on the Party was now strong, based as it was on the principle of personal loyalty. However, everything was not yet under his control. The crucial Ministry of Defence was under the Parchamite Abdul Qadir and the Chief of Army Staff was another Parchamite, General Shahpur Ahmedzai. The Soviet Union had earlier advised Taraki that at least 30 per cent of government and Party posts should remain with Parcham in order to safeguard Party unity. If Amin believed that by getting rid of the leading Parchamites and ousting Karmal from the Politburo and the Central Committee he would be able to root out Parcham completely, he was wrong. However, to his good fortune, a Parcham plan to unseat the Khalq government was unearthed by the intelligence agencies, according to which a coup led by Parchamite officers and supporters was to be staged in September. This provided the needed grounds for a Parchamite purge.

After the removal of the Parchamites, Khalq decided to hold a weekly meeting of the Politburo. On 16 July, the Politburo decided to transfer all Provincial Governors appointed on the recommendation of Parcham. Party Provincial Secretaries were given the powers formerly enjoyed by the Governors. This amounted to strangulating provincial autonomy in decision-making and centralizing executive authority.[22] Somewhat later, district and sub-district administrations were also put under the control of Party functionaries. Years earlier, the PDPA manifesto had promised that 'the Party government will use all its authority to decentralize power and hand it over to the people'.[23]

However, when the Party actually took office, instead of handing over power to the people, it merely decided to 'exercise' it in the name of the people. It would have been unrealistic, in any case, to expect a Party which was so insecure and power-hungry to trust the common people to run their affairs themselves. Having made no effort to change the existing state structure or bring in administrative reform, the Marxist intellectuals of the PDPA virtually pitched themselves against the people through this greedy act of annexation of all local authority and initiative. The rural population of Afghanistan had traditionally been allowed to live in a semi-autonomous state. Direct central control and the Party's new administrative role were nothing short of political suicide.

Political parties which have known democracy neither within their ranks nor outside in their social surroundings generally end up cutting their own throats when called upon or forced to take a democratic decision, internally or externally. The great tragedy of 'popular' and 'progressive' political parties in the Third World has been their inability to practise democracy within their ranks. They are run – and with disastrous results – on the principle of centralism, 'discipline' and subservience to the person of 'the leader'. The model for all this is Stalinism. The PDPA is a classic case. Only twice in its life did it make the 'mistake' of taking democratic decisions – in 1966 on the question of Karmal's resignation and in June 1978 on the formation of the single government. The result on both occasions was bitter discord and factional warfare. All its disputes were finally settled in battle. Karmal did not accept the 24 June Politburo decision which virtually ousted him from the government. Before leaving for Prague, he prepared a plan to take over power. After 1980, Khalq leaders and workers languishing in Pulcharkhi prison often cursed the day the decision was taken to send Karmal into diplomatic exile. They attributed his survival to 'that ill-omened democratic decision'.

According to the Khalq group, before leaving for Prague, Karmal arranged with Qadir, Rafi, Gen. Shahpur, Kishtmand, Dr. Mir Akbar, the head of the Jamhooriyat Hospital, and the Sitm-e-Milli leader Tahir Badakhshi that Parcham would stage a coup and take over power on 4 September 1978, the day of the Muslim festival Eid.[24] This particular day was chosen because soldiers and officers of the armed forces would be on leave and the general atmosphere would be relaxed and free of suspicion. A law and order situation was to be created and, assuming that the army would be called in to deal with it, it was thought this would give Qadir and Shahpur an opportunity to take over power while pretending to fight in defence of the Khalq government. The six

Parchamite ambassadors – Karmal, Anahita Ratebzad, Noor, Baryali, Najibullah and Wakil – according to Khalq sources, were to have secretly returned to Kabul a few days before to activate their Parcham workers. After the coup, a 'United National Front' government was to be formed with Qadir as its head. Tahir Badakhshi of the Sitm-e-Milli party and Abdul Wahid Haqooqi, former Chief Justice of the Supreme Court, were also to be included, as well as any Khalq members who agreed to support the Front.[25]

The conspiracy was blown in August when the Afghan ambassador in Delhi tipped off Amin and Taraki. Qadir, Shahpur and Dr Akbar were arrested, followed by the arrests of Kishtmand, Rafi and Badakhshi.[26] It did not take Sarwari, the intelligence chief, long to break Qadir who was said to have 'sung like a canary'. He stated that he never had the intention of putting the Parcham plan into action because the majority of officers in the armed forces consisted of Khalq supporters. Detailed confessions of Qadir, Rafi and Kishtmand were published on 23 September 1978 by the *Kabul Times.*

In political terms, the 'Eid plan' was both ill-considered and premature. In military terms, it was impractical. Qadir, who was to have played the central role, was a non-Pushtun. He came from Herat province and was a Shi'a by religious faith and a supporter of Parcham by political conviction. The majority of army officers were Pushtun, Sunni and solidly Khalq. The same was true of the Air Force where Qadir had spent all his life. The fact that the Air Force had played practically no role in the Revolution was due to his limited influence among the officers. How could he then have used Khalq cadres in the army – where his influence was negligible – to overthrow a Khalq government?

The confessions of Qadir, Rafi and Kishtmand were given extensive publicity by the Afghan media. In 1980 Parcham charged the Khalq government with having used third degree methods on these three officers to extract confessions, but it stopped short of saying that they were innocent. It is ironical that Sarwari, the man who had interrogated the conspirators, was Karmal's colleague in 1980. The Parchamites, while not denying responsibility for the 'Eid plan', add that had it succeeded, the Revolution would not have swerved from its natural course, namely, the establishment of a 'National Democratic Front'.

The 'Eid plan' was the answer to Amin's prayers. He went on a Parcham witch hunt, liquidating its members and sympathizers from government and Party jobs and filling the country's jails with them. Although Laiq and Shafi were not directly implicated, even they were eased out of the Politburo. Amin also tried to shift some of the responsibility on to Taraki, saying that despite Parcham's rout in the 17

June meeting, he had kept its leaders and functionaries in government and Party jobs. Amin was informed enough to know that Taraki's decision to allow Parcham to continue to occupy official positions was taken at the advice of the Soviet ambassador in Kabul, so the criticism was directed at the Soviet ambassador as well. The official press and radio were replete with 'Eid plan' stories in October 1978. A report issued by the Political Department of the Party, now headed by Amin, said:

> Comrade Taraki on the basis of his legal authority as General Secretary of the PDPA and chairman of the Revolutionary Council made these decisions [namely the retention of Parchamites in Party and government posts] in the absence of the Revolutionary Council, but he reported them in time to the Revolutionary Council, and the Politburo.[27]

The implication was clear. The Revolutionary Council, (which was really the Central Committee) had not been taken into confidence and Taraki had used his powers illegally. Only after having made his erroneous decision had he considered it necessary to inform the Revolutionary Council and the Politburo.

The Khalq government ordered the recall of the seven Parchamite ambassadors, including Karmal, but they did not return. Until December 1979, the Khalq diatribe against the Parchamite 'traitors' continued unabated in the official media. In one broadcast from Kabul radio, Anahita Ratebzad was referred to as a 'bitch'.[28] The seven ambassadors had abandoned their missions, but not before taking all the embassy funds. This 'theft' of public funds was also widely publicized. Khalq leaders and workers believed that the absconders had taken shelter in western countries. They were convinced that the 'royalist' Karmal was either in Italy with King Zahir Shah or in Germany living it up in expensive hotels. After 1980, the author heard Khalq prisoners in Pulcharkhi severely criticizing their leaders Akbar Shah Wali, Jozjani, Ghaurbandi, Hashmi and Soma for having misled them about Karmal's exact whereabouts during this period. They were being told that the 'imperialist agent' Karmal, after having 'looted' public funds, was hiding in a western country, hence the sole claimant to the Afghan Revolution and the communist ideology was the Khalq Party. Karmal's arrival in Kabul with Soviet tanks on 27 December 1980 therefore came as a great shock to the workers and leaders of the Khalq Party. A number of Khalq leaders told the author in prison that as far as they knew, Karmal had taken refuge in West Germany, not in Czechoslovakia.

During the eighteen months of Khalq rule, the Afghan Foreign Office was headed by Amin and Akbar Shah Wali in that order. It is pathetic that both men were unable to discover that Karmal was not in West Germany but an honoured guest in Prague. Part of the reason for Khalq's failure to obtain correct information, of course, lay in the fact that most important diplomatic posts were occupied by Parchamites. For instance, the Afghan ambassador in Bonn was a Parchamite, Engineer Nazar Mohammed, who kept feeding Kabul with false information.[29]

There is, however, evidence that by September 1979, Taraki at least knew that Karmal was not in the west but the east. As we will see later, in the second week of September, Taraki held a secret meeting with Karmal at Moscow airport. It is also possible that even before this meeting, Taraki knew where Karmal was, because he had some time earlier agreed to the engagement of his niece with Nazar Mohammed, the Parchamite ambassador in Bonn. (It may be added that since the death of Taraki and his brother, it has been Nazar who has been looking after the two families.[30]) Although the 'Eid Conspiracy' had come as something of a shock to Taraki, conversations with Parchamites have revealed that, had the coup succeeded, Karmal would have offered Taraki the Presidency of the country, as long as he did not object to Karmal becoming the PDPA General Secretary.

During the writer's imprisonment at Pulcharkhi, he learnt how the 'Eid Plan' had come to be blown. The source was Wafadar, whose political career really began after the Daud Revolution. In Daud's last days, he was the Afghan ambassador to India. After April 1978, while outwardly showing sympathy with Parcham, he managed to align himself with Khalq, which considered him an 'underground' Khalq follower. When the 'Eid Plan' was hatched, he was still ambassador in New Delhi. Since he was an ex-army officer, it is only natural that he was taken into confidence by Karmal. However, this was a mistake, as he immediately passed on the information to Taraki. To confirm the report, Khalq sent over some of its men to 'sniff' Qadir, who, foolishly mistaking them for Parchamites, told them of the takeover bid. And once he had been picked up, the entire conspiracy stood exposed.[31]

Khalq denounced the 'Eid Plan' as an 'American-Chinese conspiracy', a piece of rhetoric designed to bring Khalq closer to Moscow. By accusing Abdul Wahid Haqooqi and Dr Mir Akbar of being American imperialist agents and Badakhshi of being a Chinese plant, Khalq tried to impress upon Moscow that Karmal, who had aligned himself with these anti-Soviet forces, should no longer be treated as a friend. However, it is never easy to exploit great powers. In November 1978, Amin gave an interview to a *Pravda* correspondent:

Pravda: Do you have any documents and evidence regarding the intervention of foreign sources and circles?
Amin: More than you could imagine. We have got sufficient undeniable documents and evidence showing that all anti-Khalq plots are prepared, encouraged and financed by the foreign circles.[32]

A few days after this interview, Taraki informed the Central Committee in a report that 'Parcham's counter-revolutionary and anti-government activities are continuing'.[33] Amin and Taraki's assertions must have caused smiles in Moscow. These two men, who claimed to have irrefutable evidence about Karmal's collaboration with the United States and China, did not even know where he was!

The consequences of the failed 'Eid Plan' were grave for Parcham. On 18 November 1978, the Central Committee formally decided to oust Noor, Ratebzad, Baryali, Wakil and Najibullah from the Party. Qadir, Rafi, Shahpur, Kishtmand and Dr Akbar were deprived of their primary membership of the Party. Later, Dr Akbar and Shahpur were executed without the formality of a trial. Qadir, Rafi and Kishtmand survived because of Soviet intervention.[34] Sarbuland, Yorish, Tehzib and Dehnashin were demoted from positions they occupied in the Central Committee. The only Parchamites who survived as members of the Central Committee were the 'chicken-hearted' poets Laiq and Shafi. Every Parchamite who could be clearly identified as one was jailed. According to the prison guards and the security staff of those days, between 400 and 500 Parcham workers and leaders were in jail after the exposure of the 'Eid Plan'.[35] Nearly 250 Parchamites and Sitm-e-Milli workers were executed.[36] In 1980, Karmal claimed that 'thousands' of his party workers were jailed and killed by Khalq. After the crackdown on Parcham, two of Amin's men, Abdul Rashid Jalili, Rector of Kabul University, and Sahib Jan Sehrai were made Ministers. (Jalili has been in jail since December 1979 and Sehrai was hanged in June 1980.)

After Parcham's routing, Watanjar's position as Deputy Prime Minister naturally became redundant. Amin was not in favour of retaining the army as the 'third force' any longer. In July 1978, Watanjar was given the Interior portfolio in place of Noor, but after August 1978, Amin and Watanjar fell out openly on the question of the control of the Defence Ministry. Amin was not prepared to let this bastion of power be controlled by Watanjar who, on the other hand, considered it his right to hold the portfolio. Being an ex-major, this must also have been the last ambition of his life. Taraki was of the view that in order to curb Amin's spreading influence, the Defence Ministry should go to Watanjar. However, under Amin's pressure, he was not able to bring this about. The only solution he could think of was to retain the contentious portfolio himself and to make Amin his deputy. Taraki had no direct influence in the armed forces and no personal links with army officers. Postings, promotions, demotions and the like were, therefore, all left in Amin's hands. Watanjar was sent to the Ministry of Communications.

Only two months after the Revolution, the PDPA intellectuals were hatching conspiracies against one another. After Parcham's elimination, the two great political rivals were Amin and Watanjar. It should have been clear to anyone that the wild ambition of these 'revolutionaries' would soon sink the ship they were so uncertainly sailing. However, instead of trying to resolve its inner differences, the Party decided to embark on a programme of disastrous reforms. No effort was made to determine if Afghan society was ready for the reformist medicine which was soon going to be pushed down its throat. No survey or study was considered necessary before passing a rapid series of executive decrees.

11

The Contradictions of Afghan Society

To this day, all statistical surveys undertaken in Afghanistan either by governments or foreign agencies have been based on rough estimates. In the absence of any verifiable figures about the country's population or total agricultural product, or the number of landless peasants, migrant tribes or settled inhabitants, the statistics bandied around are far from reliable. Despite rural Afghanistan's feudal economy and land ownership system, the hold of time-honoured tribal customs is still very powerful. To describe the entire Afghan society as feudal in the classical sense on the strength of observed economic relations is a grave mistake – a mistake committed by the PDPA.

Afghanistan can most accurately be described as a tribal confederation comprising multi-racial groups and nationalities. The dominant nationality, both in economic and numerical terms, is Pushtun. According to one estimate, it numbers between seven and eight million, or one half of the total population. In 1978 the population of the country was said to be around 15.1 million.[1] The second largest nationality is Tajik, estimated at between three and four million. The Tajiks are mostly settled around Kabul, the Panjsher Valley and Badakhshan province. Historically, the feudal system came to Tajik areas long before it was known among the Pushtuns, which is why the tribal tradition among the Tajiks is not as strong as it is among the Pushtuns. Apart from these two major nationalities, there are a large number of smaller nationalities, such as Hazaras, Uzbeks, Turkomans, Imaqs, Farsibans, Nooristanis, Baluch and Karghez.

As a result of tribal wars stretching over several hundred years, the Pushtuns established their supremacy by driving out the once-ruling Hazaras, Tajiks and Nooristanis from their ancestral lands and grazing grounds. This Pushtun expansionism continued until the reign of Amir

Abdul Rahman Khan (1881-1901). This is the background to the deep divisions which have always existed between the Pushtuns and the Hazaras, Tajiks and Nooristanis. Unless this bitter legacy of history is kept in view and understood, it will be impossible to understand the present politics of Afghanistan.[2]

Although 99.9 per cent of Afghans are Muslim, in the field of politics regional and tribal differences take precedence over religious and ideological beliefs. Tahir Badakhshi claimed to represent the aspirations of the subjected Tajik people, while Taraki stood for the rights of the Ghilzai Pushtuns who suffered persecution over several hundred years at the hands of the ruling Pushtun tribes. While both Taraki and Badakhshi held identical political views and believed in the emancipation of the working class, they were unable to work together because one was a Tajik and the other was a Pushtun. Let us take the other side of the coin. The same historical reasons which divided Taraki and Badakhshi apply to Gulbudin Hikmatyar, who is a Pushtun, and Burhanuddin Rabbani, who is a Tajik. Religiously, they are both Sunni and politically, they are carbon copy Akhwan-ul-Muslamin. Their political parties have similar names – Jamat-e-Islami and Hizbe Islami – and follow the same objectives. Both men have been residing in Pakistan and have been actively working against the April Revolution. But their Pushtun-Tajik divide is more important than their common ideological affinity with Akhwan-ul-Muslamin. It is no wonder that they have failed to work together.

Regional differences are no less powerful. Badakhshi and Panjsheri were both Tajiks and communists. They were also founder members of the PDPA. However, despite these common bonds, they fell victim to the regional prejudices which have always existed between Badakhshan and Panjsher provinces and their inhabitants. The same is true of the 'Mujahideen' leaders Burhanuddin Rabbani, a Badakhshan Tajik, and Maulvi Ghulam Nabi, a Panjsher Tajik, who despite ties of nationality and religion have been unable to reach political agreement.

Since most western journalists and writers are not familiar with the sharp tribal, racial, nationalistic and regional divisions or contradictions among the Afghans, they try to rationalize or explain away the differences between the six reactionary Afghan parties by the use of such modern terms as 'extremists' and 'moderates'. The fact is that their differences do not flow from either 'extremist' or 'moderate' politics, any more than from varying views on the interpretation of Islam. As far as Islam is concerned, they are all equally fundamentalist. In politics, they believe in settling the Afghan problem on the field of battle. So much for their 'moderate' views. Their enmities and bitter struggles spring from the tribal, sub-tribal, nationalistic and regional differences which characterize this most backward of societies – differences which possibly escape definition in terms of modern political theory.

Ninety per cent of the people of Afghanistan are Sunni Muslims. The Qizalbash, Imaq and Buraqi people, being of Iranian origin, are Shi'as. The descendants of Ghengiz Khan and Haluku Khan, the Hazaras, are also of Shi'a faith. The Hazaras converted to Shi'aism not necessarily out of any deep religious conviction but because it seemed to be the best way of protecting their ethnic identity when faced with the Sunni Pushtun threat. To obtain a guarantee of physical survival, the descendants of the Mongols in Afghanistan turned towards the powerful Shi'a dynasty in Iran and accepted its spiritual overlordship. Kabul's largest Imambara (the organizational and spiritual centre of the Shi'a faith) is named after Afghanistan's Sunni king Nadir Shah Fashar. After the April Revolution, Iran became the headquarters of the more religiously inclined of the Hazaras, while the more politically motivated among them chose Peking as their spiritual home. Sharing their religion with the former, they were united with the latter by ties of race and blood.

The institution of *jirga* is the agreed focal point of Afghan tribal life. The *jirga* is the most ancient manifestation of tribal equality and justice. Its decisions are considered binding because they are made by members of the tribe, sub-tribe or village collectively. Local quarrels, war or peace with other tribes or the form of relationship to be established with the central authority are all debated and decided on by the *jirga*. The *jirga* system is particularly well established in those regions of Afghanistan where the tribe is still the basic social unit. In Qanduz, Balkh, Jozjan, Faryab, Koh Sufaid, Chahar Imaq and Nangarhar regions, the *jirga* system is both powerful and popularly accepted. In these areas, all land is communally owned.[3] The distribution or disposal of inherited land, called *bakhra*, is made through the *jirga*. Almost all over Afghanistan, mountains, jungles or grazing grounds adjacent to a tribal settlement or village are considered communal property. If an individual or a family is in need of fuel wood for a special occasion such as a marriage or death, it is the *jirga* which has to be approached with the request.

In practical terms, central government laws and courts have always remained confined to town and city, while the 88 per cent of the population residing in the rural areas has run its own affairs independently in accordance with ancient custom and practice. One of the Pulcharkhi prison guards, Qasim Khan, told the writer that before the Revolution there was hardly a case where a resident of the rural areas was jailed for a moral offence, because the police never interfered in local affairs, which included murders and feuds. In effect, the vast majority of Afghans always remained well out of the reach of centrally-enacted laws.

The institution of blood money is prevalent in all Pushtun areas. Blood feuds are an accepted and time-honoured Pushtun practice. The term 'debt' is employed to describe an unsettled blood feud. If, during an inter-tribal war, one tribe kills more men of the rival tribe than it has lost itself, the extra number is called a 'debt' which must one day be realized. If the aggrieved tribe fails to reclaim this 'debt', it cannot survive in the tribal environment. The Pushtun tribes have been contracting and repaying these 'debts' for hundreds of years. Sometimes, it is not even quite remembered who contracted the original debt and when. The settlement of these 'debts' is not made stealthily. Two tribes or sub-tribes or families fix a day for going to war, for it is a regular war with dug-in positions and night raids on the enemy. Women and children are considered exempt, no matter how long or bitter the fighting. After a few days, the local *jirga*, at the request of one or both of the parties, arranges a ceasefire. After obtaining the consent of both parties, the same *jirga* extends the ceasefire for a longer period which can be several years. This is called 'placing the stone' and when hostilities resume, which they must, it is known as 'breaking the stone'. The new war leads to further 'indebtedness' and so it continues from generation to generation. It is a purely tribal affair and the central government has nothing to do with it. In Afghanistan, settling a blood feud is an unemotional and impersonal act. It is like a sacred obligation which must be fulfilled. According to one Pushtun saying, 'a Pushtun curses himself for his hastiness even if the murder he has avenged took place a hundred years ago.'

The writer spent a few days in July 1979 in the Mohmand area of Nangarhar province. In the village where he was staying, a father had murdered his married daughter. The story was that the girl had become pregnant while her husband was away. Her in-laws had brought her to her father's house, in accordance with tribal tradition, so that he should punish her for her waywardness by taking her life. Had the father hesitated, they would have done the deed themselves. However, that was not necessary because he killed her with his own hands. People from neighbouring villages began to visit him in large numbers in order to offer their congratulations for the honourable deed he had performed. What was more, even the head of the local administration, called *Ilaqadar*, was among those who came to offer their tribute to the murderer. No case was registered against him and he was not questioned or arrested by the authorities. The writer was told that the government did not interfere in such traditional matters. This incident took place at a time when the government had all but given up its efforts to introduce social reforms in the country. Had the authorities arrested the murderer, it would have led to a tribal uprising. Such adherence to tribal tradition varies from area to area, but is common to all rural regions.

A survey carried out in 1978-79 placed Afghanistan's nomadic population at 2.5 million, meaning that every sixth Afghan was a nomad. The nomadic society was the forerunner of the tribal system. The first tribal settlements in Afghanistan are of fairly recent origin. Until the nineteenth century, a sizeable portion of the Afghan population was nomadic. In Amir Abdul Rahman's time, around the turn of the century, the majority of Ghilzai nomads were forced to settle in central Ghazni and the Hazara areas.

Afghan nomads can be divided into three categories: pure nomads, semi-nomads and local semi-nomads.[4] The first group comprises nomads who until recent times were engaged in the purchase and sale of camels used to transport goods. They are settled in southern Afghanistan and live in tents. With the construction of roads in the countryside and the phasing out of the camel by mechanized transport, these people re-adjusted themselves to modern times through the acquisition of trucks and buses. Although until this day they have not quite managed to say farewell to their tented nomadic existence, some of them have turned into rich traders. After the Revolution, most of them moved across to Pakistan where they continued to follow their traditional profession. Their presence in Pakistan's transportation sector is well recognized.

Semi-nomads consisted of shepherds who, along with their flocks, wintered in the east and moved north when summer came. Today, most of them are engaged in the flourishing trade of smuggling goods. They are also moneylenders. Some of them are known to have acquired agricultural land, but there is no evidence that they actually cultivate it themselves.[5] Local semi-nomads are found in Afghanistan's northern areas. Historians have traced their origins to the Euro-Mongols. Their total number has been estimated at 200,000.[6] They move between their settlements and their grazing grounds.

Whichever category a nomad belongs to, he accepts the authority of the *jirga* to settle his personal affairs. A significant proportion of the nomads and villagers still resides in tents or mountain caves. The nomadic and tribal systems are a living part of contemporary Afghan society. Even where the tribal system has given birth to feudalism, the social superstructure continues to uphold tribal traditions.

Let us examine the Afghan feudal system in some detail. Out of the country's land-mass of 160 million acres, only 12 per cent is cultivable.

However, almost 60 per cent of this arable land has not been brought under cultivation, due to a variety of factors, including lack of water or seed and restrictive feudal practices.[7] In 1978, the revolutionary government released certain statistics, according to which 5 per cent of the landowners were in possession of 45 per cent of all cultivable land.[8] About 83 per cent of owners held between five and ten acres of largely uneconomic land. However, the true dimensions of Afghan feudalism cannot be fully demonstrated by these statistics. In 1978, there were thirty families in the country whose holdings consisted of between 500 and 50,000 acres of agricultural land. The two 'Mujahideen' leaders Mujadaddi and Gilani are among those families.[9] It is also interesting to note that the number of Afghan landlords affected by the land reforms ordered by the revolutionary government did not exceed 400. These people owned about 20,000 villages.[10] Thirteen million people had no land titles. Table 5 reveals the distribution in percentage terms.

Under the feudal system in Afghanistan, the crop is divided into five portions, namely land, water, labour, capital and seed. In practice, the farmer gets only one-fifth of the yield, since the land, capital and seed belong to the landlord and the water to the *mir-i-aab,* or owner of the water.[11] A country where a 'holy war' is being waged today is unique in the sense that a natural, God-given source such as water continues to be in private ownership.

This is perhaps not surprising in a society where men belonging to the same tribe, the same racial stock and the same village have come to be reduced to the lowly status of landless cultivators, the sole beneficiary of whose back-breaking labour is the feudal landlord. The origins of feudalism can perhaps be traced to water, the source of life and food in an arid country. If a tribe successfully occupied the water source of a rival tribe, it virtually amounted to the occupation of that tribe's lands. To protect this precious source of life, sustenance and power, forts were built around the area. With the passing of time, both the forts and water sources became the personal property of the tribal

Table 5

Size of Holding	Percentage in terms of Total Number of Landowners in the country	Percentage of Landholding in terms of Total Cultivable Land
5 to 10 Acres	83 per cent	35 per cent
10 to 25 Acres	12 per cent	20 per cent
25 to 50,000 Acres	5 per cent	45 per cent

chiefs who began to charge the farmers for the use of the water. In the beginning, all landholdings in the tribe were of equal size, the owner of the landholding being called *Daftri*. However, in times of drought or the loss of agricultural livestock, the farmers were forced to borrow money from the tribal chief on interest. The only collateral they could offer was the little land they held. Once it was handed over, its retrieval was very difficult. Gradually, therefore, almost all land in the tribe came to rest in the hands of the chief. Those who were once his equals became his tenants. No member of the tribe was entitled to sell his land.[12] It could only be used as a collateral within the tribe. As for adjacent rivers, mountains and grazing grounds, they continue to be in communal ownership, but it is the tribal chief who principally benefits from them.

Even after they had lost it, the primeval ties of the former owners with what had been their land did not entirely snap. In any case, it was difficult for a dispossessed farmer to go and join another tribe, because no matter how long he lived among them, he was always treated as a stranger, if not a beggar. In his own tribe, despite his poverty, he was at least not treated as an outsider. It is important to mention here that the landless peasant never felt that the chief had dispossessed him of his land. He believed that his former land or the land that once belonged to his forefathers was in the temporary possession of his chief because he or his ancestors had failed to honour a debt. To claim ownership on property which was mortgaged was considered 'un-Islamic'. The Afghan feudal lord, therefore, was also the chief or *sardar* of the tribe. His tenants all belonged to his tribe and were joined to him in a social contract of long, historical standing. Despite the rise of feudalism, old tribal customs based on social equality were not phased out. In tribal *jirgas* or in the sardar's *hujra* or private chambers, the landless peasant was treated as a social equal.

The feudal lord in the Indian subcontinent was an outsider. The Turkoman, Mughal or Afghan kings either owned local lands personally or gave them to locals who were loyal to them. The British continued this tradition. Those who remained loyal to them were generously rewarded with gifts of land and became *zamindars* or *jagirdars*.[13] However, in India between the landlord and the peasant there were no common ties of race, tribe, caste or culture. Here the landlord was a state-appointed owner of local and indigenous wealth. The relationship between the feudal lord and the peasant was one between the ruler and the ruled. The subsequent peasant revolts in India are to be seen in this light.

In Afghanistan, by contrast, the feudal lord or the Khan was very much a part of the social and tribal system. He acted not only as the economic lord and master of the peasants, but was at the same time their unquestioned military, tribal and administrative leader. The Khan's elevated position was an immutable fact of tribal life, and it was unthinkable for his indebted and loyal followers to break their established links with him.

The role played by the institution of Mullahism in a tribal society is so important that unless it is clearly understood, any effort to analyze the tribal system will be doomed to failure. In Afghan society, the Mullah, instead of being an unemployed, unpropertied pariah, dependent for his livelihood on the crumbs he was thrown from the feudal chief's table, occupied an influential religious, social and economic position. Throughout Afghanistan, excepting Nooristan province, a great deal of spiritual and temporal authority has been associated with the person of the Mullah. (The advent of Islam in Nooristan is only a century old, hence the Mullah's lack of acceptance in that society). A careful analysis of Pushtun social history reveals that it is the Mullah who is the father of the feudal system. The Mullah came to the Pushtuns with Islam. In order to honour the man who recited the sacred word, in Pushtun tribes, a piece of communal land was earmarked for the Mullah and given over to him. This land was known as *seri*. Not only was the size of this holding larger than that cultivated by ordinary members of the tribe, but in time of war or tribal conflict, the Mullah was exempt from military duties. It was he who first established the institution of tenancy in tribal society. His tenants were members of other tribes who had either sought refuge or been vanquished. There is not a single example in Afghan history of a Mullah being dispossessed of his *seri* lands. He cannot be compared to his poor counterpart in the Indian subcontinent who is chucked out of his post if he is unable to sound the call of prayer in a mellifluous voice. In Afghanistan, Mullahism has been like a sacred dynasty. The Mullah in Afghan society was mostly of Arab racial stock and even if otherwise, he was made a Syed, or a descendant of the Holy Prophet Mohammed. Gankovsky writes:

> Here it is important to note that Muslim theologians were the first to form into a privileged estate of the Pushtun society, and it was they who made the first breach in the system of agrarian relationships based on common landownership ... *seri* – a land benefice granted to the clergy can and must be regarded as the initial form of feudal land tenure.[14]

Ideologies, systems or religions brought in from another country not only change the host environment and society in profound ways, but in the process change themselves. There are many instances in history where an imported religion left intact a large body of pre-existing custom, tradition or belief, and modified its own original character. When Islam moved beyond its Arab frontiers, it confronted such pre-existing forces, and, consequently, the Mullah interpreted and applied Islam in line with the Afghan social and ethical value system. In Islam, for instance, there is provision for the forgiveness of a murderer or acceptance of monetary or material compensation in lieu of the blood shed. Since Afghan society believed in 'an eye for an eye', the Mullah made it a part of the Islamic system of belief.[15]

Islam expressly forbids usury or the taking or giving of interest. Since in Afghanistan one basis of feudal power was the interest system which helped the tribal chief acquire and annex land belonging to poorer members of the tribe, the Afghan Mullah decided that there was nothing objectionable or un-Islamic about the institution of usury. The Afghan feudalist, taking full advantage of this divine sanction, felt free to exploit his landless peasantry at will. The average ratio of interest was a staggering 25 per cent per year. During the 1972 famine, feudal chiefs are known to have extended credit to starving peasants at up to 400 per cent of the loan taken.[16]

The role played by the Mullah in consolidating the feudal system in Afghanistan is far greater than that played by the country's Saddozai, Barakzai or Mohammedzai rulers. It is almost impossible even today to convince an Afghan peasant that what he has paid the tribal sardar by way of interest over the years is many times more than the original sum of money borrowed, for the simple reason that the Mullah has made him believe that unless he liquidates his debt to the chief, he will not be allowed to enter heaven after he dies, but hung upside down from the sky.

The position of women in Afghanistan is perhaps even more helpless than that of animals. All Afghan nationalities faithfully practise the 'Islamic' tradition of purchase and sale of women. Child marriage is also considered in keeping with the teachings of Islam. The Mullah has ordained that nothing pleases God more than that a man should take four wives. Women are sold like cattle with full 'divine' sanction.[17] In Afghanistan, it is the bride's father who receives money in return for his daughter. In the subcontinent, it is the bridegroom's father who receives both a wife for his son and gifts that must accompany her. Both institutions, although diametrically opposed, have been sanctioned as 'Islamic' by the Mullah.

By means of this integration of old tribal customs and feudal traditions into religion, the Afghan Mullah made Islam extremely simple for the common man: to the average Afghan, it consists of offering five prayers a day and fasting for one month in a year. Haj, the pilgrimage to Islam's holy places in Mecca, is beyond his financial abilities. Consequently, all the Hajis, as those who have performed the holy pilgrimage are called, in Afghanistan are either Mullahs or the big Khans who have fattened themselves on usury. Amir Amanullah Khan's failed social reforms actually ended up strengthening Mullahism. In Nadir Khan and Zahir Shah's time, the Mullah was even given the additional honour of teaching children in village schools. An American author, expressing praise for this step, writes:

> The present dynasty has achieved a large share of its stability from having successfully incorporated religious specialists into government service and by emphasizing the religious components of its authority. The regime has set out to enlist the clergy's support in the process of state building and profiting from Amanullah's example it has succeeded to a large degree.[18]

To understand Afghan rural society, it is essential to keep in view the government's administrative structure. It is based on three pillars: the province, the district and the sub-district. The sub-district is the most important unit in the sense that it deals directly with the rural population. It is headed by a junior official called *Ilaqadar* who can match the tribal sardar or feudal lord in terms neither of armed men nor tribal influence. Without the cooperation of the tribal hierarchy, he cannot collect government land revenue dues, nor recruit soldiers for the national army. He has always been seen as an 'external' presence who should not be allowed to interfere with tribal autonomy. A small misjudgement on his part can lead to a tribal uprising and, more often than not, he will be its first victim. For all practical purposes, he is half administrator, half ambassador who operates on the principle of live and let live.

To sum up, until the April Revolution, the rural population of Afghanistan lived in a free, semi-autonomous state. Secondly, due to tribal custom and tradition there existed an intricate relationship between feudal lord and the peasant which could not be understood on the mere basis of productive agrarian relations. Thirdly, the Mullah was not only the spiritual and religious force behind the feudo-tribal system, but, in a way, its creator. Without making any attempt to understand these intricacies, the Marxist intellectuals of the PDPA proclaimed in the Party manifesto that the major contradictions were those between 'the people and imperialism' rather than those between peasant and feudal lord. Such clear, compartmentalized distinctions were academic and unrealistic in the objective conditions of Afghanistan – an over-simplification of both Marxism and their own society.

In 1978, the share of industry in Afghan GNP was 17 per cent,[19] which, according to a Soviet writer, 'could meet but 10 to 15 per cent of the home demand for textiles, sugar and so on.'[20] The bulk of the industrial sector was in public ownership. Private manufacture of such goods as socks, shoes, textiles, clarified butter, sugar and cotton ginning was mostly controlled by foreign companies, many of them Pakistani.[21] The Afghan 'national trader' was confined to the traditional trade in dried fruits and carpets. What he earned through exports, he spent on importing foreign goods. The number of workers in indigenous trades was greater than that of industrial workers.[22] In 1978, total industrial labour in Afghanistan was around 40,000, nearly 70 per cent of it in Kabul alone.[23] Qanduz, with its clarified butter and sugar factories, employed 22 per cent of the workers. In other words, industry, or what there was of it, was confined to Kabul and Qanduz. 39 per cent of the industrial workers were associated with textiles and cotton ginning, 11 per cent with the cement and minerals industry and between 7 and 9 per cent with food processing, construction, minerals and power-generating industries.[24] In February 1986, a survey of privately-owned industry conducted by the Politburo estimated the number of such units at 474, representing 11 per cent of industrial production: the share of handicraft products was higher than that of industrially produced ones.[25]

One of the major sources of government revenues consisted of business and trade taxes. According to 1966 figures, the contribution of direct land revenue taxes to national taxes was 3.5 per cent, while customs duties imposed on imports and exports accounted for 27 per cent. Income tax and corporate tax brought in 8.5 per cent.[26] The meagre income from land revenues proves that large landholdings were taxed in name only. Any increase in land revenues, it was felt, would cause disaffection in rural areas. In 1977-78, despite government attempts and professions, there was no increase in income from this source. That year, direct taxes accounted for 46 per cent.[27] Fifteen per cent of the GNP was derived from trade and in terms of exports, Afghanistan was at the bottom of the list of forty-two of the world's least developed countries. The bulk of exports consisted of livestock and foodstuffs. After 1968, gas exports to the Soviet Union became the largest foreign exchange earner.[28] No Afghan city was equipped to make use of gas for private or industrial purposes. The manufacturing industry which accounted for 21 per cent of the GNP, employed only 1.9 per cent of the national workforce.[29]

In terms of per capita income, Afghanistan was one of the most backward countries in the world and the distribution of income was so uneven that 40 per cent of the population was under-nourished and ill-housed. The annual increase in national income was 0.7 per cent, while annual growth in population was 2.55 per cent. In 1971, a World Bank report, expressing dismay over Afghanistan's situation, said:

> Pessimism is justified as even in areas where development activities are undertaken with heavy inputs of capital investment and foreign advice, returns have been dismally low.[30]

Afghanistan was perhaps the world's only country where 50 per cent of the import–export trade was conducted through smuggling.[31] Afghan traders would import large quantities of luxury goods and after duly paying duty on the consignments, would just as duly smuggle them to Pakistan, where the upper and middle classes have always considered any imported item nothing short of a sacred relic, no matter how exorbitant the price.[32] The great smuggling market some years ago used to be Landi Kotal in the Khyber Pass. It has now moved and proliferated in Pakistan's principal cities, including the notorious Sohrab Goth at Karachi. From Pakistan, goods like clarified butter, sugar, flour and cotton cloth were smuggled to Afghanistan. In 1973, while there was an acute shortage of clarified butter in Pakistan, it was selling in abundance in the bazaars of Kabul. Kabul's famous illegal foreign exchange market was the backbone of the smuggling trade. It was run by Hindus and Sikhs of Indian origin. Before the establishment of the first Afghan bank in 1930, these currency traders played that role. The government could only put an end to their activities if it either had adequate reserves of foreign exchange itself or was in a position to offer a better deal. Since it was not equipped to do either, the few efforts it made to close down the black market did not meet with success. Ultimately, the government came to accept the role of the black market in Afghan trade, and today it is still allowed to operate freely. It is in the writer's personal knowledge that on several occasions, the government itself has purchased dollars from the black market in Kabul to meet its requirements.[33] Until 1980, there was hardly any difference between the official exchange rate of the dollar and the one quoted in the open market. The arrival of the Red Army and the ensuing civil war proved the last straw for the sick Afghan economy. In 1983, while the central bank of Afghanistan (Da Bank Afghanistan) was offering a purchase rate of 55 Afghanis (the unit of currency) for one dollar, in the black market it fetched 130 Afghanis.[34] In 1984, the ratio between the central bank and the open market dollar rate was 60:200.[35]

In August 1983, Afghan Finance Minister Mehrabuddin Paktiawal told the author that the government had made huge gains in external trade and was using some of the profits to subsidize export corporations. Earlier, the government had set up corporations to export carpets and Qaraquli wool which were being run by bureaucrats. On further questioning, the writer learned from the Minister that these official export corporations were paid for their exports by the central bank at the official rate of 55 Afghanis to the dollar, while the open market rate of the dollar was 130 Afghanis. This 'difference' was the 'huge gains' Paktiawal was bragging about. It was no more than a game being played with figures on a piece of paper.

In any case, in a country where 50 per cent of the goods available in stores are smuggled and where almost 90 per cent of what is sold is foreign-manufactured, it is very difficult to find 'patriotic' traders. If, against this economic background, one analyzes the most important clause in the PDPA manifesto, namely the establishment of a 'united national front', which the Party's Marxist intellectuals needed to go beyond the initial national democratic phase, the ideological bankruptcy of the Party becomes evident – as witness this 1966 Khalq call:

> In the name of the primordal national and human duty, all the progressive and democratic forces, the workers, the farmers, the craftsmen, the progressive intellectuals, small and medium-size landlords and national capitalists and traders [are] to be united to form a national government.[36]

In 1978, when the PDPA came to power, with the exception of a few 'progressive' intellectuals, it could hardly find any small and medium-size landowners or national capitalists to form a united front. The working class was unorganized and there were no professional bodies or associations of doctors, lawyers, journalists, writers, teachers or artists. The peasants, those with land and those without it, were inextricably ensnared in the feudo-tribal system. The 'progressive and democratic forces' whose unity alone could guarantee the Revolution's success, did not exist. The April Revolution had been engineered in a political and ideological vacuum. Amin was not so wrong when he said:

> If we had waited to follow the same class pattern of working-class revolution through a national democratic bourgeoisie, then we would have followed such a long and thorny road that it would have required not only years but centuries.[37]

This statement by Amin, issued only two weeks after the Revolution, despite its exaggerated tone, does convey the lack of class formation which characterized Afghan society. That is why the Khalq group said a quick farewell to the ideal of the 'united national front' after the Revolution. In June 1978, Taraki told the Iraqi News Agency in an interview that the Party would not set up a joint front with any outside group.[38] He said the formation of such a front would slow down the process of reform. In truth, however, there was simply no organized force from which to forge such a united front. All he had was his coterie of conspiring middle-class Marxists.

Under the circumstances, the only course open for the PDPA was to declare itself as the 'national government' in the name of the people. This was done a week after the Revolution. The announcement giving an outline of the government's 'revolutionary duties' stated that this 'national government' would protect the interests of peasants, workers, nomadic workers, small and middle-level traders, national capitalists, soldiers, officers and patriotic *ulema* or religious leaders.[39] Khalq and Parcham claimed that their membership at the time of the Revolution numbered between 7,000 and 10,000.[40] Within a few months, however, the Party's 'iron man' was announcing that:

> In the great April Revolution, in spite of the fact that it triumphed according to the general and particular laws of the epoch-making ideology of the working class, the army played the major role of the proletariat, that is the powerful centre of the victory.[41]

Amin also said that the Party, which was the 'vanguard' of the working class, had equipped the army with the 'ideological weapon', thus enabling it to make up for the absence of the proletariat.

The proletariat is a technical term used by Marx for industrial workers. The army comprised soldiers who were the product of a tribal-feudal system and who were in uniform because under the law anyone over the age of eighteen was obliged to do national service. Perhaps Amin thought that once an Afghan officer had completed his training with the Soviet army, he could also be said to have gone through all the historical stages in the genesis of industrial labour.

At all events, only ten months after the April Revolution, Amin had laid claim to its being a 'proletarian Revolution', a claim which did not go unnoticed in the Soviet Union. A commentary published in a Soviet journal in 1979 said:

> The national democratic revolution was carried through on April 27th by the Afghan army supported by the broad masses. It was headed by the PDPA which is, as its document records, 'a party of the working class'.[42]

Clearly, the Soviet Union regarded the April Revolution as a national democratic and not a proletarian revolution. The Afghan army had brought it about through revolutionary action, but according to Soviet thinking, the Afghan army was not a substitute for the proletariat.

Again, the PDPA was not the 'vanguard' of the working classes but a party of the working classes. The term 'vanguard' is only to be used for communist parties. However, the Soviet description of the April Revolution as a 'national democratic revolution' was generous, because it was still miles away even from that stage.

The revolutions in Ethiopia, South Yemen, Libya, Kampuchea and Afghanistan shared common tribal and social elements. In Libya, Kampuchea and Afghanistan, the army captured power and in South Yemen and Kampuchea the national liberation movement led the forces of change. Except in Libya, it was the communist parties which inherited the revolution. However, without making a scientific analysis of their tribal, pre-tribal and feudal history, they tried to impose the 'national democratic front' concept on their revolutions. The resultant famines and civil wars in these countries have made revolution a terrifying visitation for the rest of the Third World. The tragedy of these parties lies in the fact that instead of fashioning the revolution in accordance with their national requirements and priorities, they try to follow the beaten track of officially-approved Marxism which lays down that Third World revolutions have to pass through the 'national democratic phase' before reaching the socialist heaven.

If the PDPA had remembered that 85 per cent of the people of Afghanistan were still an integral part of the ancient tribal culture with its collectivism and social equality, it would not have made the mistake of jumping headlong from the mountain of 'reforms', but shown some understanding of social forces and established ways of life.

The Party should have realized that the concepts of joint ownership of land and collective exercise of power bore many similarities to Afghan custom, practice and tradition. These Marxist intellectuals should have known that the local *jirga* was the focal point of rural life in Afghanistan which could be compared to a genuine 'people's congress' or 'popular parliament'. Not only was every male member of the community a member of this people's congress or *jirga* in the Afghan system, but he expected it to protect his rights and provide him with justice. He was also bound by honour and tradition to respect its decisions. The landless peasants and smallholders the Marxist theoreticians of the Party were looking for on the streets of Kabul could all have been easily found on the platform of the local *jirga*. The rural areas already had their people's congresses. What the Party needed to do was to try to enlist their support for the Revolution. It should have declared these popular assemblies where people took their own decisions the fountainhead of power and left them to administer their areas and the lives of their people. If the Party had accepted the authority of the local congresses and given them full executive authority to manage their affairs, it could have put an end to the suspicion, uncertainty and prejudice which came to blight its relations with the rural masses. The failure of the PDPA to understand this basic fact of Afghan life created a wall between it and the masses which no amount of official directives from the Marxist leaders sitting in Kabul could ever hope to demolish. If the Party had been able to find its way to the people, Hafizullah Amin would not have had to tell his frustrated workers:

> If the people of Afghanistan do not believe in promises you should not be depressed ... work and discharge your duties in such a way that you win the confidence of the people. The confidence of the people cannot be won only through radio and newspapers.[43]

The only way the confidence of the people could have been won was through associating them with the running of the country. However, a Party weighed down by the heavy burden of all its accumulated power could hardly be expected to do anything more imaginative that make crude propaganda through radio, television and newspapers.

Traditionally, the most important task of the local *jirga* had been to distribute land among the members of the tribe in equal measure. If the Party had seriously tried to breathe new revolutionary life into this old but effective institution, its land reform programme (which involved distribution of land among the landless) could have been effectively implemented by the local *jirgas*. For them, this would have been neither new nor unknown, nor irreligious nor un-tribal. Had the Party made the tribal *jirgas* part of the power structure, it could have politicized them to the extent that they themselves would have demanded revolutionary reform. Had the Party had even the remotest idea of what people's rule stood for, it would not only have requested the local *jirgas*, which represented 90 per cent of the country's poor farmers, to decide upon the nature of the reforms needed by the Afghan people, but also asked them to implement those reforms. To sum up, the local *jirga* alone was the weapon the Party could have used to defeat feudalism. However, the romanticist Taraki, who dreamt about inducting Afghanistan's peasants into the communist party in order to free them from the stultifying hold of tribal society, was lecturing his workers on the peasantry in Kabul:

> Peasants are a nice lot. They do not nourish ill feelings in their hearts. Their only drawback is that they are illiterate. Do not talk too much about the theory, but tell them about the benefits they draw from the state and the Party.[44]

12

Reforms and their Aftermath

The old Khalq-Parcham in-fighting dominated the first two months of the Revolution. Finally, in the middle of July, the Party unveiled its land reforms through what came to be known as Decree No. 6. The declared objective of the Decree was to free landless farmers of the vicious circle of compound interest and secure the release of all mortgaged lands up to five acres. It was assumed by the government that every plot which produced two crops a year brought in enough income to pay for 20 per cent of its value. On that basis, five acres of mortgaged land could be said to have repaid to the holder its total value, or the sum of money extended to the owner at the time the mortgage was enacted, after a lapse of five years. The land, having liquidated the debt raised against it, should be returned to the original owners, who had repaid debts raised against their land at a rate of 20 per cent for a period of five years.

Agriculture Minister Saleh Mohammed Zeary was of the view that through this measure nearly 81 per cent of the rural population would stand to benefit directly. The five-acre limit was based on the fact that 71 per cent of all landholdings in the country were below that ceiling. The holders of these small units had been forced to mortgage their sole asset to big or middle-size landlords.[1] Mortgaged lands above the five-acre ceiling were not affected by the Decree. It was a wise, fair and humane decision, based as it was on the unexceptionable assumption that an owner who had paid interest against his mortgaged land for five years, could be said to have met fully his contracted financial obligations. It also had the added virtue of not being overly harsh or vengeful against the big landowning Khans. The Party must have calculated that through one single enactment it would win over the vast majority of Afghanistan's rural population, which would become the bedrock of the Revolution. Had the Party tried to win the support of the rural masses before the actual announcement, the results would not have belied its expectations.

To implement the Decree, the Party set up a committee in every district, which, in turn, was placed under the overall control of a provincial committee, headed by the Governor. The focal point of the reforms was the village, but such was the Party's lack of organization that it was not even in a position to set up sub-district committees or units to see the reforms through. The Party also announced, rather grandiloquently, that every district committee would contain two peasant representatives. As to where the Party was going to get hold of two peasants with the ability to deal with such an intricate task, let it be said that there was no intention ever to associate peasants with the operation directly. Almost everywhere, the two 'peasant representatives' were school teachers co-opted by the local district administration.[2] The education department in the district was also an *ex-officio* member of the committee, turning it, in effect, into an assemblage of Party officials and school teachers.

Since almost all land mortgage deals were made on the basis of oral contracts, nearly 80 per cent of the mortgaged lands had no written or documented record.[3] Secondly, district officials had always been considered representatives of the central authority and any form of cooperation with them was seen as nothing short of treachery to local traditions and institutions. Thirdly, in a society so deeply rooted in the tribal way of life, the arrival of district officials in the company of police and army to read out a decree issued in the remote capital Kabul, was a most inappropriate method of implementing a measure which was basically good.

The plight of more than 80 per cent of Afghanistan's population can be imagined from the fact that though the country's first agricultural bank was established in King Zahir Shah's time, it did not have a single branch outside Kabul.[4] In any case, the bank's main beneficiaries were only big landlords and feudal Khans. The smallholders and landless peasants could only seek financial help from usurious nomads, traders, tribal Khans and profiteers at inhumanly exorbitant interest rates.

One main cause of the failure of the Decree was that as soon as it was issued, professional moneylenders stopped extending loans to their impoverished clients. The government, of course, had issued the Decree first and thought about providing the peasants with fertilizer, seed or alternate credit facilities only afterwards. Not until August 1978 was the formation of a farmers' relief fund and a farmers' cooperative was announced.[5] However, because of the Party's lack of experience, rampant inefficiency and limited resources, these measures failed to fill the gap created by the moneylenders' moratorium on fresh lending.[6]

The establishment of rural banks should have preceded land reforms, but the PDPA's Marxist intellectuals were men in a hurry. The limited number of farmers who had managed to regain possession of their lands as a result of the Decree were soon forced to re-mortgage them to the old moneylenders. In some cases, they even offered to honour debts which the Decree had liquidated.

The unholy marriage between Islam and usury perfected by Afghan tribal society could only have been dissolved through careful preparation by the Party. A few primary school teachers, local bureaucrats and executive decisions were not enough to end this alliance. Those directly hit by the Decree – big Khans, feudal lords and usurers – soon joined hands to resist the change. As so often in history, it was the Mullah who agreed to lend his services to the unholy cause by declaring that the return of mortgaged land after a lapse of five years was a 'cardinal sin'. While this united the counter-revolutionary forces on one platform, the Party was unable to enlist the support of its natural friends, the farmers, landless peasants and smallholders.

Leaving the mess created by the land reform Decree where it was, the Party came out with yet another Decree five and a half months after the Revolution.[7] Decree No. 7, as it was called, related to the rights of women. Child marriages were declared illegal, the minimum marriageable age for boys being set at 18 and for girls at 16. It also laid down that the consent of the parties entering wedlock was essential. The most important – and controversial – aspect of the Decree was the maximum limit of 300 Afghanis (nine dollars) it placed on *haq mehr*, the money payable to the wife in case of dissolution of the contract. In other words, the despicable practice of purchase and sale of women was now forbidden by law. In terms of western standards of women's rights, this may have been no more than a simple reformist step, but in the context of the conservative Afghan society, it was a revolutionary change. The trade in women was perhaps the greatest tragedy of Afghan society, though it had the sanction and acceptance of all classes, tribes and nationalities. The sum realized through the sale of a woman was considered a symbol of her purity and social position. Whatever its financial and social position, every family, rich or poor, had abided by this inhuman code for centuries as if it were a providential law. Some American writers are wrong when they argue that it was the Afghan Pushtuns who, due to their dominant position, influenced other nationalities and ethnic minorities to adopt this despicable custom. The practice of selling women was prevalent in many tribal and feudal cultures which had no contact with Pushtun society. In this context, one can cite Arabs, Kurds, Uzbeks, Baluchis, Turkomans and Tajiks who were never part of Afghanistan. Before the advent of Islam, this inhuman practice was so much a part of Arab life that the greatest pre-Islamic poet, Antari, writing about the most beautiful woman of his time, says that she was married in return for a hundred white camels. To put an end to this barbaric practice, the Holy Prophet set the amount of his daughter's *haq mehr* at a most nominal figure. He maintained the ritual, and without directly challenging the traditional tribal code of honour, demonstrated through personal example that from now on, the practice was to be followed in name only.

In the more modern environment of the capital Kabul, the Decree was viewed favourably. For the first time in Afghan history, young couples were able to get married in a civil ceremony and of their own accord. There were, however, instances of Party workers misusing the new liberal legislation to enter into forced marriages. These stories were widely circulated by reactionary opponents of the regime to discredit the Party for its high-handed ways and lack of respect for tradition. The Party cadres were not entirely without blame, of course. Some of them made use of the new law to take second wives, in some cases against the wishes of the women concerned.

In the rural areas, the Decree affected both the high and the low. By tradition, marriages were made in the open atmosphere of the *jirga*, where both families had the opportunity to come to an amicable and mutually suitable settlement. Once the precise sum of the *haq mehr* was agreed between the two families, none of the parties was expected to go back on the arrangement. However, district officials began to make arrests across the country for violation of Decree No. 7. This was done indiscriminately. Many marriages objected to had been arranged before the coming into force of the Decree. As was to be expected, the majority of the victims of the enthusiasm of the authorities consisted of poor and powerless farmers and landless farm workers.

In Afghanistan, a kind of 'barter system' had also long been practised in the marriage market. Two families would exchange sons for daughters-in-law or sons-in-law for daughters on a one-to-one basis. The young people whose fate was thus decided were not asked for their opinions. The irony of the new situation was that within their own families, the Marxist leaders of the Party were not willing to abide by the Decree's provisions. A few days before the Decree's coming into force, a 'barter' marriage deal was finalized between Hafizullah Amin and his brother, Abdullah Amin. Hafizullah's eldest daughter Ghaurgati was to be married to Abdullah's son Asadullah Amin in return for the hand of Abdullah's daughter for Hafizullah's son, Abdul Rahman Amin. Amin's daughter was not interested in the marriage because she was fond of a young Kabul non-Pushtun named Rafiq.[8] Ghaurgati, under great family pressure, finally came up with what she thought was an impossible condition. She told her father that she would marry her cousin only if Ahmed Zahir, the popular Kabul pop singer, would give a concert on her wedding day at their house.[9] Zahir was in jail at the time, charged with his wife's murder. However, for Amin, this was not a difficult thing to arrange. He had Zahir released. The unhappy marriage lasted fourteen months. Asadullah was hanged in June 1980 following Amin's murder.[10]

If the American-educated Marxist Amin had not proved able to comply with Decree 7 when it came to his own daughter's choice, how could he have expected the poor, backward, illiterate people of Afghanistan to change their tribal ways when it came into force? It is a further irony that while the PDPA was issuing loud and eloquent statements about the rights of women, there was not a single member of the Central Committee or the new cabinet who was a woman.[11]

In November 1978, the Party issued another Decree (No. 8) relating to land reforms.[12] The new measure placed the size of the maximum land holding at fifteen acres. The Decree further nationalized all sources of irrigation, leaving the Ministry of Agriculture and the Land Reform Commission to determine the allocation of water resources. Locally, the work was to be handled by village cooperatives and water supply departments. These organizations were also authorized to borrow money from the Agricultural Bank to finance their operations. Since these new institutions had been created at exactly the same time as the Decree, it goes without saying that they lacked both expertise and experience.

The upper limit of fifteen acres on land holdings meant that 50 per cent of the total agricultural land in the country would be available to the government for redistribution. Under the Decree, the repossessed lands were to be given to landless peasants and those with holdings below five acres. The government believed that with the implementation of the Decree, 81 per cent of the total rural population would stand to benefit directly.[13]

In July 1978, the government had set up district-level committees on peasant problems. The real task of these bodies was to survey agricultural lands,[14] – a task which it preposterously claimed at the time of issuing Decree No. 8 in late November 1978 had already been completed.[15] It was the PDPA government's belief that 40 per cent of the country's agricultural land was never cultivated because of a lack of such basic facilities as seed, fertilizer and water, not to mention the crippling feudal factor. The Party leaders were labouring under the illusion that if, as a result of their land reforms, this uncultivated land could be made productive, Afghanistan would become self-sufficient in food.

The Party once again set up district-level implementation committees consisting of enthusiastic but inexperienced city youth, who would alight on villages, gather the poor inhabitants together and regale them with speeches dripping with praise for the 'Great Leader'. At the end of these ceremonies, peasants were handed out land title deeds. By the evening, the revolutionaries would return to base, happy in the thought that they had accomplished the ends of the great April Revolution. These over-motivated, urbanized young men, being totally unfamiliar with the dynamics of the tribal society they were trying to change, were often guilty of grave errors. In one instance, a Party worker used derogatory language about the local landlord. One of the peasants who was among the recipients of the land title deeds reprimanded him for his lack of respect for the Khan. There was an altercation and the Party worker was shot dead. The next day, the police moved in, making indiscriminate arrests. Ironically, every arrested peasant had earlier been given the title to his formerly mortgaged land.[16] According to the writer's information, many similar incidents took place across the country, again testifying to the Party's failure to understand the nature of the entrenched authority of the feudal lord.

As stated elsewhere, there were roughly 400 big landowning families in Afghanistan. These handful of feudalists inflicted a humiliating defeat on 100,000 armed soldiers, 80,000 policemen and thousands of zealous Party workers because, small though their number was, they were among the country's most influential political, social and spiritual leaders. In the last category, there were hundreds of thousands of devoted followers of men like Mian Gul, Mujadaddi, and Gilani. And, of course, the religious establishment headed by the Mullahs was fully on the side of the threatened but powerful minority.

Side by side with these basic reforms, the government also set a literacy campaign in motion. It was headed by Shah Mohammed Hussain with a woman, Dil Ara Mehak, as his deputy. This organization was staffed by 510 teachers and 60 supervisors. In July 1978, it announced that 6,000 army soldiers would be taught to read and write by their officers.[17] The government actually believed that in a period of five years, it would root out illiteracy from the country. After about eighteen months, the target date was extended by another five years.[18]

Reformist governments generally use the 'crusade against illiteracy' as a means of propagating their ideas. If the Party had used its brains and done some planning, the literacy centres it set up could have been employed to familiarize the masses with the Party manifesto and politics. This would have given its cadres an opportunity to understand rural problems and, at the same time, it would have helped create popular support for the Party and its programme among the people.

However, the PDPA's Marxist intellectuals again acted like men in a hurry.

The basic teaching materials used by the literacy programme were no more than superficial propaganda where 'A' stood for Amin and 'T' stood for Taraki. The young Party volunteers from Kabul had also been assigned the delicate task of spreading education among rural women. These volunteer teachers, instead of taking up residence in the countryside, familiarizing themselves with the people they were supposed to be imparting literacy to and wearing the same clothes they did, used to arrive in droves on official transport, guarded by soldiers and policemen. They would set up shop in the village square, and while it was possible to assemble the men, when it came to women, things were not so simple. A city girl, wearing a skirt, showing her legs, was not exactly the villagers' idea of a teacher. They felt it was all a conspiracy to corrupt the morals of their women. The first armed confrontation between the government and the rural people occurred on this very question.

It is stated that in a village in Paktia province, the people refused, when asked, to send their women to the literacy centre. The team from Kabul, enraged at such a lack of respect for its revolutionary mission, ordered the accompanying guards to bring the women forcibly to the centre. As the soldiers tried to break into homes to get the women out, the villagers started firing. All members of the Kabul party, along with their guards, were killed. The news of the clash spread quickly and in a few days the entire area was in the grip of a rebellion against the PDPA government.[19] The Mullahs, grateful for the godsent opportunity to discredit the government further, began to issue *fatwas* or religious edicts, charging the government with the spread of 'shamelessness' and irreligiosity. The Party, once again, instead of learning a lesson from the situation, denounced the reaction as counter-revolutionary. In 1979, Amin described the resistance being offered to female literacy as 'unimportant', adding that had the government not been short of resources, it would have sent every Afghan woman to school. Looking back, one can see that the Party's instant reform programme carried the seeds of self-destruction. To quote Amin:

> No matter what the cost is, we shall do away with the roots of feudalism and imperialism and have resolved to launch the first and most important projects for the advancement and well-being of the people ... namely land reforms in the interest of landless farmers and farmers with meagre landholdings.[20]

The Party, which had launched its programme on 15 July 1978, was claiming exactly one year later that it had fully implemented its package of social and agricultural reforms.[21] The PDPA intellectuals were obviously at pains to set up a new world record.[22] However, on the ground, the situation was somewhat different. In many areas, peasants had refused to take over lands given to them. There were also cases where peasants who had taken possession were punished for their 'treachery' by the landlords by having their standing crops burnt and even their ears chopped off.[23] The Party had no presence at all in the rural regions. All it could do was to order military operations which amounted to playing into the hands of the forces of reaction.

Many tribal chiefs, with their followers in tow, began to move across the border to Pakistan, where the new but tottering military regime welcomed them with open arms because it provided the junta with a cause to perpetuate and ultimately consolidate its rule. Despite its own considerable economic difficulties, the Pakistani government put every arriving Afghan on a daily stipend of four rupees (then about half a dollar), more than the average income of a common Afghan. This 'generous help' was intended to attract more and more Afghans to come to Pakistan. One cannot but recall that in 1976-77, the Pakistan government had earmarked a total sum of $24.6 million for its entire tribal areas, while in 1978 alone, it spent $145 million in 'humanitarian assistance' to the incoming Afghans. By 1978, according to official Pakistani figures, 80,000 Afghan refugees had reached Pakistan.[24]

Agricultural production was severely hit by the unrest in the countryside in reaction to the reforms and the spreading strife. However, in Kabul, the Finance Minister was announcing happily that the wheat crop had been 'satisfactory'.[25] Under normal circumstances, Afghanistan imported 200,000 tons of wheat every year. In May 1979, after the crop was harvested, the government realized that there would be an acute food shortage. Taraki therefore announced that 300,000 tons of wheat was being purchased from abroad as a 'safety measure'.[26] At the end, as much as 350,000 tons was imported, which was 75 per cent more than the normal figure.

In September 1979, Amin told the nation that the wheat crop had been 'very good' and that the country would become 'self-sufficient' in food in a few years time.[27] However, six months later, Amin's successor Karmal was telling the people that out of a cultivable area of 9.5 million acres, only 8.75 million had been actually cropped. Consequently, the average yearly yield of 6.5 million tons had been reduced to 5.9 million tons. The shortfall in the cotton crop was 30 per cent and peanut production had fallen by 40 per cent. Total agricultural yield had dipped by 9 per cent.[28]

The Mullahs used these shortages to unleash highly poisonous propaganda against the government. One story which was quite common in the provinces was that, as a young man, Taraki had told his father that he would rather marry his own sister than a girl from outside the family.[29] What stories like this were supposed to demonstrate to the simple Afghan was that a communist was not only an enemy of God and his book, but had the morality of an animal. Although at his press conference on 4 May 1978, Taraki had denied that he or the PDPA were communist, what possible impact could a press conference have in a country where 90 per cent of the population could neither read nor write? In any case, the total Afghan media estabishment consisted of a few irregular city newspapers and a pathetic radio and TV station. Justice Minister Abdul Hakim Sharai Jozjani, to counter the campaign of the Mullahs against Taraki, had obtained a *fatwa* from another group of *ulema* that Taraki was a true Muslim. This certificate of legitimacy was broadcast every day by radio and television, beginning June 1978. However, this officially obtained Islamic medal could not counter the growing movement against Taraki and his Party. The people were already being incited by the Mullahs to wage *jihad* against the godless communists. One week before the announcement of the reforms and two months after the Revolution, Amin said in a speech:

> Those [he meant the Mullahs] who defend Islam will be regarded as the pupil of our eyes. Those who are merely engaged in worship ... and do not interfere in politics will be revered by all. But those who under the sacred name of Islam plot against the April Revolution, and are in the service of the enemies of the people, will be considered as traitors. We ... will crush them to the extent that they forget the bellows of Daud.[30]

While Amin was issuing this dire warning to the reactionaries, the Party leaders were making preparations to liquidate each other. Two days after this speech, Karmal left the country, bound for Prague. The Party was cutting off its nose to spite its face. It did not have the wisdom or the vision to identify its real friends and enemies. It had no weapons to fight the Mullahs. At best, it could stop their state stipends, wherever they existed, or have the individual trouble-makers bumped off, here and there. This, of course, only increased public hostility and instead of weakening the opposition's challenge strengthened it even more.

In September 1978, Taraki made a frontal attack on Mullahism, calling its leaders *Akhwan-ul-Shaitan* (Satan's brothers), the epithet used by Gamal Abdel Nasser against the *Akhwan-ul-Muslami* in Egypt.[31] In 1979, Jozjani obtained another *fatwa* from his friends in the religious establishment, the *Jamiat-ul-Islam*, which declared that *jihad* against religious reactionaries who followed in the footsteps of the *Akhwan-ul-Muslimi* had full religious sanction.[32] While this *fatwa* proved quite effective in the cities, it had no impact in the countryside where the real challenge had been mounted. The Party also used this edict to try to inspire the army's dispirited soldiers to rise against the reactionaries. The official media were also directed to use the *fatwa* to attack the Mullahs and their campaign. On TV (whose transmissions did not go beyond Kabul), it was made the basis of skits, songs and plays. One chorus broadcast regularly by both TV and radio had the refrain:

Lannat bar tu aye Akhwan-ul-Shaitan
(May the curse of God be upon you, you brothers of Satan)

At the beginning of 1979, the government ordered the arrest of many leading religious leaders. Hazrat Shor Bazar was picked up in January.[33] One of his nephews, Sibghatullah Mujadaddi, who was running a Saudi-sponsored 'Islamic mission' in Denmark, returned to Peshawar in October 1978 to set up his counter-revolutionary camp. His niece, interestingly enough, was the wife of Suleman Laiq, head of the Aloom Academy and member of the PDPA Central Committee. Another religious leader, Mian Gul Jan, fled to Pakistan in February 1979, accompanied by hundreds of his disciples (who were also his tenants).[34]

By 14 September 1979, the Khalq group stood divided in two camps. Taraki's successor had inherited not only the Presidency of the country and the leadership of the Party, but all the *fatwas* issued in favour of the 'Great Leader' as well. The only difference was that they were now broadcast with the name changed from Taraki to Amin. During its stay in power, the Khalq group never took the trouble to make a list of either its supporters or its enemies who were killed after the Revolution. However, after extensive conversations with Khalq leaders in Pulcharkhi prison, the writer learnt that during their time in power, as many as fifteen pro-government Mullahs were assassinated by the opposition. In 1983, the Karmal regime announced that forty-six leading *ulema* had been killed by anti-government forces.[35]

The Khalq government also set up an armed body called the National Organization for the Defence of the Revolution to fight the regime's enemies. Farmers who had benefited as a result of the land reforms were trained and given arms.

13

The December Treaty

Whether a revolution takes place in a tribal society like that of Afghanistan or in the more industrialized environment of eastern Europe, it cannot be kept alive in the name of the 'people' when they are neither its makers nor its beneficiaries or inheritors. When the entire material resources of the country are placed in the hands of the state, which in turn is under the iron trusteeship of a single political party, impervious to the people and unanswerable to them, it can only lead to the further strengthening of the intrinsically cannibalistic state apparatus and the deepening of popular hatred against the 'revolutionary' party. This is the greatest tragedy of the world communist movement.

The PDPA, like its counterparts elsewhere, believed that the participation of the people in the exercise of power could be achieved by herding them together with the help of Party bureaucrats into the central city square, giving them red banners to wave and asking them to raise full-throated slogans glorifying the Party. These Afghan Marxist intellectuals also believed that the accountability of the Party to those it ruled was contrary to Marxist ideology. Marxism here, as in North Korea, became a grotesque Stalinist parody.

After the Revolution, it took the Khalqite leadership only seven months – until the last week of November 1978 – to complete its 'reforms' and get rid of its Parchamite rivals. How long the Marxist leaders were able to remain complacent about their stewardship of the Revolution – the state-controlled media being their sole source of sustenance – is difficult to say. Caught up as the Party was in the whirlpool of political and financial difficulties, not to mention the gathering storm of revolts, it is possible that in its own inner councils, it had begun to realize its vulnerability. Despite its public claims, the new government had failed to energize the masses in support of the

Revolution. It had also failed to persuade the United States, China, Pakistan and Iran to end their opposition to the new order in Kabul. While financial help from the United States, other western countries and Saudi Arabia had dried up, enough money had already begun to flow to the regime's enemies. To counter these external and internal challenges, the regime turned to Moscow, but typically not to its own people. In December 1978, Taraki and Amin arrived in the Soviet capital at the head of a large delegation. The Afghan-Soviet Treaty of Cooperation and Friendship signed on 5 December was an offspring of the Afghan government's military, political, economic, cultural, ideological and psychological needs and shortcomings. It should be noted that both political observers and the normally sensitive western press were unable at the time to appreciate the consequences of a Treaty (as were Taraki and Amin) which was to change Afghanistan in internal and external terms. The western press did not take much notice of it, treating it as a routine development. After all, it was not the first such treaty signed by the Soviet Union with a Third World country. Not long before, a similar arrangement had been concluded by Moscow with Ethiopia.

Under one of the Treaty's articles, Afghanistan could call on Soviet military assistance in its hour of need. Exactly one year later, Amin was to invoke this article, only himself to become the first victim of the invited Red Army. It took only a few months to confine the April Revolution to the privacy of the living room of the former royal palace, while the 'Afghanistan problem' came to assume grave international proportions.

According to some members of the Afghan delegation to Moscow, when the Soviet draft was shown to Taraki, he looked at it casually, as was his wont, and said: 'I find nothing wrong with the general form of the Treaty. As for the details, my deputy Prime Minister Amin should be asked to work them out.'[1] The article relating to Soviet military assistance in time of need was subject to two amendments proposed by Amin. First, that any Soviet troops sent for by the Afghan government would serve under the command of Afghan officers, and second that their eventual return would be decided in accordance with the wishes of the host government. Khalq leaders state that the first amendment was considered 'unacceptable' by other members of the Afghan delegation itself, while the second amendment was modified to read that the recall of the invited Soviet troops would be decided with the mutual consent of the two governments.

After 1980 pro-Amin leaders imprisoned at Pulcharkhi cited these amendments as evidence of Amin's 'patriotic' attitude. For the Parchamites who succeeded Amin, the two amendments in question were tantamount to treachery to the land of Lenin, lack of faith in Brezhnev's proletarian leadership and a betrayal of the international communist movement.[2] However, the amendments proposed by Amin were typical of his character and policies. While on the one hand, when in power, he sought unconditional aid from the west for his 'neutral' country, on the other, he tried to use the state's socialist credentials to keep the Red Army at his beck and call. In February 1979, in an obvious gesture of reassurance to the west, Amin, the true policy-maker of the Khalq regime, described the Treaty with the Soviet Union as a continuation of its 1921 forerunner and, as such, representing no change.[3]

During Taraki's December 1978 Moscow visit, *New Times* ran biographical sketches, complete with pictures, of Amin and Akbar Shah Wali under the caption 'This Week's Personalities'. *New Times* is published under the direct supervision of the Foreign Relations Committee of the Soviet Communist Party and distributed worldwide in more than ten languages. The fact that it projected Amin and Shah Wali as international personalities at least proves one thing, namely that until 5 December 1978, the two men were not considered 'enemies' of the Soviet Union. A year would pass before they would be denounced as traitors, counter-revolutionaries and agents of the CIA.

Even before the signing of the December Treaty, large numbers of Soviet civilian and military advisers were present in Afghanistan. In fact, much of the expenditure of running the state was met from Soviet sources. Perhaps the Treaty was concluded to send a signal to counter-revolutionary elements to the effect that the new order at Kabul was irreversible. The Treaty was also an open warning to the United States and its satellite countries that if they did not desist from their support of counter-revolutionary forces, the Red Army could be brought in to defend the April Revolution. In Pakistan by 1978 eight training camps had been set up by the new military regime to turn simple Afghan refugees into guerillas. The first contingent, armed with Chinese weapons, entered Afghanistan's Kunnarha province under the flag of the Hizbe Islami.[4] According to western sources, the number of these armed insurrectionists was around 5,000. They attacked Asadabad, the principal town of the province, and successfully occupied an important and strategically-located fort.[5]

While under normal circumstances the Asadabad garrison should have been fully capable of dealing with the attack, it failed to do so because its military commander had already entered into a clandestine deal with the rebels. When the attack came, as agreed, he signalled his Jalalabad military headquarters requesting immediate ammunition supplies. Three helicopters soon arrived at Asadabad and after they were unloaded, he had them destroyed. He killed every political assistant posted with units under his command, and also organized an attack on the office of the Provincial Governor.

The name of this soldier of fortune was Abdul Rauf. He was later made guerilla commander of Kunnarha province by the Hizbe Islami.[7] (It should be noted here that the three provinces of Kunnarha, Panjsher and Ghazni, where the Kabul regime faced increasing military difficulties after 1980, had one thing in common. In all three, the rebel forces were led by former officers of the Afghan army, all of whom had been considered Khalq followers during the Revolution.[8] While Abdul Rauf from Kunnarha and Ahmed Shah Mahsud from Panjsher joined the rebels during the Khalq regime, the Ghazni commander did so after 1980.) The division based at Jalalabad was sent to Kunnarha to deal with the insurrection, but it failed to dislodge Abdul Rauf's brigade, now grown in size and fire power with help from across the border. Another effort to deal with the rebels was made when a commando brigade was air-dropped at Kunnarha under the command of Maj. Alamyar.[9] After heavy fighting, it was successful in pushing out Abdul Rauf and his men from their stronghold towards Pakistan.

Another important development took place on 14 February 1979, when between 8.30 and 9 a.m. four terrorists abducted US ambassador Dubb from a Kabul street and removed him to room 117 of the fashionable Hotel Kabul. These terrorists, who belonged to the Sitm-e-Milli group, had staged the abduction to obtain the release of their leaders Tahir Badakhshi, Majid, Quaiz, Faizant and Behruddin Bais.[10] The same evening, after seeing off the Iraqi Deputy Foreign Minister at the Kabul airport, Amin told ambassadors and newsmen that the men who had abducted Dubb were demanding the release of Behruddin Bais, a 'narrow-minded nationalist and an extreme-left adventurist'. He further told the envoys that Bais had been arrested in Daud's time, but had escaped during the 27 April revolutionary upheaval and that the government, as such, was unable to accede to the terrorists' demand.[11]

Amin's briefing to the ambassadors was either a crude example of naivety and ignorance or simple deceit. The Sitm-e-Milli workers, or Amin's 'narrow-minded nationalists and extreme-left adventurists', were not so stupid as to run the enormous risk of abducting the US ambassador if the man they wanted sprung had escaped from prison a year before. The facts were otherwise. When Daud took over in 1973, most of the political prisoners of earlier years, including Saleh Mohammed Zeary and Ghulam Dastgir Panjsheri, were set free. However, after the April Revolution, not a single political prisoner from Daud's times was released. During the author's many conversations with Pulcharkhi prison guards, he was told that most of

Daud's political prisoners were summarily killed after the April Revolution. Those who were lucky enough not to be executed were kept confined at Pulcharkhi.[12]

Since the regime was unwilling either to accept the existence of political prisoners in the first place or to release those it held, there appeared to be no likelihood of its negotiating with the terrorists, and so giving them an opportunity to have their point of view propagated worldwide. Although in the outlying provinces uprisings against the government had by now become routine, it was the first time any such incident had taken place in the capital. It was not only against the expectations of the government but beyond its tolerance too.

It is not therefore surprising that by 9.30 that morning, only half an hour after the abduction of the ambassador was reported, the government decided to storm the room in which the diplomatic hostage was being kept. By 10.30 a.m., the security forces had taken positions outside the hotel. The US embassy staff was told to act as mediator and inform the ambassador in the German language that he should hit the floor or run to the bathroom the moment he heard the first shots ring out. Afghan sources say that the US embassy staff refused to do any such thing.[13] Had they agreed, there might have been a slim chance of saving the envoy's life. However, the Americans believed until the end that the government would negotiate with the terrorists or, at least, take them (the Americans) into confidence before ordering the storming of the hotel. Embassy officials also wasted valuable time trying to reach Amin. At 12.30 sharp, room 117 was stormed by soldiers firing away their guns. Two terrorists and the ambassador were killed in the *mêlée*. A third terrorist was injured but captured alive. However, nothing was said about him officially, which suggests that he too was later killed. There is also some evidence that the fourth terrorist was captured at 9.30 in the morning, taken to the main detention centre and shot after brief questioning.[14] Old Pulcharkhi inmates and prison guards told the author that the unsuccessful abduction of the US ambassador sealed the fate of Tahir Badakhshi and other Sitm-e-Milli leaders who were all shot without the formality of a trial.[15]

On 5 March 1979 there was a major uprising in Herat. An angry mob attacked the office of Provincial Governor Nazifullah Nuzhat, causing him grave injuries.[16] The mob also attacked the Herat cantonment, forcing the inexperienced commander to pull out. Ammunition depots were ransacked and many military vehicles set on fire. The uprising became so massive that by 16 March, the city of Herat no longer had any links with the rest of the country.[17] Afghan Air Force planes, based at Shindan, were ordered to bomb the rebel stronghold. Troop reinforcements were also sent for from Kandhar and after three days of fierce fighting, the government was finally able to recapture Herat and re-establish control.[18]

The real cause of the uprising was the return of thousands of workers from Iran after the fall of the Shah. During his time, a large number of people from Herat were resident in Iran. The Shah had used them to set up clandestine branches of his secret service Savak in Afghanistan. Many of the Herati workers had also been given military training so as to act as a restraining force in case an Oman-like situation arose in Afghanistan threatening Iranian security.[19] It is an irony of history that many of these trained Herati workers, swept off their feet by the resurgent wave of Shi'aism, took an active part in the anti-Shah movement in Iran in 1978, leading the emperor to charge that the Afghan government had sent over trained guerillas to bring him down. Had Afghanistan only had enough trained guerillas to send contingents of them to destabilize the Shah, it would first have used them to solve its own problems.

The establishment of a religious government in Iran in February 1979 had succeeded in creating a great deal of religious fervour and revolutionary zeal among these out-of-work men who, like the Iranians, belonged to the Shi'a faith. The new government in Tehran had provided them both with arms and with open political support. When the Herat uprising was at its height, Ayatollah Shariat Madari said on Iranian television and radio that the rebels would be given every help.[20] In historical, cultural and religious terms also, Herat was much closer to Iran that it was to Afghanistan. Its largely Shi'a population naturally looked up to Imam Khomeini as a deliverer. The uprising, therefore, was directly inspired by the Iranian revolution.

The Iranian consul at Herat played an active part in the rebellion. He was constantly in touch with his agents in Kabul, giving them minute-by-minute information about the situation in the city. This information, there is reason to suppose, was being passed on to the US embassy where its news-manufacturing factory, after making necessary excisions and additions, was channeling it to the world's press quoting 'western diplomatic sources'.[21] According to these reports, during the disturbances, the angry mobs massacred '400 Soviet advisers'.[22]

Years later, the rebel commander in Herat, Allauddin, told a press conference in London that as many as 24,000 people had been killed during the uprising. He also said that the city had been bombed by Soviet pilots. In addition – and this was in 1986 – he claimed that the Afghan 'Mujahideen' neither received military assistance from any source, nor did they have any training camps outside the country. When asked about US Stinger missiles, he replied that such questions could only create 'difficulties' for the freedom fighters.[23] These 'Islamic' answers given by the commander should cast some doubt on his figure of 24,000 dead as well. According to the writer's investigation, about 800 people were killed during the uprising, all Afghan apart from nine Soviet advisers.[24]

As soon as fighting broke out in Herat, Burhanuddin Rabbani of the Jamiat-e Islami announced from the safety of Peshawar in Pakistan that it was he who had inspired the 'forces of faith' to launch a holy war against the communists. The head of the Nijat-e-Milli party, Sibghatullah Mujadaddi, not to be left behind, also ordered his followers to join the *jihad.* He also claimed full credit for the Herat events.[25] However, the fact is that neither Rabbani nor Mujadaddi, much less their parties, had anything to do with the uprising. They exercised no influence over the overwhelmingly Shi'a population of the province.

The Khalq government, on the other hand, claiming one hundred per cent 'popular support', charged that the rebels in Herat were not Afghan at all, but 'Iranian soldiers'. A press note issued in March 1979 said:

> In fact, these were not citizens of Afghanistan ... but Iranian soldiers in disguise ... about 4,000 managed to settle in Herat city and its vicinity in the name of Afghan citizens with the help of the Iranian consulate and organized disorder there.[26]

The claim made by Kabul was ridiculous in the extreme. Not one dead or captured Iranian soldier was produced in evidence. It is no wonder that the average Afghan soon learnt to attach no credence to what he heard from Radio Kabul, preferring the lesser lies of the BBC and Radio Pakistan. While the misrepresentation of Afghan facts by western media needs to be highlighted, it must be said that the Party itself has shown less than a liking for the truth. To this day, it has not admitted that it was because of its wrong policies that the people initially rose against the government. Of course, once they had risen, there were many, including Afghanistan's hostile neighbours, who were happy to fuel the insurrection in every possible way. Even today, the Party considers the Afghan problem as something 'external' rather than 'internal'. While there is no doubt that certain foreign governments have done everything to aid those fighting the Marxist regime, that is only half the story.

The Herat events led to a crackdown on whatever was left of the Parcham faction, and to the further intensification of the struggle for power within the Khalq group. On the night of 17 March, when Herat lay severed from the rest of the country, a meeting of the Revolutionary Council was held. This was a good opportunity for Watanjar, Ghulabzoi and Mazdooryar to raise the vexing question of the Defence portfolio, which, while on paper with Taraki, was effectively under Amin's control. Amin was on a weak wicket, because both the Kunnarha commander and the officer in charge of the Herat garrison were his appointees. The Watanjar group argued that if the Ministry of Defence had acted in time, the tragic events at Kunnarha and Herat could have been easily avoided.[27]

As a compromise formula, at the 17 March meeting, Taraki handed over the Defence portfolio to Watanjar and some of his own powers to Amin.[28] The Party had once again tried to solve a political problem with an administrative solution through a re-apportionment of ministerial portfolios. While Amin was forced to retreat from the Ministry of Defence, he was not willing politically to distance himself from the army. He therefore suggested at the 26 March Politburo meeting that the new Minister of Defence should be accountable to a Homeland High Defence Committee. The proposal was carried. This move also enabled Amin to have his brother-in-law, Maj. Mohammed Yaqub, elevated to Chief of Staff. The head of the powerful Political Department of the army, Iqbal Waziri, was already an Amin man. In effect, though Watanjar was now the Defence Minister, two of the most important men in the army were diehard Amin loyalists. While Watanjar may have felt happy at the fulfilment of his ambition of heading the Defence Ministry, he must at the same time have realized that his post was largely ceremonial since he could not order promotions, demotions, or transfers or lay down policy.

While offering Amin the Prime Ministership as a sort of 'consolation prize', Taraki said:

> As one of our slogans is 'to everyone according to his capacity and work', therefore as a result of past performance and services, he [Amin] has won our greater trust and assurances. I have full confidence in him and in the light of this confidence I entrust him with this job.[29]

However, inside the Party, there were manifest signs of Taraki-Amin differences, and in February 1979, first reports of a rift appeared in the international press.[30] Dismissing them as hostile western propaganda, Taraki said in March 1979: 'I want to tell them [the western press] that Amin and I can best be compared to a flesh-embedded nail. It is not possible to separate one from the other'.[31]

The rustic Pushstu proverbs were not enough, however, to bridge the growing chasm between the two men. Amin believed that by patronizing Watanjar and his friends, Taraki intended to dilute his (Amin's) influence in the armed forces, while at the same time helping set up a group opposed to him. With the exception of the Watanjar group, other members of the armed forces high command identified themselves with Amin. Consequently, the 26 March changes proved to be the last chapter in the once-fraternal Taraki-Amin relationship. Like all top leaders of undemocratic parties, Taraki was obliged to counter his deputy's strength and vaulting ambition by consolidating his (Amin's) opponents within the ruling circle. But it was not easy. Amin was too powerful and the Khalq group was too small to contain him. It needed someone like Karmal. This then was what really led six months later to the Taraki-Karmal meeting at Moscow airport.

The change in Amin's public attitude towards his rivals became evident after 26 March. In the middle of April, without actually naming the Watanjar group, Amin described it as compromising enemies of the 'working class' who were trying to use Taraki for their nefarious ends:

The enemies of the working class movement are trying to penetrate into the PDPA leadership and above all woo the working-class party leader, but the people of Afghanistan take pride in the fact that the PDPA leader and its General Secretary enjoys great popularity and a strong character, and far-reaching fame, which renders him impossible to woo.[32]

By bracketing Taraki with the Watanjar group, Amin intended either to weaken and isolate him from the Party, or to force him to withdraw his patronage of Watanjar and his friends. A few days after this statement, at a meeting of the Politburo, Amin, while replying to a speech made earlier by Taraki, made an appeal for unity in Party ranks.[33] If unity appeals were being made, it was obvious that there were serious and fundamental differences. Moreover, this was also the first time such a situation had arisen in the ranks of the Khalq group.

Between April and July 1979, the PDPA government held a series of meetings with the chiefs of Jaji, Mengal, Shinwari, Afridi and Torikhel (Bhangash) tribes living on both sides of the Durand Line. To win their support, large amounts of money were distributed among them. Several million dollars had earlier been received from Moscow for this express purpose.[34] If it was the PDPA government's assessment that by bribing important tribal chiefs, it would be able to discourage them from hobnobbing with its enemies across the border, it was wrong because there was plenty of Saudi and American money on the other side of the Durand Line in Pakistan waiting to line the pockets of cooperative tribal leaders.

While the Party was embroiled in the Defence portfolio wrangle, in April 1979 a large force organized by Gilani and Mujadaddi launched a major attack on Jalalabad, Paktia and Gardez. By May and June, fierce battles were raging in Paktia and Gardez. To quell the incursion, the government brought Soviet helicopter gunships into action for the first time. These gunships had been supplied by the Soviet Union during the Herat uprising.[35]

On 23 June 1979, the Chandawal residential quarter of Kabul city, which had a large Shi'a population of the Hazara nationality, witnessed violent anti-government demonstrations. What had enraged the Hazaras were reports of merciless bombing of Hazara areas in Ghazni province by the Afghan Air Force. The second cause was a speech made by Ayatollah Syeddi Tabhatabai on Tehran Radio, calling on the Shi'a people of Afghanistan to rise in revolt against the Kabul government to reclaim their lost rights.[36] The call for *jihad* from the first Shi'a government in Islamic history now ruling Iran was like the observance of a holy duty as far as the Shi'as of Afghanistan were concerned. On 23 June the Hazaras of Chandawal hit the streets. They attacked the Jada-e-Maiwand police station and set many government jeeps and wagons on fire. The authorities responded by ordering armoured cars and light tanks to move into the troubled area. The army opened fire to disperse the crowds and the situation was brought under control after a couple of hours.

The BBC reported that eleven persons had died during the demonstrations, including, predictably enough, one Soviet adviser.[37] The *Statesman* of New Delhi estimated the number of those killed at a hundred. The government, however, described the disturbances in a press note as an 'Iranian attack' and warned the people to be careful of armcd 'Iranian saboteurs' who were said to be hiding in the city. This disclosure must have caused a certain amount of amusement in Kabul because the people knew exactly what had happened. According to eye-witness reports, the number of dead on 23 June was about fifteen. However, even this figure should be taken with a pinch of salt because some of the former Khalqite Ministers the author spoke to in Pulcharkhi prison did not know for certain how many people had actually died in the demonstrations.

According to old Pulcharkhi guards, between 23 and 24 June, the Afghan intelligence brought in around 300 people from Chandwal to Pulcharkhi, most of whom were probably executed. Among the unfortunate victims were boys aged fifteen, their only fault being that they belonged to the Hazara nationality. For Amin there was no qualitative difference between a protest made by a poor and oppressed Hazara and King Zahir Shah's son-in-law Mohammed Gilani who was making war on them. If a handful of the population decided to stage a simple, peaceful protest against the dictatorial policies of the leadership of the Party, steeped in middle-class fascism, the government considered it the epitome of revolutionary justice to respond with ruthless repression. Ironically, a religiously, politically and socially oppressed nationality like the Hazaras should have been in the vanguard of the ruling socialist Party. However, because of the aggressive Pushtun nationalistic tendencies of its leadership, the Hazaras had been forced to take to the barricades.

In May 1979, a general amnesty was declared for all those who, according to the government, had been misled by reactionary propaganda into leaving the country.[38] The date was extended once. The success of the amnesty would have spelled an end to the activities and ambitions of the Peshawar-based leadership of the rebels. Their *jihad* could only succeed if the poor Afghan refugees could all be turned into '*Mujahideen*'. Not surprisingly, therefore, they denounced the amnesty offer as an 'ugly conspiracy' to sow discord in the ranks of the refugees.[39] Before the amnesty announcement, the 'proletarian' government operating from the former royal palace in Kabul had consistently refused to accept the existence of the refugees, while the rebel leaders in Pakistan were counting them by the hundreds of thousands. After the amnesty announcement, Kabul TV began to show Afghan refugees 'returning' to their homeland in large numbers. The Peshawar-based refugee leaders countered these claims by asserting that it was not the refugees who were returning but nomads who traditionally moved from one country to the other at given times of the year. Ironically, before the amnesty, the Kabul government used to describe the refugees moving across to Pakistan as nomads or Pawindas. Neither side, in short, was much interested in telling the truth. One lied in the name of 'tactics', the other in the name of holy war.

By July 1979, the differences between Taraki and Amin, following the ministerial reshuffle of March, had reached their height. If Watanjar had believed that under his 'dynamic' leadership, the Afghan army would crush the fast-multiplying rebellions, he had been proved wrong. Nor had he apparently had much success with his attempts to disabuse army officers of their loyalty towards Amin in favour of Taraki. Watanjar had celebrated his assumption of the Defence portfolio by inviting senior army officers to a dinner with Taraki, apparently in an effort to afford the President an opportunity to establish personal links with them. Amin, on the other hand, had arranged to have one of his most loyal followers, Daud Tarun, appointed commander of the guard at the presidential palace in April 1979. The names of the officers who dined with Taraki must then have been passed on to Amin, who must have undone the damage by inviting them the next day and assuring them of his continuing favours. Since all Party organizational matters were in the hands of Amin and Shah Wali, it was not easy for Taraki to intervene directly and cultivate crucial political contacts.

The only success Taraki and Watanjar could claim between March and July 1979 was the 'recruitment' of the loyal Amin supporter, Asadullah Sarwari. He told the author later that his differences with Amin arose because of a visit made by Amin's son Abdul Rahman Amin to Japan. According to Sarwari, Abdul Rahman had sold priceless valuables taken from the national museum and precious stones from the royal palace while in Japan.[40] Members of his family confirmed that he had visited Japan twice, but insisted that both trips were of a purely touristic nature.[41] Sarwari further charged that Amin was trying to hobnob with the United States through Japan's good offices. However, even the publicity-hungry Karmal and Amin's most implacable enemy did not repeat this charge in later years. Whatever the truth, it is a fact that the Afghan national museum did lose some of its treasures after the Revolution.[42] It is also a matter of record that economic and political ties with Japan were given special priority after the Revolution.[43] (Japan was the one industrialized country which like a good shopkeeper did not scale down its links with Afghanistan following the April takeover, an attitude which the economically-cripped country could only be grateful for).

It is difficult to say whether Sarwari changed his camp because of Abdul Rahman's Japan visits or it was a result of Ghulabzoi's efforts. However, it can be stated with certainty that Sarwari's defection from the Khalq chessboard was not the handiwork of Soviet advisers. In August 1979, western sources were estimating their number at 3,000 or thereabouts, while maintaining that all civil and military matters were in their hands.[44] However, considering that in July-August 1979, Amin was being opposed by only four military officers, logically either there were only four Soviet advisers in the country, or if there really were 3,000 of them, they played no role in the Taraki-Amin quarrel.

On 14 July Taraki's birthday (which proved to be his last) was celebrated with great fervour. While in the official media Taraki and Amin were endlessly described as close and inseparable comrades, their mutual differences had reached a point where they were no longer bridgeable. In a meeting of the Politburo on 28 July, Amin held Taraki responsible for all the government's failures. Identifying Taraki's 'individual decisions' as the basic cause of the party's predicament, he called for 'collective leadership and collective decisions'.[45] Panjsheri and Zeary supported Amin's 'principled criticism'. The Politburo therefore decided that discussions [should take] place on the realization of collective leadership in the party organization as soon as possible and a realization of criticism and self-criticism and complete democratic discussions in the party meetings, and a resolution was passed in this connection by the Politburo.[46]

Had this actually taken place, then the PDPA would have become the first Marxist party and Amin the first Marxist leader to have followed the principles of 'collective leadership' and 'democratic decision'. The fact is that neither of the PDPA factions believed in the existence of a democratic atmosphere within or outside the Party. To them that would have amounted to a negation of socialism. However, the PDPA need not be blamed, because the Kremlin of those days itself maintained that 'democratic debate' was tantamount to an 'imperialist conspiracy'. The principle of 'collective leadership' was being invoked on 28 July because Amin wanted to recapture the Ministry of Defence on the basis of his new-found majority. In the name of this principle, he managed to have the desired changes made in the ministerial portfolios. The bone of contention, namely the Ministry of Defence, was returned to Taraki's charge, with Amin once again as his deputy. Amin handed over the Foreign Affairs Ministry and the Deputy Prime Ministership to Shah Wali, while Watanjar was sent back to the Interior Ministry. The Tribal Affairs Ministry was passed on to Mazdooryar. However, to keep an eye on both, Amin had Babrak Shinwari and Faqir Mohammed Faqir appointed as deputies at the Ministries of Interior and Tribal Affairs respectively. Salim Masaudi was recalled from his ambassadorial post in Bulgaria and given the Ministry of Education, while Saleh Mohammed Zeary was put in charge of the Ministry of Public Health and Abdul Rashid (ex-Rector of the Kabul University) made Minister without Portfolio. Amin also had his elder brother Abdullah Amin made 'Supervisory Governor' of the country's four northern provinces and his nephew, Abdullah's son, Asadullah Amin, Deputy Minister at the Foreign Affairs Ministry along with Shah Mohammed Dost.[47]

Through these important political and administrative decisions, Amin had effectively reduced his 'great leader' Taraki to a figurehead. Taraki was now no more than a silent mural on the walls of the presidential palace. He was not even allowed to receive newspaper correspondents or grant interviews.[48]

On 4 August 1979, the brigade based at Bala Hisar staged a revolt. Taking advantage of the lunch hour, a group of officers captured the command centre, requisitioned the tanks and armoured cars and began to move towards the presidential palace. At Mahmood Khan bridge, a bloody confrontation took place between the rebels and government troops.[49] The loyalist soldiers surrounded the Bala Hisar fort with their tanks. Two MI-24 helicopter gunships were moved into action and after five hours of intense fighting, shelling and bombardment, the uprising was put down. During the fighting, Afghan Air Force MIGs could be seen patrolling the skies over the presidential palace, the Ministry of Defence and suburban Kabul cantonments. For hours, the citizens of Kabul stood in the streets and on their rooftops and watched Afghans fighting Afghans. In the evening, they were informed by the official radio and television that the day's action was the result of an attack by 'Iranian and Pakistani guerillas' who had been routed by the brave revolutionary Afghan troops. However, as usual, the government did not consider it necessary to present any evidence in support of its claim. No dead or captured Iranian or Pakistani guerillas were shown on television or elsewhere.[50] An average Afghan citizen must have wondered what these Iranian and Pakistani guerillas were doing in the Bala Hisar cantonment in the first place. And how had they managed to capture and use Afghan tanks and soldiers? The government did not really care whether the people who with their own eyes had watched the fighting believed its authorized version or not.

Later, a large number of Afghan political groups tried to claim credit for the uprising, including Ghulam Mohammed Farhad 'Papa's' Afghan Millat party, the Hizbe Islami and the pro-Peking Shola-e-Javed group. After 1980, the Parchamites, in order to establish their 'revolutionary role' during the Khalq regime, also staked their claim to the Bala Hisar revolt.

The facts were much less dramatic. The Bala Hisar brigade had been recalled to Kabul from the eastern zone of Jalalabad, Kunnarha and Paktia because of its unsatisfactory performance. This disgraced formation had further been subjected to humiliating interrogation over several months in a bid to unearth 'disloyal' elements. It seems that finally the patience of its officers and men had run out and they had taken to the streets.[51]

With the Taraki-Amin struggle growing more and more bitter by the day, the government decided to hold an International World Peace Conference, which, as is customary, was attended by a large number of pro-Moscow intellectuals from many countries. A sort of running commentary was broadcast on state TV while the conference lasted. On the last day, while Taraki was delivering his closing address, signs of great inner tension were evident on the face of the applauding Amin. This was to be their last joint public appearance.

14

Taraki's End: Amin comes to Power

If Taraki had decided quietly to withdraw from active exercise of power after the 28 July Politburo meeting, there is reason to suppose that Amin would have with equal quietness sent him into retirement after six months. He might have even allowed him to remain President and General Secretary of the Party on paper. However, this was not to be. What came to be known as the 'gang of four' (Aslam Watanjar, Asadullah Sarwari, Sherjan Mazdooryar and Syed Ghulabzoi) was intent on forcing Taraki and Amin into the ring. For the entire month of August 1979, Sarwari continued his efforts to persuade Jozjani, Zeary and Panjsheri to come out in the open on Taraki's side.[1] However Zeary, though not on good terms with Amin, consistently resisted these moves.[2] Panjsheri, because of his Groh-e-Kargar links, was not of much consequence anyway, while Jozjani refused to turn against Amin.

In August, for the first time, bitter words were exchanged between Taraki and Amin. According to Mrs Taraki, her husband told Amin: 'We are a Marxist Party, but people accuse us of nepotism. You have appointed Abdullah Amin (who was not even a member of the Party) 'Supervisory Governor' of the four northern provinces and your nephew has been made Deputy Foreign Minister.' Amin is said to have shot out of his seat in great anger and screamed: 'So, should I murder my family?'[3] In those days, Amin supporters used to argue (apparently in all seriousness) that he was a true Marxist-Leninist, as he had only followed the example of Fidel Castro, who had appointed his brother his Minister of Defence and successor and his wife the head of the women's wing of his party.[4]

On 4 September 1979, Taraki left for Havana by way of Moscow with Foreign Minister Akbar Shah Wali, Information Minister Khyal

Mohammed Katwazi and Presidential Guard Commander Maj. Daud Tarun, all openly pro-Amin men, as members of his delegation.[5] Since the public stance of the Party continued to remain one of comradeship and unity, Amin saw Taraki off at the Kabul airport with great aplomb. Two days before Taraki's departure, Sarwari told the Soviet adviser to the Department of Intelligence who was attached to him, 'It is my information that Amin has decided to kill Taraki and take over power.' Within hours of being informed of Sarwari's remark, the Soviet adviser took a flight for Moscow.[6] After Taraki's departure, a showdown between Amin and the four military officers, Watanjar, Mazdooryar, Sarwari and Ghulabzoi, had become a distinct possibility. None of the men was any longer sleeping at his own house for fear that Amin might have them killed.[7] It was Sarwari who had taken over the 'command' of the 'gang of four' and it was now clear that the Taraki-Amin dispute would take the form of armed confrontation. From his early days, Sarwari had been a believer in what can only be described as adventurist heroism. Amin's nephew and son-in-law Asadullah Amin narrated the following story about Sarwari (whom he had replaced as Head of Intelligence after Taraki's overthrow) in October 1979 in the presence of the author:

> 'Sarwari was an adventurist. In 1977, he told uncle (Hafizullah Amin) that he had been invited by Sardar Daud to come and see him because he probably wanted to reinstate him to the Air Force. If the Party wanted to take advantage of this opportunity, he would strangle the old Daud with his own hands during the meeting and thus remove the final hurdle in the way of the revolution. The Party rejected this adventurist formula vehemently.'[8]

After Taraki's departure for Havana, Sarwari drew up a stratagem to eliminate Amin. It simply consisted of gunning him down in front of the Kabul TV station when he drove to the airport to receive Taraki. To keep it a 'closely guarded secret', he made his nephew and deputy, Aziz Akbari, responsible for its execution. He also directed him to handpick a team of ten from the Intelligence Department to assist him. The men were not to be told anything about their mission but to be given a crash course in shooting at fast-moving vehicles.[9]

It could never have occurred to Sarwari that his nephew was an agent of the Intelligence Department's Soviet adviser and the first man to know about Sarwari's 'closely guarded secret' would be no other than the Soviet adviser himself.[10] Sarwari's plan must have caused shock and astonishment to the Soviet officer because there is no evidence that at this point the Soviet Union had any plans to eliminate Amin. It is probable that the Soviet adviser, after consulting his principals, told Akbari to inform Amin about the plot and advise him to change his route to the airport on the day of Taraki's arrival from Havana. In any case, that is what Amin did. Akbari must also have informed Amin about the Soviet rection to Sarwari's bid to kill him, something which made Amin conclude wrongly that in the inter-factional Khalq struggle, the Soviet Union was on his side.[11] The fact is that the Soviet Union was not yet prepared for any dramatic actions. The Soviet adviser, it may be added, also instructed another of Sarwari's 'reliable' deputies, Nawab Ali, to keep his eyes open and remain in touch with Amin.

When Amin came to power, he appointed Aziz Akbari Director of Intelligence in place of Sarwari because he was convinced of his being 'his man'. In October 1979 he was sent as ambassador to Iraq. In 1980 the Karmal government, instead of jailing Akbari for 'helping' Amin, sent him on another diplomatic assignment, this time as First Secretary to the Afghan mission in Mongolia, so that he could keep an eye on his uncle Sarwari who had already been posted there as ambassador. Akbari's career proves beyond any doubt that his loyalties did not lie with Amin. Otherwise, he would have been sent to Pulcharkhi after the Karmal takeover.

In Akbari, Amin's prayers had been answered. With him on the inside, he was now being kept informed regularly and in detail about the doings of the 'gang of four'. Sarwari's other deputy, Nawab Ali, was also part of Amin's intelligence network. With Taraki away from the country, Amin had already begun to plan the arrest of the four men and there were all kinds of rumours floating about. Higher Khalq circles believed that the Taraki-Amin showdown was just round the corner. On 7 September, in a phone call to Taraki in Havana, Sarwari told him: 'Amin is planning to either arrest us or have us all killed, so that he can take over the government before your return.'[12]

Amin certainly had come to a decision, but instead of directly capturing power (he was already in effective control of the government), he wanted to force Taraki to dismiss and jail the 'gang of four'. What better strategy could there be than that Taraki himself should be made to snuff out Amin's rivals and follow his bidding in future?

This was the situation which forced Taraki to use the Moscow connection to establish contact with Karmal. The development must have caused great anxiety in the Kremlin, because within one year of the Khalq-Parcham break, the Khalq group was now itself split into two warring factions. The policy-makers in Moscow must have argued that it was better to arrange a Taraki-Karmal alliance so that a 'national democratic front' could be established and the leaking boat of the

Afghan Revolution kept from sinking. On 12 September, on his return from Havana, Taraki made a six-hour stopover at Moscow airport where he held what in appearance was a private meeting with Foreign Minister Andrei Gromkyo. In fact Karmal was also present at this meeting.[13] Taraki's associates Shah Wali, Katwazi and Tarun, waiting in the VIP lounge, could never have imagined that not far from them Taraki was conferring with Karmal.[14] They probably believed that Taraki wanted to seek Soviet advice following his meeting with Pakistani President Gen. Zia-ul-Haq in Havana.

After their discussions, Taraki and Karmal seem to have come to the conclusion that while Amin was around, there could be no question of either Khalq-Parcham unity or the establishment of a 'national democratic front' government. Gromyko advised Taraki to send Amin and his more recalcitrant supporters into diplomatic exile.[15] It was also decided to appoint Karmal Prime Minister and Deputy General Secretary of the PDPA, while Taraki was to continue to hold his two current posts, namely President of the country and General Secretary of the Party. Another decision taken was that half the cabinet ministers should be taken from outside the Party so as to give the impression that there was a 'national democratic' government in office.[16]

The only question that remained was: who was to bell the cat? In his simplicity, Taraki took the onerous responsibility on himself. However, both Taraki and Gromyko failed correctly to predict Amin's reaction when the showdown came. While it was true that the Parcham leadership had initially offered no resistance when sent into diplomtic exile, it should have been borne in mind that compared to Khalq, Parcham was weak on the ground. It should also have been remembered that Amin was a powerful rival if openly pitched against Taraki. Whereas Parcham had retaliated soon after being sent into diplomatic exile by hatching the Eid conspiracy, Amin, when pushed to the wall, should not have been expected to wait for a later opportunity to strike back. He was in a position to choose his own time to deal with his 'great teacher'. The Kremlin-based Taraki-Karmal alliance was based on certain assumptions which, as time proved, were utterly false.

After his meeting with Karmal and Gromyko, Taraki received a group of Afghan students. One of his remarks to them was: 'In order to ensure the good health of the Party, it will be necessary to get rid of the mosquito which has made it impossible for the party to sleep peacefully at night.'[17]

According to schedule, Taraki's aircraft entered Kabul air space at 2.30 p.m. Thousands of Party workers and government employees thronged the airport waving red flags to welcome the 'great leader'. In accordance with his uncle Sarwari's plan, Akbari had deployed two sharp-shooters in front of the TV station, while Sarwari could be seen pacing about impatiently at the airport waiting for 'the news'. Taraki's aircraft, instead of landing, began to circle the airport. There was no sign of Amin. The crowd could not understand why the President's plane was not landing. The suspense continued for a full sixty minutes. Taraki in the air and the 'gang of four' on the ground were now certain that Amin had taken over.[18] At 3.30 a calm, unruffled Amin arrived at the airport in a white Volkswagen which he was driving himself. He had changed his car, his route and his expected time of arrival. It was only then that Taraki's plane was given clearance to land. By keeping the President suspended in the air for one hour, Amin had proved that it was he who was in effective control of the government, a clear message to Taraki not to make any mistake when choosing between him and the 'gang of four'. Amin walked up to the President's aircraft and as Taraki came down, he received him quite normally. 'Where are those four?' was the first thing Taraki asked. 'I did not eat them up. They must be somewhere around,' Amin answered drily.[19] The poor workers, quite unaware of what was going on, began shouting slogans of 'Long live the great leader', 'Long live his true disciple'.

As soon as he arrived at the presidential palace, Taraki went into a meeting with the four conspirators. In a move which amounted to virtual suicide, he told them that he would invite Amin to dinner that evening and propose to him to accept an ambassadorship, or order him to do so, if necessary. However, even before the arrival of Taraki's dinner invitation, Amin knew what had transpired, thanks to Daud Tarun. He spent the next few hours preparing himself for the confrontation with the President, much like a bull readying itself for a charge.

At about eight in the evening, Amin presented himself to Taraki at the presidential palace. After an exchange of formal greetings, he placed a typed piece of paper in front of the President. It was the dismissal order of the 'gang of four'. Taraki glanced at it casually, but without betraying his reaction, smiled good-naturedly, as was his habit, and began to talk about the situation in the country and the Party, concluding with the words: 'Amin, to me you are the most important, but things being what they are in the country and the Party, I think you should go out briefly as an ambassador. As soon as the situation improves I will call you back.'

Amin did not let Taraki continue. Raising his voice angrily, he shouted: 'You are the one who should quit. Because of drink and old age you have taken leave of your senses.'[20] Then he rose abruptly and left the room.[21] The Presidency of the country was there for Amin to take whenever he wanted it and here he was being offered an ambassadorship. As soon as he reached home, he phoned Taraki and told him: 'If you do not dismiss these four men and hand them over to me, then from this moment on I will not obey a single order issued by you as President.'

On 13 September 1979, Afghanistan could be said to have two heads of government: Taraki in his presidential palace and Amin at the Ministry of Defence. The same day, Zeary and Panjsheri tried to act as a bridge between the 'teacher' and the 'student', but Amin was adamant. He wanted Taraki to sign the dismissal orders of the 'gang of four', something Taraki was in no position to do. The same day, Taraki held a meeting with a group of seventeen army officers, arranged by Watanjar and Sarwari.[22] Amin was not idle at the Defence Ministry either, but was making last minute contacts with his friends in the army and preparing for the showdown. The struggle between the two had entered the final stage.

That evening, Sarwari's fertile mind gave birth to another scheme to deal with the impasse. Accordingly, next morning Taraki phoned Amin and told him to come for lunch, adding 'I am also inviting those four and I am sure that once we have talked things over, we'll come to an amicable settlement.' The Sarwari plan was that Amin should be shot dead once he appeared at the palace.[23]

However, Sarwari had again made the old mistake. He had taken his nephew Akbari into confidence once more, who had informed his Soviet intelligence adviser and with his approval passed on the information to Amin. Daud Tarun was also keeping Amin informed by the minute of Taraki's visitors and whatever else he was able to gather. Thus forewarned, Amin declined the invitation, saying: 'I prefer the announcement of their dismissal to having lunch with them.'[24] The lunch was duly held, but without Amin. Sarwari then came up with another ruse. He told Taraki: 'Unless we involve the Soviet ambassador, it will not be possible to trap Amin. He would come if he was told that the Soviet ambassador had agreed to play the role of peacemaker in the dispute.'[25] Sarwari's thinking was not so far off the mark. In keeping with PDPA tradition, the Soviet Union and its leadership was Amin's ideal too. He was also under the illusion that he was preferred by the Soviet Union to the 'rusty' Taraki. He was strengthened in this view by the fact that Akbari had the full blessings of his Soviet adviser to keep Amin informed of the intrigue against him.[26]

After lunch, on 14 September Taraki briefed Soviet Ambassador Punzanov on the situation and invited him to the presidential palace at four o'clock.[27] This he followed with a phone call to Amin, informing him that the Soviet ambassador had agreed to act as mediator. The moment

Amin agreed to come, Sarwari, Watanjar and Ghulabzoi, who were present when Taraki called the Soviet ambassador, left. Sarwari had a new plan now, according to which they were all to return to the palace at 3.30 p.m and pounce on Amin as soon as he entered Taraki's room. They were to tie him up and lock him in the bathroom of one of the suites where a time-device hidden in the toilet was to go off after a few minutes killing Amin. In fact, it was for the purpose of procuring this time-device that the three had left the palace.[28]

Daud Tarun phoned Amin and warned him that something very odd was going on. Amin was puzzled. Suddenly, he asked Tarun if Taraki was alone. When told that he was, Amin replied, 'Then I'm coming over right away to see him.'[29] It was Amin's thinking that if Taraki was really serious about ending their dispute, he would come to an agreement with him before the Soviet ambassador's arrival. Moreover, if the four o'clock appointment was really a conspiracy, by going earlier he would upstage Taraki. At exactly ten minutes past two, Amin arrived at the presidential palace.

According to Khalq leaders, when Amin was at the main gate, Tarun tried to persuade him not to go in, but Amin was adamant.[30] Tarun and Sarwari's deputy Nawab Ali led the way to Taraki's chambers with Amin walking a few steps behind. As they went up the stairway and entered the main corridor leading to Taraki's quarters, two guards on duty suddenly opened fire on them, killing Tarun on the spot and seriously injuring Nawab Ali. Without losing his nerve, Amin rolled down the stairs, rushed to his car (which was also fired on) and managed to escape with his life. He drove to the Defence Ministry and ordered a full-scale alert in the armed forces. The die had been cast.

Taraki's two bodyguards were next day taken to the headquarters of the 4th Armoured Corps and shot dead by Col. Ahmed Jan and Maj. Shaista Khan.[31] (After 1980, these two officers were arrested for the murders. They told the writer in Pulcharkhi prison that they had executed the two men on the verbal orders of Chief of Staff Maj. Mohammed Yaqub, Amin's brother-in-law. According to them, the two guards had told them during interrogation that before leaving the palace, Sarwari and Watanjar had ordered them to shoot anyone who tried to approach Taraki's quarters. They had also been told that Amin and Tarun were conspiring to kill or do harm to the President.)

Nawab Ali was admitted to the city's Jamhooriyat Hospital, where on the night of 14 September he was murdered by Sarwari's men.[32] During his three months in power, Amin tried to build Tarun and Nawab into national heroes. The municipal corporations of their home towns were named after them and special songs were commissioned for radio and TV extolling their 'great deeds'.[33]

On the evening of 14 September, a concert of Afghan folk music was in progress on the lawns of Afghan Music, an academy next to the Indonesian embassy and barely a kilometre away from the presidential palace. Such evenings were regularly organized by the Khalq government to propagate Party programmes and achievements. As was customary, the stage was profusely decorated with large photographs of the 'great leader'. Popular artists, including Qamar Gul, Gul Zaman, Bakhat Zarmina, Master Fazal Ghani, Ahmed Wali and Hangama, were busy singing the praises of the Revolution and the Party. The well-known comic, Haji Kamran, who was acting as master of ceremonies, was dutifully leading the crowd into chants of 'Long Live Taraki' and 'Long Live Amin' whenever a new performer appeared on the stage. At about 6.30 p.m., when the concert was at its climax, tanks from the 4th Armoured Corps moved into the city, taking positions in front of important buildings and occupying major squares. The rumble of the tanks on the roads so unnerved the organizers of the concert and the artists that they ran away helter-skelter, leaving even their musical instruments behind.[34]

At six o'clock, Radio Kabul began to play a Ravi Shankar *sitar* recital, while the television displayed an unblinking portrait of Taraki with a sound recording of one of his old speeches providing the accompaniment. Off and on, excerpts from some of Amin's speeches were also being broadcast. The eight o'clock news bulletin said that 'four rebel officers' had been dismissed, namely Watanjar, Sarwari, Mazdooryar and Ghulabzoi.

On his return to the Defence Ministry after his lucky escape from the presidential palace, Amin had phoned the Soviet ambassador informing him of the day's events. The ambassador, as expected in such situations, had condemned the incident.[35] Amin was not yet ready to accept that if he had turned up at four o'clock as arranged, he would have met the same reception as he had done at two, nor could he suspect that the Soviet Union wished to remove him. He ordered Taraki to be detained in the palace, which was how he spent the remaining three weeks of his life.

The four o'clock Sarwari plan had been too wishful and another example of its author's adventurism. Even if Amin had come to the palace as arranged, it would not have been so easy to kill him.[36] Was Taraki so naive as to believe that Sarwari's ploy would succeed? In any case, by turning up at the palace at an unexpected hour, the wily Amin had upset the scenario.

Since it was Amin who had planned, organized and staffed the PDPA government, he did not have to get rid of any of the Ministers or members of the Central Committee after Taraki's attempt to oust him, barring a handful of pro-Taraki provincial officers such as Zahir

Chopan and Ghairat Hunar. On 15 September 1979, Amin summoned a meeting of the Central Committee at which he charged the detained Taraki with terrorism. This body, which should have tried to resolve the Taraki-Amin dispute, had been incapable of doing so because of its lack of familiarity with internal party democracy and its subservience to disciplinary centralism. It had simply waited for the winner to emerge. Expressing full faith in Amin's leadership, the Committee 'accepted' the resignation of Taraki on 'grounds of ill health'.[37] It was another matter that Taraki was neither ill, nor had he tendered his resignation.[38] The *Kabul Times* and *Inqilab-e-Saur* of 16 September 1979 carried a picture of Central Committee members which showed them with hands raised in favour of the new leader and smiling faces. In fact, it appeared as if they were engaged in a contest called 'who can put the biggest smile on his face'.[39] The Central Committee had once again proved to be a rubber stamp.

Let us now turn to Soviet-Afghan relations and to the conduct of foreign policy during the eighteen months of the Taraki-Amin administration. On the face of it, the two men seemed to advocate conflicting positions, but this was all a carefully arranged charade. Most of Taraki's statements were full of criticism of the United States and China and sychophantic praise of the Soviet Union, while those of Amin related to Afghanistan's independence, requests for 'unconditional' aid from the west and a reiteration of fraternal Soviet-Afghan ties.[40] Since Amin was also responsible for foreign policy, his wishy-washy statements about the United States and the west were part of a typical Khalq strategy aimed (in vain) at securing the maximum financial assistance from these sources.

The Ministry of Information used to maintain a balance between the Taraki and Amin foreign policy pronouncements. If one day the press carried a pro-Soviet Taraki statement, it also published one from his deputy which was cleverly worded to reassure the west. The last such combination could be seen in the *Kabul Times* of 12 September 1979, which carried both the text of the Taraki-Gromyko joint communique and an interview with Amin in which he ruled out the possibility of the Soviet Army being summoned to the aid of Afghanistan (ironically, he was the first man to do exactly that three months later).

In his 16 September address to the nation, Amin accused Taraki (without naming him) of working against the national interest. 'History is a witness that whenever a Pushtun leader has tried to do a deal on Pushtunistan, he has had to take leave of his office under extremely humiliating circumstances,' he said.[41] Amin was referring to Taraki's meeting in Havana a few days earlier with Gen. Zia-ul-Haq of Pakistan. He also projected himself as a Khrushchev-like 'saviour' against Taraki's Stalin and Sarwari's Beria. Criticizing his predecessors' fondness for the 'cult of personality', which he held responsible for all of Afghanistan's troubles, he condemned the atrocities committed on the people by the Department of Intelligence, promising to change its name and restrict its powers. He promised that in future this Department would not arrest anyone without due cause.[42] In fact, in Amin's time, the renamed Department picked up hundreds of people without any legal basis, having most of them shot. Amin appointed Sarwari's nephew Akbari the head of the Department (KAM), but only one month later sent him to Iraq as ambassador, replacing him with his own nephew Asadullah Amin.

Amin also ordered that a list of those in prison should be posted outside the Prime Minister's office. There were no more than a hundred names. Those missing and not on the list were declared to have been killed during Taraki's time.[43] Thousands of people with missing relatives thronged to the Prime Minister's office, but were disappointed and enraged. They started chanting slogans, first against Taraki, and then against Amin himself. The police soon moved in and dispersed the crowd.[44]

Amin's arrival should have spelt no danger to Soviet interests. Any sensible person sitting in Moscow could well see that the PDPA, presiding over a lacerated country, did not have the strength to move out of the Soviet orbit. Amin was no potential Tito, Mao or Enver Hoxha. He could only emerge as a national hero if he succeeded in ending the civil war raging in the country. And for that he required Soviet military and economic aid for many more years.

However, Amin's assumption of power was seen in at least some sections of Moscow as an intolerable development. Amin's appointment as PDPA General Secretary was announced on 16 September, but it was not until 19 September that a congratulatory message was received from the Kremlin. This was a signal for the countries of Eastern Europe to follow suit. However, Amin did not attach much importance to the delay in the Soviet message and was satisfied with the fact that he had been accepted. On 17 September the Soviet ambassador in Kabul came to call on Amin. He was at pains to reassure him that he had not been part of the conspiracy against him.[45]

There appears to have been no coordination between three important and all-powerful sections of the Soviet state machinery insofar as the Taraki–Amin dispute is concerned. Punzanov, the Soviet ambassador in Kabul and the representative of the Soviet Foreign Ministry, was certainly an integral part of the anti-Amin camp. It may be borne in mind that he had no hesitation in granting asylum in his chancery to Sarwari, Watanjar and Ghulabzoi, who had conspired against Amin.[46] At the other end of the scale, the KGB operatives in Afghan Intelligence (AGSA), acting as 'advisers', had consistently helped Amin with information through the two Afghan intelligence officials Akbari and Nawab Ali. However, Soviet military intelligence (present in the country in the form of military advisers) had completely stayed out of the Taraki-Amin struggle.

The Soviet Union is a bureaucratic state where all power resides in the central Politburo. It is inconceivable that in such a centralized and well-coordinated system, three different policies should have been followed in a most crucial area of foreign relations. One concludes that Brezhnev had become so enfeebled by disease that he had lost his hold on state policy, which was being run in different directions by different departments and ministries.

Another instance of the lack of coordination in Soviet policies at the time is provided by a failed military uprising in October 1979 in which the Soviet embassy was definitely involved. Prof. Zakriya of Kabul University was summoned to the embassy where he was taken to see the three absconders Watanjar, Sarwari and Ghulabzoi, who deputed him to carry a message to certain of their contacts in important cantonments bordering Kabul, calling for a coup on 20 October.[47]

In keeping with what had almost become Afghan style, this uprising was to get under way at midday, with low-flying Afghan Air Force aircraft signalling the start of the takeover bid.[48] While Taraki's supporters in various cantonments waited in vain for the planes to take to the skies, the Reshkhor Division decided to start the proceedings without the Air Force. It was a violent uprising which took about twenty-four hours to quell. After 1980 Watanjar, Sarwari and Ghulabzoi learnt that the failure of the coup was mainly due to Soviet military advisers who had prevented Taraki supporters from taking control of the Bagram air base. The KGB went out of its way to help Amin.[49] Officially and on record, the Amin government held Ghulam Mohammed Farhad, leader of the Afghan Millat party, responsible for the conspiracy. He was arrested, but since the government knew that he was innocent, he was not executed. Had he been behind the failed attempt, there could have been no question of his life being spared.

The dissension between three prime centres of Soviet state power also showed that the heads of all three (Andrei Gromyko at the Foreign Ministry, Dimitri Ustanov at Defence and Yuri Andropov at the KGB) were all waiting in the wings for the ailing Brezhnev to die so that they could take his place.

Amin was by now convinced that the Soviet ambassador, apart from offering asylum to his political enemies, was also engaged in hatching a conspiracy against him. After the failure of the October coup, he intensified pressure for the envoy's recall to Moscow. In May-June 1981, Jozjani was in the next cell to the author at Nazarat Khana Sadarat, the central detention centre, with only a flimsy hardboard partition separating them.[50] He was under interrogation and the writer could clearly overhear the interrogator's questions. The central point of the investigation appeared to be the role of the Soviet embassy. In November Punzanov was finally recalled, but before he left he arranged to put the three absconding Parcham men on a Soviet transport plane bound for Tajikistan.

15

Taraki's Career, and his Murder

According to Taraki's official biography, he was born on 14 July 1917 in the village of Saur Kilai in the district of Makur, Ghazni province. This was also the year of the October Revolution in Czarist Russia. In 1929 he passed his matriculation examination from the Makur High School. By coincidence, 1929 was the year of Amir Amanullah Khan's exile from the country. The events of that time must have left a deep impression on Taraki because the Ghilzai Pushtuns of Ghazni were among the king's ardent supporters.

Again according to the official biography, Taraki spent the 1934-37 period in India, where he continued his education while working as a representative of a Kabul-based Afghan businessman. (He told a press conference on 3 May 1978 that he had got himself an education by sleeping on the footpaths of Bombay.)[1] The Bombay of the 1930s was the centre of the Indian communist movement. This was the young Taraki's first brush with Marxism. It was also during his years in India that he met the famous Pushtun leader, Khan Abdul Ghaffar Khan. (In terms of Pushtun nationalism, he remained an admirer of Ghaffar Khan all his life). In 1937 he returned to Kabul and continued his association with the same businessman, Zabuli by name. He also continued his education, taking a degree in law and political science from Kabul University in 1941. He began to write short stories at about this time and worked at different periods for the Ministry of Revenue and the Government Printing Press. Between 1951 and 1953, he was Assistant Director at the Bakhtar News Agency.[2] His small house in the Karta Chahar district of Kabul was built during these years. The American author Anthony Arnold has falsely alleged that this house was made with money embezzled from the businessman Zabuli. The fact is that when the house was built, Taraki had been out of Zabuli's employ for

177

several years. The Afghan intellectual Amir Ali Ayin, quoted by Arnold as the source of the story, denied it categorically when the author wrote to him for confirmation.[3]

Because of Taraki's involvement in the Tehrik Naujawanan-e-Baidar, he was shifted from Bakhtar in 1953 and sent to the United States as the Press and Cultural Attaché to the Afghan mission. While there he contributed a number of articles to newspapers against the institution of kingship and was recalled for this reason by the Daud government. According to some reports, he made efforts to get political asylum in the United States (had he been given asylum, who knows whether Afghanistan's political future would have been different or not). Before his departure from the States he called a press conference and said that both his life and liberty would be in danger on return to his country.[4] He also addressed a press conference at Karachi airport at which he said that he was returning to Afghanistan.[5] His official biography says that on his arrival at Kabul airport, he phoned Daud and told him: 'I have returned. Should I go home or to the jail?' Daud did not put him in prison, but the doors of government employment were closed on him permanently.[6] In order to survive, Taraki opened a small Persian-English translation bureau. In 1955-58 he also performed some translation work for the US–AID office in Kabul. (It is unlikely that the Americans knew anything about his political beliefs).

According to his official biography, after his return from the States, he found himself in serious economic difficulties:

> From 1953 to 1963 Comrade Taraki primarily did odd jobs to eke out his living. However, as soon as he would land at [sic] a good job, he was suspended through [the] intelligence services. So he was forced to run a translation bureau under his own name doing translation for some people and organizations or writing for the press.[7]

Taraki's short stories revolve around the unequal and unjust social relationship between the Afghan peasant and the exploiting landlord. (In 1979, some of these stories were made the basis of a number of television plays).

In keeping with his rustic habits, Taraki, unlike city-bred intellectuals, was fond of spending an hour or two when he had time chatting and exchanging stories in the bazaar with grocers, cobblers and bakers. One Karta Chahar baker, a good acquaintance of Taraki's who used to sell contraband liquor under the counter, was picked up by the police after the Revolution on just that charge. As soon as he was let out from the lock-up, he went straight to the presidential palace. When Taraki was informed of his presence, he sent for him. The baker, simple soul that he was, said to Taraki: 'Can you tell these stupid soldiers of yours to leave me alone? There were days when you used to drink my home-distilled liquor on credit. There was nothing illegal about it then, but now that you drink imported stuff, has it become a crime to consume the local variety?' A characteristic smile appeared on Taraki's face and he told the baker to stay for dinner. That evening they both drank home-distilled liquor.[8] Before the Revolution, Taraki was often in debt to local butchers, grocers and general merchants. There was a popular joke in Kabul about Taraki. It said that a plain-clothes man detailed to keep a tail on him one day got so tired of walking behind him for hours on end that he finally approached him and said, 'I don't know where you are going, but wherever it is, let me buy a bus ticket for the two of us because my feet are killing me.' His wife told the author that all through their married life, her husband never once raised his hand to her, nor did he ever express regret at being childless. No scandals involving women were attached to his name.

Taraki performed three impossibles in Afghan history. He was the first poor man to become the country's ruler. The homeless student who had slept on the footpaths of Bombay was also the founder of the first Afghan revolutionary party and the leader of the country's first revolution. Thirdly, he was the first nomad Pushtun who challenged and defeated the powerful Barakzais, Saddozais and Mohammadzais of Kandhar. Of course, these achievements were made possible by the collective work of the Party – which was all the more reason why there should have been no need to turn Taraki's simple and home-spun personality into something super-heroic and mysterious. Taraki was neither the leader of a great historical movement, nor the victor of a war of liberation. He was a simple writer, not a single line from whose work can be presented as a new and creative interpretation of Marxism. He founded a party consisting of middle-class wage-earners which captured power by subverting the army. In personal terms, his political career was eventless, boasting of nothing more heroic than two and a half days in jail.

This simple-hearted, affectionate, honest and rootless nomad was turned into a colossus through Party propaganda which flew in the face of both reality and common sense. If Taraki's name occurred during a radio or TV broadcast five times, for instance, the announcer was under instructions to read it out in full with all the ludicrous titles appended to it: The model for this was Kim Il Sung's North Korea. Often this wordage was in excess of what was devoted to the actual news story. Taraki's Karta Chahar house and his translation bureau were turned into 'Museums of the Revolution'. There were always contingents of soldiers on guard outside and a group of guides to show visitors around.

The poor average Afghans could hardly be expected to visit this 'revolutionary shrine', but if an unfortunate delegation from abroad or a progressive from another country landed in Kabul, they were subjected to the full treatment. In the Karta Chahar Museum of the Revolution, Taraki's old shoes, shorts, pens, inkpots and a rustic cot had been put on display. The guides would spend about half an hour expounding the 'revolutionary significance' of these old shoes and shirts. You were told that on the day of a certain procession, the leader was wearing this particular shirt or that pair of shoes, or that this was the bed on which 'the teacher' used to sit while imparting revolutionary instruction to his 'true disciple'. Both these museums were under the direct charge of the 'true disciple' (Amin) and therefore the guides were always telling stories designed to prove how close the bonds between the two men were.

The man who created the living monument called Taraki was Amin. He used it as a shield to eliminate Parcham from the field and later strengthen his own grip over the Party and the state apparatus. After Taraki's fall, he threw the entire blame for the Revolution's failures on his 'great leader'. As for Taraki, he was taken in by this sycophancy and heaped identical praise on Amin. In 1980 Amin's Director of Intelligence and son-in-law, Asadullah Amin, said in answer to an interrogating officer's question: 'Taraki was a man without a personality. It was we [meaning Amin and himself] who gave him a personality.' After 14 September 1979, Taraki and his wife were put under detention in one of the rooms of the presidential palace. According to Mir Wais Amin, on two occasions Taraki expressed a desire to see Amin, but perhaps it was psychologically difficult for Amin to come face to face with his former 'teacher', now his prisoner.[10] Mir Wais told the author that his uncle Amin sent a message to Brezhnev saying 'Taraki is still around. What should I do with him? If you like, I can send him to Moscow.' On 6 October 1979, Brezhnev's answer was received. 'There is no need to send Taraki to Moscow. This is your problem. You solve it in the manner you consider best.' If the Soviet leadership had calculated what 'solution' Amin would find under the circumstances, then the message was a diplomatic way of assuring him that as far as Moscow was concerned, it had no interest in either Taraki or his faction of the Khalq group. Amin's Ministers maintained that if Brezhnev had wanted to save Taraki's life, Amin could not have hanged him.[11] It is well known that in order to please the Soviets, Amin had converted the death sentence passed on Kishtmand and Qadir to life imprisonment two days before Taraki was to be hanged.[12] After the murders of Taraki and Amin, their supporters insisted that Brezhnev had deliberately created the Taraki-Amin rift in order to clear the way for Karmal.

Mrs Taraki told the writer: 'On the night of 6 October, I was separated from my husband and sent to Pulcharkhi. I was sure I would never see him again. On 9 October a brief announcement on radio and TV said that the "ailing Taraki" had died. I ran out to the corridor wailing.' (It is an irony of history that exactly three months later Mrs Amin was to walk through the same corridor crying inconsolably for her murdered husband and two sons.)

Newspapers, much of whose column space used to be devoted to listing Taraki's string of titles, reported his death in four short sentences.[13] During his time, huge life-size posters showing his picture used to adorn almost every city wall. One near the Isteqlal School said *'Gaund au Taraki, Jism au Rooh di'*, meaning 'The Party and Taraki are like body and soul'. After his overthrow, every sign and poster bearing his name was brought down, but the one near the Isteqlal School stayed for about four days.

In 1980, in order to exploit the enmity between the Taraki and Amin groups, the Karmal regime released lurid details of Taraki's last hours. According to these accounts, on the night of 8-9 October he was choked to death with a pillow. The three men who had come to kill him were said to have been given a key to a box by Taraki, with the words: 'It contains 40,000 Afghanis [about 1,000 dollars] and my wife's ornaments which should be given to her if she is still alive.' His watch and Party card he had given to a guard. 'Give them to Amin,' he said.[14] He also expressed a desire to be buried next to his brother who was a taxi driver and had died a few months earlier. The three men who killed Taraki included Rozi Khan, the Political Commissar of the Presidential Guard, who later sought refuge in Quetta, Pakistan, along with Hakim Gondi, Assistant Director of Intelligence. (Both men remained under interrogation by the Pakistani intelligence agencies for some time).[15] The other two involved in the killing were hanged by the Karmal government.

16

Amin in Office and his Downfall

After taking over on 14 September 1979, Amin, in characteristic political style, began to put his close friends and associates in key positions. The number two slot in the Party and the government was given to Akbar Shah Wali, who was appointed Deputy Prime Minister and First Secretary of the Party. Faqir Mohammed Faqir was given Interior, while Sahib Jan Sehrai was put in charge of the Ministry of Tribal Affairs. Engineer Zarif was made Minister of Communications. In a meeting on 22 September, important changes were made in the Central Committee and the Politburo. Arif Alamyar, Mansur Hashmi and Gul Nawaz were nominated to the Party Secretariat and the number of permanent members of the Central Committee was fixed at fifty, with three additional temporary posts. Hakim Sharai Jozjani and Abdul Jalili were put on the Politburo.[1] Although the Party did not announce the names of Politburo or Central Committee members, the author's conversations with senior Amin Ministers have established that the following were members of the Amin Politburo:

1. Hafizullah Amin
2. Akbar Shah Wali
3. Saleh Mohammed Zeary
4. Ghulam Dastgir Panjsheri
5. M.K. Soma
6. Abdul Karim Misaq
7. Abdul Rashid Jalili
8. Abdul Hakim Jozjani

A fifty-member constitutional committee was set up. A handful of political prisoners were also released to establish the new government's 'humanitarian and law-abiding' credentials, but during Amin's brief stay in office, the population of the country's jails increased considerably.

In his first broadcast speech, Amin declared, in an effort to demonstrate his commitment to Pushtun nationalism, that the people inhabiting the areas lying between the rivers Amu and Abbasin were a geographical, cultural and racial entity whose homeland was Afghanistan. However, he soon began to shift from this position. In an interview to a Pakistani journalist, he said that the observation in question was not intended to stake a claim to areas which were part of Pakistan, but to stress that the nomadic tribes which moved constantly between Afghanistan and Pakistan considered Afghanistan their homeland.

Although Amin had taken over power, he was not unmindful of his delicate position. He was not strong enough to survive for a day without Soviet assistance. He also knew that the United States, China and Pakistan were not about to withdraw their support from the rebels. The Afghan army was in a mess and the Party was torn with dissensions. It was at this time that he first considered a trade-off with Pakistan: Afghanistan's acceptance of the Durand Line as the international frontier in return for an end to Pakistan's support for the regime's enemies.[2] In the first week of December 1979, he made moves seeking a meeting with Gen. Zia-ul-Haq of Pakistan.[3]

As with Daud and Taraki before him, Amin's Pushtun nationalism had cooled off. From December onwards, Zia-ul-Haq began for the first time to be referred to in the Afghan media as 'His Excellency the President of Pakistan'. On 19 December, addressing a meeting of directors of the Public Health Department, Amin announced (and the happiness on his face was apparent) that 'His Excellency Agha Shahi', Foreign Minister of Pakistan, would pay an official visit to Kabul.[4] On 22 December the Ministry of Information released the text of this speech to the press so that it should be the first story to catch Agha Shahi's attention in the papers when he arrived. However, the military regime in Pakistan was in no great hurry to settle its differences, including the Durand Line question, with Afghanistan. The existence of the 'Afghan problem' was the sole guarantee of Zia's survival because it was only on that basis that the United States was providing him with its full backing. Gen. Zia-ul-Haq was not prepared to shorten his own life in order to lengthen Amin's. The policy-makers of the Pakistani martial law government were of the view that unless the United States made a conciliatory move towards Afghanistan, Pakistan should not take any initiative.[5]

Despite stormy weather over Kabul on 22 December, Akbar Shah Wali was at the Kabul airport, waiting at the other end of a red carpet for 'His Excellency Agha Shahi'. However, instead of landing at Kabul, the Pakistani Foreign Minister's plane turned towards Tehran,[6] on what can safely be assumed to have been instructions from the White House. The 'heavy snowfall' cited as the reason for Shahi's non-arrival on 22 December[7] did not appear to cause much difficulty for the Red Army which began to land at Kabul the next day. Amin had taken a 180 degree turn.

Following Taraki's diplomatic tradition, Amin too had decided to make inviting gestures to the west while ensconced in the arms of the Soviet Union. In an interview to *Washington Post* and *Los Angeles Times* correspondents at the end of October, Amin said, 'We want that in a realistic manner the United States should study the situation in this region and provide us with more assistance.'[8] Afghan sources have confirmed to the author that at the very moment Amin was making these overtures to the Americans, some Soviet battalions were already in Badakhshan.[9]

In the middle of December, Amin was telling the world: 'No Soviet military bases will be allowed in Afghanistan because we don't need them.'[10] However, two Red Army battalions were already at the Bagram air base, and according to US sources about 30,000 Soviet troops had moved over the preceding fortnight to the Afghan border and three Soviet battalions had already landed at an air base near Kabul.[11]

While to Amin the domestic situation was gravely disappointing, the Khalq group in-fighting was a godsent blessing for the reactionaries. In Ghazni, the Afghan army and volunteers of the Defence of Revolution (NODR) had just beaten back a major attack by the rebels. However, these minor successes were not enough to secure the regime. On 27 November, rebel forces had for the first time managed to cut the Kabul-Jalalabad highway near Sarobi, and were repelled only with difficulty.[12] In the middle of November, Taraki's followers had carried out an assassination attempt on Asadullah Amin, injuring him seriously. The Afghan Deputy Justice Minister was, however, killed. On 20 December the rebels also successfully cut across the Kabul-Gardez highway.[13] Until Amin's fall, heavy fighting continued in this area between Afghan and rebel troops. Thus Amin was fighting not only the Taraki group, but a growing rebellion as well.[14]

At this point, he really had only two options: either to arrange to have rebel bases in Pakistan dismantled or invite the Soviet army to crush the forces of intervention. According to his Ministers, by the end of November he had already put in a request to the Soviet Union to send in 10,000 troops. He believed that while the Red Army would protect the capital, he would use his own troops to beat back the rebels.[15] (Deploying the Afghan army outside the capital had the added advantage of securing him against any possible coup attempt). It was under this programme that two battalions of the Red Army flew into Bagram in the last week of December. It was further decided that by 20 December the 'required number' of Soviet troops would arrive in Kabul.

However, in early December the reply from Gen. Zia-ul-Haq to Amin's request for a meeting was positive, which encouraged Amin to put a halt to further Soviet troops arrivals until Agha Shahi's visit.[16] It is reasonable to assume that had Amin lived, he would have taken the same position *vis-à-vis* the presence of the Red Army in Afghanistan as later taken by Karmal, namely that it would only go back if external support for the Afghan rebels came to an end and their bases in Pakistan were dismantled. While Amin would have been more skilful than Karmal, the problem would have remained unsolved. In contemporary politics, subject as it is to inter-superpower rivalry, if one bloc comes to the aid of a given country, the other bloc comes to the aid of its adversary – and in greater strength too.

The cancellation of 'His Excellency' Agha Shahi's visit on 22 December not only became the immediate cause of the massive arrival of the Red Army in Afghanistan, but led to an immediate change in Amin's attitude towards the Pakistan political exile groups resident in Kabul. (Earlier, he had placed restrictions on their free movement). On 26 December he sent for Mir Murtaza Bhutto, former Pakistani Prime Minister Zulfikar Ali Bhutto's eldest son.[17] The young Bhutto asked the writer to accompany him so that if any questions were asked about the Pakistan People's Party, it would be possible to answer them. So exactly twenty-four hours before Amin was to be overthrown, Hakim Gondi, Assistant Director of Intelligence, picked up Murtaza Bhutto and the writer and drove them to Qaser-e-Darul Amin, Amin's new official residence on the outskirts of Kabul.

This building which a day later was to become the scene of great bloodshed, could best be described as the world's most insecure palace. It had no protective boundary wall, nor a single standing structure within a radius of 300 yards. After Amin moved, a barbed wire was placed around its circumference. The army GHQ was about 300 yards away and the road linking the two was unpaved. Between the GHQ and Amin's residence, there were forty or fifty tanks and wireless-equipped military vehicles. Two freshly-constructed rooms at the entrance acted as the 'checkpoint'. Amin's shift to this absurdly under-protected residence had in fact been skilfully engineered by his Soviet advisers, who by inducing both Amin and his GHQ to move from the city, could be said to have completed 50 per cent of the operation designed to overthrow Amin.

After the arrival of Mir Murtaza Bhutto and the author, they were taken to ADC Jehandad's room, where Amin's six- or seven-year-old daughter Wigma was busy phoning her mother every two or three minutes. The ADC was trying gently to dissuade her from carrying on with her game, but this being the President's daughter, he was naturally not in a position to order her to leave his phone alone. While the little girl was playing with the phone, the author was wondering what sort of a young woman she would grow into if she was raised in this palace. It could not have occurred to any of the people present in that room that exactly twenty-four hours later, this residence would be bathed in blood and the playful child would be in Pulcharkhi. Nor could the author have imagined that one year later he too would be sent to the same prison, where Wigma, dressed in threadbare clothes, would come to him meekly to take English lessons.

At about 6.30 p.m. Amin sent for Bhutto, who later told the author about the meeting. In his words:

> Amin was very happy. He told me: 'You are young and you are alone. You should get married here. Soon there will be a change in Pakistan. There is no need to lose heart. Time will pass so quickly that you wouldn't even notice. Look at us, it seems as if it was only yesterday that we brought about the revolution, but two years have passed in a jiffy. One cannot believe that so much time has gone by so quickly.' In answer to a question about Asadullah Amin, he said that he had some stomach problem (he did not mention that this 'stomach problem' has been caused by a Kalashnikov). He said that an operation had already been performed and that he had spoken to him on the phone earlier, but because of the bad weather the line was not so good. Without mentioning the arrival of the Soviet army, Amin said: 'Reactionary states can do no harm to our Revolution now'.[18]

Twenty-four hours before his death, Amin was confident of his future.

The Soviet operation brought into play in Kabul on the evening of 27 December has remained a puzzle for political analysts all over the world. Not only did the Soviet Union have no need to mount a military action to get rid of their own Comrade Amin, but the timing was all wrong. In accordance with the principles of international conduct, Amin should have been given an opportunity to provide legal cover to the arrival in Afghanistan of the Red Army, so that it could later have been spared worldwide condemnation as an army of occupation and aggression. A hundred ways could then have been found of getting rid of Amin quietly. After all, the Soviet state machinery was not exactly inexperienced in these matters.

One day after Amin's murder, the radio announced that all members of the cabinet should report to the Kabul radio station at four o'clock in the evening, when, with the President dead, they should have known what was in store for them. However, all of them presented themselves at the appointed hour when they were promptly taken into custody. Had their government been removed by Karmal rather than the Soviet Union, they would perhaps have preferred to go down fighting. Since the government had been overthrown directly by the Soviet Union which to them had always remained the perfect ideal, with heads bowed they obeyed the summons to their own doom. For the Kremlin, socialism may be a scientific ideology, but for the devout and piety-ridden communists of the Third World, it is like a religion. Why had the Soviet Union considered it necessary to launch an operation against such a 'religious' party as the PDPA? Was this brutal option the only one left to the paralytic Brezhnev and the blind Soviet bureaucracy? Why did the Soviet Union want to remove Amin at all?

During his time at Pulcharkhi, the author was to discover the answers to these questions. In those two and a half years, he had the opportunity to get to know Amin's former Ministers, members of his Central Committee and Politburo and his nephew Mir Wais Amin. The writer's cell and that of Mir Wais were located in the northern part of the jail, where the rear yard was occupied by the women and children of the Amin family. The back window of the cell, though lined with bars, was often used by Mir Wais to talk to his family. This was also the cell where the Amin family children used to come to the author for English lessons. In April 1981, the Tajik interpreter of the Soviet adviser to the Intelligence Department, Watan Shah, came to visit the Amin family and told them that because of 'BBC propaganda' they might have to be moved to some other place. Only five yards away from the writer's window, Mrs Amin could be heard screaming: 'If you people were going to keep innocent women and children locked up like this, you should also have murdered us that night,' to which the petty bureaucrat replied arrogantly in Persian: 'This task is not too difficult for us even now.'[19]

During those days, the author was able to piece together the story of Amin's death through his conversations with Mir Wais Amin and Mrs Amin (through her son Babrak). Mir Wais said that at the new presidential residence there were two Russian cooks, a Russian governess to look after Amin's new-born grandson Ghamai and a Russian doctor to test the food before it was served to the President and his family. Russian cooks had been hired because the 'Marxist leader' of the Afghan masses was not willing to trust Afghan cooks, who, he was afraid, might try to poison him. On 27 December Mrs Saleh Mohammed Zeary and Mrs Shah Wali were guests at the Amin residence for lunch. (Mrs Amin was at the table though she did not eat as she was waiting for her son Abdul Rahman Amin). Amin, who had had an upset stomach since the night before, did not eat either except for a few morsels to keep his guests company. Amin's children, his daughter-in-law and the two guests heartily ate the food prepared by the Russian cooks. As soon as they had finished, they all fell unconscious, including Amin. Mrs Amin immediately sent for the commander of the presidential guard, Mohammed Iqbal, who frantically phoned the Charsad Bistar Hospital for help. By this time, Abdul Rahman had also arrived. The Afghan doctors gave the unconscious men, women and children a stomach wash and injected them with antidotes. At about 2 p.m. Amin opened his eyes, the first sign that he was regaining consciousness.

At Pulcharkhi, meanwhile, all the prisoners had been ordered to assemble in the compound of the first block to hear an 'important announcement'. The author learnt from Maj. Shaista Khan,[20] then commander of the prison, that he had received these orders from Mohammed Yusuf, an Assistant Director in the Department of Intelligence. The aim was to capture Pulcharkhi in order to save the lives of the Parchamites detained there by Amin.

The Soviet plan was that after Amin lost consciousness, he would be removed to the headquarters of the Soviet Medical Corps and the coup would then get into motion and a Parcham government be installed without firing a shot. Amin was to be given two choices: either to resign in favour of Karmal or to face a trial for Taraki's murder. Amin's wife, who was unaffected because she had not eaten, later said that the two Afghan doctors who had come from the Charsad Bistar Hospital were accompanied by a Soviet military doctor who appeared to be a senior officer, judging by his uniform. The Russian proposed that Amin should be shifted to the Soviet Army Medical Corps, a suggestion which was opposed by the Afghan doctors and the commander of the Presidential Guard on the ground that Amin was showing better signs of recovery than the others.[21] The Soviet plan, therefore, had come unstuck, since Amin could no longer be transferred to their custody (as the Soviet doctor was frantically and repeatedly suggesting). The fast-improving Amin had played havoc with the carefully worked out scenario. Although the failure of the Soviet ploy would cost Amin his life a few hours later, for the Soviet Union itself it would be the beginning of a long bloody march across the stony and hostile Afghan mountains which would – and perhaps only could – end with the death of the already ailing Afghan Revolution.

Because of Amin's improving condition, the Pulcharkhi prisoners assembled in the jail yard, instead of being taken over for protection by

Soviet troops at 2 p.m. (according to the master plan), were dismissed at 4 p.m. – without the 'special announcement' which had earlier been promised, but not before being made to listen to a short cliché-ridden speech by the prison commander, himself equally puzzled by these goings-on, in praise of Amin.[22]

On hearing of Amin's 'sickness', his brother's family (Mir Wais and others) arrived at the presidential palace at about 3.30 p.m. to see how he was. At exactly the same time a Soviet Army Medical Corps general was shown into Amin's bedroom. He must have been disappointed to see that the 'patient' was well enough to greet him. Expressing his pleasure at Amin's recovery, he left. The first thing that Amin said to his wife after coming to was: 'Believe it or not, this is the Taraki group's doing.' It did not occur to anyone, according to Mrs Amin, to suspect the Russian household staff, which had disappeared around 1 p.m. At about 5.30 in the evening, Amin walked to his office, declining his ADC Jehandad's offer to help him negotiate the steps. He was in full control of his senses now, though pale and visibly weak. The first thing he asked for was a report on every army cantonment. He was told that 'everything was okay'. He next asked the doctors when his children would regain consciousness and when told that it would be within twenty-four hours and there was no cause for worry, he seemed to relax. In the event, when they regained consciousness a day later they found themselves in Pulcharkhi prison.

According to the Amin family, the first tank shell hit Qasr-e-Darul Amin at exactly six o'clock in the evening. Amin ordered his Guard Commander Iqbal to establish contact with the GHQ. About the same time, the Soviet troops had put the central telephone exchange in Pushtunistan Square out of commission. The link between Amin's residence and the GHQ was now confined to wireless communications. Iqbal came to report a few minutes later that the GHQ was also under heavy fire, but what was strange was that not a single Afghan soldier had moved from the cantonments. 'Where then is the fire coming from?' Amin asked. Then he told his ADC, 'Get in touch with those asses at the GHQ again and ask them to recheck which particular cantonment the troops have been moved from.'

However, the GHQ was right. No Afghan unit had moved from its base, nor were there any reports of unrest or mutiny elsewhere. Both Amin's residence and the GHQ were being shelled by Soviet units based at Tapa-e-Taj Beg, some three to four kilometres away.[23] These units had moved at six in the evening and effectively surrounded both Amin's residence and the GHQ. Since it was already pitch dark, nobody was sure who was firing. Facing the east gate of the GHQ was a newly-constructed two-storey building which served as the residence of

Amin's brother-in-law and Chief of Staff. Maj. Mohammed Yaqub. It was soon turned into rubble by the attacking units.[24] At 6.30 p.m. Guard Commander Iqbal said to Amin: 'The officers at the GHQ believe that we are under attack by the "friendly army."' 'That's impossible,' Amin rasped back. 'It is our own mutineering troops. Let me speak to the GHQ.' Amin instructed that immediate contact should be established with Soviet army headquarters and assistance requested. Half an hour before his death, Amin was not even prepared to entertain the possibility that it was the 'friendly army' which had decided to kill him, the same Red Army whose stories of valour he used to narrate to his students to inspire them to join the Party.

At 6.45 p.m., the invading force was in front of Amin's residence. The resistance being offered by his guards was petering out. Amin ordered his ADC to extinguish all lights, then turning to his wife he said: 'Don't worry, the Soviet army should be coming to our rescue any minute.' Nobody claims to have seen Amin after this. (A Soviet doctor who was with him until the end was also killed along with his ADC, Jehandad.) Suddenly, there were men outside the house shouting: 'Amin, where are you? We have come to your help.' Mir Wais has said that these were Soviet Tajik soldiers who were speaking Persian in a Tajik accent.[25] Abdul Rahman ran down the stairs screaming, 'This way, come this way. This is where Amin is.' He was shot dead on the lower veranda. Mir Wais says that the Tajik soldiers then methodically searched every room with the help of hand-held torchlights looking for Amin. (They were also carrying his picture). Amin's youngest son and Mrs Shah Wali were killed while they were still unconscious. One of Amin's daughters was shot in the leg, but she survived only to become a prisoner in Pulcharkhi for many years.

According to Asadullah Sarwari and Syed Ghulabzoi, the soldiers who stormed Amin's palace were under their command. They say that when they entered Amin's office, they found him in his chair, his head resting on the table with blood flowing from his temple. They are not sure if he had received a stray bullet or whether he had committed suicide.[26] Sarwari has also affirmed that Watanjar, Ghulabzoi, other Parchamite leaders and he himself were smuggled into Kabul on Soviet military aircraft on the night of 24-25 December (they had probably been put up at the Soviet embassy). On 27 December at five in the evening they were told: 'Amin's palace is to be attacked at six o'clock tonight. Some of you will have to come along because Soviet soldiers will not recognize him.' Mir Wais's description of Tajik soldiers carrying Amin's picture is seemingly correct, as this special storm-trooper squad might have been thus 'equipped' to help identify the target. According to Sarwari, of all the Parcham leaders, only Anahita Ratebzad volunteered to go on the mission. However, her offer was not taken up because all three of them were of the view that it would not be 'proper' to take a woman along. Sarwari told this story to stress the 'cowardice' of the Parcham leadership. On the other hand, Parchamites said that since these three men had once been Amin's disciples, they were ideally suited for the assignment since it was in keeping with the Khalq tradition of patricide.

In order to secure the lives of Parchamite prisoners, Pulcharkhi was captured at exactly 6 p.m. by the Soviet army without much difficulty. The main onslaught was directed at the Kabul Radio and TV building where about twenty Afghan tanks put up fierce resistance until 8.30 p.m.[27] As soon as the attack got underway, Radio Kabul discontinued its normal programmes and began to play a Ravi Shankar *sitar* recital. The big TV booster had already been destroyed and for many days afterwards there were no TV transmissions.

Between 23 and 26 December, about 10,000 Soviet troops landed in Kabul and were accommodated in the city's major cantonments, including Kargha, Reshkhor and Bagram. Some of them were put up with the 4th Armoured Corps. The dispersal of the Red Army was considered necessary so as to rule out the chances of any Afghan troops coming to Amin's aid. The 4th Armoured Corps had a majority of Khalqite officers. On 26 December Soviet engineers, on the pretext of inspecting its tanks, divested all the mounted guns of their firing pins.[28] That the Afghan cantonments remained quiet on 27 December is therefore no surprise. The arrival of the Red Army was justified to the Afghan troops by telling them that China and Pakistan were about to launch a joint invasion of the country and this had forced the government to invite the 'friendly' Soviet army to defend Afghanistan.[29] In order to maintain the lie, the Afghan army had been kept on emergency alert for the Sino-Pakistani 'attack', by the Amin government.

Only the Reshkhor Brigade, in keeping with its traditions, offered resistance to the Soviet army. The fighting, which began on the night of 27 December, died out the next day. The Soviet army also experienced some resistance while trying to capture the Presidential Secretariat and the Ministry of the Interior.[30] After regaining consciousness, Amin had ordered Arif Alamyar, Sahib Jan Sehrai and Engineer Zarif to take charge of the control room in his Secretariat, and although they were time and again told that it was the Soviet army which was attacking the Secretariat, they had continued to resist. After some fierce fighting, the Soviet troops were finally able to gain control of the Secretariat at about 8 p.m. The three Ministers were arrested and moved to Pulcharkhi. Their resistance was to cost them their lives.[31]

Mrs Amin later said at Pulcharkhi: 'The Russian governess was very fond of our grandson Ghamai. Before 27 December whenever she would pick him up, tears would well up in her eyes. I asked her many times what the matter with her was, but every time she evaded my question. Now I understand why she was crying. She knew what was going to happen to us.'

If the events of 27 December are analyzed in detail, it is clear that the Soviet plan to remove Amin from power quietly while he was in an unconscious state came unstuck. Under a pre-arranged programme, at 6 p.m. on 27 December Radio Tajikstan broadcast a speech by Karmal at the frequency used by Radio Kabul, which suggests that according to the original plan Amin was to have been removed quietly by that hour.[32] However, since Radio Kabul had not yet been put out of commission, the speech overlapped with the on-going broadcast and had to be played about nine hours later, on the morning of 27 December at about 3 a.m.[33] Amin's regaining consciousness at 2 p.m. meant that he would not take long to unmask the real plan.[34] The Soviet doctor sent to Amin's palace must have been assigned to keep his superiors informed of Amin's condition. It must have been on the basis of his report regarding Amin's recovery that the decision to storm his residence was taken as a last resort.[35] The planned meeting of prisoners at Pulcharkhi was postponed accordingly.

The drug administered to Amin had not worked, but the tanks did. This naked military action was also sufficient to prove that it was Brezhnev and not Karmal who had removed Amin. On the morning of 28 December, the city of Kabul was crawling with Soviet troops. The Soviet military police was even controlling the rush-hour traffic.[36] According to western sources, the 27 December *putsch* was planned and executed by three Soviet bureaucrats: Minister of Defence Dimitri Ustanov, Head of KGB Yuri Andropov and head of the Communist Party Foreign Relations Committee Boris Ponamorev. The paralyzed Brezhnev had played no active part.[37] The Soviet action not only came as a blow to international Soviet prestige but also sealed the fate of the Afghan Revolution.

If the Soviet leadership had moved against Amin to exploit the hatred the Afghan people felt for his autocratic rule, then it had failed to realize that after the night of 27 December, this hatred would be transferred to the Soviet Union and its protégé, Babrak Karmal. The events of that night gave birth to a naked triangle – Amin's murder, Soviet military action and Karmal's arrival – which no fig leaf of political argument was ever able to cover. For the anti-Soviet camp, this triangle was the opportunity it had been praying for. If there can be apportionment in these matters, then it can be said that 75 per cent of anti-Soviet propaganda since 1979 has owed its origin to Brezhnev's Afghanistan adventure.

In 1962, in order to overthrow the Diem regime, the United States got itself caught in the Vietnam military and political marsh. On 27 December the Soviet Union got rid of Amin but found itself helplessly struggling in the Afghan whirlpool. Seven years after the Soviet invasion, Gorbachev was to admit that Afghanistan was a 'bleeding wound'. On the night of 27 December, nothing could have been farther from the minds of the Soviet leaders than their future leader's words seven years later.

17

Karmal: Brezhnev's own Creature

Karmal, the illegitimate offspring of the naked Soviet military operation of 27 December, was accepted as the Afghan ruler neither within his own country nor abroad. It was as difficult for him to claim the authorship of the events of 27 December as it was for Brezhnev to deny involvement in them. His first official statement was both untrue and illogical. He claimed that he had been present in the country since 14 October 1979 and it was due to his efforts that the Party Central Committee and the Revolutionary Council had 'unanimously agreed' to remove Amin.[1] He later made the even more absurd claim that it was the Central Committee and the Revolutionary Council which had appointed him head of state. He also claimed 'credit' for requesting the Soviet Union for military assistance.[2]

The first part of Karmal's statement is false: only four members of the Central Committee later sided with him. One of them, Ghulam Dastgir Panjsheri, was not in Kabul from September until December 1979. Saleh Mohammed Zeary, his second 'supporter', can hardly have 'voted' for him, for his wife was a guest at Amin's house on 27 December and had fallen unconscious with the rest of the Amin family. In that state, she had been removed to Pulcharkhi where she was kept for four days and only released after her husband had read out a statement in support of Karmal from the state-owned radio and TV.[3] Had Zeary been one of Karmal's supporters in the Central Committee, it is unlikely his wife would have been a guest at Amin's house on the day of the killings. The third member, Ismail Danish, when asked by the author if he was one of those who had voted for Karmal, only smiled mysteriously. The fourth, Abdul Rashid Aryan, was at the time Afghan ambassador to Pakistan. Karmal was not in Kabul from October 1979 as claimed, nor could any member of the Revolutionary

Council or Central Committee belonging to the Khalq faction have 'chosen' him as leader before 27 December.

Karmal was never able to clarify during his years in power how and from where he had entered Afghanistan on 14 October. Nor was he able to disclose where in Kabul he had set up his 'secret' office where these 'secret meetings' of the Central Committee and the Revolutionary Council had taken place. If Karmal had actually set up his 'secret' government during Amin's life and it was recognized by the Soviets, then how did it accord with the 1978 Afghan-Soviet Treaty that the Soviet government should simultaneously recognize two Afghan heads of state and two Afghan governments, against one of which it was to despatch troops? The first Soviet contingents arrived in Kabul between 23 and 26 December 1979 when the legal head of the government, Hafizullah Amin, was very much alive and in charge. If the Red Army had landed at the invitation of the secret government of Karmal and against the wishes of Amin, the legal head of state, then it was an army of invasion. If it had come in response to Amin's appeal, then was it empowered under the Afghan-Soviet Treaty to murder the existing head of state? In making these absurd claims Karmal could be likened to a man who has a small piece of cloth with which he is trying to cover himself but when he covers his head, his feet become exposed and when he covers his feet there is nothing left to cover his head with. The question that he never could or did answer was this: If it was not the Soviet army which had killed Amin, then who had?

One year and five months after his accession to power, addressing Air Force officers at Kabul airport, Karmal tried to clarify his position. After duly repeating his earlier statements, he made the astonishing disclosure that on the night of 27 December, 4,000 armed Party supporters under his leadership had overthrown the Amin regime.[4] He did not say from where these 4,000 warriors had materialized, nor who had trained them and where. He was never to return to the subject. Through this statement, Karmal had once again confirmed what the western press had long been saying, namely that the Red Army was present in Afghanistan before Karmal's arrival and that it had had no hand in Amin's overthrow. However, accounts in the official media were at variance with Karmal's own earlier version:

The Soviet Union in complying with the repeated requests of the legitimate government of Afghanistan [which was, of course, headed by Amin] and in full conformity with Article 51 of the Treaty of Friendship, Goodneighbour-liness and Cooperation of 5 December 1978, sent to Afghanistan a limited contingent of its troops to help the people and the armed forces of the DRA [Democratic Republic of Afghanistan] in repelling the armed intervention by imperialism and Chinese hegemonism.[5]

This officially-issued pamphlet by Karmal's own Ministry of Foreign Affairs contains three basic statements sufficient to expose the absurdity of his earlier claims:

1.   The Soviet army came to Afghanistan not in response to a request from Karmal's self-styled 'underground government' on 17 December 1979, but after 'repeated requests' from the 'legitimate government of Afghanistan'. Until 6 p.m. on the night of 27 December 1979, Amin was the legal head of the Afghan government.

2.   The Afghan-Soviet Treaty of 5 December 1978, under Article 51 of which the Soviet army entered Afghanistan, had Amin and not Karmal as one of its authors. It was in accordance with this Treaty that Amin had requested Soviet military assistance.

3.   Amin's purpose in summoning the Soviet army was to 'help the people and the armed forces of the DRA in repelling the armed intervention by imperialism and Chinese hegemonism'.

Not only are these three conclusions in accordance with known and ascertained facts, they are confirmed by Amin's Ministers and close companions. In 1985, completely forgetting his story about the 4,000 guerillas, Karmal told the Pakistani journalist Mushahid Hussain:

> But if by mentioning the 'December events' you are referring to the timely military assistance of the USSR which was rendered in response to the requests of the legitimate government of the DRA ... I would like to once again point out that it was due to this fraternal help of the great friend of our people that the territorial integrity, independence and sovereignty of revolutionary Afghanistan was saved.[6]

Once again, trapped in his circular logic, Karmal confesses that the 'December events' involved the operation mounted by the Soviet army which had entered the country in response to a request from the 'legitimate government' whose head at that time was Amin.

Karmal also made the preposterous claim (without the formality of any evidence) that had Amin not been removed from power, he would have handed over half the country to Gulbudin Hikmatyar and Pakistan. He charged Amin with being an agent of the Central Intelligence Agency and went so far as to write a letter to the President of the United States demanding to be handed over his predecessor's relevant record from the Agency's files. This letter was well publicized by him through the official Afghan media.

On several occasions, Karmal charged that Amin, in league with

Gulbudin Hikmatyar, wanted to set up an anti-socialist government in Afghanistan. He further claimed that the government was in possession of 'incontrovertible evidence' in this regard.[7] However, and not surprisingly, during his six years in power he failed to make public his 'incontrovertible evidence' damning Amin. His controlled media spent the entire duration of his rule putting out similar political fiction.

> On 23 September 1979 the CIA confidentially prepared the ground for a secret meeting between representatives of Amin and Gulbudin in the province of Kunnarha. On 14 October 1979 Amin held a secret meeting with his closest colleagues [no names are mentioned though all of Amin's closest colleagues had been in Karmal's jails five years before these lines were printed] and discussed the holding of a meeting on 23 October. On 15 October Amin met with the Chargé d'Affaires of the US embassy in Kabul. In this meeting the plan related to [the] Amin-Gulbudin understanding was discussed and reaffirmed. [Neither the minutes of the meeting nor any other documents verifying the claim are reproduced or cited. The conspiring American Chargé d'Affaires, who was still in Kabul when Karmal came to power, was not expelled either.] As a result of this meeting the special envoy of Amin [once again no names] paid a visit to Peshawar and Karachi between 22 and 24 December 1979. During this visit the date of the coup d'état which was to bring about [the] Amin-Gulbudin government was fixed for 29 December 1979 ... As disclosed in the press [of which country, in what paper, on what date, the document does not say] the CIA had assured both sides, if necessary, they would be supported by the American forces.[8]

This absurd story is its own contradiction. If Amin wanted to set up a new government in association with Gulbudin Hikmatyar on 29 December 1979 and the CIA had extended assurances of military support to the conspirators, then instead of the Red Army landing in Kabul between 23 and 26 December, it should have been the US marines. Was Amin so stupid as to have conspired with the Americans, while asking the Red Army to move into Afghanistan?

After 27 December the Soviet position in Afghanistan was as untenable as that of its protégé, with the difference that the former seemed to have come to the conclusion that the less it said the better. Nevertheless, it took three contradictory stands at different times to justify the presence of the Red Army in Afghanistan. The first Soviet comment appeared in *New Times* three weeks after Amin's assassination. At the time, Moscow had not yet fully realized the consequences and fallout of its intervention. Without making a direct reference to the physical intervention of its army in the country, it proudly proclaimed that it had only fulfilled its 'revolutionary duty':

> Refusal to come to the aid of the Afghanistan Revolution would have

amounted to contributing to its defeat, which would have come as a blow to all communist and national liberation struggles.[9]

However, the violent popular reaction in Afghanistan to the Soviet intervention, and the international outcry it created, soon forced the Soviet Union to go back on this gallantly-worded revolutionary statement. Three months after Amin's murder, the Soviet media were trying to defend the 'innocence' of the Red Army:

> The revolt against Amin and the arrival of the Soviet army were two purely coincidental developments, bearing no mutual link. The Soviet Union played no role in the internal politics of Afghanistan [meaning Amin's removal and Karmal's accession to power].

But even the Soviet Union could not continue to pretend for long that it was pure coincidence that as soon as its army entered Afghanistan, Karmal overthrew Amin (Karmal had yet to come up with the 4,000 guerillas story). Nor could the fact that a Soviet radio station had broadcast Karmal's speech while Amin was still in power be explained away as a coincidence. Again, the 'coincidence' of Soviet recognition of the Karmal regime at 3 a.m. on the morning of 28 December was not so easy to explain either.

After this profession of 'innocence', the Soviet Union thought it best to say no more about the events of 27 December 1979, being merely content with rationalizing its continued military presence in Afghanistan. The basic Soviet position was that it had come to the assistance of an ally at the ally's request in accordance with its Treaty obligations and in keeping with the provisions of the UN Charter. Without making any mention of the events of 27 December, Brezhnev in an address to the 26th Party Congress in March 1981 said: 'The Soviet Union cannot tolerate provocations on its southern frontiers, therefore, unless peace is established there [namely in Afghanistan], the Red Army will not be recalled.'[10]

What an irony of history, if not one of its jokes, that exactly seven years and three days after the Soviet military action, Karmal's successor Dr Najibullah invited Gulbudin Hikmatyar and all other reactionary elements to join him in a 'national government',[11] while Brezhnev's successor Gorbachev was declaring in New Delhi that in a 'neutral' Afghanistan it will be the people who will form the government.[12] Gorbachev was virtually admitting that the government in Afghanistan was not a people's government. The fact is that the Afghan Revolution died on the night of 27 December 1979. It was left to Gorbachev, as an honest politician, to announce its death. Once the Soviet army had moved into Afghanistan, there could be neither peace, nor revolution.

The Soviet military intervention and its rejection by the Afghan people was the best 1980 new year gift for the United States, Western Europe and China. Unlike ordinary new year gifts, it has retained its value in the years that have followed. The anti-Soviet camp, while denouncing the Soviet move as the 'invasion' and 'occupation' of a neutral country, threw in its own choice reasons for the development.

The 'warm waters' theory was bandied about so much that the average person believes that this was the only reason the Red Army came to Afghanistan. It might seem a major objection to this theory that Afghanistan itself is a landlocked country, surrounded neither by warm nor cold waters. But against this, it has been argued that Afghanistan was only the 'first step' and Iran and Pakistan were to be the next in line. The 'theory' however, still rests on a geographical absurdity given that the distance between the warm waters of the Persian Gulf and the Soviet-Afghan border is almost exactly the same as that between the Gulf and the Soviet-Iranian border. However, despite its absurdity, this argument proved effective against the Soviet Union. While it did not much impress the religious regime in Iran, Pakistan and the Sheikhdoms of the Gulf felt persuaded to get under the blankets with the United States. Pakistan even permitted Washington to build air bases in Baluchistan. International press reports also allege that American U-3 aircraft regularly use Karachi's Mauripur air base to conduct surveillance flights.[13] China too felt no hesitation in accepting the warm waters argument:

> In pursuit of its strategic interests in the region, the Soviet Union apparently intends to penetrate into the Indian Ocean and Persian Gulf areas via Afghanistan.[14]

On the other side of the coin, three weeks after the 27 December Soviet action, US President Jimmy Carter came out with the Carter Doctrine which described the Persian Gulf area as integral to American strategic interests. There is no need to mention at this point that the White House is located exactly 14,000 kilometres away from the Persian Gulf on a separate continent. The *Washington Post* wrote applaudingly:

> Carter's unilateral declaration of a new defence perimeter – in effect placing the Persian Gulf on the same footing as Western Europe – was a bold exercise of Presidential authority. The US has no security treaties with any Persian Gulf nations.[15]

The United States, while accusing the Soviet Union of reviving the old Czarist dream, was in the same breath putting the world on notice that its greatest democracy reserved the right to declare any area, close to home or distant, integral to its 'strategic interests'.

Since the entire American and western media establishment had failed to understand the real background of the Soviet military action of 27 December, it was not short on fanciful interpretations of the Soviet move. Amin, until then described as a 'diehard communist, butcher and Russia's puppet', became overnight a 'great nationalist' and 'martyr'. It was said that the Soviet Union had invaded Kabul because Amin had refused to allow Soviet bases on Afghan soil: in order to get rid of the nationalist Amin, the USSR had invaded Kabul and put its real pawn (Karmal) on the Afghan chessboard. It was also argued that by taking the US embassy staff hostage in November 1979, the Iranian students had created a situation where armed American intervention in Iran could take place any time. The Soviet Union, it was alleged, had demanded the Shindan air base near the Iranian border so that it could exercise effective control over the Gulf region and perhaps also discourage the US from attacking Iran. Amin's rejection of the Soviet request for the Shindan base, it was stated, had become the direct cause of his fall.[16]

It is illogical to suggest that Amin, who had felt no hesitation at all in inviting the Red Army to Afghanistan to protect his power, basing it in the capital itself where it could slash his throat if it so wished, would have been unwilling to hand over such a far-flung outpost as Shindan to his Soviet benefactors. The entire theory that the Soviet Union was seeking bases in Afghanistan is supported neither by history nor by geography. The Soviet Union has a long common border with Iran. Why should it have gone to the trouble of marching its army into Afghanistan just to gain control of Shindan?

Years later, the present General Secretary of the Soviet Communist Party, Mikhail Gorbachev, was quoted as telling Indian journalists in Moscow that his country had no bases there (Afghanistan), nor was it exploiting Afghanistan's mineral resources or raw materials. About the arrival of the Soviet troops in Afghanistan, he said: 'We entered Afghanistan on the request of its government.'[17] After signing the Treaty of 5 December 1978, the Afghan government was entitled to summon the Soviet army any time it felt the need to do so (such military movements are allowed under Article 51 of the UN Charter). The arrival of the Soviet army during Amin's time confirms that it did so in response to his request. The internal situation which forced Amin's hand has been explained in detail elsewhere in this book. However, two basic questions remain to be clearly answered. Why did the Soviet Union despatch the Red Army to Afghanistan? Why did this Army overthrow the Amin government?

It was clear from the beginning that if reactionary Afghan elements continued to receive external patronage and the bitter in-fighting in the ruling PDPA Khalq faction did not come to an end, the Soviet Union would not remain a silent spectator for any length of time. Afghanistan was situated in an area of great Muslim sensitivity where any successful religious Islamic movement was bound to affect Soviet Muslim Republics in a direct manner. (The Soviet Union's lack of unease over the Shi'a revolution in Iran may be explained by the fact that not only was this revolution anti-American in its character but the majority of Soviet Muslims were Sunnite by faith.) The three leaders of the PDPA – Taraki, Amin and Karmal – all seem to have failed to understand Soviet sensitivities. To the first two, Soviet help was part of the country's 'international obligations', while Karmal considered it a 'personal favour' done by Brezhnev.[18]

Since early 1979 the Soviet Union had been openly expressing its views on the external patronage being given to reactionary Afghan forces. The United States was never under any illusion about the Soviet Union not jumping into the Afghan fray at any moment. In March 1979, during the Herat uprising, it had issued a warning to Moscow to stay out.[19] By April 1979 the western press was full of reports about two divisions of the Red Army having moved close to Afghan borders.[20] These reports also noted that for the first time the Soviet Union had described 'non-aligned' Afghanistan, passing through the 'national democratic phase' as a member of the 'socialist family'.[21] The message was obvious: in Afghanistan, as in the Eastern European communist states, the Soviet Union would brook no interference.

In June 1979 there were reports in the Soviet media warning that because of the blatant patronage being accorded to reactionary forces in Afghanistan by external powers, a war-like situation was being created between Afghanistan and Pakistan. It was also said that in the event of war, the Soviet Union would not remain a 'silent spectator' because 'it involves the question of aggression against a country [meaning Afghanistan] which shares a common border with the Soviet Union.'[22]

After the Herat uprising, the first Soviet Deputy Defence Minister, Gen. Alexei Yepishov, visited Afghanistan. During his stay, he exchanged views about the internal situation of the Afghan army with Iqbal Waziri, the army's Political Commissar, and the Chief of Staff, Maj. Mohammed Yaqub.[23] On 17 April the Soviet general met Taraki and Amin. In August 1979 the Commander of the Soviet Land Army, Gen. Pavlovsky, visited Afghanistan, according to reports in the western press (the Soviet and Afghan media remained silent about the visit). According to western observers, the purpose of Gen Pavlovsky's trip was to make an assessment of the rapidly deteriorating law and order situation in Afghanistan.[24] If this was true, it only proved that the Soviet Union could not remain insensitive to developments in the neighbouring country.

On 6 September 1979 the *New York Times*, quoting 'diplomatic sources' in Kabul, predicted in a lengthy report that the Soviet Union was inexorably moving towards military intervention in Afghanistan. The paper said that if the assumption were correct that under no circumstances would the Soviet Union let go of Afghanistan, and the fact was also taken into account that the Afghan government machinery was incapable of dealing with the rebellion and the deteriorating law and order situation, then the conclusion was inescapable that the Soviet Union would enter Afghanistan in full force.[25] In other words, long before December 1979, the United States and the west in general expected the Soviet Union to intervene in Afghanistan. At that time, western newspapers were not citing either 'warm waters' or 'military bases' as reasons for the expected Soviet intervention, but arguing that Afghanistan's internal situation would force the Soviet hand.

Events have shown that the Soviet Union was anxious to stem the rising tide of reaction in Afghanistan with its military might. When Brezhnev and his comrades decided to send Soviet soldiers into Afghanistan, they seem to have tried to kill two birds with one stone: crush the Afghan reactionary elements and remove the Amin government so that a joint Khalq-Parcham government could be brought to power under Karmal's leadership. The Brezhnev government was under the illusion that after Amin's departure, it would not only be able to unify the PDPA, but also wipe out the growing rebellion with the aid of military power. Moscow also planned to make the return of Soviet troops from Afghanistan a *quid pro quo* for an end to external support for the Afghan rebels, a goal it has been unsuccessfully pursuing since it first entered the country.

18

Karmal's 'New Phase'

In Karmal's political mint, there was never any shortage of newly-struck coins. He described his arrival as the 'new phase' of the Afghan Revolution. In his first broadcast on the night of 27-28 December 1979, he piously intoned the opening Quranic verse, obviously in an effort to present himself not as a 'blood-shedding communist', but as a believer in Islam who was also a liberal progressive. After castigating Amin, he expressed a desire to embrace all elements of Afghan society, among which he listed:

> Muslims of Afghanistan, Sunnis or Shi'ites, pure and pious religious scholars and leaders of the country, heroic soldiers and officers of the homeland, national traders ... patriotic landowners, hard-working artists, brave clans and tribes of Afghanistan, fugitive shepherds and nomads of the homeland, government officials, vanguard intelligentsia and youth, working men and women, peasant men and women ...[1]

He mentioned Taraki's name with great reverence, declaring him a 'martyr' (the first and last time he did so),[2] and speaking of

> That historic murderer and rogue [Amin] who even did not have pity on Noor Mohammed Taraki, our dear leader and noble founder of our Party, the first General Secretary of the PDPA Central Committee and our first President and Prime Minister, whose name will last forever.[3]

To create the impression that the change he had brought about was total, he threw open the gates of the Pulcharkhi prison.[4] The government claimed to have released 15,000 detainees (this was an exaggeration because the two then completed blocks of the prison could not hold more than 5,000 prisoners).[5] Karmal did not benefit from this liberal move because those released included Hazrat Shor Bazar, the Mujadaddi family, members of the former royal family and the men like Taj Mohammed Khan Baluch who left the country and immediately assumed command of anti-government movements from abroad. As time passed, the empty cells of Pulcharkhi began to be filled again and three years after Karmal's assumption of power the number of inmates was twice that during Amin's time.

Three months after coming to power, on the occasion of the Afghan new year (20 March 1980), Karmal addressed the nation in wildly optimistic terms:

> I hope it will be a year of well-being and happiness, tranquillity and security – a year in which the wounds inflicted on our people will be palliated ... The black spectre of fear has been permanently ended in Afghanistan. Do not be scared any longer of what may happen tomorrow. I assure you that your revolutionary government has power and imperturbable will to decisively defend your dignity, honour, human and Islamic position as well as your property and families.[6]

Karmal was obviously under the illusion that with the backing of the Kremlin and the enormous power of the Red Army, he would be able to bring the country back to normal. In the same speech, he tried to impress the reactionary Pakistani military government with empty threats:

> All allies of imperialism and reaction in Pakistan are warned hereby that any conspiratorial decision made against revolutionary Afghanistan will be met with a strong reaction on the part of the entire heroic people of Afghanistan and the progressive world and the consequences thereof should be borne by the reactionary authorities of Pakistan.[7]

The main reason for this threat was the conference of Islamic Foreign Ministers which had recently been convened in Islamabad at Pakistan's request and at which Afghanistan had been declared a country no longer in control of its own sovereignty. It was on this basis that its membership had been suspended. However, Babrak Karmal's tough words neither impressed Pakistan nor enabled him to re-establish normalcy in the country. In 1983 his brother Mahmood Baryali was to write:

> The counter-revolutionaries have so far destroyed 2,812 schools (more than 50 per cent of the national total), 32 hospitals (more than 60 per cent of the total), 111 basic health centres (more than 75 per cent of the total), 800 big-capacity public vehicles (more than 14 per cent of the total), 14,000

kilometres of communication lines together with the communication facilities and devices. In addition, 906 peasant cooperatives (more than 70 per cent of the total) have been destroyed – and partial destruction done to some of the hydropower plants and distribution networks – and tens of industrial production projects. The total estimated value of these is more than 35 billion Afghanis (about one billion dollars) which is equal to 50 per cent of the total development investment in 20 years before the Revolution.[8]

The tragic balance sheet drawn up three years after Karmal's assumption of power did not include roads, bridges, military vehicles, tanks and, last but not least, human lives. Six months after the Soviet action the roads leading out of Kabul were full of gaping holes due to anti-tank mines. In 1980-81 private traffic between Kabul and other Afghan cities was only allowed to move once a day in the form of a convoy. Although these convoys used to operate under the protection of tanks and helicopters, it did not prevent the rebels from attacking them in hilly areas and often inflicting heavy damage. In 1983 the Red Army set up checkposts at every two kilometres on important inter-provincial roads. This dire situation notwithstanding, the Karmal government kept bragging about the agricultural advances made in the country:

> 6,657 hectares of land have already been distributed free of charge to 296 peasant families and at present more than 70,000 hectares of land are ready for distribution. 1,217 peasant cooperatives were set up but due to [the] destructive actions of counter-revolution only 207 units are operating ... The measures explained above [i.e. mechanized cultivation, supply of cheap seeds and fertilizer to the peasants] have been instrumental in [the] increase of gross agricultural and gross livestock product by 5.2 per cent and 9 per cent respectively. In the year 1982 average yield per hectare of land for good grain has increased to 1,340 kilograms and for potatoes [by] more than 11.5 per cent.[9]

Because of intense fighting, nearly four million of the country's rural population had already migrated to Pakistan and Iran. Under the circumstances, the increase in agricultural production must be either a miracle or a statistical trick. (Later – in November 1983 – Karmal was to admit to the failures of the government's economic and agricultural policies).[10]

In order to create the impression of an independent economic policy, Karmal brought back Sardar Daud's Minister of Trade Mohammed Khan Jalalar to his old post. Jalalar, who was not a member of the Party, reorganized the Chamber of Commerce. In 1981 Karmal claimed notable successes in both trade and the private sector.[11] According to official figures, Afghanistan's external trade in 1982 was 1,355 million dollars (against 729.6 million in 1973). The people were also told that exports had gone up by 20 per cent and imports by 13.7 per cent.[12] The facts were otherwise. Because of the establishment of state export and import corporations, disruption of communications in the country and the closure of Iranian and Pakistani ports to Afghan goods, the country's main exchange earners, namely carpets and fine lamb wool, often lay rotting in local bazaars. Goods exported through Soviet ports faced long delays which naturally affected the export performance.[13]

In an address to the Party's 9th Congress, Karmal told his comrades with undisguised pride:

> For instance, during the [Afghan] year 1360 (ending March 1982), national income increased by 3.4 per cent as compared to preceding years and amounted to Afghanis 94.3 milliard.[14]

In the same speech Karmal made the startling disclosure that 150,000 workers were employed at the country's 300 industrial establishments.[15] These figures were highly exaggerated: the catastrophe which had hit Afghanistan was of such proportions that the country could at best be compared with a patient who was still somehow managing to breathe. After Brezhnev's death, a decline in Soviet aid and an increase in political pressure finally forced Karmal to retract his earlier claims:

> Reports on trade brought to me have sometimes been encouraging and at other times disappointing. In the field of internal and external trade, whatever is happening today is not enough.[16]

In 1985 the 14th Plenum of the Party announced support for private enterprise in the national economy. That year Afghan banks extended 199.2 million dollars in credits to help private industry, an increase of 77 per cent over 1984. On 3 February 1986, under Karmal's chairmanship, the Politburo gave the nation the glad tidings that in the next five-year plan (1986-90), national income would increase by 26 per cent, industrial production by 38 per cent and agricultural produce by 14.6 per cent. (This plan was dependent on Soviet assistance to the extent of 70 per cent).[17] The Politburo also announced in February that those who tried to weaken private enterprise would be severely dealt with.[18] It is obvious that Karmal, whose name literally meant the 'workers' friend', was directing this threat at the weakest and most exploited section of Afghan society, the workers. The Party's new General Secretary, Najibullah, addressing the 19th Plenum of the Party, expressed the hope to Abdul Sattar Purdilli that the workers under his charge would create conditions for industrial peace in order to increase national production.[19] The wheel which had never moved forward was now being pushed back.

How did the people react to Karmal's 'new phase'? In the third week of February 1980, two months after the arrival of the Soviet army in Afghanistan, a nationwide movement called Allah-au-Akbar (God is great) started against Karmal. Daytime processions began to take place at which slogans were chanted against Karmal and the Soviet army. At night the entire population including children would get on the rooftops and intone the *azan*, the Muslim call to prayer (this novel form of protest had been imported from Pakistan where it had been widely employed in 1977 to bring down the government of Ali Bhutto). Anti-government organizations put into motion an organized campaign involving the night-time, door to door distribution of pamphlets full of false and exaggerated news claiming that such and such town had been 'liberated' from the Soviet army.[20]

The Karmal government, following in the Taraki regime's footsteps, denounced this popular reaction as the handiwork of 'external elements'. In a raid on a Kabul hotel, a group of Pakistani 'saboteurs' was arrested, and on radio, TV, newspapers and wall posters, these 'foreign saboteurs' were held responsible for the February agitation.[21]

Instead of making an objective analysis of the situation, Karmal's senior functionaries were often heard saying in private that the popular unrest was in protest against the 'blood-shedding murderer Amin', and that the imperialists were trying to use it against 'our revolutionary government'.[22] Soon after these events, the Soviet Union began to repatriate soldiers drawn from its Muslim republics so that they should not get infected by the religious upsurge in Afghanistan. In the midst of the continuing unrest, the Karmal government announced the formation of 'resistance groups'. Party and local functionaries were used to form small armed units in urban areas to deal with night-time terrorist activities. As for the rural areas, the government was in no position to do anything. In order to break up the Khalq leadership, leading Khalq figures had been picked up and sent to Pulcharkhi soon after Karmal's arrival. Minor workers were divested of their arms after being charged with pro-Amin sympathies. These defenceless Khalqites were thus purposely made an easy prey of the rebels' terrorist activities. Taking the cue from their Parcham leaders and Ministers, those assigned to lead the 'resistance groups' moved to the safer Kabul district of Makrwaryan, thus drawing the curtain on Karmal's attempt to fight anti-government forces in the city.

While stray nightly terrorist incidents were common in urban localities,[23] some western press reports claimed that in the summer of

1980, about ten to fifteen Party workers were being murdered every night.[24] At the same time, according to American 'Afghan experts', the Party had no more than 2,500 members in December 1979.[25] Assuming that the number had doubled after Karmal's arrival, with between ten and fifteen Party members being 'murdered' every night, perhaps the only member still alive in 1980 was Karmal himself!

In April 1980 girls' colleges were swept by a wave of anti-Karmal and anti-Red Army agitation. The basic cause of the troubles was a 'letter' supposedly written by an Afghan girl student in Moscow which said that she, along with eight other Afghan girl students, was being kept in an experimental laboratory where they were being forcibly co-habited with in order to perfect a new hybrid race. She had further written that if the Soviet infidels were not pushed out of Afghanistan, every Afghan woman would meet the same fate. Almost as soon as photocopies of this so-called 'letter' were distributed in girls' educational institutions, as was to be expected, they took off their veils and came out on the streets. Because of these demonstrations, life in Kabul remained suspended for three days. Two girl students were also killed in police firing. Hardly had this agitation died out when the drinking water in girls' colleges was found poisoned. Hundreds of the unconscious students had to be rushed to hospitals.[26] The 'night letters' distributed after this incident alleged that the government had taken revenge on the students for their earlier agitation. In June 1980, Mohsin Rajai, a young Iranian, was caught along with his Afghan companions: it turned out that not only was he the author of the Moscow 'letter', he was also responsible for poisoning the girls' drinking water.[27]

Immediately after Karmal's installation at Arg, the presidential palace, there was a revival of the old Khalq-Parcham struggle. The first dispute arose over a cartoon published in a paper edited by Sultan Ali Kishtmand's younger brother (the cartoon was captioned 'Teacher and Disciple' and poked fun at Taraki and Amin). Sarwari had all copies of the publication withdrawn from news-stands, denouncing it as gross disrespect shown to Taraki. A meeting of the Politburo called to discuss the case led to pandemonium after Sarwari slapped Kishtmand across the face.[28] The Taraki group, henceforth led by Sarwari, put so much pressure on Karmal that he was forced to put Kishtmand's brother in detention for three days. Sarwari ordered Taraki's portrait hung over the central entrance to the Prime Minister's office in Sadarat so that all Parchamites, including Kishtmand, should be obliged to pass under it before proceeding to their offices. Taking this as a cue, minor Khalqites in government also put up Taraki's portrait in their offices.[29]

In February 1980 the question of changing the national flag led to a bitter inter-group struggle. Karmal wanted a new tricolour, while the Khalqites were unwilling to give up their traditional red. However, since the majority of the Central Committee membership was now in Karmal's pocket and he had Brezhnev to protect him, Sarwari and his friends were no longer strong enough to stop him.[30] On 19 February, in a 'people's ceremony' broadcast live over radio and TV, Karmal raised the new national tricolour; but the reaction of Khalqite officers in the army to the change was one of undisguised hostility which was what prompted Karmal to call a meeting of senior army commanders in March 1980 where he stressed the need for Party unity. It was widely noted that only a few of the tanks, armoured cars and anti-aircraft batteries which took part in the march-past on the second anniversary of the Revolution on 27 April 1980 displayed Karmal's new national standard. The message was clear. Loyal Khalqite officers had refused to bow before Karmal and his 'new phase'. However, Khalq was in no position to make use of its support in the army and remove Karmal.

Sarwari and others who had cooperated with Karmal to oust Amin were perhaps still labouring under the illusion that the Red Army, after installing Karmal in power, would salute him smartly, turn around and march back to Moscow. With the Red Army no longer around to protect him, Karmal would be so weakened that he would have no option but to stay under their thumb. It was well known, after all, that Karmal's influence in the army was limited. Once the Soviet troops were out of Afghanistan, they argued, it would even be possible to remove Karmal altogether. However, since the Red Army had entered Afghanistan to 'unite' the PDPA under Karmal's leadership and to 'protect the Revolution', Karmal and the Khalq group had no option but to tolerate each other. The obligation to stay together notwithstanding, the Parchamites were not about to forgive Khalq for what it had done to them during its days of power. By the same token, the Khalqites could not for a moment forget that they had been removed from power through brute military action.

Karmal, meanwhile, was trying to keep his balance on a tight rope, one of whose ends was held by Khalqite army officers and the other by the Red Army, with the people of Afghanistan throwing stones at him from down below. Had the Brezhnev administration only taken the trouble of studying the PDPA's past before the 27 December action, it would have realized that Karmal was no less controversial a figure than Amin. It might also have come to the conclusion that Moscow-imposed unity could never act as a substitute for genuine internal reconciliation within the Party. For Karmal and his Parchamites, the 'new phase' was an opportunity at last to settle across with Khalq, which was why the

Parchamite leadership watched silently as defenceless Khalq workers kept getting murdered. During Karmal's rule, never even once was the murder of Khalq workers and sympathizers, in or out of uniform, reported accurately by the government-controlled media. The commonly bandied-about epithets 'hero' and 'martyr' were not for them.[31]

While Karmal was able to eliminate Khalq from the body politic without much difficulty, he could not strike at its real source of support, which was the army. He could neither disarm Khalqite officers, nor send them to Pulcharkhi. However, after he watched in embarrassed silence Afghan tank commanders flying the old red flag on Revolution Day, he decided to make changes in top army leadership. Seven commanders heading provincial formations, including those at Paktia and Ghazni, were ordered transferred; but when Parchamite officers arrived to take charge, the Khalqites refused to honour the orders. No action was taken against them for fear that it might lead to a revolt in the army. Karmal swallowed this bitter pill in silence. The western press reported the episode in its usual ill-informed and distorted style.[32]

Thanks to Karmal's one-sided policies, based wholly on his hatred for Khalq, old Khalqites soon found themselves united under Sarwari's leadership. In factional politics, workers tend to back the leader who is tough and uncompromising and prepared to fight, if necessary, to defend their political interests. Sarwari was one man who met this description. As early as March 1980, he had begun to say openly that the Soviet army should hand over power to 'us' and return, a demand which fully reflected the feelings of nationalist army officers.[33] Karmal, being an old hand at such games, sought the Kremlin's help instead of staging a showdown with Sarwari. In June 1980 he had him sent over to Moscow for 'treatment' and a bit later dispatched to Mongolia as ambassador.[34] According to Azamuddin, Karmal told Sarwari on the phone from Kabul: 'You were like one of my arms and I am deeply saddened by your departure, but you know it was not my decision.'[35]

The political education of an average Khalqite officer did not extend beyond a few simple slogans. As Karmal began to close in on them, many fled to join the rebels.[36] Taking full advantage of this internal weakness, the rebels decided to put the names of known pro-Khalq officers on lists they had started to maintain. Whenever a rebel was arrested by government agencies, such lists were found on him, leading to the arrest of more Khalqite officers than of actual anti-Karmal elements. According to one estimate, in January 1981 as many as 600 military officers were sent to Pulcharkhi on conspiracy charges, though many of them were released later for lack of evidence and sent back to their units. Needless to say, these men could hardly be expected to fight for Karmal and his 'new phase'. One major reason for the disenchantment of the Afghan army with Karmal was these open and often useless vendettas against Khalqite officers.

In August 1980 there were reports in the western press that Khalqite officers had tried to overthrow Karmal.[37] In other words, the political battles of the regime were now being fought inside the Afghan military establishment where the Defence Minister and the political commissars were without exception Parchamites whom no loyal pro-Khalq officer was willing to obey. In September 1980, Karmal announced the formation of Sipahiyan-e-Inqilab (Soldiers of the Revolution), an armed outfit drawn from Party volunteer cadres. These men, according to the media, were to fight anti-government rebels.[39] As expected, Radio Kabul and TV went to town with their glowing accounts of the "heroic deeds" of the new revolutionary force.[40] Had Karmal been serious about the success of this 'revolutionary' force, he would not have kept the Party's rural-based Khalqite cadres and his own ivory tower Central Committee out of his new formation. However, secure in the belief that the Brezhnev regime was now committed to pay the price for the folly of intervention through the continuing sacrifice of its resources, blood and national honour in the mountains of Afghanistan, Karmal was not willing to exert himself beyond empty and futile gestures. These Kabul-bred Parchamite volunteers were almost all wiped out in the stony, hostile, battle-weary Afghan countryside by July 1981. There were no replacements, because there were no motivated Party cadres.

Karmal's 'new phase' had pushed the army beyond the limits of tolerance. In the first year of its rule, the Karmal regime was not even in a position to demob soldiers who had already completed their compulsory one year service and were being kept in the army against their will. On 27 December 1980 (which was also the birthday of Karmal's 'new phase'), 600 drafted soldiers who had completed their obligatory service threw down their weapons in front of Willayat-e-Kabul, the main police building, and formed themselves into a procession which went round the streets of the city demanding immediate discharge from military duties. The angry soldiers smashed traffic lights and damaged government buses. By the evening, most of them had been brought in under armed escort to the main detention centre. Even the commander of the Kabul Constabulary, Saifullah, and his political commissar were kept in detention for some days. In the evening news, the demonstration was described as an 'imperialist plot' which had been effectively dealt with by the patriotic, law-enforcing agencies (no mention was made of the just and legal demand made by the drafted soldiers). However, the incident forced the government to demob all those who had completed their obligatory period of service.

In 1981 emergency recruitment was ordered to fill the country's emptying cantonments. A new law running into eight sections and ninety articles was brought in under which men who had already completed national military service were recalled. However, the Soviet military presence had created such a hostile environment in and outside the army that no Afghan was willing to join; if forced to do so, he could be expected to desert at the first opportunity. It did not go unnoticed that no-one belonging to the families of Party cadres was made to join either the Sipahiyan-e-Inqilab or the armed forces under the new regulation. The sons of senior Party leaders were either in the Soviet Union or Eastern Europe for higher education, if not chasing girls on the streets of Kabul.[41]

During Karmal's time the inter-factional rivalry between Khalq and Parcham was most clearly manifested in the bitter struggle between the Ministry of the Interior and the Department of Intelligence. In order to weaken the Interior Ministry which was headed by Taraki's 'adopted' son Syed Gholabzoi (who was also a known Khalq supporter), Karmal brought about the separation of the Intelligence Department (KHAD) from the Ministry, setting it up as an independent entity. He also patronized Najibullah who belonged to Gholabzoi's province, Paktia, to keep the latter under pressure. All matters relating to the country's political detainees, interrogation of prisoners, arrests and the like were transferred from the Ministry to KHAD which was headed by Dr Najibullah (the police were only competent to deal with ordinary criminals). To further improve the image of his talented disciple, Karmal made Najibullah a brigadier in 1982 and a lieutenant general in 1983. KHAD was also equipped with an army division complete with helicopters, tanks and armoured cars. Despite his general's uniform, the civilian Najibullah did not find it easy to control his troops, which was why Gen. Ghulam Qadir Miankhel was appointed Military Adviser to him (Najibullah later made him a member of the PDPA Central Committee).[42]

The in-fighting between KHAD and the Interior Ministry continued quite openly with no holds barred. Because of Gholabzoi's patronage of Khalq, old Khalqites began to encourage their sons to join the police (which was under Gholabzoi's charge) rather than the army. According to one estimate, in 1984 the size of the police was twice that of the army:

> The police are numerically more powerful than the army and on top of it are led by a member of the Khalq faction (Gholabzoi). The head of the secret police is Najibullah, an adherent of Karmal. The police and the secret police are

inimical to each other and armed clashes between the two are not uncommon.[43]

Karmal spent six years intriguing against Gholabzoi and looking for ways to get him out of the Interior Ministry, but was unable to dislodge him because of his effective performance in his job. Every Karmal speech used to have one part devoted to those who were trying to destroy Party 'unity' (which to him meant complete subservience to Parcham). But if Karmal's arrival led to the intensification of the old Khalq-Parcham dispute, his departure in 1986 broke Parcham up into two groups. In the middle of 1986 Karmal's successor Dr Najibullah, following his deposed patron's example, was still mouthing the same clichés about Party unity:

> However, the fanning of discord by some members of the PDPA (meaning Karmal and his loyal followers who were opposing his nomination by the Kremlin as PDPA General Secretary) culminates in serving the interest of the enemies of the Revolution, imperialism and those who resist the progress of Afghanistan. Therefore, we should regard the resistance to unity as a betrayal of the interests of the Revolution, Party, people. Apart from that, resistance to unity is a betrayal of the friendship with the great Soviet Union.[44]

One of the main goals of the Soviet Union in sending its troops to Afghanistan was to unite the PDPA's two factions under one leadership to enable it to fight the reactionary forces. In this context, what Najibullah was speaking was the truth though, without realizing it, he was also reconfirming the continuance of the Party's internal contradictions.

Here, we must mention the internal changes brought about in the leadership of the Khalq group by Karmal's 'new phase'. After Taraki and Amin, Saleh Mohammed Zeary should have been the natural and agreed leader of the group, but because of his unhappy relations with the two, he was unable to dissociate the post-Amin situation from his own person (which is why after the 'new phase', the Parchamites liked to describe him as a man of 'balanced views', while the Khalqites called him a 'chicken-hearted opportunist'). He may have believed that in the event of the PDPA's reunification, he, as the senior Khalqite, would naturally come to occupy the number two position – the fulfilment of an old dream. Karmal, mindful of this ambition, began to invite him to sit next to him at official state functions. He wanted to create the impression that the real Khalq leader was Zeary and not Gholabzoi or Sarwari. However, within the cabinet it was Kishtmand, and within the Party Noor, who were actually preferred over Zeary. To keep Zeary happy, Karmal made him the head of a quasi-organization, the Qaumi

Pidar Watan Mahaz (the National Fatherland Front). Zeary, it should be mentioned, did nothing to save the lives of poor and unimportant Khalq workers who were now the target of Parcham's revenge. Therefore while on the one hand he lost respect among his Khalq comrades, at the same time he failed to fulfil his life ambition of becoming the number two figure in the Party. Had Zeary's two senior colleagues Panjsheri (a Tajik) and Danish (an Arab) tried to assume the leadership of the group, it is doubtful if the preponderant Pushtun majority of Khalq supporters would have accepted either of them. As for Mazdooryar and Watanjar, it was obvious that they had decided to lie low, which was why after Sarwari's exile in June 1980, it fell to the young Syed Gholabzoi to assume the leadership of the Khalq group.[45] He was not only the youngest but also of lowly rank (a mere junior commissioned officer) and ideologically much less educated than the others.

In the middle of 1981 Karmal announced that Party membership had reached 70,000, which was really due to the fact that he had begun to draft government employees, corporation workers, school teachers and petty functionaries into its ranks.[46] The fact that until now these civil servants had stayed out of the Party proved that they were not interested in it or its work. Karmal had pushed them like driven cattle into the Party to swell its ranks. He also claimed that 28 per cent of PDPA membership consisted of those born in the families of peasants and workers.[47] This figure was misleading because these members were only petty government officials and humble army soldiers who had been anointed with the working-class label almost overnight. Even if Karmal's figure was accepted, 72 per cent of Party members still belonged to the middle class (when no more than 10 per cent of the Afghan population could be said to belong to this class). Karmal was at the same time confessing that in the twenty-two-year history of the Party, its membership had contained no peasants or workers:

> The absorption of a considerable number of workers and peasants is a new phenomenon in the history of the Party and of course a number of the Party officials do not adequately ... perceive various aspects of the phenomenon.[48]

However, the forced induction of "peasants and workers" was a psychological shock for the Party and unacceptable to its bureaucrats. Two decades after the founding of the PDPA, Karmal had to tell his comrades that 'this approach within the Party of mistrust and dissatisfaction as regards this portion of Party members ["peasants and workers"] must be discarded decisively.'[49]

Addressing the 19th PDPA session on 10 July 1986, Dr Najibullah claimed that the membership of the Party now stood at 155,000, with peasants and workers representing 34 per cent of the total.[50] It goes without saying what the new leader meant by 'peasants and workers'. After the 'new phase', the main recruiting ground for the Party consisted of government ministries and departments where clear divisions between those who favoured Khalq and those who supported Parcham remained a fact of life. Consequently, the new membership did not represent unity but the same old diversity; the Party remained divided along the old battle-lines.

After coming into power, Karmal decided to associate non-Party individuals with the administration in order to widen his influence. By May 1980, of the 191 important official appointments made, 78 of the beneficiaries were not PDPA members.[51] While the Khalq group saw these 'new faces' as a hangover from Sardar Daud's days, Karmal saw their inclusion as the fulfilment of his old ambition of setting up a 'national democratic' government. Karmal also declared a 'general amnesty', promising that all those who returned would be given back their houses, lands and properties.[52] To make his offer doubly attractive, he announced that even if the real owners did not return, their close relatives would be treated as the real owners. To benefit from Karmal's offer, rebels who had left properties in Afghanistan and were now living in Pakistan sent harmless members of their families back to the country, where they reclaimed the properties, mortgaged them to local residents (to rule out any future takeover) and returned to Pakistan, their pockets lined with money. To stop this 'heads I win tails you lose' practice, the government made it incumbent on all Afghans who wished to sell any property valued at or above Rupees 300,000 (about $20,000) to obtain a clearance certificate.[53]

In order to go back on the agricultural reforms of the Taraki period, the Karmal government announced a set of exemptions in the summer of 1981.[54] According to the new rules, land reform laws were no longer applicable to the following categories: officers of the armed forces, tribal leaders who supported the government and landowners who were willing to undertake mechanized farming and sell the excess produce to the government, landowners who returned to the country under the government's general amnesty, and smallholders and landless peasants who voluntarily offered to send their sons for national service in the Afghan armed forces (the last category was also to be given special preference in the allotment of distributed lands).

Karmal had cleverly tried to offer to return the confiscated lands belonging to Afghanistan's big Khans and landlords on condition that they should put an end to their anti-government activities. Had he not been involved in the events of 27 December 1979 and had the reactionary camp not been able to convince the common Afghan that he had come to power riding a Soviet tank, this package of concessions could have turned the tables. Despite these widespread reservations about Karmal, his announcement did have an appreciable effect in areas where the military presence of the government was substantive; but in areas where the rebels were in control and where the landless peasants continued to work for absentee landlords (who were in Pakistan enjoying income from their lands) Karmal's announcement did not cut much ice.

By offering partially to return nationalized property into private ownership, was Karmal also not announcing the 'partial withdrawal' of the April Revolution – which after all was officially committed to the conversion of private into nationalized or state-owned assets? And yet this was nothing compared to the declaration made seven years after the Soviet intervention by Karmal's successor that neither he nor his Party were socialist,[55] and that he was willing to return to their rightful owners all confiscated assets (lands, houses, factories, companies and banks) if they returned to the country in the next five years.[56]

19

'Leninist Tactics'

Until 1981 neither Karmal nor his benefactor Brezhnev had despaired of 'complete and final victory'. There is no indication that they were even faintly aware of the terrible future which awaited their political and military misadventure. Every Karmal speech used to end with warm praise on behalf of the Party, the people and himself for Brezhnev's 'fraternal' assistance. The Kremlin, for its part, believed that by promoting Karmal's image, it would win him worldwide acceptance (Karmal's address to the 26th Soviet Party Congress and his frequent trips to Eastern Europe were all part of this strategy). When with the approval of Moscow Karmal began to go back on Taraki's land reforms, his Parchamite apologists justified the move as being the old Leninist tactic 'one step forward, two steps back'.

Perhaps as a continuation of this tactic, on 18 June 1983 the Revolutionary Council announced an amnesty for all those who would lay down their arms. The amnesty even extended to those who had deserted the Afghan army and gone over to the rebels. There was an additional guarantee that those who took up the offer would be entitled to full government protection of their lives and properties – a lofty boast by Karmal considering the circumstances. According to government claims, by the end of 1983, taking advantage of the amnesty, 4,000 families had returned to Afghanistan, while 25,000 rebel fighters had laid down their arms.[1] Exaggeration is always part of such claims: moreover, the number of those who picked up arms against the government in the first three years of Karmal's rule was much, much larger. According to the author's personal estimate, until the end of 1983 no more than 2,000 to 3,000 rebels had actually surrendered to the government.

The man assigned the responsibility of overseeing this operation was

217

Dr Bahar, an assistant to the then KHAD head, Dr Najibullah. Bahar had an office next to Darul Aman, but the building where the surrendering rebels were brought and kept was situated in front of the Rabia Balkhi School.[2] Dr Bahar's agents, posing as rebels, would join the fighters and, exploiting their internal rivalries and contradictions, sometimes succeed in winning over a certain section to the government side. This was risky business and many valuable agents were lost during these operations. The rebels did admit, however, that Dr Najibullah's agents were present at every level in their camps.

Among the PDPA's various failures was its inability to give the country a constitution in the nine years of its rule. The fifty-member Constitutional Committee appointed by Amin had not even held its first meeting when Karmal arrived on the scene with his 'new phase'.[3] In 1980 he announced a provisional constitution under the title 'Basic Principles', but that was as far as he went, and for six and a half years, Afghanistan remained without a permanent constitutional document. Karmal's provisional constitution consisted of ten chapters, sixty-eight articles and about six thousand words.[4] Under one of its provisions a National Fatherland Front was to be established consisting of associations of youth, teachers, women, journalists, artists, workers and scholars (these associations did not exist). Declaring that the Front would be the bastion of future political power, the government promised popular participation in the running of the state at every level. But what were the steps Karmal actually took to fulfil his promise?

Not unexpectedly, one of the articles (No 5) was devoted to the supremacy of Islam and the role of religious scholars. Addressing a conference of Islamic leaders in 1980, Karmal declared that 'after the triumphant uprising of 6th Jaddi (coinciding with the Soviet military action of 27 December 1979), respect to the holy religion of Islam has been granted by the government.'[5] To impart an Islamic colour to his government, he set up a separate Department of Islamic Affairs (later turned into a Ministry). The first religious Ministry in the history of Afghanistan was thus set up by the communists. By the end of 1984, in the city of Kabul alone, there were 34 new mosques, all constructed under Karmal's orders. As many as 523 mosques in different parts of the country were renovated. In 1983 salaries paid to mosque *imams* or congregational heads ran into 65 million Afghanis.[6]

However, neither the decrees nor *fatwas* broadcast every day by radio and TV during Taraki's and Amin's times, nor Karmal's mosques and his creation of a Ministry for religious affairs, could smother the fires of so-called religious fanaticism in the country. During its time in office, the Khalq government surrendered the powerful Islamic weapon to its opponents, while Karmal, brought into power by the Red Army, ended up creating a situation where this weapon could be used effectively against his government. Without making any effort to understand why the Afghan people had turned against him, Karmal was always at pains to establish that the rebels were doing no service to Islam:

> We must explain to the people that the slogan [Islam] is merely a cover and a pretext for strangulating our Revolution.... The masses must know that the so-called slogan of defence of Islam is being used hypocritically.[7]

By intervening in Afghanistan, the Brezhnev administration had however made an offering of the flag of the defence of Islam to the Afghan reactionaries. Previously, the slogan of Islam was only raised against the government's reforms, but after the Soviet military action, it was transformed into one of *jihad* in defence of national liberation. Taraki had been no wiser than Karmal. His answer to the resistance being offered to him by reactionary elements was given in the form of *fatwas* favouring his government, when he should have turned to the masses to bail him out. In 1987 the fourth General Secretary of the PDPA, Dr Najibullah, was to be seen appearing at public rallies with a copy of the Quran in his hand. All four leaders of the Party, failing to identify the real cause of the people's resistance to their rule, have instead kept making naive attempts to use Islam as a weapon of defence.

Under Article 6 of Karmal's provisional constitution, a National Fatherland Front was to be set up; however, it could not provide the solution required, given the incomplete class structure characterizing Afghan society. For more than a year and a half, Karmal continued his efforts to set up professional organizations of poets, writers, journalists, teachers and religious scholars outside the Party to fulfil his dream of an 'ideal' national front. He also set up rural cooperatives and workers' trade unions. Nearly 90 per cent of these bodies consisted of people associated with middle-class professions, which meant that they had no existence outside the city limits of Kabul. On top of this, the leadership of these bodies was not in the hands of professionals but of various Party leaders. Panjsheri was made president of the society of writers and journalists, while Abdul Sattar Purdilli was declared the 'leader' of all Afghan workers. Kishtmand and Noor were similarly in charge of other professional organizations. Anahita Ratebzad was not only the head of the women's organization, but also of the Soviet-Afghan Friendship Association, the World Peace Council and the Council for Peace, Progress and Solidarity.

On 19 June 1981 the inaugural session of the National Fatherland

Front opened with 945 delegations in attendance. Saleh Mohammed Zeary was 'elected' as its president.[8] The vast majority of the participating delegations comprised paper organizations created by Karmal. The Front claimed that it represented a cross-section of Afghan society, but instead of turning to the masses, it contented itself with sending a telegram to the UN Secretary General to the effect that the Karmal government was legal, the 'limited' contingent of Soviet troops (it was three times the size of the entire Afghan army) had come to Afghanistan at the invitation of the legally-constituted government, etc., etc. The congratulatory messages received from the 'national fronts' of Vietnam, Kampuchea and Bulgaria were sombrely broadcast by Afghan radio and TV. While this was good enough for the insatiable propaganda appetite of the official Afghan media, it could not extricate the government from the crisis in which it was engulfed.

In October 1981 the Karmal regime passed legislation relating to local government institutions, under which the powers of the central government were to be transferred to local and autonomous bodies. The new law declared that the ultimate repository of state power would be the Loya Jirga or the Grand Assembly of all Afghan Tribes. However, it was announced at the same time that until conditions were ripe for free elections to the local bodies and the holding of the Loya Jirga, all powers would rest with the Revolutionary Council.[9]

Had the Party followed its original constitution or taken the material conditions of Afghan society into account, its first act in office should have been the establishment of local bodies and the holding of the Loya Jirga. However, and not surprisingly either, what the Party should have done first, it tried to do last. While the local bodies' legislation was drafted in 1981, it took Karmal four years to give it practical shape. In 1985, possibly on Moscow's advice, Karmal staged 'elections' to the two institutions.[10] On 23-24 April the Loya Jirga was called to session. According to the government's own version, the class background of the 'elected representatives' to the Loya Jirga was as follows:

> Of the total elected delegates, 11.6 per cent were workers, 26 per cent peasants, 23 per cent scholars, teachers, university professors, physicians, engineers and civil servants, 3 per cent national bourgeoisie and tradesmen, 11 per cent religious scholars and preachers, 25.4 per cent were elders, leaders of tribes and ethnic groups ... There were sixty women elected as members of [the] Loya Jirga, while 21 per cent of the elected members belonged to the PDPA.[11]

This Jirga, claiming to be the unanimous representative of the Afghan people, also sent a telegram to the UN Secretary General in support of Karmal. Peasants, who formed 80 per cent of the country's population, had been given only 26 per cent of the seats on the Jirga, while traders, big businessmen and tribal chiefs, who represented no more than one per cent of the Afghan population, had been accorded 28.4 per cent of the seats. The majority of the Jirga's members belonged to the middle class (and amusingly enough the burden of representing peasants and workers had also been placed on the shoulders of this class). Karmal claimed that the Loya Jirga was the true repository of state power, while in fact it hardly had any hand in running the government or influencing its decisions. Ironically, one of the members of Karmal's Jirga – Haji Mohammed Chamakni – took over Karmal's job as President of the country one year later.

It must be pointed out that in Afghan tradition, the Loya Jirga has always played a crucial role during times of national crisis. The situation created by the events of December 1979 made it possible for the rebels to call for a Loya Jirga of their own. In May 1980 Afghan rebels based in Peshawar organized one which was attended by 916 representatives. However, with the exception of Mujadaddi and Gilani, all other tribal leaders rejected the genuineness of the gathering and the Jirga died its own quiet death.[12] Thus neither the rebels nor Karmal could organize a genuine and successful Loya Jirga.

The greatest problem facing Karmal was how to seal the country's long common border with Pakistan to stop rebel attacks and incursions. Militarily, his efforts had failed, and thus his only chance was to induce tribes inhabiting the Pakistani side to make it impossible for the rebels to cross to and fro at will as they were doing. In 1985 such an opportunity at last arose. Since the arrival of Afghan refugees in Pakistan, the Khyber Agency had become the world's largest centre of heroin traffic. The Pakistan government, in order to please the White House (Nancy Reagan being the head of a drugs fighting programme), had begun to undertake minor military operations in the area to stop the production and smuggling of heroin, and this had naturally caused a great deal of resentment among the tribes. Jumping at this chance, on 13-14 September 1985 Karmal organized a Loya Jirga of border tribes.

According to the government announcement, 3,700 representatives of Pakistan's border tribes took part in the Jirga, 65 per cent of whom were tribal chiefs, 18 per cent religious leaders, 5 per cent traders, 5 per cent nomads, 5 per cent former members of parliament and 2 per cent Afghan tribal unit commanders.[13] (Earlier, a Tribal Force had been set up by Karmal to deal with the rebels.) The well-known tribal leader from the Khyber Agency, Sardar Wali Khan Kokikhel (Afridi), was represented in this Jirga by his son. A month later, Karmal claimed in an interview that 'it is not our brother Wali

Khan Kokikhel alone who fights the ruling regime in Pakistan.'[14]

The Pakistan government, it was feared in Kabul, might induce the tribal leaders to support its actions with the help of generous handouts, which was exactly what happened. In 1986 Karmal's 'brother' Sardar Wali Khan Kokikhel was enjoying Pakistani hospitality in Islamabad. Despite earlier propaganda campaigns about local self-government and the 1985 Loya Jirga, Karmal's disciple and successor Dr Najibullah was claiming by 1986 that the study of the situation testifies to the fact that new organs of power have not become the real organs of action.[15]

20

The Red Army and Soviet Advisers

On the night of 27 December 1979 there must have been a sense of satisfaction in the Kremlin over the success of the action in Kabul. However, before long the number of Soviet troops in Afghanistan had to be increased from 10,000 to 100,000 and later to 150,000 to fight a futile war on Afghanistan's arid and hostile soil. The number of non-military Soviet advisers (including college and university teachers) was around 10,000 in 1984[1] (in every department of the University of Kabul, there were Soviet teachers who used to lecture their classes with the help of Tajik Farsi-speaking interpreters).[2]

After Karmal's 'new phase', there were Soviet advisers in every government department and ministry (from the offices of cabinet Ministers to those of mere section heads) to help in reorganization. For all practical purposes, the government was run by these men. The Afghan bureaucracy could only take important decisions or bring about changes in administrative and economic policies after 'consulting' these advisers. While this process was supposed to be accomplished behind closed doors, the weak and gutless Afghan bureaucracy made no secret of the fact that real power lay in the hands of the Soviet advisers. When an ordinary citizen visited a government department of ministry to get something done, he was almost invariably told that decision-making powers lay with Soviet advisers and not Afghan officers. In 1984 Karmal advised the sick Afghan bureaucracy to

> take full advantage of the experience and wisdom of our Soviet brothers and comrades. However, it is for you to take the ultimate responsibility [because] only you are fully conversant with your country's customs and traditions, its tribes and nations and its mountains and passes. Only by bringing our own experience in line with the wisdom and experience of our Soviet comrades will we be able to bring our joint efforts to the highest level.[3]

Karmal's remarks were an admission that Party and government functionaries, instead of accepting responsibility for decisions taken, were content with leaving everything to the Soviet advisers so that if something went wrong, the Soviets should get the blame.

For the Soviet advisers, war-torn Afghanistan struggling with Karmal's 'new phase' was a happy place. A Soviet head mechanic working without respite eight hours a day in his home country must have felt like a king when posted to Afghanistan where his arrival at the factory in the morning was treated as no less than a state event. It is difficult to assess at this point what, if anything, the PDPA learnt from the Red Army and its Soviet advisers. However, the influence of the PDPA and Afghan society on Soviet soldiers and civilian advisers is not so difficult to ascertain. Many of them, especially advisers attached to civilian or military outfits, actually became partisans in the Khalq-Parcham dispute.[4] The Soviet troops and civilian advisers had been brought to a country where graft, bribery, dishonesty and malingering were common. The Afghan bureaucracy did not take long to infect its Soviet guests with these diseases. There were few Soviet advisers in Kabul who did not possess a personal Japanese or German car – which clearly could not have been purchased out of the meagre salaries they received. How had they come by these cars? It should not take much imagination to answer the question.[5]

It has been normal for soldiers of the Red Army to buy American cigarettes in exchange for Kalashnikov bullets on the streets of Kabul. In October 1980 an eighteen-year-old Afghan by the name of Abdul Hamid was caught making such an exchange. He was brought to Pulcharkhi and soon given the name 'Marlboro' by other Afghan prisoners. He said he had been buying bullets from Soviet soldiers for the last six months before his arrest. There are many Afghans in Pulcharkhi because they were caught doing this barter trade but there is not a single Soviet to be found in any Afghan jail on this count.

Adelbert Eskala, an elderly Austrian prisoner, told the author in Pulcharkhi that while he was being kept at the central detention centre in the city (Nazarat Khana Sadarat), some Soviet soldiers burst into his cell at night and robbed him of his wedding ring, watch and electric shaver. (This part of the Nazarat Khana Sadarat consisted of underground cells which were commonly known as *Tashnabha* or toilets. Until the end of 1981 one Soviet detachment was based at Sadarat to guard the prison. 'Dangerous' detainees like Majid Kalakani and Asadullah Amin were kept in these underground cells.)

Young Soviet soldiers were also much given to writing graffiti on the walls of Sadarat. There were even inscriptions on the tank which supplied water to the detention centre. The graffiti typically recorded the names of their friends, sweethearts, family members and cities of birth.[6] The most prominent inscription on the water tank said in Russian: *O Moscow, may you live forever, but when will I see you again?*

Another common sight in Kabul was Soviet soldiers selling tyres and spare parts at throwaway prices to owners of small auto workshops. In 1983, the author himself saw Soviet soldiers selling tyres taken from official Volga cars to private workshops run by Afghans.[7] In 1981 a Sikh currency trader was arrested at Kabul airport trying to smuggle out about 30 million roubles. He was released three days later because it was rumoured that he was acting on behalf of senior Afghan officials and Soviet advisers.[8] Petrol shortages in Kabul were common after 1980 (one cause being guerilla raids on oil-transport convoys) and it was public knowledge that Soviet officers were selling entire oil tankers to traders of the Hazara nationality. Some Hazara traders were caught and sent to Pulcharkhi, but the 'party of the second part' was, of course, above local laws.

If Afghan refugees have been able to turn Pakistan into one of the world's major heroin suppliers in a matter of a few years, it is only logical that the Afghan locals should have brought some changes in the life-style of their Soviet 'guests'. Smoking hashish is not considered so objectionable in Afghanistan and Afghan soldiers smoking 'pot' are a common sight. The habit has caught on and Soviet soldiers have become increasingly partial to it.

Soviet soldiers have also been involved in episodes of violence. In May 1981 one Hazara taxi driver was brought to jail with serious injuries. He was charged with murdering two Soviet soldiers. The story was that they had hailed him on the street and asked to be taken to the Soviet embassy, but had refused to pay the fare. There had been a violent argument and the driver had killed both of them.

The same year, in Kabul's Darul Aman district, three Afghan women were found raped and murdered and Soviet soldiers were held responsible for the outrage in the *shabnamas* or night letters circulated by the rebels.[9] It was further reported that the Afghan Defence Minister, Mohammed Rafi, had insisted on stern action and been removed from his post for his pains.[10]

Not everything about the Soviet soldiers is bad, however. Those taken prisoner by the Red Army in battle speak in warm terms of their treatment at the hands of their captors. There were four or five men in Pulcharkhi who had been left for dead by their 'Mujahideen' comrades after a battle and who were later captured by the Soviets. They had been taken to hospital and given blood donated by Soviet soldiers which had saved their lives. Ziauddin Mahmood, an Egyptian adherent of the right-wing Akhwanul Muslimeen captured in Kunnarha province, was full of praise for his teatment in the Soviet prison camp. While it is true that any Soviet soldier or officer caught committing an illegal act is court martialled and sent home, probably to Siberia, the Soviet rulers do not understand that it is only the cold Siberian winds which reach Afghanistan, not the news of the punishment meted out to Soviet offenders for their misdeeds. Taking advantage of this silence, rebel *shabnamas* are always full of stories listing the crimes committed by the Red Army on Afghanistan's soil. Many of these stories are pure fabrication, but the way things have gone in Afghanistan, people tend to believe what they hear about the Soviets.

The history of the Great October Revolution of 1917 records numerous incidents where soldiers of the Red Army suspected of committing atrocities against the population during the civil war were tried and, if found guilty, put against the wall and shot. These were Lenin's express orders because he wanted the peasants to be able to draw a distinction between the Red and White Armies. If some criminal elements in the Red Army, guilty of atrocities against the Afghans, had been tried and publicly punished in Kabul the effect would have been dramatic and the people would have no longer accepted every anti-Soviet rumour as fact. Unfortunately, however, the Kabul administration would not even give a traffic ticket to a drunken Soviet driver.[11]

The Soviet advisers were most active in the Afghan intelligence establishment which they tried to reorganize and modernize, teaching Afghans to employ more humane interrogation methods. During Taraki and Amin's time, there were two to three resident Soviet advisers at the Department of Intelligence, but it seems their advice was disregarded, the prime task of the Department being the liquidation of political opponents. During this period, Syed Abdullah, Superintendent of the Pulcharkhi prison, was known to have a liking for having prisoners shot dead in the cells. He once had about 300 prisoners assembled on the lawn of the first block and mowed down with machine-guns fired from all four directions. Some were able to escape and hide in offices, but on Syed Abdullah's orders the guards are said to have brought a ladder, put it against the wall of the room where the prisoners were hiding, climbed up and lobbed enough hand grenades through the ventilator to destroy everyone. Marks of this 'revolutionary action' could be seen on the walls of that room.[12]

The Khalq government never considered it necessary to have prisoners tried by a court of law. After 1980 the situation definitely changed to some extent:

In 1978-79 the Pulcharkhi prison in Kabul was without doubt a kind of Buchenwald. Thousands of innocent people were tortured and killed there without any legal proceedings. Things improved a bit after the arrival of the Soviets. But an enormous number of arrests are still being made. Prisoners are still being tortured. Electric shocks have, however, been abolished and nobody is executed without a proper trial.[13]

During Karmal's time the interrogation centre operated by the internal section of the Intelligence Department was situated in Kabul's Shashdrak quarter and prisoners who were moved from there to Pulcharkhi said that until December 1980, they were given electric shocks by their interrogators to obtain information. When this came to the notice of Soviet advisers, they had the practice discontinued.[14] Until 1983, interrogating officers often beat up their prisoners, but it became less common after that, partly because nearly 80 per cent of these officials had by that time returned from the Soviet Union after completing six months of training in interrogation techniques.[15] One glimpsed a change in their attitude if not in their psychological makeup.

There were in Kabul about twenty secret interrogation centres from where, after initial questioning, detainees were transferred to the central intelligence facility at Sadarat. Soviet advisers were always present when foreigners or rebels captured in battle were interrogated. The detention law, enacted during Daud's regime, made it obligatory on the authorities to produce a detainee before a court of law within two months of his arrest. The maximum detention period could not exceed nine months. Officers from the Special Revolutionary Courts used to tour the prisons and detention centres after every few months to obtain lists of prisoners who had not been produced before a court. (The author was an exception. For the two and a half years that he was in jail, no investigation was carried out and no charges framed, and his final release was ordered without any reasons being given.) However, Afghan prisoners were generally given early trials. In the Special Revolutionary Courts, the accused could offer his own defence without a lawyer. The author knows of no case where the death sentence was pronounced without at least a year's court proceedings.[16]

It can be said with complete certainty that after the arrival of the Soviet army, no Afghan prisoner was hanged without due process. Those sent to the gallows between 1980 and 1983 numbered 200 and 250 each year. Given the situation in Afghanistan, these figures might appear low, but they are accurate.[17] (According to Amnesty International, the number of hangings in Pakistan during this period exceeds 400 a year, a finding which by comparison does 'credit' to war-torn Afghanistan.)

In the entire history of Afghanistan, it was never considered necessary to draft a jail manual. In 1982 – under Soviet advice, one assumes – Karmal announced the first jail reforms in Afghan history. It was no longer permitted to beat up prisoners, nor could jail officials keep a prisoner in solitary confinement for more than fourteen days. Prisoners were allowed to meet their families in private every fortnight, and to receive food, small gifts and letters. Under the new regulations, jails were to be transferred from the administrative control of the Department of Intelligence to the Interior Ministry (though since the Interior Ministry was under the charge of Syed Gholabzoi, the effective control of the country's jails stayed with the Intelligence Department). However, the Afghan intelligence service could not be expected to implement Karmal's reforms. In May 1982, when prisoners went on a strike against the attitude of the Pulcharkhi administration, they were in some cases beaten up.[18]

While according to modern standards the conditions in which prisoners are kept in Afghanistan are pathetic, the country's history and traditions have been such that no miracles should have been expected. It is against the Afghan temperament to forgive or take pity on political and personal opponents, Karmal's prison reforms, therefore, can only be credited to his Soviet advisers. A bad law is better than no law at all, said the British philosopher David Hume and in this spirit the changes brought about in Afghan prison laws can be welcomed.

21

External Interference

A survey of the political parties active in Afghanistan before the April 1978 Revolution will show that the estimated membership of the two PDPA factions was around 10,000[1] a figure in line with western estimates. There is no question that the largest political party in the country before the Revolution was the PDPA. Despite its middle-class membership, it contained representatives of almost all of Afghanistan's nationalities, regions and races. By contrast, rebel parties even today are confined to regional, racial or nationality-oriented groups. While the political blunders of the PDPA, no less than the adventurist policies of the Kremlin, contributed to the distortion and, ultimately, betrayal of the Afghan Revolution, the unprincipled support lent to the undemocratic and religiously bigoted rebel forces by the United States has played a major role in bringing Afghanistan to its present predicament.

Long before the arrival of the Soviet army – in fact, only one week after the Revolution – the *New York Times* declared the change in Kabul as a calamity for Gen. Zia-ul-Haq of Pakistan and the Shah of Iran. It also predicted that the Afghan refugees of the future would offer tribal resistance to the new order, leading to much bloodshed. As if providing a tip to Afghanistan's neighbours about their future course of action, the paper asked 'countries in the region [namely Iran and Pakistan which had not yet recognized the new Kabul regime][2] to lend a hand [to help the future Afghan refugees?] and the wealthier nations to help them carry the burden'.[3] The message was clear and a 'high-ranking' Iranian official was soon after quoted by the *New York Times* in a news report:

Tehran felt that Mr Taraki's declaration of non-alignment is absurd in view of the dominant role the Russians are playing in Kabul [the 'high-ranking' official forgot to mention the 'role' being played in Iran by the Shah's 25,000 American advisers]. ... Speaking of Iranian intervention in Oman, he went on to warn of the possibility of [Iranian] military intervention in Afghanistan.[4]

The new military order in Pakistan, for its part, saw the Afghan Revolution as a good opportunity to seek more US aid and wasted no time in sending a signal to Washington. A 'senior official' told the *New York Times*:

For all practical purposes, the Soviet Union now has a border with Pakistan [a proclamation that from now on Pakistan was a 'frontline' state]. The United States must realize that there has been a historic readjustment in this part of the world and act accordingly.[5]

In effect, long before the Soviet 'military occupation' of Afghanistan, Pakistan was calling on the United States to 'act'.[6] Only a month and a half after the Revolution, the western media's news-assembly line sent out the first report of 'Mujahideen resistance' to the new government in Kabul.[7] Barely fifteen days later, the right-wing Mohaz-e-Najat-e-Milli (National Salvation Front) opened an office in Peshawar.[8] The offices of the three other reactionary parties – the Hizbe Islami, the Jamiat-e Islami and the Harkat-e Islami – were already active there. The Pakistan government now began to extend open military and financial assistance to these groups and parties. It was thus Pakistan which initiated the 'holy war' in Afghanistan. According to one author:

While some [border] tribes resisted Islamabad's blandishments, others succumbed and allowed the rebels to establish guerilla bases on their tribal territory. The most important of these were at Miran Shah ... and at Parachanar (adjacent to Afghanistan's Paktia province) ... The others were located in Mohmand and Bajur Agencies (bordering the Afghan provinces of Kunnarha and Nangarhar). Pakistan denied the existence of these bases ... however, guerilla operations against Afghanistan were carried out from these areas of Pakistan ... The evidence also suggests that Pakistan's roads and rail system were also used to transport arms to the rebels.[9]

After a visit to Pakistan, the same author wrote about the 'holy war' being waged by the rebels against the Kabul government:

None of these, neither Gilani's ambitious plan, nor the insurgency that developed in Kunnarha, Nangarhar and parts of Kabul valley (in 1979) would have been possible without the active assistance of the Martial Law regime in Pakistan. Pakistan officially denied that it did more than offer 'humanitarian assistance' to the refugees who crossed the 'porous' border into Pakistan's tribal areas ... In fact, Pakistan did much more. The Afghan [rebel] politicians were able to hold press conferences [in Pakistan] ... The Pakistani media, carefully controlled (by the military government) gave publicity to the rebel statements ... It is clear tht the [rebel] propaganda campaign had Islamabad's blessings.[10]

According to some reports, before the Soviet intervention, there were twenty-three camps in Pakistan[11] where 35,000 men were given military training for periods ranging from three to six months.[12] To better understand Pakistan's role in Afghanistan, it will be useful to review the political changes in the region during 1977-79. In July 1977 Ali Bhutto's progressive government was overthrown in Pakistan and replaced by a right-wing military regime. A year earlier, Mao Tse-Tung had died, but not before laying the foundations of Sino-American friendship. In 1977, too, Mrs Indira Gandhi lost power in India. In 1978 Sardar Daud Khan was overthrown, and the Shah of Iran met the same fate one year later. The Shah's ousting was the greatest setback suffered by the United States since Vietnam, because as the region's 'policeman' he had successfully protected US interests. While the Shah was around, Pakistan in Washington's eyes was no more than an unimportant reference point on the map. But after the Shah's departure, Pakistan's new military ruler quite correctly assessed his value and cashed in on it. It is interesting that neither China under Deng Xiao-Ping, nor India under Morarji Desai found any cause for complaint over Pakistan's 'new role'.

The steps taken by the martial law regime in Pakistan in 1978 in the name of 'humanitarian assistance' to Afghan refugees laid the foundations of the biggest reality of the decade two years later. The United States needed Pakistan after the Afghan and Iranian revolutions as Pakistan's new military order needed the United States. This convergence of US-Pakistan interests led two months after the Shah's fall to the execution of Ali Bhutto following a controversial and legally untenable trial. It was clear that after 'losing' Iran, the United States was not prepared to risk the restoration of democratic rule in Pakistan. Bhutto was hanged on 4 April 1979 and it became an obvious necessity for the military regime to create tension on its Afghan border to forestall any possible outbreak of popular unrest in the country. According to an official protest lodged by the Afghan government, Pakistani regulars invaded its territory on 7 April 1979.[13] The controlled Pakistani press carried prominently-displayed stories on 11 April alleging Afghan air attacks on Chitral in the north of the country.

The American attitude towards Afghanistan in recent years can be divided into three distinct phases. The first covers the period between the Saur Revolution and the overthrow of the Shah of Iran. While adopting a negative, if not hostile, attitude towards the Afghan Revolution, the United States did not get directly involved in the conflict, but encouraged Pakistan to play a meddlesome role. Only in the summer of 1979 did the United States begin to take an active interest in Afghan events. According to the *Washington Post*, senior US officials for the first time received a rebel representative, Zia Nassery, in May.[15] During the same month, there were reports in the American media of an important meeting held by the Carter administration about 'secret intervention' in Afghanistan.[16] In July 1979 US Deputy Secretary of State Warren Christopher visited Pakistan. Later that summer, a US Congressional delegation toured the country. This delegation praised Pakistan for its support of Afghan rebels and also met some rebel leaders.[17] However, throughout 1979 the United States kept making public denials that it was playing any role in Afghanistan, even while it was secretly patronizing rebel groups and leaders. A US State Department spokesman, Tom Roston, denied in June 1979 'that any US personnel or arms are being used in training and equipping the Afghan rebels in Pakistan or any place elsewhere.'[18]

In 1980 the *Washington Post*, commenting on American assistance to Afghanistan before Soviet military intervention, wrote:

> US government aid prior to the December invasion ... was limited to funnelling small amounts of medical supplies and equipment to scattered rebel tribes, plus what is described as 'technical advice' to the rebels about where they could acquire arms on their own.[19]

After the Soviet military intervention of 27 December 1979, the United States finally decided to enter the Afghan fray openly. Accusing the Soviet Union of aggression against a small, non-aligned Islamic country, it declared its full moral and material support for the rebel forces. By 1985 the United States had invested nearly 625 million dollars in the Afghan rebels.[20] In that year alone, the Reagan administration provided them with 250 million dollars. According to the *Washington Post*:

> Congress has nearly tripled the Reagan administration's original request for covert aid to support the rebels. The estimated 250 million dollars expected to be provided to the rebels this fiscal year is part of the largest CIA military support application since the Vietnam war.[21]

The newspaper went on to add that the CIA was training the rebels in the use of mortars, rocket grenades, ground-to-air missiles and Russian-made AK-47 rifles. It also disclosed that the Soviet weapons (which the rebels claimed to have captured from Soviet and Afghan troops) were being bought from China, Egypt and Israel (the Israelis possessed vast quantities of Soviet arms captured during various Middle East wars). The Soviet weapons, the newspaper further wrote, were crated to Karachi via the Gulf states, from where they were transported by truck and train to the NWFP and Baluchistan provinces bordering Afghanistan.

There were reports in the American press in 1986 that in order to aid the Afghan rebels, the CIA was providing them with funds lodged in Swiss banks. According to the *Washington Post,* the US government had deposited a sum of $250 million in Swiss banks for the use of Afghan rebels. An equal sum was said to have been lodged there by Saudi Arabia. The money was spent on acquiring Soviet and Chinese weapons.[22]

The United States supplied the rebels with 200 Stinger missiles in 1986. An American journalist who spent some days in Nangarhar province wrote that he had personally witnessed US experts training Hizbe Islami 'Mujahideen' in the use of Stingers. Between 6 and 8 October 1986, these missiles were used to bring down Soviet helicopters in Bast and Kaka inside Afghanistan. According to the journalist, the 'experiment' was 80 per cent successful. He also added that the 'Mujahideen' had been promised two Stingers for every Soviet aircraft brought down. Operators who failed to aim correctly were given additional training.[23] If this account is correct, the implication is quite clear. By 1986 the United States was so deeply involved in the Afghan war that Soviet aircraft were being brought down under the supervision of American 'experts', in a move which considerably diminished the superiority of Soviet helicopter gunships in the Afghan theatre of war.

China's role in Afghanistan also requires examination. Mao's successor Deng Xiao-Ping had decided to jump into the Afghan fray even before the United States. Accordingly to the *Boston Globe,* in order to learn more about the change that had taken place in Afghanistan after the April Revolution, China opened consultations with the United States in the summer of 1978. At that time, the United States had a reliable intelligence presence in Afghanistan. A detailed report was eventually passed on to the Chinese about the situation.[24]

Indeed, Afghanistan became a point of friendly convergence between the two countries. Instead of hypocritically distorting the teachings of Marx and Lenin, Deng used a rustic Chinese metaphor to explain his position. He said it did not matter if the cow was red or black; what mattered was its ability to provide milk (no matter that he belonged to a generation which had fought wars about the colour of the cow, regardless of its ability to provide milk). The pragmatic Chinese leader was obviously only interested in the udders of the American cow, not the colour of its hide. The Afghan situation was his best opportunity to lure this cow into his backyard. Mutual Soviet enmity finally brought the two countries together. After a visit to Peking by a senior State Department official, as US TV commentator noted that 'for the first time in history, an American representative publicly admitted the possibility of concluding a military alliance between the United States and China.'[25]

Even before the Soviet intervention, China had begun to supply arms and provide training facilities to the Afghan rebels. One week after the Red Army's arrival in Afghanistan, the *Daily Telegraph* reported:

> China is flying large supplies of arms and ammunition to the insurgents in Afghanistan. According to diplomatic reports, supplies have arrived in Pakistan from China via the Karakurram Highway ... A major build-up of Chinese involvement is underway – in the past few days [since the Soviet military action]. Scores of Chinese instructors have arrived at Shola-e-Javed camps.[26]

According to the Karmal administration, during 1983-85 there were eight training camps near the Afghan border operated by the Chinese in Sinkiang province. Afghan media also disclosed that in the same period China supplied the rebels with a variety of weapons, including 40,000 RPG-7 and 20,000 RPG-II anti-tank rocket launchers.[27] However, following its neighbour Pakistan's example, China did not publicly admit its involvement in the Afghan conflict: in 1985, the Chinese mission at the United Nations distributed a letter denying that China was extending any kind of help to the Afghan rebels.

In 1987, for the first time in many years, there appeared signs of a Sino-Soviet détente – which was what must have prompted the new Afghan leader, Dr Najibullah, to declare China a 'great socialist' country. Until then, China had been described by the PDPA as 'non-socialist and nationalist'. Najibullah said: 'China is a great socialist country. We have great respect for the Chinese revolution. We hope the Chinese will be more amenable to a political settlement in Afghanistan.'[28] However, two days after this fulsome tribute, Gen. Nabi Azami, the Afghan Deputy Defence Minister, said in an interview:

> Despite the improvement in China's relations with the Soviet Union, there is

no change in the Chinese attitude towards our country. They continue to support the guerillas at the same level as before.[29]

The Arab role in the Afghan conflict also needs to be analyzed. The credit for turning the Afghan Revolution into the Afghan 'problem' goes to the successors of Mao, Nasser and Bhutto. Without Deng, Sadat and Zia, it would not have been possible to stage even the opening act of the great Afghan tragedy. All three were obliged to jump into the Afghan conflict by their internal and external circumstances, but perhaps none of them needed to do so as urgently as Sadat. After signing the Camp David accords, Sadat may have managed to win the Nobel Peace Prize, the Sinai desert and American goodwill, but as far as the Islamic world was concerned, he was a 'traitor to the cause'. By joining the Afghanistan *jihad,* Sadat could re-establish his 'Islamic' credentials, or so he believed. He could thus not only please the Muslim nations, but also place the United States and Israel in his debt. His Defence Minister Gen. Kamal Hassan said in January 1980: 'Army camps have been opened for the training of Afghan rebels; they are being supplied with weapons from Egypt.'[30]

Sadat, keen to claim credit for his role in Afghanistan, told an American TV interviewer in 1981 that for the last twenty-one months, the United States had been buying arms from Egypt for the Afghan rebels. He said he had been approached by the United States in December 1979 and he had decided to 'open my stores'. He further disclosed that these arms were being flown to Pakistan from Egypt by American aircraft.[31] Egypt had vast supplies of SAM-7 and RPG-7 anti-aircraft and anti-tank weapons which Sadat agreed to supply to Afghanistan in exchange for new American arms. The Soviet weapons, being light, were ideally suited to guerilla warfare. They had the additional virtue that the 'Mujahideen' could easily claim to have captured them from Soviet and Afghan troops in battle.

Sadat's successor Hosni Mubarak had no political need to fight in Afghanistan; as time passed, he extricated his country from the Afghan imbroglio. The Saudi and Gulf rulers, on the other hand, became the financial patrons of the Afghan rebels from the very start of the conflict. It is Afghanistan's good fortune that Khomeini's Iran got embroiled in war, otherwise Kabul would have also had to contend with the full might of the Islamic revolutionaries.

The United States and its friends see Afghanistan not only as the first test case of a Marxist revolution suffering popular defeat, but also as an opportunity to ignite the fires of religious reaction and anti-Marxism in the Muslim Republics of the Soviet Union. The Afghan 'holy warriors', fighting under the 'sacred' leadership of the CIA, made two raids into Soviet territory in 1987.[32] Such acts are clearly inspired by the idea that it may one day become possible to incite the Muslim Republics of the USSR to rise against Moscow for the 'defence of Islam'.

The remote possibility that this might happen at some point in the future may have induced the Red Army to march into Afghanistan in 1979. If so, then the intervention, contrary to Soviet wishes or expectation, had by 1987 turned the half-imagined danger into a nightmarish possibility. The millions of dollars sunk into Afghanistan by the United States have not, therefore, been to no purpose.

22

The Afghan 'Mujahideen'

Well before the Soviet army moved into Afghanistan in December 1979, a number of right-wing Afghan groups and parties were active on Pakistani soil against the social and economic reforms brought in by the Khalq government. Despite Khalq's blunders, the popular appeal of these reactionary elements was extremely limited; internationally they were unknown or ignored. Dick Downy, an American journalist who spent four months with the rebels in Kunnarha province before the arrival of the Red Army, said of them that 'they were leaderless, bitterly divided and fought mainly for loot.'[1]

The Soviet *putsch* came as a gift from heaven for the rebels, not only bringing them generous American support but turning the Afghan civil war into a 'war of national liberation' and winning them the sympathies of the majority of Afghans.[2] The Afghan people saw the Red Army as an army of aggression and occupation. This became the main cause of rebel success. It contributed to the transformation of the Peshawar-based splinter groups into major national parties, which were soon turned into money and armament pipelines from abroad to keep the fires of war burning in Afghanistan.

A brief survey of the Afghan refugee leadership in Pakistan is essential here. Before 27 December 1979, the rebel groups could be divided into two categories. The first consisted of 'religious and spiritual' leaders like Sibghatullah Mujadaddi and Mohammed Gilani who commanded a certain following, but who could on no account be called political leaders, nor their organizations political parties. In the second category fell men like Gulbudin Hikmatyar, Burhanuddin Rabbani, Maulvi Mohammed Nabi and Maulvi Mohammed Yunus Khalis, who claimed to lead political parties but the total strength of whose following did not exceed a few hundred.[3]

In 1979 the Pakistan government itself estimated the number of Afghan refugees in the country at 80,000, a figure which was neither large nor unexpected. Before December 1979, the Pakistan-based Afghan parties and refugee organizations had no public following to speak of. The intrinsically tribal Afghan society had never been conducive to the formation of political parties. The Pakistan government, which had placed debilitating restrictions on Pakistani political parties, went out of its way to encourage the formation of Afghan political parties in Peshawar. It brought in a new law which required that all Afghan refugees should register with one Afghan political party or another:

> As a rule, a refugee has to be registered with one of the parties to get food rations ... people who are unregistered do not get rations [and thus] can starve or have an extremely difficult time keeping themselves and their children fed.[4]

According to the author's information, if an Afghan refugee refuses to join the '*jihad*' when ordered to do so by the party he has been forced to become a member of, his membership is immediately cancelled – and with that his free rations too.[5] What a tragic choice for the innocent Afghan this is. On the one hand, the Afghan regime tries to recruit him into the army; and when he comes across to Pakistan, the Afghan political parties in exile turn him into a 'holy warrior'. However, despite all these efforts, the Afghan groups and parties have no future among the people, according to a rebel commander:

> The parties sit in Peshawar fighting among themselves, giving themselves fat jobs, cars. If we won our war tomorrow, the parties would simply disappear. No one wants them.[6]

These warring factions have portioned out Afghanistan into separate areas of influence sharing nothing in common but hatred and lack of trust. Bloody clashes between 'Mujahideen' are the norm, not the exception. In late 1980 a Hizbe Islami commander was killed after a battle between two rival factions in Paghman province. Later, Afghan government troops attacked the area and routed the rebels. The rebels' mutual rivalries are sometimes so rabid that they will even use the enemy to settle a score:

> In their mutual hatred they don't even hesitate to provide information to the Soviets against their own countrymen. All successful Soviet military operations are a result of intelligence provided to them by the rebels.[7]

Even rebel leaders confess that bloody clashes among their followers are common. According to the *Washington Post*, Sibghatullah Mujadaddi said in 1985 that arms were being given to extremist groups (such as Hizbe Islami) which were using them to fight their rivals and enemies instead of the Soviets.[8] A rebel commander admitted in 1987 that 'groups of Mujahideen may fight each other (in some areas).'[9] It is this almost primeval mutual hatred which often induces captured 'Mujahideen' in Afghan government jails to report on each other to the authorities or spy on their 'Islamic brothers'. The tragedy of Afghanistan lies in the fact that the followers of both Marx and Mohammed are divided and at one another's throats. If the Red Army decided to march out of Afghanistan today without leaving any arrangements in place, the rebels would not take much time to fill the Afghan valleys with rivers of blood and paint the streets of Kabul red with the blood of their comrades.

All wars are tragic, but the Afghan war is more tragic than many others in recent history. In Afghanistan today any group which carries arms has its own laws of war. According to the teachings of Islam, it is forbidden to disfigure a dead body even if it is that of your bitterest enemy. However, to the 'Mujahideen', it is the observance of Islam itself to torture and mutilate the bodies of their captured enemies by chopping off their ears, noses, arms and legs before finally killing them. The author heard from captured rebels lodged at Pulcharkhi blood-curdling accounts of how Soviet soldiers taken prisoner after a battle or an ambush were tortured before being killed. The Afghan Press International does not report these stories because it does not wish liberal opinion in the west to learn of the barbaric methods the 'soldiers of Islam' use against their enemies. Tass will not report them because this would lead to the demoralization of the Red Army and might even turn popular opinion in the Soviet Union against the war in Afghanistan. The facts are most unpleasant:

> If one is travelling through the provinces of Nangarhar and Kunnarha, he will be told terrible stories about the fate of Soviet soldiers taken prisoner by the rebels. They put rings through their noses and pull them along as if they were performing bears. However, both sides have good reason to keep these inhuman practices secret.[10]

Evidence of torture and murder of Red Army soldiers is also indirectly provided by the fact that in the first four years of the war, the rebels handed over to the Red Cross no more than eight captured Soviet soldiers.

In 1985 it became public knowledge that all Afghan political parties based in Pakistan were maintaining their own separate jails and torture cells where captured Soviet and Afghan soldiers – and suspects from 'Mujahideen' ranks – were kept. On 27 April 1985 there was a massive explosion in an ammunition dump located next to a detention centre run by one of the rebel groups. It shook the entire city of Peshawar and the neighbouring town of Baraber. The tame Pakistani press tried to explain the explosion away as the result of an earthquake, but the true story came out through western reporters. It turned out that Rabbani's Jamiat-e Islami was keeping twelve Soviet soldiers prisoner in a detention centre near Peshawar. One day they managed to pounce on their guards and disarm them. They then occupied the nearby arms dump, demanding to be put in touch with Soviet or Pakistani officials. The Rabbani group procrastinated for a few days and finally decided to storm the hideout, which resulted in the catastrophe. Once the story was out in the international press, the Pakistan government said that no Soviet soldier had been killed in the explosion. The Afghan press, which had hitherto lacked the courage to admit the loss of even a single Russian life, began to print details of the incident, lionizing the dead Soviet soldiers as war heroes. Special adulatory articles and reports were carried about them and their deeds of valour.[11]

Those lucky enough to obtain their release or escape from 'Mujahideen' captivity tell of atrocities committed on defenceless men which have few parallels. On 14 May 1984 the author saw, in the office of the Governor of Nangarhar province, Nasir Shimladar, a young former student of the Jalalabad Medical College who spent two months in a jail run by the Maulvi Mohammad Yunus Khalis group. His captors and interrogators had peppered his face and body with burning cigarettes.[12]

The rebels maintain their jails all over Afghanistan and even right up to the suburbs of Kabul. Quite often they make night raids in the capital and capture government officials and supporters of the regime. Those released are reluctant to report their abduction and treatment to the authorities for fear that their families may be victimized.[13] The 'Mujahideen' have no compunction even about jailing women and children.[14] One of the most notorious rebel jails in Panjsher province is known as Chah-e-Ahu (which means 'the deer well'). In 1982, following a successful military operation, the government forces captured from there a former local official by the name of Abdul Rashid, along with five others.[15] Rashid, the Jamiat-e-Islami-appointed 'judge' for the whole area, was also in charge of Chah-e-Ahu. With a big smile he told an interviewer on Afghan TV that 150 men had been executed on his orders. He repeated the claim during his interrogation and in conversations with other prisoners.[16] He was hanged, a fate he seems to have accepted stoically.

For some reason, teachers have become the favoured target of the 'Mujahideen'. As the author wrote in 1984:

> Fundamentalist rebels are not only the major enemies of the Soviets, but also of music, education, art and literature which they consider inventions of the devil. Musicians like Fazal Ghani and Khan Qarra Baghi and the well-known TV woman presenter Saima Akbar were all killed by the rebels after 1980. Dr Mohammed Usman, the only Afghan novelist of note, survived through sheer luck after an attack. It can be safely said that the rebels have launched a crusade against modern knowledge.[17]

What do the 'Mujahideen' do with the arms they receive? It is no secret that many are sold off in Pakistan, one reason that country has become one of the world's largest centres of contraband arms. Things have reached a point where modern automatic weapons are fired to celebrate weddings, religious festivals, political rallies and even birthdays.[18] Rebel leaders regularly accuse one another of profiteering through the sale of arms meant to fight the Soviets. In 1985 Hikmatyar charged that the Mujadaddi group was trading in arms, a compliment duly returned by the latter.[19] A newspaper in London published a 'rate card' in 1987, listing weapons easily purchasable in Pakistan's border areas. The Pakistan prices, it should be noted, are about 50 per cent lower than those prevailing internationally.[20]

	(Price in Pakistan Rupees)
T & T mine	50
Kalashnikov tracer bullet	30
Anti-aircraft bullet (Egyptian made)	150
Rocket launcher shell	300
American rifle	5,000
Chinese rifle	18,000
Russian rifle	22,000
Sten gun (Russian) 30-bore	3,500
Anti-tank rocket launcher	25,000
Kalashnikov AK-47 rifle	15,000 to 16,000
G-3 automatic rifle	13,000 to 25,000

(One US$ = Pakistan Rupees 17 to 18)

The Afghan 'Mujahideen' have helped Pakistan become self-sufficient in illicit arms and heroin. The Pakistani bureaucracy is, of course, integral to this lucrative trade. Some of its critics even mention the names of a number of the most important men in government: Air

Marshal Asghar Khan, a right-wing Pakistani politician, has charged that the Pakistan government itself is part of the racket.[21] Rebel leaders complain that no more than 20 per cent of the arms sent for them actually reach them.[22] As the principal supply channel is the Pakistan government, it must bear responsibility for the alleged disappearance of 80 per cent of the weapons. One rebel leader asked, in an American journal:

> Would it not be in American interest as well as ours to find out where these supplies of money and arms go? They send it; we do not receive it. In the middle there is some kind of a hole into which most of the things vanish.[23]

The hole in the middle, it is quite clear, is the Pakistani government, but this must also involve important figures in the 'Mujahideen' community.

It ought to be a matter of some concern to the United States that despite its generosity, rebel leaders have failed to unite. They are not even agreed about the future of their country or the interpretation of Islam.

Three of the rebel commanders – Ismail Toran in Herat, Jalaluddin Haqqani in the east and Ahmed Shah Masaud in the north – are acknowledged even by the Afghan government.[24] However, none of them has been able to emerge as a national leader. The western media, ignorant of Afghanistan's tribal and nationalistic contradictions, have been heavily tipping Ahmed Shah Masaud as the man to watch as far as the future of Afghan leadership is concerned. Little do these 'experts' know that even if Masaud were able to defeat the Red Army fifty times over, he, being of Tajik nationality, would never be acceptable to Afghanistan's Pushtun majority. The same goes for Ismail Toran of Herat. As for Haqqani, though he is an eastern Pushtun, he does not have the political clout or social background to be accepted as a national leader. To quote a rebel commander in Kabul:

> The west says we are disunited because you (the west) are seeing things through your eyes. You are always looking for a single command all over Afghanistan. That is why you are always building up Masaud or someone else, speculating whether he will become a national leader. It is not the Afghan way.[25]

Both the Kremlin and Washington have failed to read or understand the 'Afghan style', which is why the former has been unable to unite the PDPA under one leadership and the latter the warring rebel factions around a common leader. The roots of the Afghan style lie deep in the Afghan tribal psyche. If two Afghans, for example, are equally well armed, neither of them will even conceive of walking behind the other as it would seem to him to constitute an insult to his family, his tribe and his own person. Although a special kind of anarchy born out of this very tribal attitude has always characterized Afghan society, the massive flow of foreign arms into the country since the Soviet intervention has immeasurably deepened that state of mind and way of life. The anarchic Afghan temperament has not only managed to stalemate the Red Army, but made it impossible for any future government to deal with a situation where every individual citizen is armed with modern weapons. Afghan rebels like to claim that it is they who determine the course and conduct of the war, but the greatest damage to the Red and Afghan armies has been done by hundreds of small disparate groups which accept no-one's leadership, and least of all that of the Peshawar-based parties. In Pulcharkhi at least 60 per cent of rebel prisoners owed allegiance not to any of the major political parties, but to these small, independent, unknown and uncoordinated groups which are a law unto themselves. (In 1981 a mosque *imam* was brought to Pulcharkhi. It transpired that he had a following of no more than four men and yet he was charged with the murder of nine government officials. His story was published in the local press.)[26]

Eight years of unremitting war have tired out not only the Afghan people but the Kabul government, the Soviet Union and the rebels themselves. A rebel commander admitted in 1987 that morale was low after eight years of conflict:

> Their [the Soviet] morale is low because the war goes on with no result, and our morale is lower too. We have been fighting for seven years, and we are tired, and we feel that you do not help us.[27]

The Soviet Union came to Afghanistan with an ideology. There is no doubt that Marxist ideas have exercised a certain influence on the literate sections of the Afghan middle class and youth, but today, even if the Soviet Union were still interested in converting the Afghans to its ideology, it would take, if not centuries, then decades of conflict and war.[28] Had Brezhnev only doubled Soviet economic assistance to Afghanistan instead of involving his country so disastrously in its internal affairs, not only would its backward and small neighbour been spared unspeakable suffering and devastation, but the Soviet Union would not have had cause to repent its actions, as it is doing today.

23

Karmal's Deposition and the Future Outlook

After the Red Army moved into Afghanistan on 27 December 1979, there were only three possible ways of restoring peace and ensuring the success of Karmal's government. A positive change in Pakistan's attitude was one. However, this miracle could not be expected, given America's intransigence and the spineless military regime in Pakistan.

The second option was to bomb Peshawar, besiege the city Beirut style and flush out the rebels. Had Peshawar been bombed, Pakistan's military government would have moved even closer to the United States and China. Internationally, the cold war would have intensified and anti-Soviet propaganda been given a new lease of life. Militarily, however, the step might not have proved unsuccessful from an Afghan point of view: Pakistan's military government might have been forced to discontinue its patronage of the 'Islamic *jihad*' in Afghanistan.

The rebel bases in and around Peshawar were not bombed, although the Kremlin intensified its pressure on Pakistan by holding out threats of reprisal. The third option for the Soviet Union was somehow to seal Afghanistan's long common border with Pakistan, bottle up the rebels and wipe them out. This was easier said than done. Effectively to patrol and secure the unnaturally-drawn Durand Line would have required at least one million troops. Since the Soviet Union was in no position to do so, its 'revolutionary' struggle became confined to the bombardment of Afghan villages. This failed military strategy not only added to the number of refugees but, consequently, swelled the ranks of the 'Mujahideen'.

The rise of Gorbachev in 1985 was the beginning of the reconstruction of the petrified Soviet system, as it was of industrial modernisation, restoration of at least some democratic rights and the desire to end the superpower stalemate. Afghanistan was at the top of

Gorbachev's reform agenda. One of his first decisions was to get rid of Babrak Karmal and his forcibly-installed government. The new Soviet leader was quick to assess that while Karmal was around, there could be neither peace in Afghanistan nor even a remote likelihood of opening negotiations with rebel forces. As early as November 1985, he was helping Dr Najibullah to the post of Deputy Prime Minister. In April 1986 Karmal was summoned to Moscow a few days before the anniversary of the Saur Revolution – a simple ruse to enable Najibullah to take the salute at the big military march-past in Kabul.

On Revolution Day itself, Karmal was subjected to harsh criticism for the first time by *Pravda*.[1] The message was clear: the time had come to sacrifice the man who had always insisted on being flown by Soviet pilots in Soviet aircraft because he did not trust his own Afghan countrymen.[2] One day after Karmal's return to Kabul and a week following the anniversary of the April Revolution, the PDPA 'accepted' Karmal's resignation on grounds of 'ill health'.[3]

In keeping with past practice, Karmal sent his written resignation to the Central Committee. He made no effort to attend the meeting personally.[4] Anahita Ratebzad and Mahmood Baryali did not attend the meeting either. Perhaps the old tactician wanted to make it abundantly clear to the Committee that he had resigned under pressure. According to newspaper reports, it was Sultan Ali Kishtmand who proposed the name of the new General Secretary which the Committee approved in an atmosphere of 'complete democracy and freedom'.[5] In his acceptance speech, Najibullah (who used to devote one-half of every speech to mouthing the 'great comrade' Karmal's sayings) disposed of him in one sentence of thanks. The significance of what was said and what was left unsaid was clear to both teacher and pupil.

On the day the news that Karmal had resigned was published, Anahita Ratebzad's Women's Organization organized a procession, mainly comprising the students of the Malali Girls' College, which marched through the streets of the city shouting slogans against Najibullah and Gorbachev.[6] This was the beginning of the further fragmentation of the Parcham group. The PDPA, which Brezhnev had hoped to unify through military intervention, now stood divided into four groups led by Karmal, Najibullah and the political heirs of Taraki and Amin.

In July 1986 the 19th Plenum of the PDPA Central Committee was held. In keeping with tradition, the new leader began his speech with a denunciation of the Karmal period which he now attacked as lacking serious analysis, self-criticism and discipline – failings which had encouraged certain of the Central Committee, government and social organizations to start believing that they were beyond accountability.

Karmal, Ratebzad and Baryali did not attend the 19th Plenum, as mentioned earlier. Najibullah, after speaking about the services rendered to the Party by Ratebzad, declared that he was ordering the 'freeing' of the Women's Organization from 'personal' control and placing it in the 'collective' hands of the Party.[8] The Plenum upgraded forty-four Alternate Central Committee Members into Permanent Members and thirty-seven new Alternate Members were nominated.[9] Najibullah also paid warm tribute to the new Soviet leader Gorbachev.[10] One year after coming to power, Karmal had announced that 'complete peace' prevailed in the country. Najibullah told the Afghan people to wait until the tenth anniversary of the Revolution for peaceful and normal life to return to the country: 'And we must celebrate the tenth anniversary of the Revolution ... in conditions of peace and tranquillity.'[11]

Karmal was no Gromyko to step gracefully aside when overtaken by a much younger Gorbachev. There can, however, be no question that within the Parcham group he was far more popular than Najibullah. Of the senior Party leaders, Ratebzad was openly with Karmal, while Suleman Laiq chose to go with Najibullah. Kishtmand and Noor asked no questions because they knew that the decision to get rid of Karmal had come from the Kremlin. However, while accepting Najibullah unhesitatingly, they did not wish to join the anti-Karmal campaign. The younger Parchamite generation was sympathetic to Karmal, which was why Najibullah found it necessary to juggle around ministerial portfolios every couple of months.

Although Karmal had resigned, he continued to campaign against his resignation within the Party (not the first time he had done so). He was unable to do any harm to Najibullah, however, thanks to the presence of the Red Army. In November 1986 he was finally divested of the country's Presidency – to the great delight of the Peshawar-based Afghan Press International, which could now send him at will to Pulcharkhi or have his loyal followers hatching conspiracies to overthrow Najibullah. In May 1987 Karmal was sent to Moscow for 'treatment': so ended his political journey, exactly at the point where it had begun on 27 December 1979.

Dr Najibullah's nomination in May 1986 was seen by the Pakistani and international media as an indication that the Kremlin had decided to harden its attitude towards a political solution of the Afghan crisis. However, when the bag was opened, it was a dove and not a hawk which flew out of it. Neither Moscow nor Kabul was in a position any longer to pursue hawkish policies.

In May 1986, soon after coming to power, Najibullah stated his objectives in terms exactly similar to those Karmal had been using for the last six years:

> To ensure peace in the country [we want to] decisively crush the last bands of counter-revolution, peacefully solve the situation created around Afghanistan and put an end to the undeclared war being waged against the DRA. We shall approach with mercy, kindness and reconciliation those who have unconsciously stood in the ranks of counter-revolution ... The ring-leaders of these treacherous bands are traitors to the national interest and are committing crimes against our people and homeland every day.[12]

Najibullah's early statements proved beyond doubt that he neither understood why he had been brought to power, nor did he have any idea of Gorbachev's new foreign policy which was aimed at reducing international tension by coming to a *modus vivendi* with the United States and establishing normal relations with China. The new Afghan leader did not seem to realize that the Soviet Union was determined to cut its losses and retrieve what national honour it could from the unfriendly mountains of Afghanistan. Its two objectives now were: national reconciliation between the warring Afghans and the establishment of a 'national government' in Kabul. The present author pointed out in 1984 the possibility of forming a national government in Afghanistan[13] (at that time, the mere mention of the phrase 'national government' was tantamount to treachery in Kabul):

> The only way would be a compromise, a dialogue between East and West (including the United States), resulting in the establishment of a national government which should be independent and not under the thumb of any single group. It should consist of the PDPA and non-extremist factions and be under international guarantees. However, even such a national government will need years to disarm guerilla groups and make the country self-dependent up to a certain degree.[14]

But Najibullah did eventually latch on to the fundamental policy changes brought in by Gorbachev and proceeded to take back almost every word that he had spoken since being brought to power. In December 1986 he offered 'national government' to the rebels after 'national reconciliation' had been achieved. This offer he made to the very people he had earlier denounced as 'traitors to the national cause'.[15] He also declared a unilateral ceasefire in January 1987, when only six months earlier he had been bragging about crushing 'those bandits'. And China, which he had declared to be 'counter-revolutionary' and outside the socialist fraternity, came to be described in March 1987 as a 'great socialist country'.

The Mujahideen's rejection of both Najibullah as an independent and sovereign head of state and his unilateral ceasefire offer could not have come as a surprise to Gorbachev. The new Soviet leader had, meanwhile, sent a clear signal to the Afghan refugees and other actors in the drama that he was serious about ending the war in Afghanistan and pulling out Soviet soldiers. The Kabul government, in keeping with its style, began issuing euphoric claims about the success of the ceasefire offer and the 'surrender' of thousands of rebel fighters.

Gorbachev's honest moves did have a positive effect on the Afghan refugees and for the first time since the conflict, western diplomats had to admit that a 'number of people' from Afghan refugee camps were prepared to return home;[16] but they had quite a different effect on the demoralized Afghan army. Opportunists and fortune-hunters, afraid for the first time that the Red Army might quit and a 'national government' be set up, decided to jump the sinking ship of the PDPA government. Some tried to establish links with the rebels, while ordinary Party workers felt that there was no point in risking their lives for a Party which had begun to go back on everything it had said it stood for. The defence of the April Revolution, they realized, was an exercise in futility. Najibullah was seeking peace and they well knew that only the weak seek peace when a battle is in progress. Nor did it help Najibullah when the rebels rejected his ceasefire offer contemptuously and used the opportunity to intensify their attacks and consolidate their military positions.

The ball called 'national reconciliation' which Gorbachev had lobbed into the court of the 'Mujahideen' caused bitter disputes in their camp. In another move, the Kremlin initiated unofficial contacts with the deposed King Zahir Shah and rebel leaders in exile, leading to a spate of rumours that the former King was the future head of a national government in Afghanistan. The King refused to confirm or deny that he had been approached by the Russians.[17] In May 1987 stories began to circulate that senior Pakistani officials were also secretly in touch with Zahir Shah.[18] Mujadaddi and Gilani, the two rebel leaders whom the western press had already declared 'moderate', began to organize rallies and demonstrations in Pakistan's Afghan refugee camps as speculation about Zahir Shah's future role grew. Addressing a meeting of his supporters at Charsadda near Peshawar on 27 April 1987, Mujadaddi said:

> The Afghans would welcome any Afghan Muslim, be it former King Zahir Shah ... who could bring peace and independence through the establishment of an Islamic government.[19]

While Gilani also welcomed the King's entrance on the scene, Hikmatyar declared that under no circumstances would the return of Zahir Shah be acceptable. Repeating old allegations, he said that it was during his reign that communism had come to take root in Afghanistan. On 27 April 1987 his supporters held a public meeting at Warsak near Peshawar where one of Hikmatyar's lieutenants, Engineer Obaidullah, told the audience:

Zahir Shah committed so many crimes against the Afghans that it [is] not possible to pardon him. Those thinking in terms of recalling Zahir Shah from retirement [are] day-dreaming.[20]

In other words, long before the establishment of a 'national government', the 'Mujahideen' leadership was in complete disarray on the question of who should head it. The head of the international communist movement in the Kremlin bending backwards to bring a deposed king to power, while the reactionary Hizbe Islami was dead set against it. The objective conditions of Afghanistan had forced the two extremes to exchange their ideological garb.

A government of 'national reconciliation' which would ultimately lead to a 'national' government is subject to three conflicting, if not paradoxical, interpretations. Gorbachev, it is obvious, is hoping for the creation of an atmosphere of compromise which could lead to the formation of joint PDPA–'Mujahideen' government willing to hand over to Zahir Shah.[21] To Hikmatyar, the inclusion of the PDPA or the exiled King in any future national government is out of the question. However, to the 'royalist' Mujadaddi and Gilani a 'national' government is one headed by the old King, minus the PDPA and Hizbe Islami.

The 'royalists' have taken care to assure the Soviet Union that if a government is set up on the lines suggested by them, it would be friendly to its giant neighbour. In May 1987, Gilani said: 'Even now if the Russians settle the war fairly we will be prepared to have normal, neighbourly relations with them.'[22] Zahir Shah himself told the BBC that he 'was of the view that the (future) government under him would cooperate with the Soviet Union on the principles of co-existence.'[23]

Zahir Shah's former supporters announced the formation of an electoral 'Majlis-e-Shoora' (parliament) in 1987.[24] It is quite clear that if such a body comes into existence, it will have a majority of 'royalists'. If this forum invites the King to 'play his role', he will have no hesitation in doing so, as he has repeatedly indicated.[25]

Gorbachev may have successfully opened channels of communication with 'moderate' rebel leaders, but he needs the help of the United States. Without US blessing, neither the 'Mujahideen' nor Pakistan are in a position to make a decisive move. President Zia-ul-Haq has been talking since 1986 about a 'political settlement' in

Afghanistan and has also paid tribute to Gorbachev's political honesty.²⁶ However, he has remained silent about the strong and decisive pressure being exerted by the Americans on him and his government: Zia, it should be understood, is no longer in a position to jump across the restraining line drawn for him by the United States. Meanwhile, Congressional leaders have extended assurances to India that after any settlement of the Afghan problem, US policy towards Pakistan would be reviewed.²⁷ Pakistan's lack of enthusiasm for the Soviet initiative is thus understandable.

In what way, how and when does the United States want the Afghanistan problem to be settled? There are three schools of thought among the Americans. A section of American politicians is impressed by Gorbachev's conciliatory gestures and believes that if the Afghan issue remains unresolved for any length of time, it may harm US interests. Former President Richard Nixon seems to be among them:

> Both Pakistan and the Persian Gulf could be destabilized if the [Afghan] conflict continues, with the US facing the dilemma of being forced out of the region or forced into war.²⁸

US Secretary of State George Shultz is said to be of the same view as Nixon, and believes that Gorbachev's gestures are worth responding to.

However, a powerful section of the US administration, backed by the popular media, is bent upon turning Afghanistan into a 'Russian Vietnam'. It is argued that the longer the Afghan conflict continues, the greater the economic, military and political damage the Soviet Union will suffer. From available evidence, especially the decision to supply Stinger missiles to the rebels, it can be concluded that this school has won the day. It may be added that Stingers were supplied at a time when peace was for the first time being seriously explored by the warring parties. A State Department report published in 1987, which also gives the impression that there are many in US administration who believe in 'teaching the Soviets a lesson' in Afghanistan, 'the Mujahideen resistance will remain steadfast ... They are prepared to fight for a decade or more.'²⁹

To belittle or diminish the effect of Gorbachev's conciliatory moves, a section of the American press has been running stories which the hawks in the establishment can only see as pointers that even harder times await the Soviet Union in Afghanistan. In May 1987 *Time* reported the start of guerilla activities in Soviet Tajikstan. This was reproduced under blazing headlines in the Pakistani press. Quoting an Afghan 'Mujahideen' commander who claimed to have operated inside Soviet territory, *Time* stated that Uzbek and Tajik Soviet citizens had been supplying the guerillas not only with intelligence, but with food and shelter as well. The commander said that Soviet Muslims were beginning to form themselves into guerilla groups and that the Afghan 'Mujahideen' raids had managed to create a new political consciousness among ordinary Soviet citizens in these areas. He even claimed that a number of Soviet Muslims had been hanged by the authorities for aiding the guerillas[30] – a claim based neither on evidence nor on the truth. One Pakistani newspaper, quoting a British contemporary without naming it, reported in May 1987 that because of these raids, the activities of the 'Islamic Movement' in Soviet Turkestan had intensified. One Muslim clergyman had been arrested and protest demonstrations had been staged at various places.[31]

There are also those in the United States who maintain that the Afghan problem should be left untouched during Ronald Reagan's Presidency. This could perhaps reflect the views of the 'lame duck' President himself, especially after the damaging Iran arms scandal. He cannot afford any further setbacks. In any case, after the Iran fiasco, he seems to be in no position to take major foreign policy decisions or initiatives.

If the United States does indeed decide to have the war in Afghanistan continue, it will also mean that Pakistan, the spring-board for the 'Mujahideen', will have to be left undisturbed. Although Zia's hold over power is not as strong as it was, there is no apparent danger to American interests in Pakistan. Whenever the United States wishes, it can move a few pawns across the Pakistani chessboard to instal a 'helpful' government. In other words, the United States is in a position to continue to be able to rub the bloodied nose of the Kremlin a while longer in Afghanistan's stony soil.

Moscow's keenness to pull out of Afghanistan and help set up a PDPA-rebel government at Kabul are signs of fatigue and frustration. Any government formed now will obviously have to step down after Soviet troop pull-out. If elections are held the PDPA should know (as should Moscow) that it can stand little chance of success. A 'national government' is the only possible bulwark against a civil war, once the Soviets leave. It goes without saying that the national government should enjoy external and internal support if it is to succeed.

The United States and its allies have paid no serious attention so far to the spectre of civil war in Afghanistan once the Red Army pulls out. If civil war breaks out, its victims will not be the communists alone, as they tend to believe. In keeping with Afghan tradition, all mutual feuds were set aside once the bigger enemy appeared on the scene. They will be settled at the first opportunity. It is doubtful if even an agreed interim government will be able to stop the bloodbath which is likely to follow the departure of the Red Army. King Zahir Shah has ruled out the possibility of a civil war in his BBC interview, but what he probably forgot was that the Afghan people he was among in 1973 have changed.[32] They have more and better arms than the regular Afghan army. Due to the long war the circle of social, personal and tribal enmities has greatly widened. The King has an optimistic assessment of the role he can play in Afghanistan, but it is doubtful if even he would be able to avert a fratricidal civil war in which all scores would be settled. The tragedy of Afghanistan would continue.

The 'Mujahideen' have tried to derive political advantage from the Soviet peace overtures. They all seem to agree that no future Afghan government should include the PDPA.[33] The Jamiat-e Islami leader, Burhanuddin Rabbani, sees the interim government on the following lines:

> The first step is to dissolve the present regime, especially the military, police and KHAD. The Deputy Minister could carry on the affairs of the Ministers for an interim period. A team of ex-military generals, lawyers and workers of the Ministry of Justice could be appointed and they can have someone as their head. This would not be a government but an interim administration responsible for internal security. It would have military power but only be armed with light weapons.
>
> This administration will not enter into international agreements or send out ambassadors. The Mujahideen will give assurances that they will not take any action against the administration or the Russians during the period of (troop) withdrawal. And also there could be observers from Pakistan, Iran and other Muslim countries and maybe the UN. After the withdrawal of the Soviet troops there will be elections and a new constitution.[34]

However, any interim, national or elected government of the future will have immediately to deal with two vital problems: first, to guarantee a secure withdrawal to the Soviet army, and secondly to disarm the Afghan tribal people and political parties to lessen the chances of a civil war. The truth is that even if a national government consisting of all major rebel groups was formed, it would not be able to deal with these two problems. In a society where every group and every citizen is armed, no government can possibly function.

During the Vietnam war, the United States had the Pacific and the Atlantic oceans between its enemy and its own landmass, but between the Soviet Union and Afghanistan there is only the thin line of the Amu river which cannot block the political fallout of the Afghan war on the Soviet Muslim Republics of central Asia. In May 1987 Gulbudin Hikmatyar and Qazi Hussain Ahmed, Secretary General of the Pakistani Jamiat-e Islami, told a public meeting of Afghan refugees in

Peshawar: 'If the Mujahideen continue to fight persistently, the day is not far when the occupied areas of Soviet Central Asia will also be liberated.'[35]

Inside the Soviet Union, even the bitterest critics of Brezhnev's military policies are seriously worried about the security of their southern borders even after the war in Afghanistan has ended.[36] According to an American journalist, a Soviet observer told him: 'What we did in 1979 I was opposed to. I believe it was a great mistake. However, I am not in favour of the unilateral withdrawal of the Soviet army. We would need to obtain certain guarantees about our southern borders.'[37]

Is the Soviet option then confined to the possible establishment of a government in Kabul which should remain under its sphere of influence? After eight years of a terrible, divisive and devastating war, no future Afghan government can openly appear to be a Soviet supporter. Gorbachev has himself rejected as baseless the western analysis that Moscow will only agree to a political situation in Afghanistan which guarantees the continuation of its influence in the country. However, while Moscow may no longer expect to set up a subservient government at Kabul, it will try until the end to have one which is not hostile. It will also demand a guarantee that the future Afghan state would remain non-aligned and stay out of military pacts. A government formed by the 'Mujahideen' would be required to give an undertaking, for example, that the fires of religious reaction would be kept confined to its own side of the Amu river. If assured on these counts, the Soviet Union can be persuaded to withdraw its troops. If a round-table conference on Afghanistan, held under the auspices of the United Nations, or by the countries involved, could furnish the Soviet Union with the basic guarantees it seeks, it would, in all likelihood, be glad to fling the PDPA into the Amu river and pull out.

Notes

Chapter 1: Early History

1. Herodotus, *Istoria*, ed. by K. Abicht, Leipzig, 1869, Chap. IV, p. 44. Also edition edited by C. Hude, Oxford, 1913-14, Chap. VII, p. 67.

2. Gordon, D.H., *The Pre-Historic Background of Indian Culture*, Bombay, 1958, p. 94. Also, Shahidullah, M., 'The Philology of Pashtuu Language', *Journal of the Asiatic Society of Pakistan*, Vol. 2, Dacca, 1957, pp. 25-28.

3. Gankovsky, Yuri V., *The People of Pakistan*, Moscow, 1971, p. 126.

4. Jarring, *On the Distribution of Turk Tribes*, Lund, 1939, pp. 38, 56.

5. Babur, Zaheeruddin, *Babur Nama*, ed. by A.S. Beveridge, London, 1905, p. 166.

6. According to H.W. Bellow, *The Races of Afghanistan*, Calcutta, 1880, a considerable number of the Yusufzai Khans and Maliks possessed slaves, with some of them having more than a hundred of them. For details, see his *A General Report on Yousafzais*, Lahore, 1864, p. 184.

7. Raverty, H.G., *Notes on Afghanistan and Part of Baluchistan*, London, 1880, p. 569. Also Hayat Khan, M., *Hayat-i-Afghani*, Lahore, 1867, pp. 119-21.

8. The man who converted the Pushtun tribes to Islam may indeed have been called Qais Abdul Rashid, which is an Arab name. However, if the story is to be credible, one would also have to believe that the Pushtuns bore Arab names even before the advent of Islam – and this is quite impossible. It is, of course, possible that the first Pushtun to become a Muslim was given the name Qais Abdul Rashid, and this may be why the Armuri tribes used to call the Pushtuns Qais (cf. Morgenstierne, G., *Indo-Iranian Frontier Languages*, Vol. I, Oslo, 1929, p. 312). There is historical evidence that until the end of the 10th century, the majority of Pushtuns were non-Muslim. Wide-scale conversions to Islam only took place under the Ghaznavis and Ghauris when the Pushtun areas came under their control (see Nahmatullah, *History of the Afghans*, Santinketan (India), 1958, Vol. II, p. 41. Also, *Hadood-al-Alam* trans. V. Minorsky, London, 1937, Sheet 25b).

9. Gankovsky, Yuri V., *op. cit.*, p. 133.

10. A commonly known verse of Ahmed Shah Abdali.

Chapter 2: The British and Afghanistan

1. Khalfin, Nafatula, *British Plots Against Afghanistan*, Novosti, Moscow, 1981, p. 18.

2. *Ibid*, p. 24.

3. Ghubar, Mir Ghulam Mohammed, *Afghanistan dar Maseer-i-Tarikh*, Government Printing Press, Kabul, 1981 (probably). The term 'friendly army' was also used by Shah Shuja for the British troops.

4. Khalfin, Nafatula, *op. cit.*, p. 26.

5. Rishtia, Qasim, *Afghanistan dar Qaran-i-Nauzdham*, (publisher not known), Kabul, (published between 1950 and 1955). A Russian translation was published in Moscow in 1958.

6. Khalfin, Nafatula, *op. cit.*, p. 30.

7. Marx, Karl, *Notes on Indian History*, Moscow, 1960, p. 164.

8. *Ibid*, p. 37.

9. Khalfin, Nafatula, *op. cit.*, p. 37.

10. Baha, L., 'Politics in NWFP 1901-1919', *Peshawar University Review*, Vol. I, No. I, Peshawar, 1978, pp. 12-31. Also, Core, O., *The Pathan Borderland*, Hague, 1963, pp. 142-44.

11. Buckle, G.E., *The Life of Benjamin Disraeli, Earl of Beaconsfield*, Vol. VI, London, 1920, p. 390.

12. The British officer who defeated Sardar Ayub Khan was honoured by being made a Knight of the Grand Cross. He was also presented with two ceremonial swords and given a cash award of £12,500, all of which goes to show the extent of the hatred the British government felt towards Sardar Ayub Khan.

13. When the British built the India Gate memorial arch in New Delhi to honour their First World War dead, mention was also made of those who had fallen in the Second Afghan War.

14. Sadat, Asmat, *Afghanistan, Land of Jirgas*, Kabul, 1986, pp. 13-15.

15. The author was allowed to visit this prison by the Afghan authorities in 1979.

16. Ghubar, Mir Ghulam Mohammed, *op. cit.* for details.

17. Arnold, Anthony, *Two Party Communism*, University of Stanford, California, 1983, p. 2.

Chapter 3: Into Modern Times

1. Since both Amir Amanullah Khan and Nasrullah Khan were in favour of invading the British, they were popularly known as the Jang (war) Party.

2. Ali, Mohammad, pp. 151-52.

3. *Afghan-Soviet Relations*, Afghan Government Publication, Kabul, November 1984, p. 6.

4. Khalfin, Nafatula, *British Plots Against Afghanistan*, Novosti, Moscow, 1981, p. 85.

5. Sadat, Asmat, *Afghanistan, Land of Jirgas*, Kabul, 1986, p. 38.

6. Jaenson, Erland, *India, Pakistan or Pakhtunistan?*, Stockholm, 1981, p. 28.

7. Spain, J.W., *The Pathan Borderland*, Hague, 1963, p. 186.

8. The author is here drawing on information provided in a number of long and detailed meetings during 1979-80 with Amir Amanullah Khan's brother-in-law, Tarzi (the author cannot recall his first name), who was also the son of Mohammud Beg Tarzi, Amir Amanullah's Foreign Minister. Though only 14 years of age at the time, he had been told of these events much later by his father. He was also interviewed on Kabul TV on 17 June 1982.

9. As above.

10. As above.

11. The Tajiks deny these allegations and maintain that all such stories are Pushtun fabrications. According to their version, Bacha Saqao was a poor worker and a nationalist.

12. Author's conversations with Tarzi (see note 8).

13. In 1978 the author spent three months at Landi Qila, an Afridi village, and this information is derived from extensive conversations with tribal elders, some of whom had

fought in Nadir Khan's army. A central pillar in the village still carries an engraving of the name of the British officer who quelled the Afridi revolt of 1906 and was later killed in this village.

14. Paullada, L.B., *Reform and Rebellion in Afghanistan: King Amanullah's Failure to Modernize a Tribal Society*, Cornell University Press, Ithaca, New York, 1973, pp. 165-95.

15. Given this background, Gilani's and Mujadaddi's war against the Afghan Revolution is quite understandable.

16. Author's conversations in 1982 with Sultan Kalakani, a Maoist Tajik in the Pulcharkhi prison, Kabul.

17. The law of compulsory military service was not applicable to the inhabitants of Paktia province even during Babrak Karmal's time.

18. Shore, Bashir in *Kabul Times*, 20-21 May 1978.

19. Author's conversations with influential Afghans.

20. Even Anahita Ratebzad's enemies confirm this fact.

21. Gregorian, Vartan, *Emergence of Modern Afghanistan, Politics of Reform and Modernism*, University of Stanford, California, 1969, pp. 239-40 and 338-39.

22. Information obtained from Qasim Khan, currently a warden at Pulcharkhi prison in Kabul, who had also served as warden in Deh Mozang during King Zahir Shah's rule. At the time of Nadir Khan's murder, Qasim's father was a warden at Deh Mozang prison. Because of this long family association with the Afghan penal system, Qasim was extremely well informed and full of inside stories. He even talked of writing a book himself. Until 1983 he was not a member of the PDPA.

23. Author's information gleaned from highly-placed Afghan sources.

24. *Afghanistan, the Target of Imperialism*, Party Printing Press, Kabul, November 1983, p. 13.

25. In an interview broadcast by the West German TV Channel ZDF on 18 December 1986, King Zahir Shah said that despite pressure he did not oust the German ambassador to Kabul during the Second World War.

26. *Afghanistan, the Target of Imperialism.*

27. Gregorian, Vartan, *op. cit.*, pp. 163, 187-88 and 309-10.

28. *Babrak Karmal's Speech to the 9th Plenum of the People's Democratic Party of Afghanistan*, Government Printing Press, Kabul, 1982 (probably), p. 33.

29. Jaekel, Klaus, 'Noor Mohammad Taraki', *Afghanistan Journal* 5 No. 3, 1978, pp. 105-8.

30. Author's information gathered from highly-placed Parchamites.

31. Dupree, Louis, *Afghanistan*, Princeton, 1980, p. 495.

32. Author's conversation with Engineer Latif Mahmoodi, nephew of Dr Rahman Mahmoodi in Pulcharkhi prison. Latif, a pro-China communist, was executed along with four of his political comrades in Pulcharkhi in 1981.

33. *Kabul Times*, 13-14 June 1973.

34. Akhramovich, R.T., *An Outline History of Afghanistan After World War II*, Moscow, 1966, p. 496.

Chapter 4: Genesis of the Pushtun Problem

1. Arnold, Anthony, *Two Party Communism*, University of Stanford, California, 1983, chapter 1.

2. Jaenson, Erland, *India, Pakistan or Pakhtunistan?*, Stockholm, 1981, p. 213. Also, Payarelal, *Mahatama Gandhi, The Last Phase*, Ahmedabad (India), 1958, p. 275 and Tandulkar, D.G., *Abdul Ghaffar Khan*, Bombay, (year unknown), p. 439.

3. Weekly Intelligence Summary, 5 July 1947, IOL 1/P and S/12/3201, India Office Library, London.

4. Jaenson, Erland, *op. cit.*, p. 214. Also, *Tribune*, Lahore, 21 July 1947 and

Hindustan Times, Delhi, 24 June 1947.
   5. *Tribune*, Lahore, 24 July 1947.
   6. Jaenson, Erland, *op. cit.*, p. 210.
   7. Under the Treaty, Afghanistan also received aid totalling $27 million.
   8. Arnold, Anthony, *op. cit.*, p. 9.
   9. *Le Monde*, Paris, 29 August 1973. Also see *Afghanistan and the Non-Aligned Movement*, Afghan Government Publication, Kabul, February 1983, pp. 6-7.
   10. *Afghan-Soviet Relations*, Afghan Government Publication, Kabul, January 1984, p. 20.
   11. *Ibid*, p. 28.
   12. Frank, Peter, *Afghanistan Between East and West*, National Planning Association, Washington D.C., 1960, pp. 73-74.
   13. *Afghan-Soviet Relations, op. cit.*, p. 28. Also, Vinogradov, V.M., *Soviet-Afghan Relations 1919-69*, Moscow, 1971, pp. 129-205.
   14. Paullada, L.B., 'Afghanistan and the United States: the Crucial Years', *Middle East Journal*, 35 No. 2, (USA), p. 189.
   15. Berner, Wolfgang, 'Der Kampf um Kabul' in Vogel, Heinrich, *The Soviet Intervention in Afghanistan*, Baden-Baden (West Germany), 1980, p. 332.
   16. *Afghan-Soviet Relations, op. cit.*, pp. 23-24.
   17. *Ibid.*
   18. Bhutto revealed this during his election campaign of 1970.
   19. Author's conversations with Kabul University professors.
   20. Paullada, L.B., *Reform and Rebellion in Afghanistan 1919-29: King Amanullah's Failure to Modernize a Tribal Society*, Cornell University Press, Ithaca, New York, 1973, pp. 17-18 and table I.

Chapter 5: The Birth of Afghan Communism

   1. Author's conversations with knowledgeable Afghans.
   2. Conversations with PDPA Politburo and Central Committee level Members.
   3. Conversation with Engineer Latif Mahmoodi in Pulcharkhi prison.
   4. Conversation with Ismail Danish and others.
   5. Arnold, Anthony, *Two Party Communism*, University of Stanford, California, 1983, p. 32.
   6. *Kabul Times* of 5 July 1978 carried a biographical sketch of Noor which stated that he became a Khalq member while still a student at the Kabul University in 1963.
   7. Anahita Ratebzad had taken a nursing degree in Chicago in 1950 and a medical degree from Kabul University in 1963. Parcham sources say that Karmal played an important role in the formation of the Kabul University Students' Union in 1950, which was why he was refused admission that year. He joined in 1951.
   8. Author's conversations with PDPA leaders.
   9. See *Kabul Times*, 30 October 1978. Information also gathered from conversations with PDPA leaders.
   10. Arunova, M.R., *Democratic Republic of Afghanistan*, Nauka, Moscow 1981, p. 60.
   11. Private meeting between the author and Mrs Taraki in 1983.
   12. Karmal himself claims to be a Pushtun, but the author's research has established that he is a Tajik. Both his parents' families have long been resident in Kabul. He has no close or even distant relationship with any Pushtun family. It was probably his father who began to identify himself as a Pushtun.
   13. Conversation with Ismail Danish in Libya in September 1986.
   14. *Khalq, PDPA's Platform*, People's Democratic Party of Afghanistan, Kabul, 11 April 1966. See also Arnold, Anthony, *op. cit.*, appendix C.
   15. *Ibid.*
   16. *Ibid.*

17. *Ibid.*
18. *Kabul Times*, 5-6 May 1978.
19. PDPA's Constitution, Article 3.
20. After Gen. Ne Win's release from prison, the pro-Soviet Communist Party of Burma expressed support for him.
21. From a Khalq group pamphlet issued in 1975-76.
22. Conversation with Mrs Taraki in 1983.
23. The author heard Khalq group leaders in 1979 accusing Karmal of informing the Royal Court of Taraki's visit to Moscow which, they said, was why his book could not be published in the Soviet Union. Such charges and counter-charges were frequently exchanged by the two rival factions. However, it further confirms that the visit to Moscow did take place.
24. Conversation with Khalil Zimer in Pulcharkhi prison, Kabul. Zimer was present at the demonstration and was an admirer of Karmal at the time.
25. Dupree, Louis, *Afghanistan*, Princeton, 1980, pp. 590-97.
26. Maiwandal was the leader of the Musawat Party and editor of the Party organ, *Musawat.*
27. Aqrab is the eighth month in the Afghan calendar.
28. Zimer was not prepared to accept the allegation when the author brought it up during a conversation in Pulcharkhi prison.
29. The author told Zimer that not only the head of the Kremlin, but even a humble worker at the Moscow steel plant serves his nation or the socialist ideology in the same measure, and reminded him of Lenin's refusal to attend a ceremony organized to celebrate his birthday. Lenin instead sent a message saying that an individual's birthday was his personal affair.
30. Author's information from highly-placed Khalq and Parcham sources.
31. Conversations with Khalq leaders in Pulcharkhi prison, Kabul.

Chapter 6: The Karmal-Taraki Break

1. This is the same Sibghatullah Mujadaddi who emerged as a rebel leader after the Revolution.
2. Jilani Bakhtiari resided in the Karta Parwan quarter of Kabul.
3. In some parts of Afghanistan, families of Arab origin have been settled for hundreds of years. Danish's family was resident in the suburbs of Jalalabad and that of Hashmi in Badakhshan.
4. Conversations with Khalq leaders. The Khalq group issued several pamphlets on this subject at the time.
5. This speech was used by the Khalq group in many of the publications to attack Karmal. See also Arnold, Anthony, *Two Party Communism*, University of Stanford, California, 1983, appendix C.
6. *Hizbe Democratic Khalq Afghanistan*, pamphlet issued by the Khalq group, 1976.
7. Pro-Amin Khalq workers told me in Pulcharkhi that Amin had made this speech with the permission of the party as a 'defensive tactic'. On the other hand, the Parchamites claim that since Karmal had opted for this 'defensive tactic' years earlier, Khalq apologists have no right to accuse him of being a 'royalist'.
8. Conversations with Khalq leaders in Pulcharkhi prison, Kabul.
9. Arnold, Anthony, *op. cit.*, appendix C.
10. According to Mrs Taraki, her husband used to caution his followers during King Zahir Shah's time: 'Don't discuss politics openly. Instead, "smell" the situation carefully.'
11. Following renewed unity between Taraki and Karmal in July 1977, Karmal was once again appointed Taraki's 'heir apparent'.
12. Author's conversation with Khalil Zimer in Pulcharki prison, Kabul.
13. In March 1986 the students of Malali School — at Anahita Ratebzad's instance — staged a procession demanding that Karmal's resignation should not be accepted. They

shouted slogans denouncing Dr Najibullah and the Soviet Union. I learnt of this from Afghan diplomatic sources in West Germany.

14. Khalil Zimer and Khalq sources.

15. *Hizbe Democratic Khalq Afghanistan, op. cit.*

16. Khalq and Parcham sources.

17. Khalil Zimer and Parcham sources.

18. Not only was the Royal family incarcerated during Taraki's time, but various plays satirizing the imperial Afghan house were shown on TV.

19. Khalq and Parcham sources.

20. *Hizbe Democratic Khalq Afghanistan, op. cit.*

21. Conversations with high-level Khalq sources in 1979 and with well-informed Parchamites in 1983.

22. The author was in prison at the time.

23. From Afghan diplomatic sources.

24. The Jamiat-e-Inqlabyun or Revolutionary Party, was set up in 1968. Also see *Foreign Affairs Bulletin*, Vol. 5, No. 7, Afghan Government Publication, Kabul, 1986, pp. 40-53.

25. At the time the author was Adviser for Student Affairs to Prime Minister Zulfikar Ali Bhutto of Pakistan.

26. For the text of Karmal's speech, see *Da Watan da Paigham*, No. 1, Afghan Government Publication, Kabul, 1984.

27. Arunova, M.R., *Democratic Republic of Afghanistan*, Nauka, Moscow, 1981, pp. 42-61.

28. *Ibid.*, pp.44-45 and 61.

29. Dupree, Louis, *Afghanistan*, Princeton, 1980, p. 4.

30. Conversation with Engineer Latif Mahmoodi (Dr Abdul Rahman's nephew) in Pulcharkhi prison in March 1981. He was executed in June.

31. Dupree, Louis, *op. cit.*, part IV, p. 4.

32. Berner, Wolfgang, 'Kampf um Kabul' in Vogel, Henrich, *The Soviet Intervention in Afghanistan*, Baden-Baden (West Germany), 1980, pp. 338-39

33. Conversations with Engineer Latif Mahmoodi and Khalil Zimer.

34. The author found evidence in jail that there were a number of other pro-China splinter groups in Afghanistan.

35. In 1980 the different pro-China groups set up a joint central committee for action, which consisted of one member from each faction. One of its members, Syed Bashir, got in touch with the Afghan secret service KHAD through his sister whom he had talked into joining the PDPA. Having obtained assurances of his own safety, he had the entire committee arrested. He was also picked up and during the jail investigation he continued to cooperate with the authorities. However, in March 1981 he discovered in court that the promise of safety had been a deception. In his last court appearance, he begged his 'comrades' to forgive him and asked for the sentence of death to be passed on him. In May 1981 he was hanged along with Engineer Latif Mahmoodi and others. They went to the gallows shouting communist slogans. In those days, many jail guards were PDPA's freshly-recruited 'revolutionary soldiers' who were extremely surprised when they heard the condemned men shouting these stirring slogans. They had been told that pro-China communists were all 'narrow-minded nationalists'. One of the 'revolutionary soldiers' who was on duty when these men were hanged, did not touch food for three days after watching the grisly ceremony. He could not understand why 'communists were murdering communists'. During the writer's internment in Pulcharkhi lasting nearly two and a half years, there were at least thirty Maoists executed.

36. *Afghan-Soviet Relations*, Afghan Government Publication, Kabul, November 1984, p. 4.

37. Conversations with pro-China communists in jail. After 1980 this group of communists declared that its only basic difference with pro-Soviet communists was the support of the latter for Moscow and the Red Army in Afghanistan.

38. Engineer Latif Mahmoodi told the author that SAMA had been renamed Sazeman-e-Azadi-Baksh-e-Millathai Afghanistan.

39. Conversations with prisoners of the Khorasan group.
40. Conversations with Khalq leaders.
41. Dupree, Louis, *op. cit.* See also *Problems of a Free Press*, AUFSR, South Asian Series, Vol. XII, No. 6, August 1969, p. 6.
42. Karmal, Babrak, 'On the Strategy and Tactics of the PDPA', *Parcham*, No. 9, Kabul, 1969. See also Attar, Ghafur, *Das Volk an der Macht*, Antiimperialistische Informationsbulliten Marburg, West Germany, No 7/3, July-August 1978.
43. Dupree, Louis, *Afghanistan Continues its Experiment in Democracy*, South Asian Series, (USA), Vol. XV, No. 3, July 1971.
44. The Khalq claim is not borne out by known facts.
45. Conversation with Mir Wais Amin, Hafizullah Amin's nephew in Pulcharkhi prison.
46. As above.
47. As above.
48. Abdul Mohammed and Ismail Danish had already been put on the list of alternate candidates.
49. Conversations with Khalq leaders in jail.
50. As above.
51. Conversation with Ismail Danish in Libya, September 1986.
52. PDPA sources.
53. *Razakar*, Issue No. 1, Kabul, 29 September 1971. Also conversations with pro-Amin Khalq leaders in Pulcharkhi prison.
54. *Ibid.*
55. Conversations with Khalq leaders in Pulcharkhi prison.
56. *Razakar*, Kabul, 22 October 1971, 17 November 1971 and 24 November 1971.
57. *Da Watan da Paigham*, Issue No. 1, Kabul, 1984, pp. 11-13.
58. *Ibid,* p. 12.

Chapter 7: The End of Kingship

1. Smith, Harvey, *Area Handbook of Afghanistan*, Government Printing Office, Washington D.C., 4th Edition, 1973, p. xxvii.
2. The same night when a police party arrived at the Paghman rest house to arrest Shah Wali's father, the old Marshal Shah Wali, according to Din Mohammed, an attendant at the rest house, the first question asked by Nadir Khan's brother was, 'Has Abdul staged the revolution?' (The police had not told the Marshal that he was being arrested, only that he was being summoned to Kabul for important consultations.) When he was told that it was Daud who had brought about the revolution, he is reported to have said, 'After all, he too is our son.' But Daud was made of different clay; blood ties did not mean much to him. He threw both father and son in jail without giving the matter a second thought.
3. According to Daud, four policemen and two army soldiers died during his 'revolution'. One tank operator died when by mistake he put his tank in the reverse gear and fell into the Kabul river. For Daud's press conference, see *Republic of Afghanistan Annual* 1973-74, Kabul, p. 15.
4. Conversation with Faiz Mohammed Faiz, Minister of Border Regions in 1980.
5. *Republic of Afghanistan Annual* 1973-74, *op. cit.*, for text of the letter.
6. Sarwari and Faiz were generally present at these meetings and, according to them, they first met Karmal at one of them. Author's conversations with Sarwari and Faiz at different times.
7. Conversation in jail with Khalil Zimer.
8. *Anis*, Kabul, 30 October 1973, *Jamhouriat*, Kabul, 30 October 1973 and *Kabul Times*, 30 October 1973.
9. *Republic of Afghanistan Annual, op, cit.*, p. 82.
10. Conversations with Parcham leaders.

11. Conversations with Khalq leaders. Khalq literature of the period also mentions these allegations.

12. Parcham sources.

13. *Hizbe Democratic Khalq Afghanistan*, pamphlet issued by the Khalq group, 1976.

14. Conversation with Sarwari, July 1979.

15. Yaqubi told the author that he had first seen him at an official banquet in Lahore, Pakistan.

16. In 1983 when I was released from Pulcharkhi prison after two and a half years, it was Yaqubi who was first sent over to inform me of the decision.

17. Youth from the Marri tribe continue to remain at the Kandhar camp under the command of Mir Hazar Khan Marri whom the author met in Kabul in 1979-80.

18. The Pushtunistan Day has been celebrated without fail since 1973.

19. Two Peshawar University students were implicated in Sherpao's murder. The writer saw them in Jalalabad in 1979. The Afghan government was paying them a monthly stipend of about $90 each. One of them had lost his mental balance, while the other later migrated to West Germany.

20. The former Shah of Iran had sent a number of helicopters to assist the Pakistan army in its anti-insurgency operations in Baluchistan. It was believed that they were flown by Iranian crews.

21. The anti-Daud leaders living in Pakistan were in contact with Maj. Gen. M. Imtiaz, Prime Minister Bhutto's Military Secretary. According to my information, Gulbudin Hikmatyar of the Hizbe Islami was paid about Rs50,000 per month (roughly $5,000).

22. Conversation with Prime Minister Bhutto at a dinner.

23. Bhutto's speech on return from the Soviet Union.

24. Conversation with Khalil Zimer, who at the time of the incident was in Daud's good books.

25. The author was among those included in the official delegation for Bhutto's visit but because of an indisposition was unable to go to Kabul. He had recently returned from a trip to China and North Korea as part of the Pakistani Prime Minister's official entourage. Bhutto had done his 'home work' for the Kabul visit during that trip. He had told his Foreign Secretary Agha Shahi in Pyonyang: 'Finalize all the papers for the Kabul talks. Remember we are not going there to eat *chappal kebab*.'

26. *Republic of Afghanistan Annual 1977*, Kabul, p. 296.

27. *Ibid*, p. 297.

Chapter 8: The Takeover Plan

1. *Afghanistan, Multifaceted Revolutionary Process*, Afghan Government Publication, Kabul, 1982 or 1983.

2. *Ibid*, p. 1.

3. *Ibid*, pp. 1-8.

4. *Ibid*.

5. *Ibid*.

6. *Ibid*, p. 3.

7. Conversations with Khalq leaders in Pulcharkhi prison, Kabul.

8. As above.

9. *Hizbe Democratic Khalq Afghanistan*, pamphlet issued by the Khalq group, 1976.

10. The author has prepared this list after extensive conversations with Khalq and Parcham leaders. Much of this information has never been collated or published before.

11. Jaekel, Klaus, 'Nur Mohammad Taraki', *Afghanistan Journal 5*, No. 3, 1978, pp. 105-8.

12. Parcham sources.

13. Jaekel, Klaus, *op. cit.*

14. Parcham sources.

15. Meeting with Sarbaz in Kabul in May 1983 at the house of a mutual friend, Ghulam Ghaus Sarwari. Sarbaz was at the time the Afghan army's commander for recruitment. The author found him balanced in his judgments and extremely well read. A committed communist.

16. *Biography of Nur Mohammad Taraki*, Afghan Government Publication, Kabul, August 1978.

17. Conversations with pro-Amin Khalq workers.

18. Berner, Wolfgang, 'Der Kampf um Kabul', Vogel, Henrich, *The Soviet Intervention in Afghanistan*, Baden-Baden, West Germany, 1980, p. 32.

19. *Biography of Nur Mohammad Taraki, op. cit.*, pp. 19-20. Also, *Short Information About the PDPA*, Afghan Government Publication, Kabul, 1978, p. 11.

20. *Kabul Times*, 3 May 1978 and Karmal in *New Kabul Times*, 8 January 1980.

21. *Afghan-Soviet Relations*, Afghan Government Publication, Kabul, November 1984, pp. 29, 31 and 32.

22. *Afghanistan, Multifaceted Revolutionary Process, op. cit.*, p. 4.

Chapter 9: The April Revolution

1. Khalq and Parcham sources.

2. *Revolutionary Afghanistan Through Honest Eyes*, Ministry of Foreign Affairs, Kabul, 1982 or 1983, where an American magazine *Counter Spy* is quoted.

3. Conversations with pro-Amin Khalq workers in Pulcharkhi prison, Kabul.

4. Conversation with Mir Wais Amin, Hafizullah Amin's nephew, and with Mrs Hafizullah Amin in Pulcharkhi prison, Kabul.

5. Since Faqir was a frequent visitor to the Amin home, it was easy for Abdul Rahman to take the 'plan' to him without arousing any suspicion.

6. *On the Saur Revolution*, Political Department of the Armed Forces, Kabul, 1978, p. 23.

7. Conversation with Khalil Zimer. Also confirmed by both Khalq and Parcham sources.

8. Khalq and Parcham sources.

9. Khalq sources.

10. Col. Ahmed Jan (Captain at the time) says that he was with Watanjar that morning. This is confirmed by other Khalqites.

11. *On the Saur Revolution, op. cit.* (Persian Version), p. 8.

12. Conversation with Sarwari in July-August 1979. He was a frequent visitor to Mir Murtaza Bhutto's house in Kabul. Sarwari had joined the Khalq group in 1975, having previously been a Parchamite supporter.

13. According to Parchamites, Qadir was locked up in his office by Daud's supporters.

14. Author's conversation with Sarwari (see note 12).

15. After the Revolution, Watanjar's tank was placed on a raised platform in front of Arg, Daud's palace, to commemorate the Revolution.

16. Asadullah Sarwari took over the Department of Intelligence after the Revolution. This information was obtained during his interrogations of Daud's Ministers.

17. Arnold, Anthony, *Two Party Communism*, University of Stanford, California, 1983, p. 59.

18. Khalq sources.

19. Conversation with Shamsuddin in 1982.

20. Khalq sources.

21. The author heard pro-Amin Khalq leaders advancing the same argument in jail.

22. *On the Saur Revolution, op. cit.*, (English version), pp. 32-33.

23. Conversations with Khalqites in the army.

24. Amin wanted Parcham to share the failure in case the bid to stage the Revolution failed; but now in the event of victory, he wanted the glory to belong to Khalq alone.

25. Conversations in jail with pro-Amin Khalq leaders.

26. Officers of the 4th Armoured Corps told him repeatedly that they were connected with the PDPA.

27. Arnold, Anthony, *op. cit.*, p. 59. How Arnold was able to receive this detailed operational information while safely sitting in America is not difficult to understand. Obviously, all is fair in love and war.

28. The day the communists learn the art of facing criticism, the crisis facing the communist world will be lessened.

29. After watching this amusing show, the writer came to the conclusion that while a good actor might just make a successful politician, even a bad politician is a good actor.

30. The author first saw this film in jail. Television sets were provided to the inmates for the first time in April 1981.

Chapter 10: Taraki's Tryst with Destiny and the First Conspiracy

1. *Babrak Karmal's Address to the 9th Plenum of the PDPA Central Committee,* Government Printing Press, Kabul, 1983 (probably), p. 4.

2. *Kabul Times,* 4 May 1978.

3. Conversations with Khalq leaders in Pulcharkhi prison, Kabul.

4. *Kabul Times,* 13 May 1978.

5. Conversations with Khalq and Parcham leaders in Pucharkhi prison.

6. Conversations with Khalq leaders in Pulcharkhi prison.

7. *Kabul Times,* 5 May 1978.

8. Amin and his wife spent their evenings either being entertained by senior army officers or playing host to them. Sarwari told the author that after the Revolution, Mrs Amin gave her children (and those of several army officers) 20,000 Afghanis each by way of a "gift".

9. Conversations with Khalq leaders in Pulcharkhi prison.

10. *On the Saur Revolution,* Political Department of the Armed Forces, Kabul, 1978.

11. Conversations with Iqbal Waziri, head of the Political Department of the Armed Forces, in Pulcharkhi prison.

12. *Kabul Times,* 25 May 1978.

13. Saur, the second month in the Afghan calendar, runs from 20 April to 20 May. The Revolution is named after it as it occurred on 27 April.

14. Author's meeting with Ismail Danish in Libya, September 1986.

15. Parchamite sources.

16. *Kabul Times* of 18 June 1978 reported that at this meeting of the Politburo, important decisions had been made. The newspaper, however, did not say what those 'important' decisions were. Since the Party was not using the appellation Central Committee at the time, its meetings were described in newspapers as the 'Revolutionary Council's' sessions.

17. *Foreign Affairs Bulletin,* Afghan Government Publication, Kabul, July 1978, p. 37.

18. Karmal was sent as ambassador to Czechoslovakia, and Ratebzad to Bulgaria.

19. These reluctant Parchamite envoys were a disappointment to the left-wing supporters of the April Revolution (at any rate in Iran and Pakistan).

20. *Inqilab Saur,* Kabul, 9 July 1978.

21. Conversations with Khalq leaders in jail.

22. See *Kabul Times,* 19 July 1978 and *Inqilab Saur,* 19 July 1978 for details.

23. 'The PDPA Platform', *Khalq,* 11 April 1966.

24. *Kabul Times,* 23 September 1979.

25. *Ibid.* See text of report by Noor Mohammed Taraki, p. 5.

26. General Shahpur was an Ahmedzai like Dr Najibullah. He was hanged in jail without a trial at the orders of the Khalq government.

27. *Report of Five Months' Performance by the PDPA*, Publicity Bureau of the PDPA Central Committee, Kabul, October 1978, pp. 5-6.

28. In July-August 1979 the writer was present on many occasions when Khalq leaders openly used abusive language about Anahita Ratebzad.

29. Parcham sources.

30. Information based on author's meetings with Mrs Taraki and Engineer Nazar Mohammed's sister-in-law, Gulali, in 1983.

31. Khalq sources,

32. *Kabul Times*, 14 November 1978.

33. *Kabul Times*, 29 November 1978 contains the text of a report presented by Taraki to the Political Bureau of the PDPA Central Committee on 28 November 1978.

34. Khalq sources.

35. One of Karmal's brothers (who had no interest in politics) was also in jail. Many members of the families of leading Parchamites such as Kishtmand, Rafi and Qadir were also under detention.

36. Information obtained from prison officials and inmates (conflicting Khalq and Parcham versions are not always reliable). Two Pakistanis, Sardar Khan and Javed Akhter, were in jail in Kabul during the rule of Taraki, Amin and Karmal. While Sardar was released in 1981, Javed was still in Pulcharkhi when the author left Afghanistan in January 1984. A great deal of the information relating to Pulcharkhi during the Khalq years was verified by them.

Chapter 11: The Contradictions of Afghan Society

1. Conversations with Khalq leaders in Pulcharkhi prison, Kabul.

2. Some historians think that the Nooristanis are the descendants of Alexander the Great's soldiers who stayed behind. Until 1890 they were called Kafirs. As for the Hazaras (which means thousands), it is said that when Ghengis Khan invaded the area, the local people who had never seen such hordes before, called them 'hazara'. Over time, the word came to describe the local nationality itself.

3. Smith, Harvey H., *Area Handbook for Afghanistan*, 4th edition, Government Printing Office, Washington D.C., 1973, p. 272. Also, Dupree, Louis, *Afghanistan*, Princeton, 1980, chart No 6.

4. Male, Beverley, *Revolutionary Afghanistan: a reappraisal*, Croom Helm, London, 1982, pp. 78-79.

5. *Ibid.*

6. *Ibid.*

7. Saleh Mohammed Zeary in *Kabul Times*, 15 September 1978.

8. Saleh Mohammed Zeary in *Kabul Times*, 19 July 1978.

9. Author's meeting with Abdul Quddus Kandhari, Assistant Director, Land Reform Commission (set up by the Khalq government), Pulcharkhi prison, Kabul, 1981; cf. Dupree, Louis, *op. cit.*, p. 153.

10. *Distribution of Lands in Afghanistan*, 1978, p. 222. Also, Male, Beverley, *op. cit.*, p. 124.

11. In most cases the *mir-i-aab* is the feudal landlord himself. Any farmer who has his own seed stocks and animals is considered a 'rich peasant'.

12. The system of mortgaging land began with the end of the tribal *wesh* system under which neighbouring tribes exchanged their lands after every thirty years.

13. *Chiefs and Families of Note in the Punjab*, Vol I-II, Lahore, 1940.

14. Gankovsky, Yuri V., *The People of Pakistan*, Moscow, 1971, p. 132.

15. One of the inmates of Pulcharkhi at the time the author was there was an Egyptian named Ziauddin Mahmood, a member of the Akhwan-ul-Muslimin, and a graduate of the Al-Azhar University, Cairo. He had entered Afghanistan with the help of the Jamiat-e Islami for '*jihad*'. He told the author that barring the daily ritual of prayer

(*nimaz*) and the observance of the month of *Ramadhan* (fasting), he had found very little in common between the Islam practised in Afghanistan with that prevalent in the rest of the Islamic world. However, the Afghans believed that their peculiar blend was the real Islamic faith. Mahmood often said, 'If this is Islam, then there is no difference between faith and apostasy.' He was released in 1983. Perhaps the Afghan authorities had come to hear of his views.

16. Saleh Mohammed Zeary in *Kabul Times*, 19 July 1978.

17. In August 1983 the author was in Laghman (Afghanistan) where he witnessed an engagement ceremony in the *hujra* (private chambers) of the chief between a boy of six and a girl of three. The girl's family was demanding 100,000 Afghanis (about $1,000), while the boy's family wanted to pay less. Finally, a deal was struck at 70,000 Afghanis. In accordance with custom, the boy's family was to pay this sum in instalments to the girl's family until she reached the age of ten or twelve when she would be handed over to the boy's family. The mullah who helped make the settlement raised his hands solemnly in prayer afterwards, thus sanctifying this blatantly un-Islamic deal. The two little children, quite unaware of what was happening, meanwhile kept playing in a corner of the room.

18. Newell, Richard, *The Politics of Afghanistan*, Cornell University Press, Ithaca, New York, 1981, p. 75.

19. Statistical Information About Afghanistan, Afghan Government Publication, Kabul, 1978, pp. 169-80.

20. Akhramovich, R.T., *An Outline History of Afghanistan After World War II*, Moscow, 1966, p. 109.

21. The author was Pakistani Prime Minister Zulfikar Ali Bhutto's Adviser for Student Affairs from 1973 to 1977. In December 1974 he personally handed over to the Prime Minister a list of industrialists who had taken their money out of Pakistan, afraid that the Pakistan People's Party government would confiscate it and nationalize their enterprises. The powerful Watan Group had not only transferred its money to Afghanistan, but the industrial machinery it owned as well.

22. Author's conversations with Khalq and Shola-e-Javed leaders in Pulcharkhi prison, Kabul.

23. *Afghanistan Statistical Information*, Afghan Government Publication, Kabul, 1977-78, pp. 3 and 170-96.

24. *Royal Government of Afghanistan, Ministry of Mines and Industry Report*, Kabul, 1969-70.

25. *Foreign Affairs Bulletin*, Kabul, March-April 1968, pp. 32-33.

26. Smith, Harvey H., *op. cit.*, p. 359.

27. *Statistical Information 1977–78*, Afghan Government Publication, Kabul, p. 8.

28. Baryali, Mahmood, ed., *Afghanistan. Multifaceted Revolutionary Process*, Afghan Government Publication, 1982 or 1983, p. 3.

29. *Ibid.*, p. 5.

30. *Ibid.*

31. Smith, Harvey H., *op. cit.*, pp. 344–58.

32. In 1976 a number of illegal textile mills were set up in the tribal areas which put 'Made in Japan' markings on their product, selling it profitably to the imported-item crazy Pakistanis.

33. Conversation with two Kabul currency dealers, popularly known in Kabul as *Chachha Bhatija* (uncle and nephew).

34. The author himself purchased foreign currency in Kabul's open market at these rates before leaving Afghanistan in January 1984.

35. Conversations with Afghan exiles in Europe.

36. 'The PDPA Platform', *Khalq* weekly, Kabul, 11 April 1966.

37. Amin in *Kabul Times*, 15 May 1979.

38. Taraki interview with the Iraqi News Agency, *Kabul Times*, 10 June 1978.

39. *Basic Lines of the Revolutionary Duties of the Government of the Democratic Republic of Afghanistan*, Government Printing Press, Kabul, 9 May 1978.

40. Conversations with important Khalq and Parcham sources.

41. Amin's address to the Academy of Sciences, *Kabul Times*, 23 February 1979.

42. *International Affairs*, No 3, Moscow, March 1979, pp. 46-47.
43. *Kabul Times*, 11 January 1979.
44. *Kabul Times*, 13 March 1979.

Chapter 12: Reforms and their Aftermath

1. *Kabul Times*, 17 July 1978.
2. Conversation with Zahir Chopan, who after the Revolution was appointed one of the district heads of administration. This made him an *ex-officio* member of the committee set up to implement Decree No 6. Chopan was a pro-Taraki Khalq supporter, later arrested by Amin. When Karmal came to power, he was appointed PDPA General Secretary for Herat city. However, in July 1981 he was re-arrested, tried and jailed for fourteen years on the charge of 'factionalism'.
3. Conversation with Chopan (see note 2) and Abdul Quddus Kandhari, former Assistant Director, Land Reform Commission, in Pulcharkhi prison, Kabul.
4. *Kabul Times*, 15 August 1978.
5. *Ibid.*
6. Conversations with Chopan and Kandhari.
7. *Kabul Times*, 18 October 1978.
8. Muhammad Rafiq now lives as a political exile in Hamburg, West Germany, and is married to an Afghan girl by the name of Sultana. However, Ghaurgati, after being widowed in 1980, and having been imprisoned in Pulcharkhi, kept waiting for her lover, unaware of his marriage.
9. Ahmed Zahir, son of King Zahir Shah's former Prime Minister Mohammed Zahir, was murdered in June 1979. Some maintained that Maj. Daud Tarun, brother-in-law of Zahir's murdered wife, was behind the killing.
10. Amin's youngest son-in-law and nephew, Mair Waiz Amin, shared the author's cell in Pulcharkhi. He was bitter about his brother Asadullah Amin's marriage to Amin's daughter, Ghaurgati, whom he accused of keeping the marriage issueless.
11. Dil Ara Mehak, the new head of the women's wing of the Party, unlike the disgraced Anahita Ratebzad, was not a full but an Alternate Member of the Central Committee.
12. See *Kabul Times*, 2 December 1978 for details.
13. *Ibid.*
14. Conversations with Zahir Chopan and Abdul Quddus Kandhari, (see note 3).
15. *Kabul Times*, 2 December 1978.
16. Male, Beverley, *Revolutionary Afghanistan: a reappraisal*, Croom Helm, London, 1982, p. 20.
17. *Kabul Times*, 18 July 1978.
18. *Kabul Times*, 27 October 1979.
19. Conversation with Faqir Mohammed Faqir who was Governor of Paktia when the incidents happened.
20. *Kabul Times*, 22 June 1978.
21. *Kabul Times*, 2 July 1979.
22. Conversations with Khalq leaders in July-August 1979.
23. Conversation with Kandhari. Also see *Time* magazine, New York, 28 April 1980, p. 11.
24. Male, Beverley, *op. cit.*, p. 174. This is by far the best account of Pakistani intervention in Afghanistan.
25. See *Kabul Times*, 25 May 1978 for Finance Minister Karim Misaq's statement.
26. *Kabul Times*, 3 May 1979.
27. *Kabul Times*, 1 September 1979.
28. *Babrak Karmal's Speeches: 27 December 1979-April 1980*, Ministry of Information and Culture, Kabul, 1980 or 1981, p. 50.
29. Conversations with Khalq leaders.

30. *Kabul Times,* 4 July 1978.
31. *Kabul Times,* 23 September 1978.
32. *Kabul Times,* 11 August 1979.
33. Male, Beverley, *op. cit.,* p. 121.
34. *Nawai Waqt* (Urdu), Lahore, 5 May 1979.
35. Baryali, Mahmood, ed., *Afghanistan, Multifaceted Revolutionary Process,* Afghan Government Publication, Kabul, 1982 or 1983, pp. 106-14. This contains the names and biographical sketches of important *ulema* killed by the rebels.

Chapter 13: The December Treaty

1. Conversations in Pulcharkhi prison with Khalq leaders who accompanied Taraki to Moscow. It was Taraki's habit to leave Amin to work out details.
2. After 1980 Parchamites used to express these views openly.
3. *Kabul Times,* 21 February 1979.
4. Information obtained from senior Afghan civil servants.
5. *Daily Telegraph,* London, 22 January 1979, *The Economist,* London, 31 January 1979.
6. Conversations with Khalq leaders in Pulcharkhi prison.
7. In March 1980 an Egyptian volunteer worker of the Akhwan-ul-Muslimeen, Ziauddin Mahmood, was arrested and brought to Pulcharkhi. He told the author that Abdul Rauf was appointed commander of Kunnarha province rebels by Hizbe Islami.
8. Conversations with Khalq leaders in Pulcharkhi prison.
9. Conversation with Maj. Alamyar in Pulcharkhi. The major was one of the four Alamyar brothers.
10. Author's meeting with Sitm-e-Milli workers, Kabul, 1983.
11. *Kabul Times,* 21 February 1979.
12. Marjan, a Hizbe Islami worker, was arrested during Daud's time. He was in Pulcharkhi prison until 1983. The only reason he was alive was that he had lost his mental balance soon after being put into prison. He was charged with a murder attempt on one of Daud's Ministers.
13. Male, Beverley, *Revolutionary Afghanistan: a reappraisal,* Croom Helm, London, 1982, p. 149.
14. Conversation with Abdul Qadir, an old guard at the Nazarat Khana Sadarat (Kabul's central detention facility). Qadir had also served as orderly to the Centre's Political Assistant.
15. Conversations in Pulcharkhi with long-serving prisoners like Haji Latif and old prison guards.
16. Nuzhat was also the Provincial PDPA Secretary. He was later transferred to Ghazni and replaced as Governor of Herat by Haye Yatim. After the fall of Karmal, both of them were jailed.
17. *Morning News,* Karachi, 18 March 1979. See also, *The Statesman,* New Delhi, 23 March 1979.
18. Conversations with Khalq leaders in Pulcharkhi.
19. Conversations with Khalq and Parcham leaders and various well-informed Afghans.
20. The *New York Times,* 23 December 1979, quotes excerpts from Shariat Madari's radio and TV address.
21. Male, Beverley, *op. cit.,* p. 162.
22. *Ibid.,* p. 169. If there were 400 Soviet advisers to be massacred in Herat alone, that would imply a total of 10,000 distributed throughout the country as a whole – a totally absurd figure.
23. *Jang* (Urdu), London, 10 April 1986. These preposterous claims were also carried in the western press.
24. Conversations with Khalq leaders in Pulcharkhi prison.

25. *Times of India*, New Delhi, 12 March 1979.
26. *Kabul Times*, 19 March 1979.
27. Conversations with Khalq leaders in Pulcharkhi.
28. *Kabul Times*, 18 March 1979.
29. *Kabul Times*, 28 March 1979.
30. *Financial Times*, London, 22 February 1979. See also, *Jasarat* (Urdu), Karachi, 23 February 1979.
31. *Kabul Times*, 11 March 1979.
32. *Kabul Times*, 19 April 1979.
33. *Kabul Times*, 22 April 1979.
34. Conversation with an officer of the Tribal Affairs Ministry in 1979. This officer was assigned the task of distributing funds among tribal leaders.
35. Khalq sources.
36. Radio Tehran broadcast on 21 June 1979, and BBC report, 22 June 1979.
37. BBC broadcast quoted by daily *Nawai Waqt* (Urdu), Lahore, 26 June 1979.
38. *Kabul Times*, 7 May 1979.
39. *Nawai Waqt* (Urdu), Lahore, 10 May 1979.
40. Author's meeting with Sarwari on 6 September 1979 at Azamuddin's house in Kabul. This was at a time when Taraki-Amin relations were at their lowest ebb.
41. Conversation with Mir Wais Amin in Pulcharkhi in 1981.
42. Khalq leaders claimed that many valuables were damaged when they were shifted from Qasr-e-Darul Aman to the National Museum.
43. Afghanistan's first TV station was completed after the Revolution with Japanese help. Cooperation with Japan also continued in other sectors.
44. Male, Beverley, *op. cit.*, p. 180.
45. Conversations with Khalq leaders in Pulcharkhi prison.
46. *Kabul Times*, 29 July 1979.
47. *Ibid.* However, the appointments of Amin's brother and nephew were not announced.
48. In July 1979 Bashir Riaz, editor of the London-based Pakistan People's Party organ *Musawat*, arrived in Kabul. The author and Mir Murtaza Bhutto both tried through Taraki's secretary and Sarwari to obtain an interview for the paper with Taraki. After a few days, Sarwari told the author that it was only Amin who could 'clear' Taraki's press interviews. On 26 August 1979 it was Amin himself who agreed to grant an interview to Riaz. It was carried in the *Kabul Times* on 28 August 1979.
49. This bridge is hardly 200 metres from the presidential palace, the old royal residence.
50. The police raided various Kabul hotels and took two Pakistanis into custody. Busy with its own internal squabbles, the Party sent them to the Pulcharkhi 'warehouse'. One of the detainees, Sardar Khan of Charsadda, NWFP, was released in April 1981. This young man was a political asylee, but was arrested because of mistaken identity. He was finally released at the recommendation of Gen. Abdul Qadir with whom he had shared a cell during the Khalq period.
The other young man, Javed Akhtar from Lahore, was in jail until January 1984. He had once tried to escape and broken one of his legs in the attempt. While the Karmal regime had no record of why he had been arrested in the first place, it brought him to trial for his escape attempt. After being released from Pulcharkhi, the author raised the question of Javed's release at a meeting with Dr Najibullah who told him that a number of letters had been addressed to the Pakistan Embassy in Kabul, asking it to reclaim its national, but no reply had ever been received from the Embassy.
51. According to Iqbal Waziri (who was at the time head of the Political Department of the Armed Forces, as well as responsible for 'screening' the officers), there were Hizbe Islami and Shola-e-Javed sympathizers in that Brigade.

Chapter 14: Taraki's End: Amin comes to Power

1. Conversation with Azamuddin.
2. In terms of seniority, Zeary should have been number two to Taraki, but Amin had relegated him to fourth position. However, Zeary was still not prepared to accept Sarwari's 'leadership'.
3. Conversation with Mrs Taraki in Kabul in 1983.
4. Conversation with Babrak Shinwari in August 1979.
5. Daud Tarun was killed when Taraki's guards opened fire on Amin. Shah Wali and Katwazi were sent to prison after Amin's murder.
6. Conversation with Azamuddin who maintained that Brezhnev had no interest in saving Taraki's life.
7. It was Azamuddin's responsibility to make safe overnight arrangements for them.
8. Conversation with Asadullah Amin at Mir Murtaza Bhutto's residence in Kabul.
9. Conversation with Azamuddin.
10. Conversations with Khalq leaders after 1980. It should be mentioned that at the time every officer in the Department, from Sarwari down, was assisted by a Soviet adviser.
11. Conversations with pro-Amin Khalq leaders in Pulcharkhi prison.
12. Conversations with Khalq leaders and Azamuddin.
13. High-level Parcham sources.
14. Conversation with Katwazi in Pulcharkhi prison.
15. These exchanges were reported to the author by Mrs Taraki and informed Parcham circles.
16. As above.
17. Conversation with Shah Mohammed who was a student at the time and part of the group which welcomed Taraki at the Moscow airport.
18. Conversation with Azamuddin soon after his return from the airport.
19. Katwazi heard this exchange himself, as he told the author in Pulcharkhi prison.
20. This story was narrated to the author in 1983 by Mrs Taraki who was present when this exchange took place.
21. As above.
22. Conversation with Azamuddin who slept at the author's house in Kabul on the night of 13 September 1979 because of the uncertain situation in the city.
23. Conversation with Azamuddin on the night of 13 September 1979. The same night Sarwari borrowed a revolver equipped with a silencer from Mir Murtaza Bhutto. He only returned it to him in January 1980 after Amin's overthrow, telling him that he had borrowed the gun to kill Amin. It should also be noted that though Sher Jan Mazdooryar was part of the 'gang of four', he was not privy to their conspiracies. Effectively, the 'gang' consisted of Sarwari, Watanjar and Ghulabzoi.
24. Based on conversations with pro-Amin Khalq leaders in jail and with Azamuddin on 13-14 September 1979.
25. Conversation with Azamuddin.
26. Conversations with pro-Amin Khalqites in Pulcharkhi prison.
27. Azamuddin told the author that he had learnt this from Sarwari.
28. As above.
29. Conversations with pro-Amin Khalqites in Pulcharkhi prison.
30. As above.
31. Cf. chapter 9, 'The April Revolution', p. 105.
32. During this attack three hospital doctors were also killed. Azamuddin told the author that because of the 'treachery' of Akbari and Nawab Ali, every plan was regularly brought to Amin's knowledge.
33. The author heard these songs broadcast on Kabul radio and TV.
34. This concert was taking place not far from the author's house which was what had encouraged him to join the audience.

35. Conversations with Amin's family members and pro-Amin Khalqites.

36. According to Sarwari's plan, after Amin's destruction through the time device, he was to be presented to the people as the 'great martyr' and Tarun executed for his 'murder'.

37. Shah Wali spoke for three hours in Amin's support.

38. Author's meeting with Mrs Taraki, 1983.

39. *Kabul Times* and *Inqilab-e-Saur*, 16 September 1979.

40. See Amin's statement on US Ambassador Dobb's abduction and killing in which he also expressed a desire for good relations with the United States. In his speech at the World Peace Conference he said that Afghanistan wished to establish friendly relations with China.

41. Amin's address on radio and TV, 16 September 1979.

42. The old name of the Department of Intelligence was AGSA which stood for 'Afghanistan de Gato Satalo Adara'. Amin changed it to KAM or 'Kargarano da Itlaati Mossassa'.

43. To whip up public anger against Taraki, the names of many living prisoners were not included in this list. According to the author's information, some of these people were later discovered in prison.

44. This was the first and last time during the Khalq regime that it was considered necessary to inform the families of prisoners about their welfare. In Afghanistan such niceties were not adhered to. Even meetings of prisoners with members of their family were not the norm.

45. Conversations with pro-Amin Khalq leaders in jail.

46. Their fourth companion, Sher Jan Mazdooryar, was jailed on Amin's orders.

47. Prof. Zakria, Azamuddin's elder brother, was a committed pro-Taraki communist. After this abortive coup, he was arrested and shot.

48. The author's relations with Azamuddin were fairly close at the time. He told the author a day before, 'Don't leave the house tomorrow. There could be trouble.' After the failure of the coup, two of his brothers were arrested, but Azamuddin was left alone as he was thought to be harmless.

49. Sarwari told the author in February 1980 that it was the Soviet advisers in the Air Force and various cantonments who had contributed to the failure of the uprising by refusing to cooperate.

50. The writer was shifted from Pulcharkhi to Nazarat Khana Sadarat (the central detention facility) to enable him to meet Dr Najibullah.

Chapter 15: Taraki's Career and his Murder

1. Conversations with Khalq leaders.

2. Conversation with Mrs Taraki.

3. The writer is in possession of this letter.

4. *New York Times*, New York, 12 November 1953, p. 9.

5. *New York Times*, 17 December 1953, p. 6.

6. The probable reason Taraki was not arrested was because he had in a small way 'internationalized' his case and Daud did not wish to get a bad name by putting him in jail.

7. *A Short Biography of Comrade Noor M. Taraki*, Afghan Government Publication, Kabul, 23 August 1978.

8. Mrs Taraki narrated this incident to the author.

9. Conversation with the officer, Syed Zahur, who was responsible for the Asadullah Amin investigation.

10. Mir Wais was of the view that if his uncle Amin had gone to see Taraki, perhaps both of them might have lived because Taraki would have filled him in on the Soviet plan and its objectives.

11. Conversations with Khalq leaders in Pulcharkhi prison.

12. *Kabul Times*, 6 June 1979.
13. *Kabul Times*, 10 October 1979.
14. *Hiqaqat-e-Inqilab-e-Saur*, 23 January 1980.
15. Parcham sources.

Chapter 16: Amin in Office and his Downfall

1. *Kabul Times*, 20 September 1979.
2. Conversations with Khalq leaders in Pulcharkhi prison.
3. Gen. Zia-ul-Haq's interview with Kuldip Nayyar, *Indian Express*, New Delhi.
4. Kabul TV, 19 December 1979.
5. *Inqilab-e-Saur*, 22 December 1979 and *Kabul Times* of the same date.
6. Male, Beverley, *Revolutionary Afghanistan: a reappraisal*, Croom Helm, London, 1982, p. 204.
7. In its 22 December TV news bulletin, stormy weather over Kabul was cited as the reason for the cancellation of Agha Shahi's visit.
8. Interview with Amin, *Kabul Times*, 28 October 1979.
9. Conversations with Amin's Ministers in Pulcharkhi prison.
10. *Kabul Times*, 17 December 1979.
11. *New York Times*, 23 December 1979.
12. On 25 December a group of Pakistanis was refused permission to travel to Gardez on account of the on-going battle.
13. Traffic remained suspended on this highway for three days.
14. Mir Wais Amin told the author that after the attempt on Asadullah Amin's life, all children in the Amin family were accompanied by police guards to and from their schools and colleges. Before the incident they used to go without any special security arrangements.
15. Conversations with Amin's former Ministers in Pulcharkhi prison.
16. As above.
17. Mir Murtaza Bhutto formed the Al-Zulfikar Movement in March 1981 to liberate Pakistan from military rule.
18. Amin made no inquiries during the interview about the Pakistan People's Party.
19. Watan Shah had merely bragged. The real reason the Amin family was brought to Pulcharkhi was that when it was released in January 1980, a month after Amin's murder, a number of assassination attempts were made on some of its members. To save itself from the responsibility of protecting the family, Afghan intelligence had thought it best to bring it back to the safety of Pulcharkhi in April.
20. This is the same Maj. Shaista Khan who was arrested along with Col. Ahmed Jan for the execution of Taraki's guards. In January 1980 Mir Murtaza Bhutto and the author called on Mohammed Yusuf. At the time he had as his adviser a Soviet intelligence officer named Olayov from Azarbaijan. Yusuf introduced him by saying that he had helped 'us a lot in getting rid of that butcher Amin'. He also disclosed that the Soviet operator had been expelled from Iran for his political activities within twenty-four hours at the orders of the Shah of Iran. This man spoke Persian with an Azarbaijani accent. He was short and dapper with big bright eyes and looked extremely friendly and well-mannered.
21. Until then the Soviet Medical Corps had no hospital of its own, though every battalion had a number of doctors and nurses attached to it. The real purpose of the Soviet doctor was to place Amin in the hands of the Red Army.
22. Conversations with prisoners, including the Pakistani Sardar Khan.
23. Tapa-e-Taj Beg was a hillock with nothing between it and the Amin residence.
24. The rubble of this building was later cleared, and no trace of it now remains.
25. Until June 1980 there were a lot of Tajiks in the Soviet army in Afghanistan.
26. Conversation with Asadullah Sarwari in February 1980.
27. This building was about 300 to 400 yards from the author's residence, which enabled him to have a ring-side view of the battle.

28. Conversation with Capt. Shafiq Alamyar of the 4th Armoured Corps in Pulcharkhi.

29. Conversation with Capt. Shafiq Alamyar (as above) and Col. Ahmed Jan.

30. Although Amin had himself shifted to the new residence, the main secretariat was still based at Sadarat.

31. During the first year of the Revolution, Sehrai and Zarif were posted outside Kabul as Provincial Governors. The Ministries given to them on return to the capital were unimportant ones. It was absurd to sentence them to death for killing Parchamites. The real charge against them was that they had offered resistance on 27 December.

32. Parcham sources.

33. After speaking to Parcham leaders, the author came to the conclusion that the texts and subject matter of the two speeches also differed in many respects. This also suggests that the Soviet Union's real plan had misfired. Consequently, Karmal had to make a new speech after the Soviet action.

34. Amin would have found out because the Russian cooks had run away without eating the food served to the family.

35. According to Mrs Amin and Mir Wais Amin, the doctor was getting on the phone to his superiors every few minutes.

36. Author's personal observation.

37. *Washington Post,* 22 January 1980.

Chapter 17: Karmal — Brezhnev's own Creature

1. *Kabul New Times,* 14 January 1980.

2. *World Marxist Review,* Moscow, Issue 23, No 4, 8 April 1980, p. 56.

3. Conversations with the Amin family in Pulcharkhi prison.

4. Karmal's speech carried a large number of references from western newspapers. The Afghan Foreign Office was incapable of collecting or presenting such detailed and documented arguments. Amin's former Ministers who heard the speech were also of the same view. However, the author heard them openly make fun of Karmal's '4,000 armed volunteers'. The jail commander later put Shah Wali in solitary confinement for ten days for 'lack of respect' shown to Karmal.

5. *White Book,* 'China's Interference in the Internal Affairs of the DRA', Ministry of Foreign Affairs, Kabul, 1985, p. 15.

6. *Babrak Karmal's Interview Granted to a Pakistani Journalist,* Government Printing Press, Kabul, November 1985, p. 16.

7. *Kabul New Times,* 22 January 1980.

8. *The Secret War of the CIA Against Afghanistan,* Government Printing Press, Kabul, November 1984, pp. 39-40.

9. *New Times,* No 3, Moscow, 18 January 1980, p. 9.

10. Brezhnev's speech on Kabul TV, 6 March 1981.

11. ZDF, West German TV channel, 30 December 1986.

12. ZDF, 11 December 1986.

13. *Jang* (Urdu), Karachi, 5 November 1986.

14. Xinhua News Agency, Peking, 24 December 1984.

15. *Washington Post,* quoted in *Revolutionary Afghanistan Through Honest Eyes,* Ministry of Foreign Affairs, Kabul, (year unknown), p. 134.

16. In early 1984 Anthony Mascarenhas, a self-styled Afghanistan 'expert' from the *Sunday Times,* London, arrived in West Berlin to interview the author. He appeared to be keen to strengthen his theory of Soviet bases and tried to persuade the author to make a statement confirming it. Earlier, he had published a story (*Sunday Times,* 21 March 1981) claiming that the author had been killed at the hands of the Red Army. By way of offering a 'deal', he told the author, 'If you are prepared to confirm my theory about Soviet bases by quoting Amin's former Ministers in prison, I will have a denial of the report of your death published.' The author refused the deal, and complained to the editor of the *Sunday Times* about Mascarenhas's unprofessional conduct. While in the columns of the *Sunday*

Times the author continues to be 'dead', Mascarenhas left the paper some time later.

17. *Dawn*, Karachi, 25 November 1986, p. 8.

18. Today, Karmal — stripped of all Party offices and state honours and living in the Soviet Union (as reports suggest) — may perhaps find solace in the fact that the Kremlin is no longer led by communists like Brezhnev.

19. *New York Times*, 24 March 1979, p. 4.

20. *Daily Telegraph*, London, 24 April 1979, p. 5.

21. *Daily Telegraph*, 31 May 1979, p. 6.

22. *New Times*, No 25, Moscow, June 1979, p. 13.

23. It was a result of this visit that Afghanistan received MI-24 helicopter gunships, the first country to do so outside the Warsaw Pact. Conversations with Khalq leaders in Pulcharkhi prison.

24. Arnold, Anthony, *Two Party Communism*, University of Stanford, 1983, pp. 81-82. Also, Monks, A.L., *Soviet Intervention in Afghanistan*, 1981, p. 27.

25. *New York Times*, 6 September 1979.

Chapter 18: Karmal's 'New Phase'

1. *Kabul New Times*, 2 January 1980. The speech was broadcast by Radio Kabul on the night of 27-28 December 1979.

2. The word 'late' was subsequently employed by Karmal as a prefix to Taraki's name.

3. *Kabul New Times* and Radio Kabul, *op. cit.*

4. Despite the announcement, about twenty Afghans and five Pakistanis failed to obtain their release (author's information from Pulcharkhi prison sources).

5. Baryali, Mahmood, ed., *Afghanistan, Multifaceted Revolutionary Process*, Afghan Government Publication, Kabul, 1982 or 1983, p. 49.

6. *Babrak Karmal's Speeches, 27 December 1979-April 1980*, Ministry of Foreign Affairs, Kabul (year uncertain), pp. 59-68.

7. *Ibid*, p. 66.

8. Baryali, Mahmood, ed., *op. cit.*, p. 7. Baryali, Karmal's step-brother, had a degree in economics from Moscow. Being a member of the Politburo and an economist, he had undertaken this study to assess the damage caused by the civil war to the Afghan economy.

9. *Ibid*, pp. 12, 13 and 15.

10. See *Da Wattan Paigham*, Democratic Youth Organization of Afghanistan, Issue No 1, Kabul, 1984, pp. 7-8.

11. *Kabul New Times*, 6 June 1981 and 5 July 1981.

12. Baryali, Mahmood, ed., *op. cit.*, p. 20.

13. Author's meeting with Kabul's Hindu and Sikh exporters in 1983.

14. *Babrak Karmal's Speech to the 9th Plenum of the PDPA Central Committee*, Government Printing Press, Kabul, 1982 (probably), p. 7.

15. This also implied that the average number of workers employed at every single Afghan industrial establishment was around 500 – which was palpably untrue.

16. *Da Wattan Paigham*, *op. cit.*, pp. 7-8.

17. *Foreign Affairs Bulletin*, No 3/4., Ministry of Foreign Affairs, Kabul, April 1986.

18. *Ibid.*

19. See *Foreign Affairs Bulletin*, *op. cit.* No 7, July 1986, for text of Najibullah's speech, pp. 32-40.

20. These pamphlets were popularly known as *shabnamas* or night letters. On the activities of the US embassy in this propaganda campaign, see *CIA is Getting Disclosed*, Afghan Government Publication, Kabul, October 1983, pp. 4-5.

21. Baryali, Mahmood, ed., *The True Face of Afghan Counter-Revolution*, Afghan Government Publication, Kabul, 1982 (probably), carried a picture of these 'foreign saboteurs'.

22. Conversations with Mahmood Baryali and Najibullah in March 1980.

23. A large number of teachers, petty civil servants and minor Khalq workers were killed during this period. The situation was also used by the Afghans to settle old personal scores.

24. *The Economist,* London, 21 June 1980, p. 40. See also, *New York Times,* 4 August 1980.

25. Arnold, Anthony, *Two Party Communism,* University of Stanford, California, 1983, pp. 118-119.

26. According to government sources, a number of girl students also died of the poisoning.

27. Rajai was arrested by a police officer named Farooq Hotak who was later rewarded by being made Political Commissar of Pulcharkhi. After Rajai's confession, his entire group was rounded up by the police and he himself sentenced to death in May 1981.

28. Sarwari was a member of the Politburo in Karmal's early days.

29. The author noticed Taraki's portrait hanging in the office of the Governor of Jalalabad, Nasir Shimladar, in 1980.

30. Until the end of 1980 Soviet soldiers were to be seen guarding Ministers' offices. As for Karmal's palace, it continued to be protected by Soviet soldiers until the end.

31. The official media remained completely silent over the murder of artists known for their sympathies with the Khalq group. Under this Parchamite conspiracy of silence, the news of the murders of Master Fazal Ghani, Khan Qarra Baghi and TV woman announcer Saima Akhtar was not published. However, news of the death of ordinary but non-controversial artists such as Ustad Sarang and Bakhat Zarmina was broadcast and published. In fact, Suleman Laiq delivered a speech at the funeral of Ustad Sarang.

32. *The Economist,* London, 21 June 1980.

33. Author's meeting with Sarwari at Azamuddin's house. Sarwari believed that the Afghan masses would turn against the Revolution because of the Soviet military action.

34. *Kabul New Times,* 21 June 1980.

35. *Kabul New Times,* 18 August 1980.

36. Sarwari wanted Azamuddin to join him but the Karmal government instead sent over his nephew, Aziz Akbari. The liquidation of the Khalq group was now taken up in earnest by the regime. Nasir Shimladar, Governor of Nangarhar province, and three other pro-Taraki Governors were reduced to the rank of ordinary soldiers and ordered to do compulsory military service. Hundreds of other Khalqites were locked up on one pretext or the other.

37. Rumours were rife in Kabul that Khalqite officers had attempted an uprising in the capital against Karmal in June and in Ghazni in July. The Ghazni commander was said to have set off for Kabul, before he was attacked and defeated by Soviet troops. This commander is now head of a pro-China group of rebels active in the Ghazni area.

38. *New York Times,* 4 August 1980. See also, *Washington Post,* 24 July 1980.

39. *Kabul New Times,* 21 September 1980, 24 September 1980 and 13 October 1980.

40. The singer Mashoor Jamal sang a number of songs in praise of these 'revolutionary soldiers'. Fifteen soldiers who had taken part in the protest march were given two-year sentences. The story was blacked out in the press.

41. The sons of Karmal, Zeary and Panjsheri were exempted from compulsory military service and sent to Moscow for studies, an example followed by less important Party leaders. Since 1978 no senior or junior Party leader has lost a son in battle. Cf. an article by the author in *Der Tagesspiegel,* West Berlin, 25 March 1984, whose criticism of the 'disgraceful escapists' was to be echoed two years later by Dr. Najibullah (see *Foreign Affairs Bulletin,* No 7, Vol. 5, Afghan Government Publication, Kabul, July 1968, p. 44). However, there has been no appreciable increase in the size of the Afghan army since Najibullah came to power.

42. *Foreign Affairs Bulletin, op. cit.,* p. 40.

43. *Der Tagesspiegel, op. cit.*

44. *Foreign Affairs Bulletin, op. cit.,* pp. 46-47 for text of Najibullah's speech.

45. Although these Khalqite Ministers had provided 'shelter' to some members of the

group in their Ministries, this fell far short of protecting the Khalq group as such.
46. Karmal's speech to the 9th Plenum of the PDPA Central Committee.
47. *Ibid.*
48. *Ibid.*
49. *Ibid.*
50. *Haqiqat-e-Inqilab-e-Saur* (Persian daily), Kabul, 11 July 1978.
51. *Kabul New Times*, 5 March 1980, 31 March 1980 and 14 May 1980.
52. *Kabul New Times*, 12 August 1981. He also announced that compensation for damage caused to the properties returned would be paid in instalments over a twenty-year period.
53. There was no legal requirement to do so, but this was the standard backdoor practice.
54. *Kabul New Times*, 12 August 1981.
55. *The Muslim*, Islamabad, 26 February 1987 for Najibullah's interview.
56. *Ibid*, 25 March 1987.

Chapter 19: 'Leninist Tactics'

1. Baryali, Mahmood, ed., *Afghanistan, Multifaceted Revolutionary Process,* Afghan Government Publication, Kabul, 1982 or 1983, p. 100.
2. At one time, this building had also served as the headquarters of the Al-Zulfikar organization (set up in Kabul by the deposed Pakistani Prime Minister Zulfikar Ali Bhutto's sons, Mir Murtaza and the late Shahnawaz Bhutto).
Ghulam Farooq Yaqubi (present Afghan Minister responsible for the Intelligence portfolio) while introducing the author to Dr Bahar at a dinner in 1983 said that the doctor had once spent two months with the rebels pretending to be one of them. At the time he told the story Yaqubi was number three to Dr Najibullah, the head of KHAD.
3. Conversation with Pakistani hijacker Islamullah Tipu in Kabul in May 1983.
4. Conversations with Khalq leaders in Pulcharkhi.
5. *Kabul New Times*, 20-21 April 1980.
6. Ratebzad, Anahita, ed., *Afghanistan Today*, Afghan Government Publication, Kabul, July-August 1985, p. 18.
7. *Ibid.*
8. Karmal's speech to the 9th Plenum of the PDPA Central Committee.
9. *Kabul New Times*, 20 June 1981.
10. *Kabul New Times*, 3, 4 and 6 October 1981.
11. Pictures released to the press by the government of local elections showed people with arms raised high. The author was told that the 'elections' were arranged by the local administration and totally stage-managed. For pictures, see Sadat, Asmat, *Afghanistan, Land of the Jirgas,* Afghan Government Publication, Kabul, January 1986.
12. Ibid., p. 15. See also, *Afghanistan Today, op. cit.*, p. 7 and *Kabul New Times*, 24 and 26 April 1985.
13. The *jirga* was presided over by a former Afghan Justice, Mahmood Barakzai.
14. *Afghanistan, Land of the Jirgas, op. cit.*, p. 17.
15. *Karmal's Interview Granted to a Pakistani Journalist*, Afghan Government Publication, Kabul, July 1986, p. 45.

Chapter 20: The Red Army and Soviet Advisers

1. Conversations with well-informed government and Party functionaries.
2. The author was a frequent visitor to the Department of Philosophy at the University of Kabul and even in this small department, there were three Soviet lecturers.
3. *Da Wattan Paigham*, Afghan Government Publication, Kabul, 1984, p. 19.

4. The author met one of the Afghan Air Force's Soviet advisers at the house of a Khalqite Air Force officer. The Russian said jokingly, 'If Asmat (the host) had a Kalashnikov and he ran into Karmal, he would kill him on the spot without giving the matter a second thought.' The author further learnt that most Soviet advisers had become partisan.

5. The author learnt in 1983 that the Soviet advisers had discovered a loophole in Soviet law which enabled them to send these cars to Tajikstan and Uzbekistan from where they were 'purchased' for onward shipment.

6. This garrison was transferred in 1981 because of persistent complaints.

7. These transactions never seemed to take more than a few minutes. A Soviet military jeep or Vega would screech to a halt in front of one of these workshops with the owner waiting outside with a fistful of money. This would be snatched without being counted and the tyres or other spare parts would be thrown on the ground and the vehicle would take off.

8. Information gathered by the author in jail.

9. Conversations with rebel prisoners in Pulcharkhi.

10. The author is unable to state with certainty those responsible for the rape and murder of these women.

11. Conversation with a senior traffic police officer in December 1983.

12. Earlier, the author had believed these charges to be no more than Karmal government propaganda. However, in 1981 Farooq Hotak, Pulcharkhi's Political Commissar, showed this room to the author. The walls were still pock-marked with hand grenade shrapnel (despite having been painted). Many of the jail's cells told the same story. Prison guards and old inmates also confirmed these brutal practices as having taken place. Syed Abdullah was later attacked by a group of prisoners and repeatedly stabbed in the stomach. However, he survived and was sent to Moscow for treatment at Amin's orders (his attackers were shot dead on the spot).

Within days of his return to Kabul, following his successful treatment, Karmal took over. In June 1980 he was hanged along with Asadullah Amin, Abdullah Amin, Sahib Jan Sehrai, Engineer Zarif and the Alamyar brothers. Qasim Khan, assistant jail commander, told the author that Syed Abdullah was very popular with jail staff despite his inhuman treatment of prisoners. Before being hanged, he said, 'I am not a murderer, but if I get another life, I will deal with the enemies of the Revolution in the same way. It is Karmal who should be ashamed of himself because I am being hanged at his orders.'

13. *Der Tagesspiegel*, West Berlin, 25 March 1984.

14. Ziauddin Mahmood, an Egyptian, told the author that he had brought this to the notice of the Soviet adviser who had assured him that such practices would cease from now on.

15. In Nazarat Khana Sadarat, Kabul's central detention facility, there were six investigation branches until 1980. By 1983 they had increased to twelve, a sign that the number of detainees had gone up proportionately. In 1981 Mukhtar Ahmed, officer-in-charge of branch No 4, reprimanded one of the investigating officers in the writer's presence for having slapped a prisoner during interrogation. However, not all branches played the game according to the rules.

16. With the exception of the pro-China communist Majid Kalkani and ten of Amin's Ministers and supporters who were sentenced to death after no more than a couple of months of legal proceedings.

17. This figure does not, of course, include those who have died in the war from the two sides.

18. One month after this strike, an International Red Cross team came to Kabul to inspect prison conditions. Since the prisoners were still furious over their treatment during and after the strike, the authorities wanted only a few handpicked men from among them to present to the Red Cross team. However, since the Red Cross insisted on inspecting all prisoners, the visit was cut short.

Chapter 21: External Interference

1. Karmal said more or less the same thing while speaking at the 22nd anniversary of the PDPA. For details, see Ratebzad, Anahita, ed., *Afghanistan Today*, Afghan Government Publication, Kabul, July-August 1985, pp. 1-2.
2. Pakistan recognized the new government in Kabul on 5 May 1978 and Iran did so a day later. The hesitation of the two was quite extraordinary.
3. *New York Times*, 5 May 1978, p. 28.
4. *New York Times*, 20 May 1978, p. 4.
5. *Ibid.*
6. During his visit to the United States in 1985, Gen. Zia-ul-Haq of Pakistan while presenting the *Tamgha-e-Khidmat* (Medal for Services Rendered) to the editor of the *New York Times* praised the newspaper's advocacy of the Afghan cause.
7. *Daily Telegraph*, London, 5 June 1978.
8. Van Hollen, Elizabeth, *Afghanistan, a Year of Occupation*, Special Report No 79, US Department of State, Washington D.C., February 1981, p. 3.
9. Male, Beverley, *Revolutionary Afghanistan: a reappraisal*, Croom Helm, London, 1982, pp. 174-5.
10. *Ibid.* pp. 173-4.
11. According to an Indian magazine, by 1980 the number of these camps had risen to 120. See *Blitz*, Bombay, 12 January 1980.
12. Press Trust of India report, 18 January 1980.
13. *Kabul Times*, 9 April 1980.
14. For details of this high-level NATO symposium on the changed strategic environment, see *New York Times*, 24 June 1978, p. 5.
15. *Washington Post*, 5 May 1979.
16. *Newsweek*, New York, cited in *The Secret War of the CIA Against Afghanistan*, Afghan Government Publication, Kabul, November 1984, p. 6.
17. *Ibid*, p. 7.
18. *Afghanistan Through Honest Eyes*, Ministry of Foreign Affairs, Kabul, 1982 or 1983, p. 142.
19. *Washington Post*, 15 February 1980.
20. *Ibid*, 7 February 1985.
21. *Ibid.*
22. *Jang* (Urdu), London, 4 December 1986 quoting *Washington Post* and Reuters reports.
23. *Imroze* (Urdu), Lahore, 25 November 1986, p. 6.
24. *The Boston Globe*, 17 January 1980.
25. NBC (New York) broadcast, 7 January 1980.
26. *Daily Telegraph*, London, 5 January 1980.
27. *White Book*, Ministry of Foreign Affairs, Kabul, 1985, p. 20.
28. Interview with Dr Najibullah, *The Muslim*, Islamabad, 27 February 1987.
29. Interview with Gen. Azimi, *ibid.*
30. *Afghanistan Through Honest Eyes, op. cit.*, 148-49.
31. NBC (New York) broadcast, 22 September 1981.
32. *The Muslim*, Islamabad, 'What Next on Afghanistan', *op. cit.* According to the writer, Ms. Lodhi, 'the Pakistan Foreign Office is also believed to have conveyed to the Soviets their disapproval of the two Mujahideen attacks inside Soviet territory.'

Chapter 22: The Afghan 'Mujahideen'

1. *The Times*, London, 3 December 1979.
2. Based on a close study of the pre and post-27 December 1979 situation.
3. According to the author's recollection, the total number of Gulbudin Hikmatyar's Jamiat-e Islami adherents was between 150 and 200. If it is assumed that there was an

increase in this number after the Revolution, 600 seems to be about the limit. One reason for Hikmatyar's poor showing may be attributable to the fact that he started his 'crusade' against communism before 1978 when there was no communist government in Afghanistan.

4. Lessing, Doris, *The New Yorker*, 'A Reporter at Large', 16 March 1987, p. 82.
5. Author's conversations between 1980 and 1983 with Afghan 'Mujahideen' who left their country as refugees and were sent back as 'God's own warriors fighting the Red infidels', after being trained by Afghan political parties 'in exile' in Pakistan.
6. *The New Yorker, op. cit.*, p. 78.
7. *Der Tagesspiegel*, West Berlin, 25 March 1984.
8. *Washington Post*, 7 May 1985.
9. *The New Yorker, op. cit.*, p. 78.
10. *Der Tagesspiegel, op. cit.*
11. Ratebzad, Anahita, ed., *Afghanistan Today*, Afghan Government Publication, Kabul, July–August 1985, p. 16.
12. This young man was in a bus travelling to Kabul when it was waylaid by a group of 'Mujahideen'. He was picked out because of his long hair which was for some reason interpreted as evidence of his being a government supporter.
13. Members of the government who were not aligned with the PDPA were generally released by the rebels after a few days, but not before they had been forced to pay a 'fine'. They were also made to promise that they would not support the communists in future. A more cruel fate awaited Party members. Their limbs were chopped off one by one and they were done to death in the most inhuman and barbaric way. Even young students suspected (often wrongly) of PDPA sympathies were shown no mercy.
14. Mir Nazir, a Pakistan People's Party worker from Peshawar, was caught by the 'Mujahideen' while he was on his way to Kabul (having escaped the martial law authorities who would surely have rounded him up). After spending nine months in different 'jails' operated by the 'Mujahideen', he managed to reach Kabul. Later he was given political refuge in Libya and when the writer last knew, he was living in Benghazi.
15. After this attack, a one-year ceasefire agreement was signed between Ahmed Shah Masaud and the PDPA government. Abdul Rashid believed that Masaud had treacherously encouraged, if not invited, the Red and Afghan armies to occupy that part of the Panjsher Valley which was under the control of his rival Rabbani group. Rashid maintained that Masaud was acting hand in glove with the Afghan government and had assured it that if its troops advanced up to a certain point in the Valley, he would neither offer any resistance, nor come to the rescue of Rabbani's fighters. Having succeeded in this 'conspiracy' and caused a large number of casualties among his rival group, he had signed a one-year peace treaty with the Kabul administration 'on the dead bodies of his co-fighters'.
16. *Judge for Yourselves*, Government Printing Press, Kabul, 1983 (probably), pp. 12-13 and 22-28 for details. The Afghan media reported the incident in their usual untruthful and distorted manner.
17. *Der Tagesspiegel, op. cit.*
18. In 1986 the birthday of an old Pakistani politician, with a following of some 15,000, was celebrated by firing Kalashnikovs in the air. According to another Pakistani politician, Air Marshal M. Asghar Khan, the residents of the relatively small city of Abbottabad (where the Air Marshal lives) greeted the new Eid moon (a twice-yearly Muslim festival) by firing machine-guns in the air as if the city had been invaded. See the Urdu weekly *Akhbar-e-Watan*, London, 28 January-4 February 1987, p. 16.
19. *Washington Post*, 7 May 1985.
20. *Akhbar-e-Watan, op. cit.*
21. *Ibid.*
22. *Washington Post*, 7 May 1985.
23. *The New Yorker, op. cit.*, p. 79.
24. Interview with Gen. Azimi, *The Muslim*, Islamabad, 28 February 1987.
25. *The New Yorker, op. cit.*, pp. 77-78
26. Baryali, Mahmood, ed., *The True Face of Counter-Revolution*, Afghan

Government Publication, Kabul, 1982, p. 39.

27. *The New Yorker, op. cit.*, p. 78.

28. Amir Mohammedi, an Afghan rebel leader, said that those among the young who had been contaminated by Soviet ideas would be killed by their own parents. See *New Yorker, op. cit.*, p. 78.

Chapter 23: Karmal's Deposition and the Future Outlook

1. ZDF, West German TV Channel, quoting Pravda, 27 April 1986.

2. During his time in office, Karmal did not once travel by Ariana Afghan, the national airline.

3. *Anis*, Kabul, 15 Saur 1365 (5 May 1986).

4. *Ibid.* On Karmal's resignation the date given was 13 Saur 1365 (3 May 1986). His resignation was accepted the next day, 4 May 1986.

5. *Anis*, Kabul, 5 May 1986.

6. Referring to the 'provocative slogans' raised by the students, Dr Najibullah felt obliged to ask Karmal two months later, 'It is right to cut the tree on which we are sitting? I mean those provocative slogans by some of the girls ...' For text of Najibullah's speech, see *Foreign Affairs Bulletin*, No 7, Afghan Government Publication, Kabul, July 1986.

7. *Ibid.* The main targets of this attack were: Baryali, Ratebzad, Sarwar, Mangal and Majid Sarbuland.

8. See *Foreign Affairs Bulletin, op. cit.*, for the text of Najibullah's speech.

9. *Ibid*, pp. 39-40.

10. *Ibid*, p. 52.

11. *Ibid*, p. 51.

12. *Ibid*, pp. 54, 57 and 58.

13. After being released from Pulcharkhi in March 1983, the author spent nine months in Afghanistan. In those days, the Kabul rulers were not even prepared to listen to suggestions that at a future date a government might be formed by the PDPA in association with the rebels. The author found that even a mention of this possibility on a social occasion was enough to put government people off.

14. *Der Tagesspiegel*, West Berlin, 25 March 1984.

15. ZDF, West German TV Channel, broadcast on 30 December 1986.

16. *The Muslim*, Islamabad, 30 April 1987.

17. BBC quoted by *The Muslim*, Islamabad, 14 May 1987.

18. Lodhi, Maleeha, *The Muslim*, Islamabad, 4 May 1987.

19. *The Muslim*, Islamabad, 28 April 1987.

20. *Ibid.*

21. Gorbachev's interview to an Italian journal quoted by *Jang* (Urdu), London, 22 May 1987.

22. *The Muslim*, Islamabad, 17 May 1987, (Maleeha Lodhi's interview with Gilani).

23. BBC quoted by *The Muslim*, Islamabad, 14 May 1987.

24. *The Muslim, op. cit.*, (Maleeha Lodhi's interview with Gilani).

25. BBC quoted by *The Muslim*, Islamabad, 14 May 1987.

26. Gen. Zia-ul-Haq's interview (reproduced from the Observer, London, 7 April 1986), *Jang, op. cit.*

27. *Jang* (Urdu), Lahore, 16 May 1987.

28. *The Muslim, op. cit.* (Maleeha Lodhi's article on Afghanistan quoting Richard Nixon, 4 May 1987).

29. *Ibid.*

30. *Time*, New York, report reproduced by *Jang* (Urdu) Lahore, 12 May 1987.

31. British press reports quoted in *Jang*, Lahore, 17 May 1987.

32. BBC quoted by *The Muslim*, Islamabad, 14 May 1987.

33. The head of the Jamiat-e Islami, Afghanistan, Prof. Burhanuddin Rabbani, said: 'People responsible for atrocities cannot be included in an administration which is

supposed to bring peace and a just solution of the problem.' See *The Muslim*, Islamabad, 20 May 1987.
    34. *Ibid.*
    35. *Jang* (Urdu), Karachi, 22 May 1987.
    36. *Ibid*, 22 May 1987.
    37. *Ibid.*

Index

Note: n indicates footnote reference; page numbers in italic indicate Tables

Abdali tribe 2-8
Abdul Rahman Khan 14, 15, 126
Abdul Rauf, guerilla commander 153-4
Afghanistan
  peoples and language 1-3, 38, 125-40
  economy 69, 84-5, 135-7, 205-6
  early kingdom 3-8
  British rule 9-16, 17-18
  independence 18-20
  post-war international relations 30-7,
    39
  Daud's 'Republican revolution' 37-8,
    39, 59, 69-73
  dispute with Pakistan 77-82
  April Revolution 92-109
    historiography 103, 108-9
    middle-class character 134, 137-40
  PDPA forms government 110-15,
    118-19
  revolutionary reforms 134, 141-50, 218
  Khalq and Soviet Union 152-3, 173,
    195-6
  Amin leadership 160-1, 182-93
  reasons for invasion 194-202
  effects of Soviet presence 207, 223-8
  foreign influences on rebels 229-35
  Intelligence Department 226-7
  Loya Jirga try at parliamentarianism
    220-1, 222
  possible effects of Soviet withdrawal
    251-3
  see also PDPA; Soviet Union; tribes
Agha Shahi', visit cancelled 183-4, 185
agriculture 130, 148
  see also land
Ahmed, Qazi Hussain 252-3
Ahmed Shah Saddozai 3-5, 6, 7
Ahmedzai tribe *see* Abdali tribe
Aimaqs 1
Akbari, Aziz 166-7, 168-9, 170, 174
Akhramovich, R.T. 29
Alamyar brothers 93, 182, 193
Ali, Nawab, protects Amin 167, 171
Amanullah Khan 7, 17, 18, 22-3
  reforming government 20-1, 24, 27,
    134
Amin, Abdul Rahman 104, 118, 162
  passes message 94, 95
Amin, Abdullah 163, 165
Amin, Asadullah 144-5, 163, 166, 174,
  180, 184, 186

Amin, Hafizullah 154, 158
  early career and background 7, 27,
    42, 45, 64
  April Revolution 92, 94, 95, 102,
    104, 108
  Eid conspiracy advances 120-1,
    122-4
  reforms and 144-5, 147
  importance in Khalq faction 54, 57,
    87-90, 180
  on working-class revolution 137, 140
  rivalry with Karmal 65, 111-15, 118,
    196-7
  visits Moscow 152-3
  overthrows Taraki 161-4, 165-76
  presidency 160-1, 182-6
  personal trust in Soviet Union 172,
    175-6, 201
  Pushtunistan policy 183
  overthrow 186-93
  responsibility for Soviet invasion
    194-8, 200
  see also Khalq Party; PDPA
Amin, Mrs Hafizullah 181, 187, 192
Amin, Mir Wais 187, 190
amir (king/ruler) *see under individual*
  names
armed forces 112-14
  Air Force 94, 97-8, 101, 102-3
  Defence of Revolution volunteers 184
  Karmal and 210-12
  role in April Revolution 89-90, 94-5,
    96-103
  Soviet training 35, 71, 83, 89
Arnold, Anthony 103, 177-8
Arunova, M.R. 57, 58
Ataturk Mustafa Kamal 20-1
Auckland, George, 1st Earl of 9-10
Ayub Khan (Sardar) 13, 14
Ayub Khan, Mohammad (of Pakistan)
  36-7
Azami, General Nabi, on China 234-5

Bacha Saqao 21-2, 23
Badakhshi, Dr Tahir 29, 40, 42, 126, 154
  founds Sitm-e-Milli 56-7
  Eid conspiracy 119-20
  executed 155
Baghdad Pact (CENTO) 33-4
Baluchistan *see* Pakistan
Barakzai 18, 31, 115

281